'Luck Was Lacking, But Valor Was Not'

The Italian Army in North Africa, 1940–43

Ralph Riccio & Massimiliano Afiero

Helion & Company Limited

Helion & Company Limited
Unit 8 Amherst Business Centre
Budbrooke Road
Warwick
CV34 5WE
England
Tel. 01926 499 619
Email: info@helion.co.uk
Website: www.helion.co.uk
Twitter: @helionbooks
Visit our blog http://blog.helion.co.uk/

Published by Helion & Company 2022
Designed and typeset by Mach 3 Solutions Ltd (www.mach3solutions.co.uk)
Cover designed by Paul Hewitt, Battlefield Design (www.battlefield-design.co.uk)

Text © Ralph Riccio & Massimiliano Afiero 2021
Photographs © as individually credited
Colour figures drawn by Anderson Subtil © Helion Company 2021; colour vehicle artwork drawn by and
© David Bocquelet 2021
Maps by George Anderson © Helion & Company 2021

ISBN 978-1-913336-16-5

British Library Cataloguing-in-Publication Data.
A catalogue record for this book is available from the British Library.

For details of other military history titles published by Helion & Company Limited contact the above
address or visit our website: http://www.helion.co.uk.

We always welcome receiving book proposals from prospective authors.

Contents

List of Maps

List of Colour AFV Plates

Lit of Colour Uniform Plates

Preface

For generations since the Second World War, there has been the perception in Anglo–American literature that the Italian Army, or *Regio Esercito*, performed poorly everywhere during that conflict. Casual readers of military history as well as, in all too many cases, serious students of military history have been led to believe that the Italian soldier was unwilling to fight and was quick to surrender. With a few notable exceptions, most British, American and German accounts either give scant attention to, are dismissive of, or otherwise cast negative aspersions on the performance of Italian ground forces. This is especially true of the desert war in North Africa, which commonly is seen largely as a conflict between Rommel and his *Afrika Korps*, on the one hand, and Montgomery and the Eighth Army, on the other. The reality is that the great bulk of the Axis forces in the desert were not German, but Italian, and that whatever their faults and shortcomings may have been, after their initial trouncing at the hands of the British in late 1940 and early 1941, the Italians fought hard and fought well, both as individual soldiers and as units.

In this book we have endeavoured to shed as much light as possible on the Italian military effort on the ground in North Africa, and because of that, the presentation necessarily pays relatively little attention to the German participation there, or to the British and Commonwealth part in the struggle. In that sense, this book admittedly is somewhat biased in favour of the Italians, just as most English-language works that deal with the *Afrika Korps* or the British side of the story pay little heed to Italian accomplishments in the desert war. Our aim in writing this work was, rather, to present a general background on the Italian soldier's capabilities and an account of Italian operations in North Africa and their overall contribution to the joint Italo–German effort; in the simplest of terms, it is to tell a story that has not been told before. We hope that we have succeeded at least in some small part in bringing to light the vital role played by the *Regio Esercito* in the fighting in North Africa.

Acknowledgments and Sources

The sources consulted in our research consist largely of Italian sources, among them the official histories produced by the Italian Army Historical Office, as well as a number of books written shortly after the war by officers who had been participants in the fighting in North Africa. Paolo Caccia Dominioni was an especially prolific and articulate chronicler of the events, especially of those at El Alamein, as was Igino Gravina in his *Le tre battaglie di Alamein*. Other particularly good descriptive and informative books were those by Dino Campini (*Nei Giardini del diavolo*), Alberto Bechi-Luserna (*I ragazzi della Folgore*) and Giuseppe Rizzo (*Buche e croci nel deserto*) which gives a good account and overview of the fighting in the desert from early 1941 onwards. English-language works which are worth mentioning are Ian Walker's *Iron Hulls, Iron Hearts*, which, although it focuses on the Italian armoured formations, is a superbly researched and written piece of work; and John Joseph Timothy Sweet's *Iron Arm*, which deals with the mechanization of the Italian army and is likewise an excellent study. Paolo Morisi's *The Italian Folgore Parachute Division* and Rex Trye's Mussolini's *Afrika Korps: The Italian Army in North Africa, 1940–1943* are also good sources of information.

With respect to the photographs in this book, many of them come from period magazines and newspapers and have not been previously published in any English-language works. Some official Italian photographs have been used in other publications, but we have included them because they represent the best images available for some of the specific pieces of equipment used in the desert.

Although several Italian sources relate essentially the same narrative for specific actions, there are some inconsistencies between sources, especially when it comes to statistical information such as the number of tanks available before or during a specific battle; we have used what we consider to be the best or most credible information available but are cognizant of the fact that there may be some inconsistencies with accounts and numbers quoted in other works. We have also, in many cases, used the term 'British' to refer in a general sense to British as well as Commonwealth forces, although we have sought to identify national units engaged in specific actions, such as Indian, New Zealand or Australian, whenever we have been able. We have avoided the use of footnotes and endnotes, but have indicated the source of information, especially of quotes, where appropriate.

Our sincerest thanks to the following individuals and organizations who provided information and photographs not available elsewhere: Giancarlo Garello (who sadly passed away in June 2020), a well-known and respected author of many works relating to the *Regia Aeronautica*, for his insightful help regarding RA ground support operations in North Africa, as well as for some excellent photographs of Italian aircraft employed to support the ground forces; Daniele Guglielmi for his willingness to read through and suggest corrections to an interminably long draft and to provide a number of photographs of German and Italian equipment; Enrico Finazzer for providing photographs and helping identify at least one anomalous artillery piece; Maurizio Brescia for photographs of Italian vessels involved in the North African convoys; the Tallillo brothers, Andrea and Antonio, for information on a few obscure points; Gianluigi Usai for his well-reasoned observations concerning the initial draft; and Dott. Federico Cioni for his gracious consent to draw liberally from previously published work relating to Italian armoured equipment and organization.

Special thanks go to the library staff at Bovington Tank Museum, including Vivian the registrar, Stuart Wheeler and Jonathan Holt, for their assistance in providing a selection of images of tanks in British service in the desert.

We would also like to thank the staff of the Queen's Own Royal West Kent Museum (Maidstone Borough Council), Samantha Harris BA (Hons) and Steve Finnis, Regimental Historian, Queen's Own Royal West Kent Regiment, as well as Steve Erskine, Assistant Curator, The Green Howards Regimental Museum.

We are especially indebted to Duncan Rogers of Helion, whose enthusiasm for this project was especially welcome, and to Victoria Powell for her gentle guidance.

Finally, we would like to acknowledge the patience and unstinting support of our wives, Charlene and Nicoletta, who suffered while we neglected our household duties while we devoted most of our waking hours to this book.

Italian Unit Naming Conventions

The Italian system of naming and numbering units was fairly consistent, although there were some exceptions. Depending on the echelon, unit numbers were either Arabic numerals or Roman numerals: armies, divisions, regiments, brigades and companies were referred to by Arabic numerals, whereas corps and battalions were referred to by Roman numerals. The numerals were always expressed in ordinal numbers, for example, *132a divisione corazzata* (132nd Armoured Division). Infantry divisions bore either a single or a double-digit numerical designation and ran from 1 through 80; motorized divisions were in the 100-series (101 and 102) and the parachute divisions had 180-series numbers from 183 to 185. In addition to being numbered, divisions and regiments typically bore names as well. There were also several other types of divisions, such as alpine, coastal and occupation divisions, all with their own distinct numbering blocks. In North Africa, the 60-series divisions generally bore names associated with North Africa, such as the 61st 'Sirte' and 62nd 'Marmarica'. With few exceptions, infantry and motorized divisions bore the names of cities; in the case of the infantry and motorized divisions that served in North Africa, all of the city names were of cities in northern Italy (Bologna, Brescia, Trieste, Trento, etc.). Regiments similarly usually bore names as well as numbers, such as the 66th Regiment 'Valtellina', but *Bersaglieri* regiments bore only single or double-digit numbers. Battalions within the regiments bore Roman numerals. Self-propelled and truck-mounted artillery groups (battalions) likewise were identified by Roman numerals in the C (100) or D (500) series.

Glossary of Italian Terms and Abbreviations

ACA: *Armata Corazzata Africa* (Italian designation for *Panzerarmee Afrika*)

ACIT: *Armata Corazzata Italo–Tedesca* (Italian designation for *Deutsch–Italienische Panzerarmee*)

Africa Settentrionale (AS): North Africa

Articelere: Designation for mobile artillery units

Artiglio: Military truck tire with large treads ('*artiglio*' is 'claw' in English)

Ascari: Native Libyan troops in Italian service

Autoblinda, autoblindo (AB): Armoured car

Autocannone: Self-propelled gun on wheeled chassis

Autocarro unificato medio: Standardized medium truck

Autocarro unificato pesante: Standardized heavy truck

Autogruppo: Transportation battalion

Autoraggruppamento: Echelon consisting of several *autogruppi* (transportation battalions)

Autoreparto: Transportation battalion

Autosezione: Motor transport section

Battaglione: Battalion

Bersaglieri: Elite light infantry. In the context of armoured operations, usually motorized infantry. Comparable to the German *Panzergrenadier*

CAM: *Corpo d'Armata di Manovra* (Manueveur Army Corps); precursor organization to XX Corps

Camionetta: Light truck

Cap.: *Capitano* (captain); alternatively, *caporale* (corporal)

Carrello elastico: A single-axle two-wheel bogie trailer on which antiquated artillery pieces were placed in order to make them suitable for high-speed towing

Carro armato: Tank

Carro veloce (CV): Fast tank (tankette)

CCNN (*Camicie Nere*): Blackshirts

Celere: Fast, in reference to a unique type of Italian division consisting of cavalry and armoured elements

Celerflex: A type of truck tire

Col.: *Colonnello* (colonel)

Comando Superiore Forze Armate dell'Africa Settentrionale: Armed Forces High Command North Africa

Comando Supremo: Supreme Command; the Italian military command headquarters in Rome

Compagnia: Company

Corazzata: Armoured

Delease: *Delegazione Africa Settentionale*; the liaison element between ACIT and the *Comando Supremo* in Rome, responsible for dealing with administrative and non-operational matters

Divisione: Division

Dovere: Duty, obligation

DSSTAM: *Direzione Superiore del Servizio Tecnico Armi e Munizioni* (Technical Services Higher Headquarters for Weapons and Munitions)

Elektron: An alloy of magnesium and aluminum used for wheels on Italian artillery pieces

EP: *effetto pronto* (Italian term for HEAT/High Explosive Antitank ammunition)

EPS: *effetto pronto speciale* (Italian term for HESH/High Explosive Squash Head ammunition)

Fanteria: Infantry

Fanteria carrista: Armoured infantry

Gen.: *Generale* (general)

Generale: General

Generale di brigata: Brigadier general

Generale di corpo d'armata: Lieutenant general

Generale di divisione: Major general

Graduati: Corporals (various grades)

Gruppo: An artillery or cavalry echelon equivalent to a battalion; also, an air force echelon equivalent to a US or British group, usually with 24 aircraft

Guastatori: Sappers, assault engineers

Magg.: *Maggiore* (major)

Milizia Volontaria per la Sicurezza Nazionale (MVSN): Volunteer Militia for National Security, a Fascist militia organization

MILMART: *Milizia Marittima di Artiglieria*; naval artillery militia, normally coastal artillery, but also manned truck-mounted naval guns

NM: *Nafta Militare* (Diesel Military), used to describe military trucks powered by diesel engines

Polizia dell'Africa Italiana (PAI): Italian Africa Police (Italian colonial police)

Raggruppamento: A tactical organization of flexible size and mission, comparable to the US task force or German *Kampfgruppe* concept

RECAM: *Reparto Esplorante Corpo d'Armata di Manovra* (Manuever Army Corps Reconnaissance Group)

RECO: *Reparto Esplorante Corazzato* (Armoured Reconnaissance Group)

Reggimento: Regiment

Reggimento carrista: Tank regiment

Regia Aeronautica (RA): Italian Royal Air Force

Regia Marina (RM): Italian Royal Navy

Regio Esercito (RE): Italian Royal Army

RSI: *Repubblica Sociale Italiana* (Italian Social Republic)

Semovente: Self-propelled gun (tracked)

Sottufficiali: Non-commissioned officers, NCOs (various grades)

SPA: *Società Piemontese Automobili*, a subsidiary of FIAT

Squadriglia: Air force squadron, usually consisting of 12 aircraft; naval squadron

Squadron: Cavalry echelon equivalent to a company

S.ten: Second Lieutenant

Stormo: Air force echelon equivalent to a US or British wing, usually consisting of 72 aircraft

Ten.: *Tenente* (lieutenant)

Ten.col.: *Tenente colonnello* (lieutenant colonel)

Glossary of Arab Terms

Abu: father
Ain: spring
Alam: landmark, sign
Bab: gate, door
Bir: well
Bu: short for Abu (father)
Chott: swampy salt lake
Dahar: escarpment, peak, ridge
Deir: depression
Djebel (Gebel): mountain, hill, slope
Gabr (Qabr): grave
Garet: village
Gasr: castle, palace
Gebel (Djebel): mountain, hill, slope
Ghibli: a hot Saharan wind
Ghot (Got): lowland, depression
Giof: hollow
Got (Ghot): lowland, depression
Hagfet: bend, curve
Hagiag: ridge
Marsa (Mersa): anchorage, anchor
Mersa (Marsa): anchorage, anchor
Naqb: pass
Qaret: small hill
Quabr (Gabr): grave
Ras: headland, cape
Rugbet (Rughbet): wish
Rughbet (Rugbet): wish
Sebkha: marsh, brackish pond, beach
Sidi: lord, master
Tariq (Trig): track, route, trail
Tell: hill; an artificial mound made of accumulated refuse material
Trig (Tariq): track, route, trail
Uadi (Wadi): dry riverbed, valley, gully
Wadi (Uadi): dry riverbed, valley, gully
Zaulet: corner, small mosque

Introduction

Mancò la fortuna, non il valore ('Luck was lacking, but valor was not'). These words are inscribed on a marble plaque erected at the furthest point of the Italian advance into Egypt by the 7th *Bersaglieri* Regiment 111 kilometers (69 miles) from Alexandria and in a way encapsulate the story of the Italian army during the desert campaign in North Africa from 1941 to 1943. There was no lack of valor, courage or self- sacrifice on the part of Italian soldiers of all ranks during the campaign, but what might be defined as 'luck', especially in terms of manpower, equipment and supplies was indeed bad more often than not.

There are many detailed accounts, in English as well as Italian, of the British counteroffensive against the Italians that ran from 9 December 1940 to 7 February 1941 during which outnumbered British forces under General Richard O'Connor won a stunning victory over a much larger Italian force in Libya. To the misfortune of the Italians, of the scores of books that have been written in several languages, the battles fought during those 61 days are the only ones that adequately document the combat operations of Italian forces in the desert between 1940 and 1943. The Anglo–Saxon historiography that does relate to the North African campaign is almost universally uncomplimentary with respect to the organization, equipment, leadership and performance of Italian troops and units in the desert; with few exceptions, it is difficult to find detailed or accurate accounts, either by unit or by battle, of the accomplishments of Italian units in North Africa from early February 1941 to the end of the campaign in Tunisia in May 1943. In the 22 months between February 1941 and November 1942 when the Axis forces were defeated at the Second Battle of El Alamein, of the 11 Italian divisions operating in the desert after February 1941 it was not until January 1942 that an Italian division, the 'Savona', was destroyed at Sollum. Another division, the 'Sabratha', was destroyed six months later in July, during the First Battle of El Alamein. Four months later, in November 1942 during the Second Battle of El Alamein, most of the remaining Italian divisions were destroyed. It might be noted that during the period from February 1941 to September 1942 the Italians were primarily responsible for the destruction of the 3rd Indian Motor Brigade, for severely mauling the British 22nd Armoured Brigade during the battle of Bir el Gobi, and for being instrumental in the capture of Tobruk in June 1942, which netted some 32,000 prisoners.

Similarly, there is scant literature in Italian that chronicles the operations of Italian forces in the desert in any systematic, coherent or all-encompassing fashion. Italian writing seems to focus largely on a few high-profile units, especially the 'Ariete' armoured division which, because of its mobility operated in close conjunction with the two armoured and one mechanized divisions of the *Deutsches Afrika Korps* (DAK); and of the 'Folgore' parachute division, which played an important and illustrious role, although its overall participation was limited to only a relatively brief period. There is a decent amount of coverage by several Italian authors, primarily Paolo Caccia Dominioni, Alberto Bechi-Luserna and Igino Gravina, devoted to the Alamein battles, focusing largely on the 'Folgore' and the armoured divisions. The infantry divisions, which represented the bulk of Italian units in the desert but which, because of their lack of mobility were limited largely to either static siege operations against Tobruk or to maintaining defensive positions to hold critical areas chosen by Rommel, are accorded only scant mention in both English-language and Italian works. Indeed, there are virtually no works in Italian that deal specifically with the history of any of the infantry

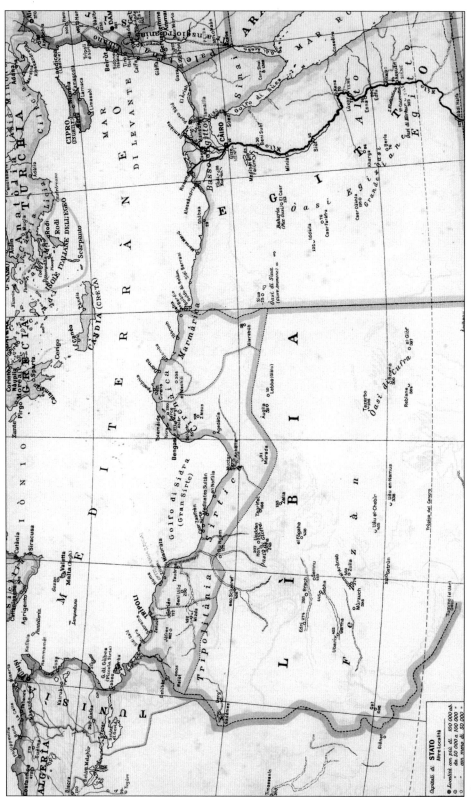

Contemporary Italian map of North Africa. Note the various regions of Libya: Marmarica, Cirenaica, Sirtica, Tripolitania and the vast interior area of Fezzan. (Courtesy Giancarlo Garello)

divisions in the desert. Although their achievements may have been less spectacular than those of the German and Italian armoured divisions, the Italian infantry divisions did, however, manage to stand up against much better equipped and mobile British and Commonwealth forces. Perhaps the attitude displayed by Gabriele Verri, the major who commanded the XI Tank Battalion in the 'Trieste' motorized division, gives us a clue as to why there is a scarcity of Italian accounts based on firsthand experience. When asked to recount his experiences, Verri answered by saying: 'For whom? For the few survivors? I don't believe it is necessary, because like me, they carry their stories in their hearts and in their scars. For anyone else, it's not worth the trouble.'

Overall, the degree to which the Italians participated in operations in the desert and the results they achieved have been ignored, minimized, denigrated, maligned or otherwise cast in mainly negative terms, especially in English-language publications. Indeed, in many accounts, it seems that the Italians were either completely absent from the fighting, or, if present, were merely passive bystanders and contributed nothing noteworthy to the generally chaotic brawl going on between the Germans and the British. The reasons for this are varied and stem from a wide range of some-times disparate and sometimes interconnected factors. The genesis of this largely negative view and assessment of Italian forces in North Africa undoubtedly had its beginnings in the offensive carried out by Wavell beginning in December 1940 and ending at Beda Fomm in February 1941, which, at a time when the British were reeling from losses at Dunkirk and in need of something resembling a victory, was portrayed as an example of superior British strategy, tactics, equipment, leadership and operational capability over the Italians. Almost inevitably, the campaign began to be seen as very capable, motivated, well-trained, well-led and courageous British forces making easy work of inept, badly led, ill-equipped Italians. Ultimately, this led to the portrayal of the individual Italian soldier as unable or unwilling to fight, or as an outright coward who was all too eager to surrender at the earliest opportunity. While it is an historical fact that the offensive by the British Western Desert Force against the Italians was a stunning success that badly mauled the Italians, destroying ten divisions, it is likewise historically true that this was far from being an irreparable calamity or a total annihilation of the Italian forces in the desert, as the Italians still maintained sizeable forces further west in Tripolitania in Libya and soon sent reinforcements to the area. Thus, when the Germans under the energetic commander, Erwin Rommel, appeared on the scene in February 1941 virtually days after the debacle at Beda Fomm and the British began to suffer defeat at the hands of the combined German and Italian forces, the British were afforded an opportunity to save face by ascribing their reverses as due to being beaten by the Germans, generally regarded as worthy and capable opponents, rather than by the Italians who, heaven forbid, should be taken seriously as soldiers. Thus, quite often in accounts that describe a given battle or action when Italian troops were exclusively or preponderantly involved in the defeat of British or Commonwealth units, such as the virtual destruction of the 3rd Indian Motor Brigade and its surrender to the Italians at Mechili in April 1941, the Italians are not given specific credit but rather are referred to as 'Axis forces', or as at Sceleidima in January 1942 which is not even acknowledged in English-language texts. Indeed, at least one German account paints the action at El Mechili in April 1941 as an entirely German affair and makes no reference at all to the role played by the Italians. The Italians, along with the Germans who came upon the scene in February 1941, fought long and hard, displaying resilience, stoicism, stubbornness, skill and courage in the face of increasingly larger and better-equipped British and Commonwealth (and ultimately American) forces until their ultimate surrender in Tunisia in May 1943. Their story deserves to be told in its proper perspective.

1

The Italian Soldier

General Considerations

Of all the factors such as organization and unit structure, equipment, training, doctrine, tactics and the nation's capacity to support its military forces that combined to define Italy's military potential, the one factor that was paramount to waging war, and without which all the other considerations would be useless, was the human element, or the soldier himself. The Italian soldier, writ large, to include enlisted, non-commissioned officer (NCO) and officer ranks, has often been maligned, joked about and described in less than flattering terms. Objectively, however, compared to the combatants of other nations or viewed strictly in the prism of the performance of the Italians themselves, they were more than capable as a fighting force in North Africa. The Italian infantry divisions were essentially foot-borne, and the case could be made that the Italian infantry soldier, who often had to walk miles across the desert rather than ride in the comfort of a truck, was a much physically tougher individual than any of his opponents or even than his much-vaunted German allies. It should also be borne in mind that in the 1930s and 1940s, Italy was still a primarily agricultural society and that much of the conscript population was accustomed to hardship and privation even before being subjected to the rigors of military life and combat. The army's emphasis on physical fitness as well as their generally hardy stock led the Italian soldier to be able to cope relatively well with extended periods in theater and poor diet. Some indication of the ability of Italian soldiers to endure privation and still function effectively may be inferred by hospital records: hospitalizations in September 1942 were relatively low (4,569 soldiers of all ranks), compared to widespread sickness among newly arrived German troops.

Italians in general and southern Italians (who comprised a disproportionately large percentage of the infantry divisions in the desert) in particular, have long been known for their ability to improvise; the Italian word '*arrangiarsi*' ('make do') conveys the sense of doing the best one can with whatever is at hand. With respect to the situation in North Africa, the Italian soldier certainly had to improvise and make do more than any other combatant: the opposing British and Commonwealth troops were blessed with an astounding wealth of food, equipment, ammunition, fuel and everything else needed to conduct operations, and the Germans seemed always to have enough of almost anything or, failing that, would resort to commandeering whatever they needed from the Italians. In stark contrast, the Italians, often undermanned, underfed and undersupplied, described themselves as beggars and '*straccioni*' ('ragamuffins'). Faced with such penury, Italian soldiers often came up with extremely innovative ways to improve their lot. An example is furnished by the 'Folgore' parachute division, which was notoriously short of vehicles, due in part to its organization as a parachute division and in part to the general paucity of vehicles throughout the *Regio Esercito* (Italian Royal Army, RE) in North Africa. The troopers of the 'Folgore', however, who were not at all inclined or resigned to having to lug their food, water and other supplies on their own shoulders, showed a special genius for salvaging vehicles from the battlefield. The soldiers identified all in their midst who had been mechanics and drivers prior to becoming paratroopers and created several 'salvage

Off duty *Bersaglieri*, April 1942. They are armed with Model 1891 cavalry carbines and sport
mustaches and goatees, a very popular combination among Italians in the desert.
(Massimiliano Afiero)

teams' who scoured the area for the remains of any type of vehicle. Having done so, within ten days
they managed to cobble together a Ford V8 truck and were then able to increase the area which they
could search for other vehicles. Within a month they were able to patch together four Chevrolets,
three Fords, six Austins, two Lancias and a Morris truck, as well as an American vehicle (probably a jeep) for the colonel, a German water tanker and four motorcycles. Gathered together, they
looked more like a Gypsy caravan than any kind of known military motor pool. Every once in
a while, when one of these vehicles (some of which consisted of only a frame and an engine and
possibly a driver's seat) broke down, the driver would make repairs and discard some piece or other,
saying: 'This piece serves no useful purpose.'

British, and later Allied, propaganda tended to attribute most, if not all, of their own defeats in
the desert to action by German forces; it was more palatable to attribute defeat to an enemy who
stereotypically was regarded as competent and whose military prowess was respected, rather than
to admit that one could suffer at the hands of an enemy who previously had been easily beaten and
whose military capabilities were looked upon with little respect or even with contempt. Because of
the often confused nature of the fighting in the desert, when German and Italian units frequently
used captured British vehicles and resorted to wearing captured British uniforms because their
own were in tatters, it is understandable that on occasion the British could mistake the Italians for
Germans. But instances such as these aside, there was an ingrained prejudice against admitting that
the Italians could perform as well as the Germans, in either defense or offense, or that they could
beat the British, Australians, New Zealanders or Indians when in fact, during various engagements, the Italians bested each of those nationalities. Somewhat illustrative of this condescending
attitude is the behavior of the commander of the New Zealand 6th Brigade, Brigadier George

Herbert Clifton, who during the battle of Alam el Halfa, blundered into a patrol of the 'Folgore' parachute division and was taken prisoner by the Italians, who subsequently turned him over to Rommel. Clifton was so embarrassed at being caught by the Italians that during his meeting with Rommel, he asked to be considered a German captive, and indeed, many accounts refer to Clifton as having been captured by the Germans rather than by the Italians. Campini states that several times Clifton claimed that he had to relieve himself and tried to escape but was unsuccessful; he was sent to a POW camp in Italy. This rather petulant behavior by Clifton, who in his memoirs repeatedly refers to the Italians as 'Wops', highlights an enduring, and especially under the circumstances, anachronistically misplaced sense of contempt for the Italians who had captured him.

That the Italian forces in North Africa (and in other theaters as well) suffered from a number of shortcomings, including often muddled leadership at the higher echelons; poor and insufficient training prior to being committed to combat; often (but not always) outdated, inadequate or inferior equipment; shortage of major end items such as artillery and armour and motor transport; and a shortage of supplies, is undeniable. It should also be noted that following the early 1941 victory over the Italians, British and Commonwealth forces in the desert suffered many of the same problems: their leadership was often in disarray, with bickering between senior commanders of different nationalities, new units arrived in the desert untrained and inexperienced and equipment, especially tanks, not significantly, if at all, better than the opposing German and Italian equipment. It was not until arrival of the Grants and Shermans from the United States in 1942 that the British finally had tanks markedly superior to those of the Germans and Italians. When taking all the negative factors into consideration, and when examining the actual performance of Italian soldiers and units, their combat performance in the field becomes quite impressive and, one might hazard to say, was in an overall sense even better than that of comparable British, Commonwealth, German and, later, American units. All the combatants, regardless of nationality, were faced with the same harsh desert environment of daytime heat and nighttime cold; lack of readily available water or of tainted water that led to high rates of dysentery; an overabundance of flies, lice, scorpions, poisonous spiders and other insects; and the ever-present sand and loose stone that necessitated constant repair and maintenance of weapons and equipment. Added to all of this, however, the Italians had to deal with other factors such as flawed strategic thinking at the highest levels, poor structure of their infantry divisions, many classes of outdated equipment, and almost endemic shortage of most classes of supplies.

Nonetheless, as events bore witness, after mid-1941 the Italian divisions in North Africa fought well, and in many cases, extremely well, against British, Commonwealth and, later, American, forces. The troops of the core Italian units in North Africa (132nd Armoured Division 'Ariete', 101st Motorized Division 'Trieste', 102nd Motorized Division 'Trento', 17th Infantry Division 'Pavia', 25th Infantry Division 'Bologna', 27th Infantry Division 'Brescia' and 55th Infantry Division 'Savona') became quite experienced, tough and battle-hardened by virtue of their prolonged service in the desert and displayed remarkable resiliency until the October–November 1942 battle of El Alamein. Although some units such as the 'Ariete' and the 'Trieste' as well as the 185th 'Folgore' parachute division were especially noteworthy, the other Italian divisions acquitted themselves well against more numerous and larger mechanized and armoured formations blessed with an abundance of more modern and capable equipment. In fact, both on their own and in concert with German forces, the Italians scored a number of successes and captured significant numbers of enemy combatants in engagements such as El Mechili, Bir el Gobi and Point 175.

All in all, throughout most of the campaigning, the Italians were outnumbered, outgunned, underequipped and undersupplied. Yet in spite of that, they, like the Germans with whom they fought alongside in the desert, were outfought not because of any inherent martial shortcomings, but because they simply could not stand up against the unrelenting and overwhelming numerical and material superiority of the Allied forces on the ground, as well as the fact that as the campaign wore on neither the *Luftwaffe* nor the *Regia Aeronautica* (Italian Royal Air Force, RA) could support or protect the Axis forces as the Allies had achieved near total air superiority over the battlefield. To overlook or minimize the role played by the Italian component of the Axis forces in North Africa and to devalue or trivialize the contribution of the Italian soldier in those campaigns is a distortion of historical fact and leads to a fundamental misunderstanding of the events as they transpired at the time.

Italian officers and soldiers in all branches of service performed well, judged by most objective standards. Perhaps the fact that the crews of many of the medium tank battalions consisted of university students contributed to the high level of performance of Italian tank units. Italian tank crews were taught to react as violently as possible when attacked and were not averse to charging headlong into the enemy when engaged. They consistently faced off against usually superior forces, increasingly equipped with more modern tanks and antitank guns, heedless of the odds and the dangers they faced, and often fought their tanks rather than abandon them even though they had suffered damage. The behavior and actions of Italian tank crews at times bordered on fanaticism. There was more truth than met the eye to the motto of the Italian tankers, '*Ferrea Mole, Ferreo Cuore*' ('Iron Hulls and Iron Hearts').

The *Bersaglieri*, or light infantry, with their distinctive plumed headgear, who were integral to the armoured and motorized divisions, were well-suited for desert warfare and operated effectively with the armoured units. They could be either truck-borne or rode motorcycles; later in the desert war they were also equipped with the AB41 armoured car. They were aggressive in the attack, and when they were attacked, even when surprised, often reacted quickly to defend and counterattack. Rommel said of the *Bersaglieri* that: 'The German soldier has astonished the world, the Italian *bersagliere* has astonished the German soldier.'

Throughout all the campaigns in North Africa, including the late 1940–early 1941 British desert offensive, Italian artillery crews performed very adequately, especially considering the age and obsolescence of most of their artillery pieces, whose range more often than not could not match the range of opposing British artillery. In fact, the most frequently encountered positive remarks to be found in British reports or postwar memoirs or accounts relate to the skill with which Italian gunners handled their pieces and the accuracy of their fire. It is generally acknowledged that Italian gunners were quite effective in providing supporting fire to the infantry and armoured units to which they were organic or attached and that when the proper guns were available were also able to deliver accurate counterbattery fire. Overall, losses among artillery officers, NCOs and gun crews were high, as it was not uncommon for Italian artillerymen to stick to their guns until they were overrun. As famous and often quoted as the final message on 4 November 1942 by 'Ariete' is in the annals of Italian armoured history lore, there was a similar final message a few hours earlier, at about 1300, transmitted by the artillerymen of 'Trieste' which read: '*Munizioni quasi esaurite. Le spareremo tutte sul posto*' ('Ammunition almost all gone. We'll stay right here and fire everything that's left').

As somewhat of a subset of the artillery, the self-propelled guns (*semoventi*) armed with the 75/18 gun/howitzer performed yeoman service against British armour, including against the 75mm M3 Lee and M4 Sherman tanks supplied by the US, but as with much of the Italian equipment in the desert, the numbers of *semoventi* available were pathetically small and not enough to significantly affect the outcome of most operations.

Somewhat less visible in the overall context of operations were combat support and support and service troops, such as the engineers, battlefield recovery and field repair units; supply, logistics and transportation units; and intelligence and intercept units. Italian military engineers seem to have had DNA inherited from their Roman ancestors, who were well-known for their ability to build roads wherever they went, bridges such as the one built by Caesar's legions at Ricomagus to cross the Rhine, walls such as Hadrian's Wall on the Scottish border, and some amazing feats of

Egypt, October 1942. Italian sappers preparing to breach a barbed wire fence. The soldier on the far left seems to be armed with a Model 40 flamethrower. (Massimiliano Afiero)

tunneling in the Carso during the First World War. In North Africa, Italian engineers built elaborate defensive works and positions such as those at Tobruk and Bardia (later used to good effect by the British), cleared minefields and were responsible for the impressive feat of building a hard-surface asphalt bypass road around Tobruk that was some 75 kilometers (about 45 miles) long in the space of a couple of months. Italian battlefield recovery units were skilled at recovering damaged vehicles and seemingly worked miracles to repair damaged tanks or cobble together parts of several vehicles to come up with one running vehicle. The Italians had a major vehicle and tank repair facility, the *12o Autoraggruppamento Africa Settentrionale*, at Villaggio Berta (El Guba, today's Al Qubah, west of Derna) run by Colonel Tullio Nicolardi, who reportedly liked his wine, but was an absolute genius when it came to motors. Transportation units managed to juggle available transportation assets, routinely pooling trucks from several units, in order to ferry the vehicle-poor infantry divisions from one location to another. The Italian intelligence office at *Comando Superiore* level, headed by Major Mario Revetria, a cavalry officer, was not only able to intercept enemy radio traffic, but apparently was quite astute at analyzing the data and providing accurate information to Italian field commanders.

Illustrative of the Italian capability for several arms to work effectively in concert is the action between the 132nd 'Ariete' armoured division and the British 22nd Armoured Brigade at Bir el Gobi on 19 November 1941 during Operation Crusader. The opposing forces were roughly equally matched in terms of force size, with the British having a slight edge in the number of tanks fielded. Despite several gallant but ill-advised charges by the British, their attacks were roundly trounced, with almost half of their tank force being destroyed, forcing them to withdraw. During this encounter, Italian armour, artillery and *Bersaglieri* elements worked as an integrated, harmonious team, each supporting the others. Another noteworthy but not often acknowledged aspect of that particular action was that the Italian XX Corps commander, General Gastone Gambara, had been ordered by Rommel to pull out of Bir el Gobi that morning, but Gambara, putting his faith in Italian rather than German intelligence assessments, refused to move, with the result that the action there later in the day upset the entire timetable of the British Operation Crusader offensive.

Morale Factors

One persistently recurring theme in much English-language literature is that the hearts and minds of the Italians were not in the struggle, or that they could not accept the desert and the hardship of an unwanted war. These sentiments go hand-in-hand with assertions that the Italians often surrendered quickly; adverbs such as 'eagerly' and 'willingly' and phrases such as their 'tendency to surrender or retreat when the going got really tough' are often used gratuitously when describing the surrender of Italian soldiers. It is interesting to note that while much use is made of the word 'surrender' in conjunction with Italians, it is not as easy to find accounts of the use of that word in conjunction with the defeat of British, Commonwealth, or even German units, who are usually described as having been 'captured'. Surrendering evokes images of someone raising their hands in submission, whereas being captured evokes a somewhat more positive image of someone who is forced to give up unwillingly.

The negative characterization of the Italian soldier is, however, quite wide of the mark when viewed in an historical context and compared to the performance of the combat records of the forces of several other European nations during the war. Between 1 September and 6 October 1939 Germany conquered Poland after the tough, courageous Poles put up a heroic defense against both German and Russian forces but were nevertheless overwhelmed in little more than a month. In 1940 the French army, with some 48 divisions and whose tanks generally outclassed the opposing German armour, lasted only about 45 days (10 May to 25 June), and about 1,900,000 French soldiers were taken prisoner. In February 1942, a mixed British/Australian/Indian force of about 80,000 troops in Singapore surrendered to a much smaller Japanese force (about 30,000) after about a week of fighting. The Belgian, Dutch and Norwegian armies also folded in the face of German attacks after brief resistance. By comparison, between February 1941 and May 1943 Italian forces, assisted by a much smaller German force, fought it out in the desert for more than two years against numerically superior and much better equipped and supplied British and Commonwealth, and later American, forces.

It should also be noted that often, if not almost always overlooked, is the role played by the Germans in North Africa in placing the Italians in a position which left them little choice but to surrender. On repeated occasions the Germans, rather than standing and fighting, turned tail and ran as fast as they could to save their own skins and thus avoid surrender, leaving the Italians to stand and fight, essentially buying time for the retreating German units. Retreat or withdrawal for the Italians was not possible because of the lack of suitable transportation assets, so the only options were to fight as long as possible and be annihilated or to surrender, and in fact, Italian infantry elements did normally resist as long as they could and were either wiped out or surrendered – the case of the 40th Infantry Regiment of the 'Bologna' infantry division, left behind by the Germans during their retreat from El Alamein in November 1942, which fought until it had literally expended its last cartridge, is perhaps the classic example of the predicament of many Italian units. There was no more shame in the surrender by Italian units than there was in the surrender of British or Commonwealth units who were captured by Italian forces, but that simple fact seems to go unnoticed in much of the historiography relating to the desert campaigns.

Concomitantly, there is somewhat of a recurring theme in non-Italian publications to the effect that, generally speaking, the morale of the average Italian soldier was low, and he wished for a speedy end to the war and wanted to go home. Reading Italian texts that deal with the war, especially regarding the campaign in North Africa, supports neither the assertion nor the conclusion that morale was consistently or universally low, or that it was any lower than that of any of the other combatants. Morale in most units remained acceptable, or even high, even when the overall situation was bleak. In July 1942, even after having suffered some major setbacks, General Ceriana-Mayneri, the interim commander of the 'Littorio' armoured division, recorded that his troops, though ill-armed and generally poorly equipped, were nevertheless in high spirits. Even as late as the Second Battle of El Alamein, when it was clear that victory for the Axis was impossible, morale among the paratroopers of the 'Folgore' remained high; unit pride and putting a good face on things led to situations in which the 'Folgorini' would rather run the risk of being killed than give enemy observers the impression that they were afraid of enemy fire. In one instance one of the officers, Guido Visconti, who insisted on shaving every day despite the scarcity of water, very calmly strolled along a ridgeline, with his walking stick in hand, naturally drawing enemy fire. When one of his paratroopers told him that it would be advisable to take cover, his response was: 'My dear man, the Viscontis are not in the habit of dodging Windsor lead.'

Contributing largely to good or high morale in units were a number of factors, including leadership, unit cohesion and a widespread sense of devotion to duty ('*dovere*'). Anecdotes of high morale are often, although not always, associated with units considered elite, such as the XXXI Sapper Battalion and the 'Folgore' parachute division, where unit cohesion was very solid. However, morale seems to have been high in other units such as the 'Ariete' armoured division, in many of the *Bersaglieri* units and in almost all artillery units, as well as in some of the more prosaic non-motorized infantry units such as the 40th Infantry Regiment of the 'Bologna' division, all of which maintained surprisingly high morale even under the most trying of circumstances. Undoubtedly, a major factor impacting both unit cohesion and morale was what appears to have been a very conscious sense of duty, or doing the right thing under the circumstances, especially when it came to standing by or assisting one's fellow soldiers. Even when exhausted, as in the case cited by Caccia Dominioni when 19 of the 23 officers, and a similar proportion of the troops in his XXXI Sapper Battalion, were sick with dysentery, they nevertheless made superhuman efforts to stay in the line. In reading accounts by Italian combatants, there are very few references to acting in obedience to orders (the German concept of '*Befehl ist Befehl*', or 'Orders are orders'), while there are frequent references to the concept of '*Il dovere è il dovere*' ('Duty is duty'). The attitude of many, if not most, Italians was much more along the lines of doing what was innately right rather than doing something without question just because one was told to do it.

Probably contributing to this sense of duty was the markedly strong Italian concept of community. Italian society has always been characterized by a distrust of centralized power; Italians are not known for allegiance to the central government, which they do not perceive as particularly benevolent towards its citizens. Family relationships in Italy are very important and traditional as well as incredibly strong. Allegiances stem outward from the family unit, progressively to the street one lives on and immediate neighbors, then to the town or city that the family lives in, and then possibly to the province or region of residence. This phenomenon is known in Italian as '*campanilismo*' – a reference to the local bell tower, around which like-minded Italians gather. The English term 'parochialism' comes close to describing the Italian attitude. What all these societal attitudes translated to in the life of the Italian soldier was that in many respects his squad was a surrogate for his immediate family, the platoon for his street or neighborhood, and the company for his province. This led to strong bonds of loyalty to his fellow soldiers and a desire not to 'let the family down'.

Even in situations where unit morale remained high, it did not impair the almost sacrosanct duty of the common soldier to complain about his lot in life and to make acerbic observations and comments about how operations were being managed, especially by officers in the rear echelons. The discontent felt by the troops was laid out rather well by Caccia Dominioni with respect to his XXXI Sapper Battalion. The troops complained that the supply situation was not adequate for the needs on the front line; that the *Regia Aeronautica* and *Luftwaffe* did little to alleviate the constant

Italian assault engineers, September 1942. The officer in the foreground is wearing the popular Sahariana jacket. The typical hard, flat, rock-strewn desert terrain offered little or no opportunity for concealment. (Massimiliano Afiero)

enemy air attacks; that the food was often spoiled, insufficient and disgusting; that what water was available was often tainted from being stored in containers that had previously held other liquids such as fuel; that the battalion was not employed as it should be in its specialized role as sappers, but rather in more mundane tasks such as laying mines; and finally, that the rear echelon had an over-abundance of staff and men to the detriment of troop numbers in the front line. In this instance, the Italian sappers on the line noted that the German engineer headquarters consisted of a colonel, a captain, a lieutenant and a small staff, whereas its bloated and overly bureaucratized Italian counterpart consisted of ten different overlapping and redundant headquarters and offices manned by four generals, 11 engineer colonels and a correspondingly large number of staff.

It should be noted that following the setbacks suffered after Operations Brevity and Battleaxe, the British refer to the low ebb of morale among their own troops. No nationality is immune from periods of depression following unexpected defeat, and to single out the Italians for low morale and infer that they suffered more than anyone else in that respect ignores the reality of human nature. Likewise, with respect to assertions by some authors that the Italians would rather go home than serve in the desert, there can be little doubt that many, if not most, of the Italians serving in the desert longed to return to hearth and home and be with their families and loved ones, but it is just as true that British, Australian, Indian, South African, New Zealand, French and German soldiers felt the same way. There are no accounts of soldiers from any nation expressing unrestrained joy and happiness at being stuck in the inhospitable desert environment and looking forward eagerly to being shot at while enduring searing heat, swarms of flies, bad food, thirst and dysentery.

British works frequently reference the luxuries that Italian officers, and to some extent the enlisted men, enjoyed in the front lines. One author in particular, Alan Moorehead, goes on for several pages referencing items such as clean bedsheets, fine wines and mineral water from Italy, high quality ostentatious uniforms and all manner of desirable foodstuffs being in abundance in the front lines during the late 1940 British offensive. The general impression conveyed was that the Italians, especially the officers, were a bunch of dandies and fops who would be more at home in a comic opera than in combat. Rizzo dismisses Moorhead's claims as being ridiculous nonsense. Even allowing for the possibility that British claims in that regard may have had some basis in fact at the time, the possibility must also be considered that the claims were likely exaggerated and that, indeed, some items such as wine and mineral water, seen as luxuries by one society, could be considered entirely commonplace in another society. Certainly, there is little if any evidence that after December 1940 the Italians on the front line had any of the amenities described by Moorhead and others. It is quite true, however, that the further to the rear one went in North Africa, the more comforts officers and enlisted men were able to treat themselves to; this applied to the British as well as to the Italians. [Parenthetically, within the British Army during the North African campaign, the joke was that the initials for the rear-echelon Royal Army Service Corps (RASC) stood for 'Run Away Someone's Coming' because of their penchant for retreating as fast as they could with their field kitchens, petrol bowsers, workshops and signal vans.] That the Italians in the rear echelon, such as back in Tripoli, enjoyed whatever creature comforts they could find is unquestionable, just as it was true of the British who in Alexandria and Cairo enjoyed catered service at luxury hotels and carried on with memberships in exclusive clubs as though the war didn't exist. Because Cairo was often in relative proximity to the front, British soldiers of all ranks could avail themselves of the pleasures of the 'big city' when they were able to get leave (a 'prize' that was almost unheard of among the Italians of all ranks). Frontline Italian soldiers were well aware of the rather comfortable style of living enjoyed by the rear-echelon officers and troops and, like soldiers in every army, resented it, although they also accepted it as a fact of life. If the Germans in North Africa did not share in this rear-area sybaritism, it was only because there were precious few Germans in the rear area in North Africa, not because of any national characteristic that mitigated against such behavior; in fact, given the opportunity, such as presented itself after the fall of France, the Germans availed themselves of the finest hotels in Paris, or confiscated palatial chateaus for their headquarters. It should be noted that when the Americans and British pushed the Germans out of such luxurious and desirable accommodations, they took them over for their own use. It is axiomatic that all armies tend to behave in a similar fashion, no matter what the nationality.

Leadership

One of the oft-repeated criticisms of the Italians is that they were poorly led. This mantra again hearkens back to the initial losses suffered in the desert, when generals such as Graziani and Bergonzoli, who, compared to the British, had an overwhelming superiority in terms of numbers of divisions and troops, failed to deploy or maneuver their forces properly and who, as a result, were able to be defeated in detail by a much smaller but mobile and astutely led British force. Those facts are undeniable, although in many individual actions during that offensive there were Italian officers such as generals Maletti and Babini who did attempt to rally their troops and organize a proper defense, but overall, Italian leadership at the higher levels was ineffective. However, after February 1941 there was a marked improvement in the skills and leadership abilities of many, if not most, of the Italian corps and divisional commanders. This was undoubtedly attributable at least in part, if not in large measure, to the arrival of Rommel upon the scene, who was energetic and aggressive even by Teutonic standards and who provided the kind of leadership and example at the top that was badly needed in the Italian forces.

At the corps level and at the divisional level, commanders such as Baldassare of the 'Ariete' and later of XX Corps; Navarini of XXI Corps and who had an especially close relationship with

Rommel; Balotta of 'Ariete'; La Ferla of 'Trieste'; De Stefanis of 'Trento', 'Ariete' and then of XX Corps; Bitossi of 'Littorio' and later of XX Corps; Calvi di Bèrgolo of 'Centauro'; Gloria of 'Bologna'; and Zaglio of 'Pavia', although seldom ever mentioned, led and fought their units well throughout the campaigning in the desert. At least a few of the Italian generals enjoyed the complete respect and devotion of their subordinate officers and of the men in the ranks as well. Perhaps one of the best examples is Alessandro Gloria, who was nicknamed '*il Cipresso*' ('the cypress tree') because he was tall, dark, austere and serious as well as being a deeply devout Catholic, attending Mass in the field whenever he could. Rather than staying in a sandbagged bunker giving commands over the telephone, he often went to the front lines in the most miserable and dangerous sectors and interacted with the troops. He was also phenomenally calm in the face of danger; on one occasion, while in a meeting in his command vehicle with other senior officers, a shell from a British 25-pdr exploded

A pair of Italian armoured crewmen with the three-quarter length leather jacket. The *Bersaglieri* feathers suggest that these are the crew of an AB41 armoured car of one of the *Bersaglieri* reconnaissance elements. (USSME)

nearby and a shard flew through the vehicle a few centimeters from Gloria's head. While everyone else instinctively fell to the floor, Gloria continued his presentation without flinching and with no interruption while maintaining the same tone of voice, as though nothing at all out of the ordinary had happened. Gloria, like many, if not most, of the Italian generals in North Africa 1941 to 1943 had served as a junior officer in Libya in 1911–1912 during the Italo–Turkish war, and thus had some experience with military operations in the desert. Further down the command hierarchy, mid-grade and junior officers such as Colonel Ugo Montemurro, Colonel Gaetano Cantaluppi, Lieutenant Colonel Gino Fabris, Major Camillo Santamaria Nicolini and Captain Oderisio Piscicelli, along with the NCOs and troops in general, developed rather good combat skills and proficiency in the field.

In any discussion of leadership in the desert, note should be taken that there were problems in the German and British hierarchies as well. Rommel, who clearly was the most effective general of any nationality in the desert, was not always happy with the performance of his subordinate corps and divisional commanders, although that was in large measure due to conflicts attributable to very strong personalities rather than to any lack of competence on the part of his subordinates, broadly speaking. Rommel and General Johannes Streich, the commander of *5.Panzer-Division*, had rather heated disagreements; Streich was not one to shrink from voicing his opinions, which often were correct, and to square off against Rommel, who ended up dismissing him in May 1941. It should also be noted that Rommel had serious disagreements with his superior, Field Marshal Albert Kesselring, and that their relationship was far from cordial. Late in the campaign a rather bitter personal and professional animosity also developed between Rommel and his German colleague, General Hans-Jürgen von Arnim in Tunisia.

The British, on the other hand, had their fair share of hidebound, slow-moving, indecisive and outright bumbling and incompetent senior officers whose performance, or lack thereof, led them to be replaced, dismissed or captured. A partial list would include Noel Beresford-Pierse and Michael O'Moore Creagh for their inept leadership during Operation Battleaxe, Bernard Klopper at Tobruk, Neil Ritchie and his dithering during Operation Crusader and his subsequent dismissal. Bernard Law Montgomery, the Eighth Army commander, widely held by the British to be the paragon of military competence in the desert, was as much a product of British propaganda as Rommel was of German propaganda; the difference was that Rommel was an able, gifted and charismatic combat leader, whereas Montgomery was more of a plodding, egotistical, irascible administrator. Montgomery almost assuredly owes much of his successes to his predecessor, General Claude Auchinleck, who, along with Major General Eric Dorman-Smith, had adopted an indirect approach to defeating the Axis forces by focusing on eliminating the Italian infantry divisions, and by this attrition denying the Italo–German mobile forces of the buffer they needed against the British. Virtually any general blessed with the superabundance of resources that Montgomery had at his disposal, fighting against the resource-starved Italo–German forces, would have been able to defeat Rommel unless he were colossally incompetent. Stated in terms of the card game of poker, Montgomery held a royal flush, while Rommel held either a pair or, at best, three of a kind; Montgomery had an unbeatable hand and the odds against the Italo–German forces were unequivocally impossible.

There was also considerable mistrust and bickering among many of the British generals as well as among generals of different nationalities that represented the Commonwealth in North Africa, which in some cases were even more accentuated than that between the Germans and Italians. Caccia Dominioni relates an incident in which General D.H. Pienaar of the 1st South African Infantry Division who, after some of his troops had been mistakenly bombed by the Royal Air Force, railed at an RAF headquarters over the phone to protest the losses suffered by his troops, adding that his father had fought against the British in the Transvaal and that his family's feelings toward the English had not changed since then, suggesting that the RAF was willingly engaging in annihilation of South African forces. He concluded by asking the officer on the other end of the line if he should consider Rommel his enemy or his friend, and if, when the RAF appeared again, he should order his antiaircraft gunners to open fire, which he would do with 'indescribable enthusiasm'. The British, who tended to be quite cautious in reaction to Rommel's aggressive tactics, were often indecisive or made bad decisions and squandered opportunities to eliminate both German and Italian units.

Except for a few isolated references, there is no specific or clear documentation that reflects discord among the Italian generals serving in North Africa or that conveys any sense of substandard performance on their part, but that does not necessarily mean that such differences, animosities and shortcomings did not exist. This general lack of understanding of either the shortcomings or, conversely, the strong suits of individual high-ranking Italian officers is in large part, if not wholly, attributable to the general dearth of Italian writings relating to the war in that theater and to any specific narratives describing the individual officers themselves or their interactions with each other. Certainly, the Italians in North Africa had their share of problems with their masters at *Comando Supremo*, led by General Ugo Cavallero in Rome, and there is some indication that there was some personal animosity between De Stefanis, as commander of XX Corps, and Gervasio Bitossi, commander of 'Littorio', but other than that it is virtually impossible to find Italian accounts of any significant problems between high-ranking officers in North Africa. With respect to poor performance, one glaring example of poor, indeed incomprehensible, performance was the behavior of Major General Alessandro Piazzoni who on 1 December 1941 deliberately ignored repeated orders by Rommel to get his division moving. Although Rommel was furious over the delay, it did not seem to have much of an impact on Piazzoni's status, as he was moved up from division to temporary corps command shortly after that incident prior to being transferred to Dalmatia in command of an infantry division.

Junior officers in the tank battalions suffered very high casualty rates. On 17 April 1941, in an engagement outside of Tobruk at Ras el Madauer which involved three L3/35 and four M13/40 tanks, all the tanks were hit: lieutenants Gallo, Pileri, Pertusi and Montanari were killed, and lieutenants D'Ambra and Mazzuccato were wounded. A few weeks later, on 4 May, in an attack against strongpoint R.4 at Tobruk, Captain Accatis and lieutenants Fiori, Bertolini, Padovani, Formis and Zilli were killed and Major Gaggetti and Captain Marini were wounded. On 2 November 1942, during the Second Battle of El Alamein, Captain Vittorio Bulgarelli, Second Lieutenant Alfonso Marchitiello, Captain Mario Bartolini, Captain Alessandro Zanetti, Captain Vittorio Carraccio and Second Lieutenant Adelmo Ferrari were killed in action. Whether these high casualty rates among the tank officers were due to inexperience, especially during the earlier engagements in 1941, poor tactics, careless exposure to enemy fire, poor armour plate, or other factors is impossible to determine, but suffice it to say that regardless of losses, Italian tank officers seemed determined to do battle at almost any cost. As an example, during Operation Crusader, Captain Casale de Bustis y Figaroa of the VIII Tank Battalion made it back to the rear area with the armour plate of his tank damaged in several places by antitank fire; with his head and one knee streaming blood, he remained calm and smiling as though he had been awarded a long-sought prize. After having received some summary treatment, with his head wrapped in a white bandage and his leg stiff, he had himself hoisted aboard his tank again helped by Lieutenant Enrico Serra and went back into combat alongside his men who had not slacked off at all. De Bustis y Figaroa's attitude and actions are also an example of both the morale of the Italians under difficult circumstances, as well as reflecting the innate sense of duty shown by many officers and men alike who, although wounded, and often severely, either did their best to get back to their units or, being totally incapacitated, expressed their disappointment at not being able to get back into the fight.

Similarly, junior and senior officers in the 'Folgore' parachute division, who along with their men were in the thick of the fighting, suffered disproportionately high loss rates. During its relatively brief deployment to North Africa, and especially during the period of the Alamein battles, 'Folgore' lost at least 38 officers, the majority of whom (almost two-thirds) were lieutenants who were platoon leaders. Like the tank officers, and in common with parachute officers of all nationalities, the 'Folgore' officers led from the front and fought shoulder-to-shoulder with the men they commanded.

Succinctly stated, it is probably safe to say that all the leadership shortcomings many authors and historians ascribe to the Italians apply at least in some measure to the Germans and unquestionably in equal and arguably greater measure to the British.

Training

All Italian males were subject to military duty; exemptions were granted for several reasons including physical or mental disability and political unreliability. Compulsory military training began at age 18, when young men were subjected to intensive courses preparing them for their future military service. There was a high degree of emphasis accorded to physical fitness and training during all phases of military service.

The military education of officers was, on the whole, considered good. Regular officers (*Ufficiali in Servizio Permanente Effettivo*) generally were the product of the Military Academy at Modena or of the Turin artillery and engineer service academies and were well grounded in theory prior to being assigned to units. Conscript officers (*Ufficiali di Complemento*) were drawn from youths who met certain educational standards and were subjected to seven months of intensive instruction as cadets, then serving the remainder of their period of conscript service as junior officers. As in virtually every other army, newly minted junior officers were shipped off to North Africa with no combat experience, especially beginning in 1941 and had to learn their craft in situ. However, most of the senior Italian officers in North Africa had experienced tours of duty in Libya during the Italo–Turkish War of 1911–1912 or had served in that colony in the 1920s and 1930s, and hence, had a practical appreciation for at least some of the problems associated with operations in a desert environment.

The scope, quality and intensity of training for enlisted men varied from arm to arm. The Fascist regime placed strong emphasis on physical training and fitness, and Italian recruits adapted well to military life; early on in their service, the soldier's assignment was matched to his general skill set whenever possible. Infantry training was rudimentary and, in accordance with Fascist standards, stressed physical fitness, but the curriculum included a wide range of subjects including marksmanship training, patrolling, use of the compass, range estimation, use of terrain features in conjunction with maneuver, intelligence gathering and use of various types of communications. The soldier was taught that he was an essential part of a squad and that unit cohesion was important. Exercises were carried out up to company and battalion level, but only infrequently at echelons higher than that. In North Africa, the infantry divisions had little time to devote to supplemental formal training in theater, but rather learned their craft during the conduct of actual operations.

The 'Folgore' parachute division was assuredly the most well-trained division-size unit sent to North Africa by the Italians. To begin with, there was a rigorous selection process that weeded out all but the most suitable and physically fit young men, all of whom were volunteers for this specialty; the rejection rate was high at about 58 percent. Both officers and men completed at least five jumps from aircraft by the end of their training. The paratroopers also underwent intensive small arms and machine gun training, close-range battle tactics and antitank training. The army spent 45 times the amount to train a paratrooper than it did to create a good regular soldier. Their physical stamina, aggressive attitude and combat skills would cause the British untold amounts of grief during the Alamein battles in 1942.

Training of Italian armoured and armoured artillery crews and units varied in duration and consistency throughout the war. The large tank force that Italy fielded in 1939 provided commanders and staffs at least a rudimentary, if imperfect, understanding of armoured operations and logistical problems. It also allowed the Italians to train significant numbers of conscripts to drive and maintain tracked armoured vehicles, even though these vehicles were soon replaced by larger, more complicated machines. Armour officers continued to be trained as infantry officers at the Military Academy in Modena until 1942, when they were provided with an armour-specific curriculum. Following the very basic course at the Military Academy, they were sent to the tank training center where they finally were introduced to the medium tanks for the first time.

Training deficiencies had been noted in operations in both Africa and Spain. One of the shortcomings noted on the eve of war was that too much stress was placed upon the Fascist obsession with heroic actions and gestures, rather than having crews being well acquainted with the capabilities and limitations of the tanks themselves as well as with taking advantage of the terrain. With the imminent introduction of the M13/40 tank in 1940, a series of three consecutive training courses was planned at the tank training center at Bracciano (officers were to take courses in theory in Rome). Ultimately, only two of three planned courses were held, between December 1940 and

The crew of an M13/40 tank during a lull in the fighting, winter 1942. (USSME)

February 1941. Equipment available for training was minimal, consisting of one M13/40, one M11/39 and four L3/35s. Tank commanders fired five live rounds from the 47mm main gun and one magazine from the machine gun, while drivers, gunners and machine gunners each fired three 47mm rounds and one machine gun magazine. This very brief exposure to gunnery amounted to familiarization rather than actual training with the weapons; it was not until they arrived in theater in North Africa that the tank crews received practical training or all too often learned their duties while in combat.

Once war had been declared, the courses resumed as of 15 July 1940 and lasted 19 days each, including holidays. The courses were held at the Ansaldo factory in Genova, using only one M13/40 as an instructional aid although some tanks from the production line were used for a few hours on occasion as well. Gunnery instruction was insufficient. Three courses of this type were held, to be replaced by a resumption of month-long courses at Bracciano, with courses reaching battalion size. At the same time, a parallel program of technical courses was held for NCO mechanics, with ten days spent at the tank training center, seven at Ansaldo, and a further seven at the SPA engine plant. Following completion of these courses, personnel were supposed to receive at least three gunnery lessons at their units of assignment. Further courses followed in late 1940 and early 1941 for drivers and mechanics at Bologna. Courses were intensified in 1941, including those on the L6/40 tank and AB41 armoured car for infantry and cavalry NCOs. Beginning in April courses were begun, limited to instruction concerning the hull of the M13/40, specifically geared towards training crews for the new 75/18 self-propelled (SP) artillery systems.

Throughout 1941 many organizations became involved in various aspects of training armour crews. Various driver training centers, the Motorization Studies Center in Rome, the Tank Training Center at Civitavecchia, the Armoured Car Training Center at Pinerolo, and other specialized training centers in Bologna and Rome all provided instruction. In early 1942 supplementary training centers were established in North Africa with the aim of tailoring instruction to operational conditions in the area. Training in situ was particularly useful in retraining the two-man crews of the L3s who would be assigned to the M13s arriving in theater, which had four-man crews. A tank training center was also established at Villaggio Marconi in Tripolitania, and tank crews improved their skills as they gained experience, which enabled them to make the most of their often-outclassed equipment. 'Ariete' also developed a range that had moving tank silhouettes as targets. Training stressed teamwork between drivers and gunners and instilled a sense of aggressive behavior. Training and exercises at the divisional level normally did not occur; only the 'Littorio' armoured division carried out a division-level exercise prior to shipping out to Africa in late 1941. Otherwise, it seems that most practical training was the result of on-the-job experience in the combat theater itself. Shortcomings in training carried out on mainland Italy that were due to fuel and ammunition shortages were rapidly rectified under actual combat conditions.

Self-propelled artillery crews received basic training at each unit's regimental depot, followed by a period of training at Nettunia in Italy that included individual, unit, live fire and battery live fire training. The final training phase for SP crews was tactical training at the Artillery School at Nettuno. There is anecdotal evidence that some groups carried out somewhat intensive training for a period of at least a few weeks in northern Italy as well.

Bersaglieri and cavalry personnel who were to be assigned to AB40/41 armoured car units were trained at the Cavalry School at Pinerolo beginning in 1941. Training consisted of technical training, formal unit training at section, platoon, squadron and group levels, tactical training and specific instructions covering various other tasks.

Although overall training was marked by a somewhat fragmented effort and by limited opportunities for live fire and field exercises due to the scarcity of ammunition and fuel, as the war progressed Italian armour and SP artillery personnel seem to have been able to learn and adapt to combat conditions rather quickly. Italian commanders likewise appear to have become proficient at handling sizeable (division-size) armoured formations and were able to work well in conjunction with German armoured units in North Africa despite there being a sometimes ambiguous command relationship.

Insufficient training prior to assignment to North Africa was not confined to the Italians. Following their initial success in early 1941 when they sent many of their battle-tested troops to fight elsewhere, the British began to experience some of the same problems as the Italians. Fresh British units in the desert were often ill-trained and unprepared for the life in the desert and for the type of combat they would face. Most of the officers and men, unlike the desert veterans who preceded them, had to learn about the problems of desert movement and navigation for the first time. While most units sent from Britain had received barely enough training in their own arm, the time and resources allocated to all-arms training was completely inadequate. Montgomery himself acknowledged that his troops were not, in all cases, highly trained, which in part led to his cautious approach to battle.

Food and Rations

By and large, Italian officers shared the same food as the enlisted men, although in rear areas officer messes offered a somewhat greater variety of meals, which the officers had to pay for. This practice was far from confined to the Italian army; the British were known for their own elaborate officer messes in rear areas and it is unlikely that even in the safety and comfort of Tripoli, Italian officers were treated to the opulence enjoyed by British officers at places like Shepheard's Hotel, the Gezira Sporting Club and the Kit-Kat Club in Cairo, which were habitual haunts of British officers. Closer to the front lines, any preferences that Italian officers might enjoy began to evaporate, and the officers shared the same food (and discomforts) as the lowliest enlisted men. In November 1941 the meals served in the officer's mess tent of the 'Ariete' division were essentially those also served to the enlisted men, but on the occasion of a visit by the corps commander, General Gastone Gambara, the usual '*Chiarizia*' minestrone and canned meat was replaced by a meal consisting of pasta cooked with tomato, tinned meat and Tuscan wine, and some of the excellent water which was brought in from Derna. Given the basic ingredients to work with, based on their experience, skill and culinary inventiveness, many of the Italian cooks could turn out an appetizing meal. However, when, such as on the line at El Alamein in October–November 1942 the supply system broke down under the stress of combat, all ranks suffered from lack of food and water for days at a time; there was no two-tiered system when it came to the front lines. In the 'Folgore' division, at the far southern end of the line, far from the main Axis supply line along the coast, hunger was a constant for officers and men alike. The only fresh meat came from an occasional camel that strayed into a minefield or came close enough to be shot.

For all the complaining there may have been about the overall quality of Italian rations, it is interesting to note that, when these rations were supplemented by captured British rations, at least in some instances after the initial enthusiasm over 'foreign' foods such as corned beef and bully biscuits, the Italians greatly preferred their own biscuits and canned foods. Coffee or tea and wine were staples of the Italian diet; in North Africa, tea was often substituted for coffee, due in part to occasional windfalls of stocks captured from the British, as well as to the fact that in the desert environment tea was somewhat more thirst-quenching than coffee. Of course, the ability to have coffee or tea was dependent on the availability of water with which to brew them. Water was limited to one liter per man a day, but by the time of Alamein in October 1942 the ration was cut to half a liter a day. The degree to which water was considered precious is exemplified by the following incident: shortly after Tobruk was taken, Lieutenant Lino Leonardi of the XXXI Sapper Battalion came under machine gun fire; one of his corporals, Gianni Berthelet, suddenly saw a pool of liquid spreading in the sand. The corporal asked Leonardi if he was wounded; the officer checked himself and said 'No, I took a round in my water bottle', to which Berthelet answered 'Dammit, it's not like we have any water to spare!', almost as if to say that it would have been preferable if the lieutenant had been wounded. Wine was generally available, even if in limited quantities closer to the front and it was not, as some Anglo-Saxon authors suggest, a 'luxury' item; it was rather like the beer that British and Commonwealth soldiers expected as part of their own rations, and which the Italians consumed willingly enough when they came across it. The paratroopers of the 'Folgore' seemed especially fond of canned lager beer, which could slake a full day's thirst.

Attesting to the skill and inventiveness of Italian cooks was an incident recounted by Campini. In mid-November 1942 while the Italians were retreating after the Alamein battles, Campini began to collect stragglers from 'Littorio' near Sirte and busied himself with trying to arrange to feed more than a thousand men who paused to rest and wash themselves off in the sea. A lieutenant named Tacoli managed to find some water 20 kilometers (12 miles) distant, which added to a truckload of lard, one of flour and one of sugar that had been taken from British stores in Tobruk, provided the cooks with the basic ingredients for Italian '*frittelle*' ('fritters'). Because the only available wood was water-logged debris washed ashore that would not burn, even when soaked with gasoline, the cooks used tank engine heaters (an item certainly useful in Russia, but a totally unnecessary item in the desert heat) and set about making the fritters, reminiscent of village fairs, but which nevertheless managed to satisfy the hunger of the starving troops.

Italian field kitchens used stoves and ovens that were fired by wood rather than by oil or gasoline; while this arrangement may have been appropriate in continental Europe where there was a relative abundance of woods and forests from which wood could be scavenged, this made cooking in North Africa, where there was essentially no wood locally available, somewhat problematic. However, as with soldiers the world over, 'field expedient' methods can almost always be found by the more inventive,

Two Italian paratroopers, likely taken in Tunisia in 1943. They are armed with Beretta MAB 38A
submachine guns, which were issued extensively to the 'Folgore' parachute division. (Bruno Benvenuti)

and this proved to be the case of the cooks feeding the troops in the El Alamein area in 1942. There
was a long line of now disused telephone poles (in Italian, the '*palificata*') that ran from the coast to
the Kufra oasis; this *palificata* served as a reference point and army-level headquarters had ordered that
the poles be left intact. At some point it became blindingly obvious that these poles were an excellent
source of seasoned wood to fuel the stoves, and the temptation for the cooks, who heretofore had to
make do with occasional dry bushes, or splintered wood from derelict truck beds, or even rifle stocks
to supplement the erratic supply of wood supplied through official supply channels to get their ovens to
blaze, became too much to resist. Accordingly, they reasoned, what harm is there if instead of every 35
meters there is a phone pole to act as a reference point, there is a pole every 70 meters? So, soon every
other pole began to disappear. When that supply of poles began to thin out, the cooks began to remove
two out of three, rather than one out of two, poles. When, as had inevitably to happen, the higher
echelons noticed the missing poles, orders were given that no other poles were to be removed. In full
compliance with that edict, the cooks began to saw off the tops of the remaining poles, bit by bit, until
ultimately the poles were nothing more than stumps in the sand. With bald-faced chutzpah the cooks
then remarked at how interesting it was that the shifting sands should almost bury the poles!

Parenthetically, it might be noted that unlike the Germans, and later the British, the Italians
seem not to have issued or otherwise used synthetic stimulants such as Pervitin, a methampheta-
mine, by the Germans, and Benzedrine by the British and the Americans in North Africa in 1942.
The Germans issued Pervitin to their troops as a matter of routine and had also developed a special
'chocolate bar' ('*Panzerschockolade*') for tank crew issue. The Italians had to rely on their own natural
abilities and stamina to stay awake and cope with fatigue.

2

Organization and Structure of Italian Formations

In 1934 General Ferdinando Baistrocchi, chief of staff of the *Regio Esercito*, determined that the army as structured according to the criteria adopted in 1926 was no longer responsive to the developing European military situation and proposed that it be reorganized and re-equipped with more modern equipment. However, the war in Ethiopia and Italian intervention in support of Franco in Spain put a halt to implementation of the proposals. In October 1936 Baistrocchi was replaced by Alberto Pariani, who after studying the then current situation, concluded that Italy would eventually have to wage war against France and England in Africa, that Italy should remain on the defensive along its northern alpine border and that it should make plans to conquer Malta to ensure freedom of navigation between Italy and Africa. However, Pariani's proposals were never put into practical effect and remained in the realm of theory. While Biastrocchi had wished to create a new army consisting of a relatively small number of powerful, well-armed and well-trained divisions (about 25, plus seven Blackshirt divisions), the Pariani reforms adopted the so-called 'binary' division (which called for 80 such divisions in peacetime, to be increased to 126 in case of war). Pariani also proposed the '*dottrina di guerra di rapido corso*' ('doctrine of the quick war').

Among the many factors that contributed to a general inability of the *Regio Esercito* to fight effectively against enemy forces were the size and organization of its divisions and the numbers and types of equipment within those divisions when compared to similar types of British or German divisions. It is simplistic and misleading to conclude that there was any kind of quantitative or qualitative parity between Italian divisions and their opposite numbers. Although the Italians had a respectable number of divisions in North Africa, the infantry divisions suffered from an inherent organizational weakness, as they consisted of only two rather than three infantry regiments, an artillery regiment, a mortar battalion and numerous supporting companies and batteries. This division type, instituted in 1938, was known as the '*divisione binaria*' ('binary division'). As originally conceived, the binary divisions were to be leaner and more manageable, equipped with improved weapons and with sufficient organic transportation assets to make them highly mobile. They were essentially brigades with an attached artillery regiment, whereas the divisions they replaced were structured with three infantry regiments and an artillery regiment with four artillery groups (battalions), while the binary divisions had only two infantry regiments supported by an artillery regiment that had been reduced to three groups. What happened in practice was that the number of infantry regiments was reduced, but the modernization of weapons and equipment that was supposed to complement the restructuring was never really implemented. Somewhat of a side-effect of this restructuring was that, much to the satisfaction of Mussolini, who wanted to be able to boast of a larger army, the number of infantry divisions essentially increased by half, although the total number of infantry regiments that comprised those divisions remained unaltered. The Italians would soon learn that the restructuring had unintended negative consequences, primarily because it negated the ability of the division commander to employ two regiments forward and hold one in reserve; it was either two up front and no reserve, or one up front and one in reserve. Thus, with respect to the seven two-regiment infantry divisions that fought in the desert during 1941 and 1942, the binary divisions amounted to less than five traditional three-regiment divisions.

The Italians had several classes of infantry division, among them motorized (*motorizzato*) and semi-motorized (*autotrasportabile*). The motorized divisions employed in the desert ('Trieste' and 'Trento', although despite its structure and designation as motorized the latter was used mainly in a static defensive role) had enough organic transportation assets to move all of their artillery and a relatively high percentage of their infantry, whereas the *autotrasportabile* divisions (most notably 'Brescia', 'Bologna' and 'Pavia') had enough tractors to move their artillery but had to rely on a transportation pool to augment their own organic assets in order to move the infantry of the division. The Italians themselves joked that the term '*autotrasportabile*' meant that if the soldiers of the division were lucky enough to find someone who would offer them a ride, they would be happy to give up marching on foot. The rather inadequate organization of Italian infantry divisions contrasted markedly with the organization of Italian armoured divisions, which, although considerably smaller, compared favorably in an organizational sense to that of the standard German panzer division, unlike the British whose armoured divisions tended to be tank-heavy units without adequate organic infantry and artillery assets.

A few numbers suffice to illustrate the disadvantages suffered by Italian divisions: an Italian *Tipo AS* (North Africa Type) infantry division numbered about 7,500 men and had 52 field and antitank guns and 434 cars, trucks and tractors. An opposing British infantry division had an establishment of 18,347 men with 120 field and antitank guns and 1,675 cars and trucks. A German infantry division had about 13,000 men and 48 field guns and ten antitank guns and 942 trucks and support vehicles. Italian armoured divisions, with one armoured regiment, one artillery regiment and one light infantry regiment, had 9,887 men and 192 medium tanks and 581 trucks, depending on the specific timeframe and force structure. A German armoured division had some 12,000–15,000 men, and 141 medium and 71 light tanks. British armoured divisions numbered about 15,000 men with 290 tanks and almost 2,100 trucks. Compared to British infantry and armoured divisions, Italian divisions were much smaller and had correspondingly less equipment; on a one-to-one basis they were always at a disadvantage numerically as well as with respect to firepower.

Although at the beginning of the North African campaign there was at least some qualitative parity in armour and artillery holdings, by mid-1942 almost all Italian equipment was outclassed as well as being increasingly outnumbered, especially with the introduction of medium tanks supplied to the British by the US. Also, as the campaigning wore on and losses mounted, manning levels in the divisions fluctuated wildly; in December 1941 Italian infantry and motorized divisions were down to 1,800–4,200 men, and the 'Ariete' armoured division was down to 1,500 men with the astonishingly low number of only three tanks still in running order. The ability of the individual Italian soldier, as well as of units at all levels, to function with some modicum of effectiveness was undoubtedly attributable to the Italian art of '*arrangiarsi*' or what in English would be termed 'improvisation'; the Italians were adept at making do with whatever was at hand. Ultimately, it was the common Italian infantryman, tanker or gunner who almost miraculously managed to fight and survive, and in many cases win, despite all the shortages and handicaps he faced.

Types of Italian Divisions

Armoured Divisions
Italy was a pioneer in development of armoured units as balanced combat forces. As early as the 1920s, Italian doctrine called for armoured units that were a mix of tanks, infantry and artillery, and in 1924 an Italian colonel, Enrico Maltese, first introduced the concept of integrating self-propelled artillery into armoured formations. By 1940, Italian armoured divisions had developed

An M14/41 of the 'Centauro' division moving at speed, probably along the Via Balbia. This tank has more than the usual complement of spare track links for protection, unusually around the turret as well as on the hull superstructure and glacis. (Ralph Riccio)

into well-balanced combined arms teams consisting of tanks, motorized infantry and artillery, and supporting units such as engineers, which trained and operated in concert with each other, not unlike their German counterparts, and quite different from the British whose armoured divisions tended to be tank-heavy units without adequate organic infantry and artillery assets.

The three armoured divisions that served in North Africa were the 131st 'Centauro', 132nd 'Ariete' and 133rd 'Littorio'. The basic organizational structure of an Italian armoured division (*divisione corazzata*) consisted of a tank regiment with three tank battalions with a total of 157 tanks, an armoured artillery regiment with three groups (battalions), a *Bersaglieri* (motorized light infantry) regiment with three battalions, an engineer battalion, an antitank battalion, a transportation battalion (*autogruppo*), and medical and supply sections. This type of division was known as the '*Divisione Corazzata Tipo AS 42*' (North Africa Type 42 Armoured Division). Authorized strength was 8,600 men, although that number could fluctuate wildly as a result of combat losses. In North Africa, the 132nd 'Ariete' armoured division's tank regiment was initially equipped with L3/35 light tanks armed only with machine guns, but by July 1941 the division had reorganized, adding another tank regiment equipped with M13/40 medium tanks. The light tank regiment, with 117 tanks, was eventually phased out, but elements of it continued to serve in a combat capacity until August 1942. By 1942 the artillery regiment consisted of six groups (two 75/27, two 75/18 self-propelled, one truck-mounted 90/53 and one 105/28). The *Bersaglieri* regiment consisted of three battalions and an antitank company. When it arrived in North Africa, the 133rd 'Littorio' division was supposed to be structured as the 'Ariete', but because of the need to bring 'Ariete' up to strength, one of its tank battalions (the X Battalion), the heavy support weapons battalion of its *Bersaglieri* regiment, two self-propelled gun groups and a truck-mounted

90mm gun group were ceded to 'Ariete'. In addition, another of its medium tank battalions (the XI) was reassigned to the 101st 'Trieste' motorized division; consequently, throughout its stay in North Africa, 'Littorio' never fought as a complete division. The last armoured division to be committed to North Africa, the 131st 'Centauro', was configured as a standard armoured division. Because of their mobility, 'Ariete' and 'Littorio' worked hand-in-glove with the two German armoured divisions in Libya and Egypt; 'Centauro' did so to a lesser extent during the fighting in Tunisia.

Motorized Divisions

The Italians deployed two motorized divisions (*divisioni motorizzate*) to the desert, the 101st 'Trieste' and the 102nd 'Trento'. Authorized strength was 7,600. The motorized division was structured with two infantry regiments, each with three infantry battalions and an antiaircraft/antitank battalion; a *Bersaglieri* motorcycle regiment with three *Bersaglieri* battalions and an antitank battalion; a motorized artillery regiment with four artillery battalions and an air defense battalion; a medium tank battalion; an engineer battalion; and transportation, medical and supply detachments. Equipment included 24 75/27 field guns, 24 100/17 howitzers, 12 88mm or 90mm dual-purpose guns, 24 20mm antiaircraft guns and, in the case of 'Trieste', 52 M13/40 medium tanks. The 101st 'Trieste' motorized division, along with the 132nd 'Ariete' armoured division, were the constituent divisions of the *Corpo d'Armata di Manovra* (CAM), which later became the XX Corps. Although the 102nd 'Trento' was classified as a motorized division, it was used largely as a standard Type AS infantry division, lacked a medium tank battalion and had much of its organic transport taken from it to be used to augment higher echelon transportation units.

September 1940: A *Bersaglieri* motorcycle patrol in the desert. *Bersaglieri* motorcyclists were assigned to the motorized divisions. The lead motorcycle in this photo mounts a Breda Model 30 light machine gun. (Massimiliano Afiero)

Infantry Divisions

The majority Italian divsions committed to the fighting in the desert were infantry. Between 1940 and August 1942 all of the *Regio Esercito* infantry divisions in North Africa were the *divisione autotrasportabile Tipo AS* (North Africa Type semi-motorized division) type. Specifically, these were the 16th 'Pistoia', 17th 'Pavia', 25th 'Bologna', 27th 'Brescia', 55th 'Savona', 60th 'Sabratha', 61st 'Sirte', 62nd 'Marmarica', 63rd 'Cirene' and 64th 'Catanzaro'; the 61st through 64th divisions were all destroyed during the British offensive of late 1940–early 1941. In addition to the *autotrasportabile* divisions, two other types of infantry divisions were committed to the North Africa in late 1942: the 1st *'Superga' fanteria da montagna* (mountain infantry) and the 80th *'La Spezia' aviotrasportabile* (air transportable) division. Despite the designations 'mountain' and 'air transportable', which had been assigned when the divisions had been formed earlier, by the time of their arrival in North Africa they had taken on the structure of normal semi-motorized infantry divisions. All these infantry divisions suffered from an inherent organizational weakness, as they were structured with only two infantry regiments, an artillery regiment, an attached light tank battalion, an engineer battalion, and service and support units. The infantry regiments

A squad of soldiers aboard a Fiat 634 heavy truck. Most of the soldiers are wearing the tropical pith helmet, although at least one is wearing the M42 visored sidecap. (Daniele Guglielmi)

A pair of Breda Model 30 light machine guns manned by 'Giovani Fascisti'. The close manufacturing tolerances of the Model 30 made it very susceptible to jamming in the sand and dust of the desert environment. (USSME)

consisted of three infantry battalions, a mortar company and a heavy weapons battery with four 65/17 guns; the artillery regiment typically had two 75/27 field artillery groups, a 100/17 group, and at least one air defense battery with eight 20mm guns; and the attached light tank battalion had 46 L3/35 tanks.

The *Tipo AS* division was based on the '*divisione binaria*' ('binary division'), instituted in 1938, which had only two infantry regiments supported by an artillery regiment that had been reduced to three groups. The Type AS division had an establishment of about 7,500 men and major equipment consisted of 46 L3/35 light tanks, 24 75/27 field guns, 12 100/17 howitzers, eight 47/32 antitank guns, eight 20mm antiaircraft guns, 12 81mm mortars, 398 trucks, 249 motorcycles and 34 artillery tractors, although the equipment authorizations and holdings could vary from division to division and at different times. The artillery in these divisions was motorized, but there were not enough trucks to transport all the troops; transportation had to be borrowed from army-level transportation assets. Largely because of their lack of mobility, most of the infantry divisions were assigned to the siege of Tobruk from April to November 1941.

Parachute Division
In August 1942, the 185th 'Folgore' parachute division (*divisione paracadutista*) was sent to North Africa. The division was rather small, with an authorized strength of 5,000 men and structured with two parachute regiments, an artillery regiment, an engineer battalion, a signals company, and service and support elements. Each parachute regiment had three battalions and a regimental

cannon company with four 47/32 antitank guns, and the artillery regiment had three artillery groups with 47/32 guns (the 47/32 antitank gun was the heaviest armament in the division's inventory). During the battle of El Alamein, 'Folgore' was the southern anchor of the Axis line and covered itself with glory, being repeatedly attacked by vastly superior British forces. The division was literally wiped out, with only about 300 soldiers surviving death or capture. Of those who were forced to surrender, the Italians claim that none ever raised their hands in the traditional act of submission.

A group of 'Folgore' paratroopers in June 1942; several are armed with the excellent Beretta MAB 38A sub-machine gun. (Massimiliano Afiero)

MSVN Divisionx

The *Milizia volontaria per la sicurezza nazionale* (Volunteer Militia for National Security, MVSN) began as a militarized gendarmerie corps that was subordinate to the Fascist party, but later developed into full-fledged combat divisions that became integrated into the *Regio Esercito*. These formations were commonly referred to as '*Camicie Nere*' (CCNN, 'Blackshirts') because MVSN personnel wore a black shirt with their uniform, rather than the regulation grey-green worn by *Regio Esercito* personnel. Three MVSN divisions took part in the fighting in North Africa: the *1 CCNN '23 marzo'*, *2 CCNN '28 ottobre'* and *4 CCNN '3 gennaio'* – all of which were lost during the British offensive of late 1940–February 1941. The MVSN divisions were structured much like the *Tipo AS* infantry divisions, but there were several differences both in the size and type of units and in the terminology used to identify units. The infantry elements consisted of MVSN personnel, who were volunteers, while the support units, including artillery and engineers, were manned by *Regio Esercito* personnel. In place of the infantry regiments of the *Tipo AS* infantry divisions, the MVSN divisions had two regiments (called '*Legioni*', 'Legions') each with three battalions ('*coorti*', 'cohorts').

An antitank crew of the 4th Blackshirt Division manning a 47/32 gun in the Libyan desert in September 1940. The gun is mounted in the bed of a truck to provide mobility. (Massimiliano Afiero)

Libyan Divisions

In addition to the Italian infantry and MVSN divisions, there were also two Libyan divisions (*divisioni libiche*): the 1st Libyan Infantry Division 'Sibille' and the 2nd Libyan Infantry Division 'Pescatori', named after their respective original Italian commanders. These were part of the *Regio Corpo Truppe Coloniali della* Libia (Royal Corps of Colonial Troops of Libya). Each division was

A pre-hostilities photo of Libyan paratroopers disembarking from an SM.81 transport aircraft; the plane is from the 44th Squadriglia, 35th Gruppo, 33rd Stormo and is the commander's aircraft. The foremost paratrooper is carrying a 6.5mm FIAT Model 14 water-cooled machine gun weighing 17kg (37.4lbs) empty and without its tripod. (Courtesy Giancarlo Garello)

A group of native Libyan troops advancing across the desert sands in 1942. The rearmost soldier is carrying a light machine gun and an ammunition chest; two other soldiers, part of the machine gun team, are also carrying ammunition chests for the weapon. (Massimiliano Afiero)

authorized 7,224 men, structured with two Libyan infantry regiments each with three battalions, a Libyan artillery group with three 77/28 batteries, two batteries of 20mm guns and an antitank company with four 47/32 guns, an engineer battalion and various service and support companies. All officers and specialist personnel were Italian, but the bulk of the personnel, including NCOs, were Libyan and called 'ascari' (Libyan for 'soldiers'). The personnel of these divisions were from the Libyan coastal region and had been granted limited Italian citizenship rights by a January 1939 decree. The two divisions were well trained, professional units with a high esprit de corps; both divisions fought hard and well during the British offensive of 1940 but, along with the regular Italian divisions, were destroyed. There was also a regiment of Libyan paratroopers, the *Reggimento Paracadutisti Libico 'Fanti dell'Aria'* (Libyan Parachute Regiment 'Infantrymen of the Air'), organized at Castel Benito airfield in 1938, and was the *Regio Esercito*'s first parachute unit. The regiment's officers were Italian, while NCOs and other ranks were Libyan. There were several Libyan light horse cavalry squadrons (*spahis*) used for border patrol duties, and some Libyan *meharisti* (camel-mounted units) employed in police duties.

Manoeuvre Army Corps Reconnaissance Group

In early August 1941 the *Raggruppamento Esplorante Corpo d'Armata di Manovra* (Manoeuvre Army Corps Reconnaissance Group, RECAM) was organized, and directly subordinated to the *Supercomando Africa Settentrionale*. The RECAM, commanded by Colonel Mario De Meo, consisted of one battalion of the *Polizia dell'Africa Italiana* (PAI) with one company of armoured cars, one company of M13/40 medium tanks, one company of L3/35 light tanks, a *raggruppamento* of flying batteries, a two-battalion group of 'Giovani Fascisti' infantry, and service and support elements. The

The crew of a 20mm anti-aircraft section of a 'flying battery' posing in front of their war booty CMP Ford F15 *camionetta*. The gun is a Breda Model 39 in a static mount. The flying batteries were part of the RECAM. (Ralph Riccio)

flying batteries, commanded by Lieutenant Colonel Dissegna and whose organizational structure ultimately included some 16 improvised batteries, were equipped with a heterogeneous mix of equipment of Italian, British and Austro–Hungarian origin. Gun/truck combinations consisted of captured 15cwt Morris CS8 trucks mounting the Italian 65/17 gun, Canadian Ford CMP F15 trucks mounting 20mm Breda cannons, 75/27 guns mounted on the SPA TL37 artillery tractor, 102/35 naval guns mounted on Fiat 634N trucks, or Škoda 100/17 howitzers mounted on Lancia 3Ro trucks. Most of the guns were mated to the trucks at the rear echelon army workshops at Villaggio Berta, using mounts specially designed and fabricated there.

Italian Africa Police

Another organization that contributed combat elements to the general mix of Italian forces was the *Polizia dell'Africa Italiana* (PAI), which was a successor to the Italian colonial police corps that had been instituted in 1936 and renamed the *Polizia dell'Africa Italiana* in 1939 In addition to its role as a police force with road, rail and port security duties, it also organized a small combat element, the *Battaglione 'Romolo Gessi'*, that operated close to the front lines, providing security escorts for high-ranking Italian and German officers. [Parenthetically, Romolo Gessi (1831–1881) was an Italian explorer in the area of the Nile and Sudan, where he was known as *'Gessi Pasha'*.] The 'Romolo Gessi' Battalion was subordinate to the RECAM and was initially structured with an armoured car company with nine or ten AB41 armoured cars and two motorcycle companies mounted on Moto Guzzi 500 motorcycles, but in January 1942 the battalion was expanded with the addition of a second armoured car company and a third motorcycle company. The PAI were well trained and performed their duties in an outstanding fashion.

10th 'Arditi' Regiment

Impressed by the success of the British Long Range Desert Group raiding parties, the Italian Army General Staff decided to form a counterpart organization, initially of battalion strength but later increased to regimental strength (the 10th 'Arditi' Regiment). The staff further ordered design and production of two special vehicles for this unit, the *camionetta mod. 42* and the *camionetta mod. 43*. In May 1942 the *Gruppo Formazioni 'A'* was formed, consisting of Italian and Arab personnel, and the I *Battaglione Special Arditi* (I Special 'Arditi' Battalion). The *arditi* traced their origins back to the First World War, when special assault teams similar to commandos were formed to carry out swift raids against enemy strongpoints. The I Special 'Arditi' Battalion was formed on 15 May, structured with three companies, each of which was specialized in nature. The *101a Compagnia Arditi Paracadutisti* (101st 'Arditi' Parachutist Company) was an airborne company, the *102a Compagnia Arditi Nuotatori* (102nd 'Arditi' Swimmer Company) was a combat swimmer company and the *103a Compagnia Camionettisti* (103rd Light Truck Company) was a truck-borne raiding unit. In July 1942 the *Reggimento Arditi* was formed, its designation being changed to X *Reggimento Arditi* on 15 September. Despite the ambitious and optimistic plans for the regiment, the length of time it took to organize and train its various sub-elements precluded it ever being employed as a cohesive unit. The only segment of the regiment to see action in North Africa was the 103rd Light Truck Company, commanded by Captain Brusa, which was sent to Tunisia and integrated into a mixed unit consisting also of the CCCXL Machine Gun Battalion and the 'Novara' group of the 'Lodi' squadron, attached to the 'Pistoia' division. The company was assigned to patrol duties as well as long-range raiding actions but ended the war fighting as a normal motorized company, surrendering along with the rest of the Axis forces in May 1943.

3

Equipment Considerations

For many reasons, ranging from the lack of funding for equipment modernization programs, to lack of Italian industrial capacity to provide for the needs of all of the services, to prioritization and planning for a defensive war to be fought along Italy's mountainous frontier, *Regio Esercito* equipment was in many, but not all, cases either antiquated or in short supply. Although there were exceptions, most of the Italian equipment was either obsolete or obsolescent, as well as being far short of the numbers required. The Italian Army was acutely aware of its shortcomings in almost all types of equipment, from small arms to artillery and tanks, and had begun a series of modernization programs in the 1930s aimed at redressing the situation. Because of shortfalls in funding and shortages of raw materials, coupled with the Italian belief that war would not begin until 1943, many of these programs either did not materialize, were significantly delayed or were produced only at a fraction of the numbers required. As an example, in 1939 Italy had developed the 7.35mm Armaguerra Model 1939 semiautomatic rifle to replace the 6.5mm Model 1891 series of bolt-action rifles and carbines, but the advent of the war put an end to adoption of the 7.35mm round as well as of the Armaguerra rifle. Had Italy been able to equip its infantry with the Armaguerra, it would have been in the forefront, along with the United States, in equipping its frontline soldiers with a semi-automatic rifle. However, lack of adequate natural resources as well as a limited manufacturing base meant that Italy was unable to implement many of its planned upgrades, so everything from small arms to tanks to artillery remained outdated and in short supply. Despite the reality that most Italian equipment was outmoded and in short supply and the fact that British wartime propaganda often denigrated Italian equipment, one should not conclude that Italian equipment was inadequate across the board. In fact, the Italians produced and employed some outstanding equipment in all categories in North Africa, from small arms to artillery, which at least for a while, outclassed the British equipment it was pitted against.

Armoured vehicles, artillery and motor transport played major roles in the desert fighting. With respect to armoured vehicles – tanks, self-propelled artillery and armoured cars – there was somewhat of an uneven record. One of the many myths that has taken hold and been perpetuated in English-language publications is that Italian tanks in North Africa were greatly inferior to their British and German counterparts. That Italian tanks had their shortcomings is undeniable, but upon closer examination, however, it becomes apparent that, like many other myths surrounding Italian military capabilities, the perception does not match reality. In the early phase of the campaign Italian armour consisted of some 326 L3 turretless light tanks armed with only two 6.5mm or 8mm machine guns, an additional 72 M11/39 medium tanks armed with an ineffective 37mm gun, and a couple of battalions of the newer M13/40 mediums mounting a 47mm gun.

The Italian armour was pitted against some 134 machine-gun-armed Mk VIB light tanks and 114 cruiser tanks (A9, A10 and A13) and 45 Matilda II tanks mounting the 2-pdr gun. The L3 and M11 were completely outgunned by the 2-pdr and were hopelessly mismatched against the relatively small number of Matilda tanks, whose armour was largely impervious to even the 47mm gun of the M13. However, this disparity did not last for long, as the Italians began to field increasing

A platoon of M11/39 tanks in the desert in late 1940. Overall, design and performance capabilities of this tank were rather poor. (USSME

numbers of the M13/40 with the 'Ariete' armoured division, while on the British side the number of Matildas dwindled, leaving the M13/40s to face an array of antiquated British cruiser tanks including the A9 and A10. The M13 is almost universally decried by British and American sources as an inferior machine or even categorically as the worst tank in the desert. One British work manages to characterize them variously as 'the most despised fighting vehicles in the desert', 'substandard', 'inferior', 'toytown tanks,' tanks with 'inadequate armour' and 'the least effective tanks in the desert'. [Parenthetically, the same authors refer to German tanks as being diesel-fueled, when in fact they were powered by Maybach gasoline engines, whereas it was the Italian tanks that used the less flammable diesel fuel.] Another author, in two separate works, describes the M13 and M14 as 'the poorest in Africa in terms of armament, armour protection and performance', and states that: 'The Italian main tanks were the M13/40 and the M14/41 variant, neither of which was a great threat to the British. In terms of armament, protection and performance they remained the poorest of all of the armour in the desert.' These and similar assertions have been repeated so often that they have become accepted as fact in many quarters. However, these claims are never backed up by any explanation as to what factors they are based upon.

There seems to be very few attempts to compare the Italian mediums to the counterpart British or German medium tanks, and it is also worth noting that, although the M13 and M14 were classified as medium tanks according to Italian weight categories established in 1938, they were in fact what most other nations would consider light tanks. The M13 and the somewhat improved but essentially similar M14 were the mainstay of the Italian armoured forces from February 1941 until the end of the fighting in Tunisia in May 1943, but in the 15-month period from February 1941 to May 1942, when American-supplied M3 medium tanks mounting a 75mm main gun began to arrive in the desert, it is useful to judge the M13 against the British-produced armour they fought against. The M13 was qualitatively equal to or better than the early British A9, A10 and A13 cruiser tanks in the desert at the time in terms of firepower, mobility, protection and reliability, and was comparable to the contemporary German PzKpfw III tank with its short 50mm gun. The Italian 47mm gun was roughly equivalent to the British 2-pdr, but the Italian gun had the

August 1942, a pair of M13/40 tanks just leaving the open desert for one of the few recognizable tracks in the desert. The markings on the turret and hull identify them as belonging to the LI Battalion, 31st Tank Regiment, 'Littorio' Division. (Massimiliano Afiero)

advantage of being able to fire both AP and HE ammunition, enabling it to engage and suppress infantry, while the 2-pdr fired only AP ammunition. The Italian 47mm round was also substantially heavier than the 40mm British round (1.44kg [3.17lbs] compared to 1.08kg [2.38lbs]). In terms of armour thickness, the M13 was equal to the British A9 through A13 cruiser tanks and to the early versions of the German PzKpfw III and IV models but suffered by comparison with the British A15 Crusader and Mk III Valentine, and of course to the famously thick-skinned Matilda. However, the quality of the Italian armour plates was very bad, as confirmed by some British and Italian reports. Its power-to-weight ratio compared favorably with many of the British and German tanks at the time. Although the Italian mediums (in actuality, light tanks as noted above) could hold their own against the 37mm-armed M3 Stuart (or 'Honey') light tank supplied by the US in November 1941, the M13 and M14 were totally outclassed in all respects by the M3 Grant and M4 Sherman medium tanks supplied to the British by the US beginning in May 1942. However, as late as November 1941 the M13 could still hold its own against the newly introduced British Mk VI (A15) Crusader 1 tank, armed with the by then obsolete 2-pdr and which was notoriously unreliable, suffering from defective water pumps, engines that were prone to shaking apart and leaking oil and a tendency to throw its tracks. The British, conducting extensive technical evaluations of captured equipment, found some redeeming features with respect to the power plant of the 75/18 self-propelled gun – essentially the same engine used by the M13 and M14 tanks. A British report dated July 1943 evaluating a captured 75/18 self-propelled gun stated:

> … mechanical design, layout and construction are not to be dismissed lightly as they exemplify sound and practical automotive engineering. The power unit has many : features to recommend it. It is very compact and components liable to require frequent attention are reasonably accessible – the injectors being particularly so. The engine has been expressly designed for tank work.

The *carro armato celere Sahariano*, an Italian copy of the British Crusader tank, which never got past the prototype stage. Its major visual difference from the Crusader was the presence of four rather than five roadwheels per side, making it similar in appearance to the British Covenanter. (CSEM)

The title of 'worst tank in the desert' should probably be reserved for the early British cruisers (A9 and A10) which were ungainly, unreliable, unable to move more than a few miles without breaking or throwing a track in a sharp turn, and basically ineffective as fighting platforms. Their own crews could not wait until they could be replaced by better machines.

The Italians realized full well that the M13 and M14 were outclassed compared to tanks being developed or fielded by other nations, but their efforts to develop a better tank were essentially fruitless. In 1940, plans were drawn up for a tank which, according to the Italian classification system, was categorized as 'heavy' but, at about 30 tons, was in the same category as the medium tanks of other nations. It was to mount either a 75mm or 90mm gun and would ultimately evolve into the P40 tank with a 75/34 gun, but none were fielded until 1943 and never saw service in North Africa. The Italians also considered making an outright copy of the Soviet T-34, but that likewise came to naught, as did plans to license-produce both the German PzKpfw III and IV tanks. Interestingly, obviously impressed by the British Crusader tank, the Italians built a prototype designated the *carro M celere sahariano* in the summer of 1942. Its external appearance, aside from four rather than five pairs of large roadwheels per side, was almost a clone of the Crusader, but it never got past the prototype stage. The *sahariano*, however, still mounted a 47mm gun, albeit somewhat improved, and was powered by a 250HP engine, yet it relied on the outdated plates-bolted-on-frame construction characteristic of virtually all Italian armoured vehicles.

One bright spot in the Italian armoured vehicle inventory in North Africa was the 75/18 self-propelled gun (the *semovente da 75/18*), which made its operational debut in the desert in May 1942 and whose 75/18 gun/howitzer, using enhanced ammunition, was able to deal quite effectively with all British armour , including the US-supplied M3 Grants and M4 Shermans. The M40/M41 75/18 SP was generally a reliable weapons system, and its low silhouette made it a difficult target to acquire and engage. Unfortunately for the Italians, it was not available in large numbers; only seven eight-gun (and later 12-gun) Groups were deployed to the North African theater. Also, on the positive side of the armoured equipment ledger, the Italians fielded a good armoured car – the AB41 – which mounted a 20mm gun and was especially well-suited for operations in the desert.

Italian artillery assets in North Africa likewise were of mixed quality, with the preponderance of them being quite old and outdated. Guns included the 20mm Breda Model 35 and 39 antiaircraft guns, the rapidly outdated 47/32 antitank gun (the same gun used on the M13 and M14 medium tanks), and an assortment of guns and howitzers ranging in caliber from 65mm through 152mm. With some exceptions, most of the field guns were obsolete, many of them being Škoda guns that

An M41 75/18 self-propelled gun in the desert. The M41 was a very potent weapons system, capable of defeating all enemy armour it faced, but was available only in relatively limited numbers. (Daniele Guglielmi)

were acquired by Italy as war booty following the First World War, and which, until the 1930s, the Italians believed were adequate for their needs. When the Italians decided to modernize their artillery assets, the lack of funding delayed implementation of the program with the result that some truly excellent modern guns were never deployed in the numbers envisioned or required.

The 20mm Breda Model 35 and Model 39 light cannon were excellent weapons and were in fact sought after by the British who used them whenever they could. The 90/53 dual-purpose gun was a superb weapon that was every bit as lethal and effective as the iconic German 88mm dual-purpose gun (as one officer who served with a 90mm battery remarked: 'Once we had a tank in our sights, it was dead.'), and the very modern 149/40 gun deployed with army-level artillery in North Africa was as good as or better than any comparable gun on either side. Another first-rate weapon which the Italians used to good effect was the Model 35 81mm mortar. However, the Italians had decided as part of their modernization program that 75mm guns would be adequate to equip their divisional artillery, while most other nations had decided to adopt guns up to 105mm for their own divisional artillery. To a very limited extent, the Italians acquired some artillery from the Germans to supplement their assets. These included three battalions of the extremely effective 88mm dual-purpose gun, as well as two battalions (14 guns) of the 149mm 15cm sFH 18 howitzer which complemented the Italian 149/40 gun at army level. In addition, at least 14 British 25-pdr guns were captured and subsequently employed by the Italians (a battalion with 12 guns by 'Trento' and two guns by 'Littorio'). Photographs also show a battery of 25-pdrs purportedly in use by the 'Folgore' parachute division. In the desert, Italian artillerymen at the divisional level were almost always easily overmatched by the excellent British 25-pdr (88mm) gun-howitzer. Nevertheless, as

A captured CMP Ford F15 mounting a 20mm Breda Model 39 static-mounted gun, ready for action against enemy aircraft. (Ralph Riccio)

A 20mm Breda Model 35 gun in the winter of 1942. The Model 35 was effective both as an antiaircraft weapon and when being used to engage ground targets. (USSME)

A 90/53 gun mounted on a Lancia 3Ro heavy truck preparing for action in early 1942. The 90/53 was an extremely accurate, powerful and effective dual-purpose antiaircraft and antitank weapon. (Ralph Riccio)

we have seen, despite all the shortcomings of the Italian artillery assets deployed to North Africa, the gunners gave as good as they got throughout the campaign, exacting more than probably could be expected from their guns.

An especially weak component of the Italian artillery inventory was in the antitank field. Although at the time of its introduction, and in the early phases of the desert war, the Austrian Böhler 47/32 antitank gun was a capable piece of equipment, on a par with the British 2-pdr, but by 1942 it was outclassed as an antitank weapon. It should be noted that the 47/32 was an infantry support weapon, not specifically an antitank weapon, although it served largely in that role. Rarely if ever mentioned is the fact that the Italians also deployed 87 German 37mm PaK 35/36 antitank guns in Libya, alongside the 47/32; these were issued to the 'Ariete', 'Brescia', 'Bologna' and 'Pavia' divisions. Lacking antitank weapons capable of penetrating the increasingly heavy armour that the British were introducing into the field, the Italians often resorted to arming hunter-killer teams with rudimentary but effective devices such as the Molotov cocktail in order to at least flush enemy tank crews from their vehicles, and later to destroy the vehicles with flame throwers or explosives. There were some limited attempts to adapt the rather antiquated, but still effective, 65/17 mountain gun for use in the antitank role; it could fire enhanced ammunition which enabled it to deal effectively with some classes of armour . A number of 65/17 guns were mounted on captured British light trucks and integrated into ad hoc units designated '*batterie volanti*' ('flying batteries'). The 90/53 dual-purpose gun, like the German 88, was also used in the antitank role, but numbers were limited. However, the 47/32 gun remained the principal Italian antitank gun, and despite its shortcomings, was nevertheless able to be employed effectively by the Italians as late as October 1942 during the battle of El Alamein, especially by the 'Folgore' paratroopers who developed innovative tactics that required daring and the utmost discipline to lie in skillfully prepared positions and wait patiently until the British armoured vehicles were at almost point-blank range or could be engaged from the side or rear before firing.

A group of 'Giovani Fascisti' manhandling their 47/32 guns into position in what appears to be a static display or parade alignment of equipment in March 1942. The young soldiers are wearing the black fez unique to their unit. (Enrico Finazzer)

A 65/17 gun mounted on a modified British Morris CS8 cargo body. Although antiquated, the 65/17 proved to be fairly effective in the desert, with a range of 6,800 meters (7,400 yards). (Nicola Pignato)

A somewhat embarrassing shortcoming on the part of the Italians was the lack of sufficient radios for their ground forces, especially since as early as 1894 Guglielmo Marconi had begun to develop wireless telegraphy and in May 1897 sent his first wireless over a 6-kilometer distance – a fact of which the Italians are justifiably proud. However, during the 1940–1943 timeframe in North Africa, the Italian ground forces were the most poorly equipped with respect to radio communications capabilities. The British, despite problems of their own with respect to range, distribution and reliability, had a much better developed radio communications system, and the Germans were even better equipped than either the Italians or the British with respect to both quality and quantity. The lack of a proper radio communication capability meant that units had to rely on landlines, which are notoriously difficult to maintain in a combat situation, especially in the fast-moving environment that marked the desert campaign, or on messengers or runners, which was also fraught with a host of problems, especially in combat. Although the Italian medium tanks were equipped with Magneti Marelli RF1 CA radios, only a handful in each company were also equipped with the RF2 CA for command purposes. Because of this, Italian tank commanders were unable to direct their tanks effectively while under fire. Added to that inconvenience was the fact that the British were often able to listen in on and often interfere with Italian radio communications. On occasion they managed to address Italians on the net by name, taunting them, as well as attempting to impart orders in Italian. Although the Italians did have codes to use, they proved cumbersome, so at times they resorted to the expedient of using terms from regional dialects that were almost always impossible for a non-Italian to understand.

4

The War of the Convoys and the Supply Situation

Waging war in North Africa posed a number of problems that centered around supplying the forces in the field. Even though the Italians had established some small agricultural enterprises in Libya, when the campaigning began, what local foodstuffs and livestock that were present in the colony were either hidden by the inhabitants to the degree that they could or were soon taken over by either the Italian military or, later, by the Germans. In any event, the Axis forces could not rely on local resources to supply food. Likewise, although there were substantial oil reserves beneath the sand on which the fighting took place, it lay undiscovered, untapped and unrefined, and was therefore unable to provide fuel for vehicles. Because there were essentially no local industries or resources that could be drawn upon or exploited to furnish any of the materiel needed to fight the war, almost everything had to be brought into the theater of operations, especially vehicles, equipment, ammunition, fuel and food, as well as other items needed to prosecute the war, including clothing and medical supplies, and everything else needed to sustain life in the unfamiliar and unforgiving environment. Conducting military operations in the desert can be likened to operating on the surface of the moon. To a large extent, Italian and German operations in North Africa depended upon the ability of the *Regia Marina* (Italian Royal Navy) to ferry men and supplies across the Mediterranean from ports in Italy to ports in Libya. The *Regia Marina* was aware of this need and had developed plans as early as 1938 to supply the ground forces in Libya in the event of war. However, the plans did not envision that the war in the desert would develop to the extent that it did, and so those plans were soon overcome by events in theatre.

A significant and indeed crucial factor in the inability to provide the supplies required was that the cargo reception capacity of the Libyan ports was fairly limited. Estimates for tonnage required to support the combined Axis forces in the desert varied from a low of 70,000 to a high of 150,000 tons per month, depending on the number of divisions present in the theater. A German panzer division needed 300–400 tons per day, while an Italian infantry division needed substantially less, about 175 tons. However, even under ideal conditions, the principal Libyan ports combined could handle only about 87,000 tons per month. The most capable port was Tripoli, which could accommodate five freighters and four troopships at a time and had a capacity of about 45,000 tons per month. Benghazi had a capacity of about 24,000 tons and could handle three freighters and two troop ships, while Tobruk (which was unavailable to the Axis from January 1941 until it was recaptured in June 1942) could also handle three freighters and two troop ships but had a capacity of only about 18,000 tons. Smaller ports such as those at Derna, Bardia, Ain el Gazala and Mersa Matruh were also used, but those could be used only by smaller coastal vessels. Supplies destined for North Africa often languished on the docks in Naples, Brindisi, Bari and Sicilian ports because of the restricted reception capacities of the Libyan ports, whose ability to handle supplies was even further diminished at times by British air attacks.

Once the supplies had arrived at the various ports along the North African coastline, the Italian supply system was responsible for getting what was needed to the front lines in the quantities and timescales required. The Italian supply system consisted of various echelons: the rearmost echelon

An aerial view of Tripoli depicting ship congestion and the somewhat
limited berthing facilities. (Courtesy Giancarlo Garello)

were the rear area quartermaster depots; further forward were the forward army depots, followed in turn by the division depots and battalion depots. Supplies were classified as 'ordinary' or 'extraordinary', with the former those that were needed to maintain basic loads at the unit level and the latter those aimed at increasing logistic autonomy. Both types were built up as stockpiles as well as being supplied during operational phases, and generally were sent directly to the relevant unit (a 'push' system). The armoured and motorized divisions, however, in order to alleviate the already stressed transportation assets of the quartermaster rear area and forward army depots, generally organized their own resupply systems with their organic transportation, drawing what was needed from higher echelon depots (a 'pull' system).

Organization at the division level is exemplified by the 'Ariete' division, which was structured with an operations staff and a services staff; services included commissariat (Classes I, II and VI in the US military supply system), ammunition and fuel (Classes III and V in the US system), and personnel and medical sections. The commissariat service dealt with providing food and water as well as being responsible for the supply and repair of clothing and equipment and providing bathing facilities and laundry service. All those functions were the responsibility of a *sezione sussistenza* (commissariat section) and two *autoreparti* (transportation battalions). Fuel and ammunition were vital to keeping the division operating as a fighting force. Ammunition was drawn from the rear area and forward army depots, which tended to maintain adequate stockage levels, and could generally be relied upon to have the types and amounts of ammunition that was needed on hand. More problematic was the supply of fuel and lubricants, as stockpiles of fuel were limited and could provide only relatively small amounts for immediate needs; the bulk of fuel deliveries to the armoured and motorized divisions were made almost directly from oil tankers moored at Tripoli or Benghazi and were met by truck and bowser columns ready to shuttle the fuel back to the user units. Accomplishing this was fraught with a host of problems including vehicle availability, the distances involved and the ever-present air threat, both in the ports and along the Via Balbia. Medical services were provided by a *servizio sanitario* (medical service), which was responsible for gathering, treating and forwarding sick and wounded soldiers; burial of the dead; and maintaining adequate stocks of medical equipment. Part of the medical detachment consisted of a small surgical team. The detachment had 12 ambulances, but in order to meet the constant battlefield needs, captured vehicles were used whenever available, as well as pressing other vehicles into service when required.

Bardia port facilities were limited and only marginally useful to the overall supply effort.
(Courtesy Giancarlo Garello)

All these various entities were gathered together in a divisional logistics base, which aimed at stocking enough material to ensure that the division could fight for five days or over a range of 500 kilometers (310 miles) without external resupply. The base area was camouflaged as best as possible, given the desert environment, and everything was dug in whenever possible. All truck drivers were taught to navigate both with a compass and by the stars so that if they became separated from the rest of the convoy, they would be able to reach their destination. All resupply moves were made by night, if possible, and were timed to reach the unit to be supplied at dawn.

There is a general impression that the *Regia Marina* was unable to supply effectively the Axis forces because British air and naval forces, operating chiefly from Malta, sank a large percentage of shipping bound for Libya. In the course of escorting some 1,210 convoys to Libya, the *Regia Marina* lost close to 90 ships, ranging from cruisers to auxiliary vessels, and the merchant navy lost 342 ships, but these losses do not present the whole picture. Despite some bad periods, such as the sinking of seven ships carrying badly needed fuel and supplies in August 1942, until January 1943 a very high percentage of troops and supplies (90 and 86 percent, respectively) sailing from Italy managed to reach Libyan ports, and from November 1942 to May 1943, 92 percent of men and 70 percent of materiel reached their destination in Tunisia. The August 1942 losses came at a particularly critical time for the Axis forces in the desert, just as the battle of Alam Halfa was about to begin. At the time, the overall supply situation for the Axis forces was far from adequate; in August 65,000 tons of shipping were lost. Between 24 and 31 August, food, ammunition and fuel deliveries to the Axis over a distance of 1,000 kilometers amounted to a meager 13,000 tons, while the corresponding figure for the British, over a distance of only 100 kilometers, was an astounding 300,000 tons. Thus, Rommel went into the offensive without any fuel reserves, counting on supplies that were to arrive from Italian ships that were at sea at the time. Between 23 and 30 August, four ships (*Alberto Fassio*, *Kreta*, *Giorgio* and *Gualdi*) delivered a total of 2,322 tons of fuel for Rommel's forces. However, within the span of a few days during September, several tankers were sunk or

The liners *Victoria*, *Marco Polo* and *Esperia* (from left to right) steaming towards Tripoli in the spring of 1941. (Erminio Bagnasco collection via Maurizio Brescia)

damaged, including the tankers *Picci Fassio*, *Pozzarica* and *Abruzzi*. Only 300 tons of diesel fuel were unloaded at Benghazi by the small ship *Unione*. On 26 October the tankers *Proserpina* (4,870 tons) and *Tergestea* (5,809 tons) were sunk just outside of Tobruk by British bomber attacks, and within a few days the tanker *Luisano* and the freighter *Tripolino* were also sunk. The loss of the tankers was especially critical, as Rommel had banked on them to supply the fuel necessary to enable him to have his armoured forces maneuver to cope with the British attacks. To add to the already precarious fuel situation, German Stuka dive-bombers mistakenly attacked a convoy of captured British trucks carrying fuel.

Earlier, between February and May of 1941, the Italians had managed to deliver 325,000 tons of supplies, which were 45,000 tons more than consumption for the same period. Although the bulk of the men and supplies were carried in cargo ships or troop ships in small convoys, at times the *Regia Marina* had to resort to ferrying men and supplies aboard destroyers and submarines in an attempt to ensure that the cargo was delivered safely and quickly. Italian submarines conducted 13 supply runs through 31 December 1941. A year later, in December 1942 and January 1943 the *Regia Marina* resorted to the drastic measure of protecting convoys with battleships, cruisers and destroyers to ensure the arrival of supplies to Libya. On 16 December 1942 Operation M 41 saw the commitment of four battleships, five cruisers and 20 destroyers to escort two convoys totaling four motorships. Although all four merchant vessels made it to Tripoli and Benghazi, two of the destroyers collided while maneuvering and suffered major damage to their bows. On 3 January 1943, encouraged by the success of Operation M 41, the navy again mounted a major effort entitled 'Operation M 43' to escort six merchant ships, assembling an escort force of four battleships, six cruisers and 21 destroyers, plus five torpedo boats; the operation ended without incident. However, these operations, although successful in delivering supplies to North African ports, cost the Italian

The steamer *Caterina*, with a deck load of trucks and other supplies, sinking on 19 October 1941 enroute from Naples to Tripoli, after having been damaged by a British torpedo bomber. (Maurizio Brescia)

navy an exorbitant price in terms of their own available fuel stocks and could not be sustained. In addition to the naval convoys, there was also some movement of troops and some classes of supplies via Italian and German transport aircraft, but the numbers and tonnages involved were very small compared to deliveries by sea. Although the Germans mounted an impressive effort using tri-motor Ju-52 as well as enormous Me-323 and BV-222 six-engine aircraft (the BV-222 was a seaplane) flying from various bases in Italy, Sicily, Greece and Crete to ferry troops and supplies to North Africa, once the flights to North Africa had attracted the attention of the British and despite being escorted by twin-engine Me-110 fighters, they began to suffer heavy losses.

A critical shortcoming for the Italian forces was the lack of sufficient numbers of trucks and artillery tractors needed to move large numbers of men and equipment across the wide expanse of the desert. Although Italy had a first-rate automotive industry in terms of quality, there was not a corresponding ability to produce the numbers of trucks and support vehicles needed to meet the needs of a modern army. The Italian infantryman of 1940 literally and figuratively walked in the footsteps of his Roman legionnaire ancestors who had trod across the sands of Cyrenaica and Tripolitania at the dawn of the Christian era some two thousand years earlier. Although the implements of war had changed drastically, most of the time the infantry divisions of the *Regio Esercito* in North Africa lacked sufficient motor transport, causing the infantry to become foot soldiers in the truest sense of the word, relying on their own two legs to march from one position to the next, in contrast to the highly motorized and mobile British and German forces which were outfitted with enough trucks and other vehicles to move all of the troops speedily and in relative comfort.

The lack of sufficient transport for the infantry divisions was only part of the problem the Italians faced with respect to the number of trucks it needed. Because of the arrangements between the Italians and the Germans, the Italians were responsible for moving virtually all supplies for the German forces as well as for the Italian forces from the ports to the front lines. It was challenging enough to move supplies for the relatively light Italian divisions but adding to them the

The *Spica* class torpedo boat *Polluce* sinking in the central Mediterranean on 4 September 1942. She was fatally damaged during a convoy escort mission from Piraeus to Tobruk. (Maurizio Brescia)

requirements for the larger and much more fuel-demanding German divisions presented yet another challenge. There were many factors that impacted the ability of the Italians to provide and maintain a sufficient number of cargo trucks to meet the needs at hand. First was the overall Italian production capacity for vehicles, which did not come close to being able to provide enough to equip the combat divisions or fill the needs of transportation units. In 1940, an army plan to requisition 20,500 civilian trucks fell short by 7,900. In North Africa specifically, in July 1941, there were only about 5,200 trucks available to an Italian force consisting of 110,000 men.

Hand-in-hand with relatively limited production capacity was the fact that, despite an attempt to establish standardization within certain truck categories (the *autocarro unificato medio* and *autocarro unificato pesante*) that called for civilian truck models to be adaptable for military use, the standardization related more to weight categories and carrying capacities than to any type of engine, transmission or other component commonality. Of the half dozen or so Italian truck manufacturers, all used diesel engines of British, German or Swiss design, built under license, for their medium and heavy trucks. Furthermore, these engines and components were from different manufacturers: Fiat built its own small diesel engines, but its larger diesels were British Ricardo and Soller designs; Officine Meccaniche (O.M.), although a Fiat subsidiary, made chassis and diesels under license from Saurer in Switzerland and pumps and injectors from Bosch; Alfa Romeo made chassis under license from Büssing-Nag and diesel engines under license from Deutz; Isotta Fraschini built entire vehicles (chassis and diesel engines) under license from MAN; Lancia built chassis and diesel engines under license from Junkers; Bianchi built complete vehicles (chassis and diesel engine) under license from Mercedes Benz with Bosch pumps and injectors. The Fiat subsidiary, SPA (*Società Piemontese Automobili*) was the only manufacturer that made trucks with little or no foreign involvement.

[Parenthetically, however, the Italians were the only nationality to have developed some truly innovative and capable vehicles, such as the *camionetta desertica SPA-Viberti mod. 42* and the *SPA-Viberti mod. 43* light truck, specifically designed for desert operations, but the numbers of these vehicles and their arrival in theater were either too little or too late. In the case of the *camionetta SPA-Viberti mod. 43*, although designed from the ground up for desert operations, it did not enter production until the fighting in North Africa was over.]

This multiplicity of manufacturers, types, engines, transmissions and all other parts contributed to logistical headaches for the supply system, as well as problems trying to keep such a heterogeneous

Italian ships in Tripoli, early January 1943. From left to right, the motorships *D'Annunzio* and *Sestriere*, and the steamer *Marocchino*. (Giorgio Apostoli collection, via Maurizio Brescia)

fleet repaired and running. According to Gravina, 35 percent of available trucks were always down for maintenance.

The lack of sufficient numbers of trucks and of standardization were only part of the multifaceted transport equation. When it came to employing the available truck assets to move supplies from the ports or supply depots to the front lines, the extremely limited road network – if a single coastal road can be called a network – and the often vast distances involved posed other logistical scheduling nightmares. The movement of supplies was confined almost exclusively to the Via Balbia, the coast road running from the Tunisian to the Egyptian border, which the Italians had built in the late 1930s; this was virtually the only paved highway in Libya and the route over which almost all supplies for the Axis forces traveled from west to east during the desert campaigning. There were also several other unimproved tracks, or '*trigs*', such as the Trig Capuzzo and the Trig el Abd, that ran through the desert, but these paled in importance when it came to the movement of essential supplies to the front. The principal supply port for the Axis was at Tripoli; consequently, depending on how far the Italo–German forces advanced and distanced themselves from that port, the further the supplies had to travel to get to the front. The distance from Tripoli to Benghazi was 1,030 kilometers (640 miles), and from Tripoli to El Alamein 1,800 kilometers (1,120 miles). Alberto Bechi-Luserna provides a somewhat terse, but apt description of the role and importance of the Via Balbia in the following description:

> Collection, resupply and repair centers, the ganglia of the circulatory system, flank it along its entire length, set up in tents or makeshift sheds. It is a spectacle of logistic grandeur without equal. What we remember of military studies instinctively gave us a glimpse of the monumental organizational work that oversees this flow and ebb. A mathematical calculation of times and distances and effort: for every soldier on the line at El Alamein there are another six or seven support personnel, spread along the road; to resupply a single battalion requires at least thirty trucks moving in stages along the route; a liter of fuel brought up to the line costs, roughly speaking, ten times as much as it is worth. Multiplying these numbers by the number of units deployed at the front and we arrive at totals that are really astronomical. It is only here, observing the Balbia, that one can get an idea of the tremendous effort that Italy is achieving to maintain the front at Alamein alive through this artery. And if you think about the fact that in

the European war academies they teach that to supply an army corps via one road is already a feat of logistic acrobatics, one has to ask oneself by what miracle of organizational intelligence our supply system manages to prevent an entire army deployed 2,000 kilometers (1,243 miles) from its bases from dying of hunger and thirst.

The Axis forces needed 70,000–150,000 tons of supplies per month, depending on the tempo of operations. At the low end of the scale of 70,000 tons per month, about 2,300 tons per day were needed to fill requirements for food, fuel, ammunition and other classes of supplies. Over even the shorter distance of 640 miles, and at an average of 4,500kg payload per truck, which may be an overly generous estimate, it would have taken over 15,500 truckloads per month, or about 500 truckloads per day to provide the needed level. To put the situation somewhat in perspective, the famed American 'Red Ball Express' that ran from the Normandy beaches to the front lines in France in 1944 required a total of 5,958 trucks to haul about 12,500 tons per day over a distance of 350–400 miles. The Italian trucks of the period were not capable of high speeds, even on paved roads; an average speed of even 30 miles per hour would be optimistic. That speed would translate to a full day's travel to cover the 640 miles between Tripoli and Benghazi. The average speed would almost certainly be lower because the truck convoys were subject to attack by Allied aircraft. It was certainly no great achievement for Allied pilots to find the single road that ran along the coast and the targets along it. The drivers, even absent attack, would have to stop periodically to refuel and to eat and rest. To keep up a steady stream of trucks to the front would require easily three to four times as many trucks. Every additional mile or kilometer to be traveled meant more trucks were needed to ferry the supplies. Bechi Luserna describes the journey from the port of arrival to the front at El Alamein as follows:

> It is a long trip, as jolting and as painful as a via crucis. It takes, to make it in a truck, from four to six days in the extremely hot and dusty atmosphere of Marmarica. From dawn to dusk we roll along the scorching ribbon of the Balbia; we stop as soon as it starts to get dark, wherever we are, the trucks scatter among the scarce lentisk bushes and we bivouac. All around us are the dark shapes of other trucks, of other truck columns at a halt. There are no bivouac fires, no songs, like other wars in Africa; just immobility and silence, because the enemy air force is alert and can sweep down upon us when we least expect it. We reluctantly wolf down a tin of meat that is still warm from the noontime sun and we throw ourselves down among the stones, which are also still warm, with eyes that burn, a dry throat and limbs that are bruised from the bouncing of the voyage. We are so exhausted that we fall instantly into a deep sleep with no dreams.

To some extent, the lack of sufficient trucks was offset by cargo trailers, which effectively doubled the carrying capacity of the trucks towing them; this, however, was at the cost of decreased speed and higher fuel consumption. Also offsetting the dearth of Italian trucks was the sporadic use of captured British vehicles, although these tended to be employed by combat units at the front lines rather than being assigned to supply columns. Even so, availability of captured vehicles was problematic, as the Germans tended to either keep as many vehicles as possible that they captured, or, in some instances, such as at El Mechili in April 1941, relieve the Italians of vehicles that they had captured. Even when the Italians did manage to integrate captured trucks into their inventory, repairs could be a problem. In at least one instance, when a 'batterie volanti' unit that used captured British and Canadian trucks needed spare parts to keep their trucks running, they resorted to the obvious and effective expedient of tracking down an isolated British detachment equipped with the same pattern trucks, taking it by surprise and capturing it. The Italians made off with the British trucks but left their former owners with enough food and water to survive until they could be

The *Navigatori* class destroyer *Da Verazzano* in 1941. This destroyer was extensively employed on convoy escort duties (Aldo Fraccaroli collection via Maurizio Brescia)

rescued. However, even such acts of gentlemanly hijacking could not make up for the overall paucity of much needed transport.

To add to the problems plaguing the supply system, there were the inevitable cases of outright bureaucratic malfeasance. During the retreat to Fuqa in November 1942, a truck from the 37th Heavy Truck Company was sent to the front loaded with 200 ten-kilo cans of black shoe polish to be used for what some time previously had been the anticipated triumphal march into Alexandria. Episodes such as this, while seemingly amusing, further strained the already overstressed system. Despite the general chaos relating to transport availability and road limitations, the Italians either miraculously, or without the aid of divine intervention but by sheer skill, ability and inventiveness (the time-honored Italian principle of 'arrangiarsi' [making do with what is at hand] certainly played a part in the supply situation) managed, at least most of the time, to get the requisite supplies to the frontline troops. Perhaps a book could and should be written that recognizes the accomplishments of the Italian logisticians, transportation officers, maintenance personnel and drivers who kept the supply system running as well as it did; they were the unsung, unrecognized and unappreciated behind-the-scenes heroes of the desert campaign.

Further exacerbating the supply situation was the fact that paradoxically the more successful the Italian and German forces were in the field, the further they distanced themselves from their supply depots, leaving the ports farther behind the front lines. The problem normally was not that supplies failed to reach North Africa, but that once there, the available transportation assets could not always cope with the tonnages and distances involved. The coastal road (the 1,822-kilometer-long Via Balbia, built by the Italians before the war) was basically the only road available over which to move the supplies and was subject to enemy air interdiction. Plus, the further the supply convoys had to travel to get to the front, the more fuel they consumed in the process, resulting in even less fuel for vehicles at the front.

By the time the front had reached El Alamein in mid-1942 the Italian supply system was not only stretched to the limit in terms of distance from its principal supply ports and bases but was suffering badly in terms of the number of trucks it had to get supplies to the front. In July 1942 the Italians had one *autogruppo di manovra* (transportation group) with only a few hundred trucks left after handing over 300 to the Germans, per order of *Comando Supremo*. There was also an *autoraggruppamento logistico* (an army-level transportation logistics group) with an unspecified number of trucks, and a collection of about 1,000 civilian trucks, all high capacity and almost all with

The *Antonio Pigafetta*, in 'standard' camouflage pattern, 12 August 1942. Between November 1941 and September 1942, *Pigafetta*, as part of the XV Destroyer Squadron, was involved in 30 convoy escort missions. (Aldo Fraccaroli collection, via Maurizio Brescia)

trailers, which represented the backbone of the so-called '*servizio di linea*', or long-haul transport along the Via Balbia and to the front lines. Heavy-duty trucks, including the Lancia 3Ro and Fiat 634 types, had been requisitioned from civilian firms in Libya, along with their drivers who were 'militarized.' Most of these civilian trucks also had two-axle trailers, effectively doubling the amount of cargo they could transport, at least on paved roads. In addition to hauling fuel, water, ammunition and food, they were also used as tank transporters in order to save wear and tear on the tanks before being committed to action on the front lines. The numbers of operational trucks of all types continued to decrease due to normal wear, driving over desert tracks, high temperatures, limited maintenance, bombing and strafing. Engine life was about half of normal life. Entreaties for additional trucks by Rommel to the Italian high command were essentially fruitless; *Comando Supremo* was long on promises, but in the end, only a laughable number of trucks were provided.

The *Spica* class torpedo boat *Lupo* in late June 1941. On 22-23 May 1941, whilst escorting a convoy to Crete, *Lupo* made a daring charge against a British force of three cruisers and four destroyers and survived, although it was hit by 18 large-caliber shells. Because of this action, *Lupo* gained a reputation as the luckiest ship in the *Regia Marina*, but nevertheless was sunk on 30 November 1942. (Erminio Bagnasco collection via Maurizio Brescia)

The steamer *Aventino* as a troop transport in the southern Adriatic Sea in March 1942 with a CANT Z.501 seaplane of the *Regia Aeronautica* flying overhead. (Erminio Bagnasco collection via Maurizio Brescia)

A shipment of brand-new M13/40 tanks being offloaded in Tripoli. In December 1941 the entire complement of 52 M14/41 tanks of XII Battalion was sunk en route to North Africa. (USSME)

The end result was that the Axis forces in the field seemed to be perpetually short of many essential supplies and often were able to sustain operations only by capturing British supplies, especially fuel and food, and to some extent other items such as clothing and medical supplies. With respect to captured fuel, the Italians did not always benefit as much as the Germans as German tanks and trucks, like most British vehicles, had gasoline engines (although some British tanks had diesel engines), whereas Italian tanks and many trucks had diesel engines and could not run on normal gasoline. Over the long term, it was inevitable that the ability of the Allies to produce and deliver staggering amounts of equipment to North Africa would seal the fate of the Axis forces, no matter how well-organized and motivated they were, or how skillfully or valiantly they fought. They were simply out-supplied.

5

Regia Aeronautica Support for Ground Operations

The war in the desert was not a unidimensional battle. In addition to the role played in the Mediterranean by the *Regia Marina* to ensure the flow of supplies for the ground forces and by the British Royal Navy to impede the flow of those supplies, there was a very active air war being waged between the *Regia Aeronautica*, later joined by the *Luftwaffe*, against the British Western Desert Air Force. A subset of the air war was the role played by the *Regia Aeronautica* in providing air support to the Italian (and German) forces on the ground.

The Italians were not unaware of the need for the air arm to be prepared and capable of providing air support, including close air support, to the ground forces. The foremost proponent of developing a ground attack capability was General Amedeo Mecozzi, who began to propound his theories and train pilots for that role in 1929 when he was still a major. It is averred that pilots trained by Mecozzi were able to fly at very low level (what today would be termed 'nap-of-the earth') and were able to drop inert bombs on a target as small as a handkerchief. As forward-looking as Mecozzi's concept and training standards may have been, when the war broke out, his vision could not be fully or properly implemented because although the *Regia Aeronautica* had supported Mecozzi's theory and provided enough funding and resources to create two ground attack wings, the *5o* and *50o* that were assigned to the V Assault (Ground Attack) Brigade in 1936, the Breda Ba.65 which equipped those units was, for the Italians at the time, an innovative and complicated aircraft, the first monoplane in Italian service with retractable landing gear, a variable pitch propeller and flaps, it was not well liked by pilots who were accustomed to the simplicity and maneuverability of biplanes. There was a high incidence of accidents when the Ba.65 was first introduced because pilots wanted to engage in the same type of aerobatics they were used to with the CR.32 and other agile biplanes; as a result, more than a few pilots lost their lives.

Added to the obsolescence and scarcity of many *Regia Aeronautica* aircraft designed for the ground attack role were a host of other factors such as lack of proper radios for air-to-ground coordination, lack or shortage of appropriate munitions, and a cumbersome bureaucratic system for requesting air support – all of which negatively impacted the ability of the RA to support ground operations.

On the eve of hostilities in the desert, the Italians had a total of 300 operational aircraft in North Africa, of which 125 were bombers, 88 fighters, 34 'assault' or fighter-bombers, 14 observation, six maritime reconnaissance and 33 belonging to the *Aviazione Sahariana*. On both sides, Italian and British, the aircraft were mostly antiquated or obsolete machines. Italian bombers were the Savoia-Marchetti SM.79 and SM.81 tri-motor aircraft, fighters consisted of FIAT CR.32 and CR.42 biplanes, and, in the ground attack role, the Italians had the Caproni CA.310 and the Breda Ba.65, neither of which were particularly successful aircraft. In fact, at the time the war broke out the Ba.65 was being recalled from frontline service. On the British side, there were some 70 Bristol Blenheim twin-engine bombers, 40 Gloster Gladiators and 10 Gloster Gauntlets (both biplanes), and 24 antiquated Bristol Bombays and Vickers Valentias in the transport role, for a total of 144 aircraft.

A FIAT CR.32 fitted with rudimentary bomb racks, used in the fighter-bomber role. The fuselage marking identifies it as belonging to the *160a Squadriglia Assalto*. The initials 'CR' in the aircraft's designation referred to Celestino Rosatelli, the plane's designer. (Courtesy Giancarlo Garello)

A Breda Ba.65 ground attack aircraft. Although obsolete and in the process of being withdrawn from service at the time of the initiation of hostilities in the desert in 1940, it was recalled to service and provided ground support to the *Regio Esercito* until augmented and replaced by more capable aircraft. (Courtesy Giancarlo Garello)

Pilot climbing into the cockpit of the Breda Ba.65. The enclosed cockpit of the Ba.65 was a novelty for Italian pilots, who at the time still preferred the open cockpits to which they were accustomed.
(Courtesy Giancarlo Garello)

The extensively damaged remains of a Breda Ba.65 on a North African airfield.
(Courtesy Giancarlo Garello)

An intact Caproni Ca.310 being inspected by the crew of a British Vickers Mk VI light tank.
(Courtesy Giancarlo Garello)

A FIAT CR.42 equipped with wing-mounted bomb racks being readied for takeoff in the desert.
(Courtesy Giancarlo Garello)

Armourers loading a bomb onto the rack of a CR.42. (Courtesy Giancarlo Garello)

FIAT CR.42 fighters at an airstrip in Libya. Although by some accounts the best biplane of the Second World War, it was no match for the low-wing British Hurricane and US-supplied P40 series fighters that it came up against early in the desert fighting. (Courtesy Giancarlo Garello)

Once hostilities began in June, the *Regio Esercito* continued to request sorties by the RA against attacking British vehicles; some of these requests were frantic appeals for strikes against only a few armoured cars, which prompted the air force to quickly adopt measures to avoid the waste of scarce resources against such relatively unprofitable targets. Request procedures were cumbersome, and the mobile nature of the targets often made it difficult for the pilots to find them based on information that was somewhat old by the time they arrived on the scene. The majority of the ground support operations necessarily fell upon the *50o Stormo* (wing) which had 23 of the Caproni C.310 and 11 Breda Ba.65, but in actuality, the C.310, which was a new aircraft that was designed as a reconnaissance and light bomber aircraft, was sent to Libya as a stop-gap measure. It was not suited for the ground attack role, lacking any type of bomb rack (small incendiary bombs had to be thrown manually from the entrance door!) and in any case proved to be a flight risk and totally unsuitable for any type of combat operation. In the end, the aircraft were withdrawn from frontline service and re-roled as multi-engine trainers. This left the Italians with pathetically few aircraft to cope with the demands for air support, so they resorted to an improvised stopgap measure by re-purposing a small number of worn-out CR.32 biplanes, fitting them with jury-rigged bomb racks that enabled them to carry two 15kg bombs. Using some captured British armoured cars as targets and determining the best angle of attack to use against the angled armour, the CR.32 pilots of the *160a Squadriglia* (squadron) developed an attack technique using a dive angle of 60 degrees, which proved to be fairly effective against armoured targets. Meanwhile, another ground attack Group, the *7o*, was equipped with the Breda Ba.88, a sleek, modern twin-engine design purpose-built as a ground attack aircraft, but which almost immediately showed itself to be another totally unreliable aircraft. Like the C.310, it was soon withdrawn from service, once again placing the burden on the few remaining Ba.65s and the CR.32s, an increasing number of which had been fitted with bomb racks. The number of Ba.65s had dwindled to only a handful because of operational losses and damage to engines from the ever-present sand, which turned engine oil into something more like a paste mixture rather than a free-flowing liquid. Early in the fighting, the tri-motor SM.79 bomber was also used to support ground troops: during the first six months of operations, SM.79s dropped 120,000kg of explosives against armoured and troop formations, and a further 22,600kg of incendiary bombs. All these measures taken by the *Regia Aeronautica*, however, were unable to do anything to alter the outcome of the British ground offensive, which resoundingly defeated the Italian army at Beda Fomm on 9 February 1941.

As these operations were progressing, both sides made haste to improve the numbers and quality of aircraft assigned to the theater: on 29 January 1941 the Italians deployed the FIAT G.50 monoplane fighter, which easily outmatched the British Gloster Gladiator biplanes, but was in turn not the equal of the Hurricane which the RAF had sent to theater. Bomber inventories improved with the addition of the FIAT BR.20 on the Italian side and the Martin Baltimore on the British side. A major change in the air equation was the arrival of the *Luftwaffe* in Libya in February, initially with 66 Junkers Ju-87 Stukas and 22 Messerschmitt Bf-110 Zerstörer fighter-bombers, soon joined by the very capable Messerschmitt Bf-109 fighter and by Heinkel He-111 bombers. The German Ju-87s were also joined by a number of Ju-87s in Italian service, nicknamed the 'Picchiatello' (equivalent to the American 'Woody Woodpecker'). Three squadriglie, the *209a*, *237a* and *239a*, were equipped with the *Picchiatello*. As the campaigning in the desert resumed, in addition to conducting their own independent air operations, the Italians and Germans engaged in numerous joint efforts, especially with regards to joint operations with Ju-87s of both nationalities; many of these Stuka attacks were carried out against the defenses at Tobruk.

The Italians sought to improve their air capabilities in North Africa by introducing the FIAT G.50 and Macchi MC.200 monoplanes to cope with the Hurricane and early Spitfires but were not particularly successful against those British aircraft. In particular, the G.50 was underpowered and, lacking sand filters, was not suited for desert operations. As a result, both the G.50 and MC.200

A flight of Junker Ju-87 Stukas. The Italians had three squadrons of this aircraft, christened *Picchiatello*, in service in North Africa. (Courtesy of Giancarlo Garello)

Two Italian Ju-87s. The Italians tended to use white propeller hubs and white or yellow engine cowlings on their fighter aircraft. In the case of the Ju-87s in the photograph, the band on the cowling was painted yellow, while the tip of the propeller hub was painted red. (Courtesy of Giancarlo Garello)

The FIAT G.50 was one of the first generation of Italian monoplane fighters, but it retained a partially open cockpit favored by Italian pilots. (Courtesy of Giancarlo Garello)

A FIAT G.50 as part of a joint patrol with a German Bf-110 in the background. Joint Italo–German sorties were fairly common in the desert. (Courtesy of Giancarlo Garello)

were modified as fighter-bombers, somewhat following in the footsteps of the CR.42 which, when considered to be at the end of its useful operational life, was given a new role by adapting it to the fighter-bomber role in 1941. All three types of aircraft represented an immediate response to the need for the *Regia Aeronautica* to develop and provide tactical air support and were used intensely for close air support. The fact that these aircraft had originally been fighters enabled them, once they had dropped their bombs, to strafe enemy personnel and vehicles as well.

Regia Aeronautica capabilities continued to improve, especially with the advent of the superb Macchi MC.202 fighter in November 1941. However, even with the qualitative performance advantage of the MC.202, and the introduction of the Messerschmitt Bf.109F and G Trop versions, their numbers were ultimately outpaced by those of the British and the newly arrived Americans. Coupled with increasingly more capable aircraft, especially the later versions of the Spitfire, the air superiority enjoyed by the Italo–German air forces came to an end in the summer of 1942, at the time of Rommel's Gazala offensive, at the beginning of which the Germans had some 200 aircraft and the Italians 240, against about 600 in the Western Desert Air Force. However, the attrition caused by three weeks of constant combat, with sortie rates of 300–400 per day, coupled with the harsh desert operating conditions, greatly weakened the Axis air capabilities. The Germans were down to about 100 planes, and the Italians similarly had reduced capabilities; with fuel stocks almost exhausted, Kesselring had to tell Rommel that his forces were no longer able to provide air cover for the final phase of the advance to Alamein. It is worth noting, however, that in the overall context of the air campaign and despite the RAF devoting a significant amount of effort against the incessant supply convoy traffic along the Via Balbia coast road and causing havoc, especially when the Axis forces were retreating, the *Regia Aeronautica* and *Luftwaffe* succeeded in keeping that vital road open to two-way traffic for most of the desert campaign.

A Macchi MC.200 with two wing-mounted bombs for ground support operations. The radial-engine MC.200 was a contemporary of the FIAT G.50 and the precursor of the excellent Macchi MC.202. The plane was designed by Mario Castoldi, hence the 'MC' designation. (Courtesy Giancarlo Garello)

A Macchi MC.202 of the 84th Squadriglia that served in Libya and Egypt. Squadron aircraft bore the inscription 'F. Baracca' on the engine cowling and the '*cavallino rampante*' ('rampant horse') symbol on the fuselage band, both in reference to Francesco Baracca, Italy's top scoring fighter ace in the First World War. Overall, the Macchi MC.202 was a superlative fighter and was fully competitive with all contemporary British and US aircraft, despite the relatively weak armament of its early versions. (Giancarlo Garello)

Despite the efforts the *Regia Aeronautica* made to provide close air support to the ground forces, it was, much like the situation with the ground war, a matter of numbers and supplies, from which the Axis air forces suffered as well as the armies. In addition to the lack of sufficient numbers of aircraft fit for the role, the Italians were never able to achieve an integrated, effective, workable system of real-time requests from the ground forces and rapid aircraft reaction times due to the lack of VHF radios and procedures to relay requests or information from one force to the other.

6

The *Afrika Korps* and Italo–German Relations

Relations between Italic and Germanic people have been marked by hostility, warfare, strife and tension since their first contact during the Cimbrian War beginning in 113 BC, when Germanic tribes began to wander into what are now southern France and northern Italy and were confronted by the Romans. For literally 2,000 years, Germans and Italians (beginning with the Romans) experienced a series of alternating wars and periods of peace, truce or coexistence. The list of battles and wars between the two peoples is long, marked by events such as the Battle of the Teutoborg Forest in 9AD, the Gothic Wars of 402–403 and 534–535, the Sack of Rome by the Vandals in 410, the Lombard invasion and annexation of northern in Italy in 568–750 and the 1527 Sack of Rome by German (mostly Lutheran) troops. Only 25 years prior to the Second World War, Germany and Italy had been enemies and battled each other in northern Italy. This long historical animosity between the two cultures left its imprint on the national psyche of both sides, and it is not surprising that in North Africa they each had negative feelings, either under the surface or made manifestly obvious, towards the other. Mussolini had initially rejected offers of German assistance in North Africa, but the defeat suffered by the Italians in February 1941 forced him to swallow his pride and request assistance from the Germans.

As early as September 1940, based on studies it had made, the German Army high command began preparations to send a mixed armoured brigade to North Africa, but the Italians saw no need to accept the German offer of help, instead launching an offensive beginning on 13 September. However, the disastrous rout of Italian forces by O'Connor's counteroffensive between 9 December 1940 and 7 February 1941 led the Italians to request assistance from their German allies. In response, the Germans began by basing the *X.Fliegerkorps* in Sicily so as to attack British supply convoys and British forces in Libya. On 6 February, the day before the Italian surrender at Beda Fomm, the German *Unternehmen Sonnenblume* (Operation Sunflower) was put into effect, calling for a blocking formation (*Sperrverband Afrika*) to be attached to a German corps headquarters. The force was to consist of the *5.leichte Afrika-Division* and an armoured division under the command of General Erwin Rommel. On 12 February, Rommel arrived in Tripoli, with the first German combat forces arriving on the following day aboard the German ship *Alicante*. Rommel wasted no time at all in sending out mixed German–Italian reconnaissance patrols, advancing 150 kilometers (93 miles) to En Nofilia on 24 February. These reconnaissance patrols set the tone for what was to follow: aggressive, decisive actions by both Italian and German forces under German direction that put unrelenting pressure on the British forces – at least until time and the supply situation inexorably worked to the advantage of the British.

On 21 February the German forces in North Africa were formally designated the '*Deutsches Afrika Korps*' (DAK). Therein lies much confusion and misunderstanding about the conduct of the war in the desert, and the role played by Italian forces. While the North African campaign is frequently thought of and written about as a contest between the German *Afrika Korps* under Rommel and Montgomery's Eighth Army (which was not formed as such until September 1941) consisting of British and Commonwealth forces, in fact the bulk of the Axis forces in the desert consisted

German PzKpfw III tanks of *1.Panzerkompanie*, *Panzer-Regiment 5*, *5.leichte-Division* parading in Tripoli on 12 March 1941. (Luca Massacci)

Rommel, wearing short pants, inspecting a group of *Bersaglieri* armed with the Carcano Model 1891 carbine. On several occasions Rommel spoke highly of the *Bersaglieri* performance. (Daniele Guglielmi)

of Italian units, and overall command of all forces in the theater was vested in a headquarters commanded by an Italian general. The chain of command ran from the Italian *Comando Supremo* (Supreme Command) in Rome, to the *Comando Superiore Forze Armate dell'Africa Settentrionale* (Armed Forces High Command North Africa) and thence to the Italian and German forces in the desert. It was not until 1 August 1942 that all the Italo–German forces under Rommel were subordinated directly to the *Comando Supremo* in Rome, although in practice Rommel continued to act pretty much as he pleased.

The commander-in-chief of all forces in Libya initially was Marshal Rodolfo Graziani, who was succeeded in turn by General Italo Gariboldi and later by General Ettore Bastico. The Axis forces consisted essentially of the German DAK and the Italian *Corpo d'Armata di Manovra* (CAM; which was later designated XX Corps) and XXI Corps. The combined Italo-German forces were given different designations as the force structure changed: from 15 August 1941 to 31 January 1942 the forces were designated '*Panzergruppe Afrika/Gruppo Corazzato Africa*', from 31 January to 1 October it was known as '*Panzerarmee Afrika/Armata Corazzata Africa*', from 1 October 1942 to 4 February 1943 the designation was the '*Deutsch–Italienische Panzerarmee/Armata Corazzata Italo–Tedesca*', and from 5 February until 13 May 1943 it was known as the '*Heeresgruppe Afrika/Gruppo d'Armate Africa*', or the Italian 1st Army. The DAK numbered no more than 54,000 men at its zenith and consisted of the *15.* and *21.Panzer-Divisions* as well as the *90.leichte-Division*, augmented by the *164.leichte-Division* in September 1942. The Italian XX Corps consisted of the 'Ariete' armoured division and the 'Trieste' motorized division. Because it was a mobile force, it frequently and quite successfully operated alongside and in conjunction with the DAK as a mobile strike force. Later, XX Corps also controlled the 133rd 'Littorio' armoured division and the 136th 'Giovani Fascisti' infantry division. The XXI Corps normally consisted of four infantry divisions – 'Trento', 'Brescia', 'Bologna' and 'Pavia'– and the Italians created X Corps by mid-1941, to which 'Brescia' and 'Pavia' were subordinated. At various times those two corps also controlled the 'Pistoia', 'Superga', 'La Spezia', 'Savona', 'Sabratha' infantry divisions and the 'Folgore' parachute division.

Although on paper overall command in North Africa was vested in the Italians, in practice it was clearly Rommel, commanding the *Panzergruppe* and later the *Panzerarmee*, who planned, directed and led the conduct of operations. However, it must be borne in mind that those formations consisted of Italian as well as German units, and that neither nationality could have survived the desert combat without the aid of the other. The Germans are said to have looked down upon, indeed despised, the Italians, while the Italians had little use for the attitude of the Germans and did not trust them, with good reason, to always provide the support they needed. Although the Germans may have had disdain for the Italians and complained about their slowness on the

The Germans supplied several of the excellent 88/55 dual-purpose gun to the Italians, such as this one manned by an Italian crew in North Africa. British reports often mistook the similar Italian 90/53 for the German gun. (Enrico Finazzer)

A German Krauss-Maffei half-track towing a war booty French 15,5cm Schneider Mle. 1917
howitzer. Designated as sFH 413/414 (f) in German, 18 of these howitzers were assigned to
Heeresküstenartillerieabteilung (Army Coast Defense Battalion) 523 and 408. (DanieleGuglielmi)

battlefield, nevertheless they relied on Italian infantry divisions to act as anchors and hold ground
as well as on Italian armoured and motorized divisions to act as maneuver forces operating in
conjunction with the mobile forces of the *Afrika Korps*. In truth, Italian units performed at least as
well, if not better, than could be expected given their inherent limitations. The XX Corps particularly handled itself extremely well, and it is highly doubtful that the DAK would have been able to
achieve what it did without the support and assistance of XX Corps. Indeed, XX Corps was vital
not only to the successes of the *Afrika Korps*, but to its very survival. The reality was that it was
a symbiotic relationship that benefited both the Germans and the Italians. As far as the fighting
qualities of 'Ariete' and 'Trieste', it should be noted that they fought tenaciously and valiantly until
the time of their virtual annihilation during the battles of Alamein. In fact, in compliance with
Rommel's orders, 'Ariete' fought until it was almost completely wiped out during the fighting at
Bir el Abd on 4 November 1942, buying precious time for the battered German units to disengage
and escape. Likewise, the infantry divisions of XXI Corps, whose performance is often either overlooked completely or is referred to dismissively or disparagingly in English-language and German
accounts of the fighting, often managed to provide critical support as holding or blocking forces
while the Italo–German armoured and motorized elements acted as strike forces.

Clearly, the notion that following their arrival in North Africa it was the Germans alone, or
even primarily, who slugged it out against the British in the desert in no way reflects reality, as the
bulk of the Axis forces engaged in the desert were Italian. In this regard, the numbers of forces
involved speak for themselves: between June 1940 and May 1943 the Italians committed a total
of 25 divisions to the campaigns in North Africa, while the Germans contributed only six. Even
accounting for the disparity in size of the substantially larger German divisions, Italian participation in terms of the sheer number of troops involved was still overwhelming in comparison to

February 1942. An Italian M13/40 in the foreground, and a German PzKpfw III in the background. The staff car is German, but the motorcyclist appears to be Italian. (Massimiliano Afiero)

the German forces involved: the highest number of Germans in the desert up to the time of El Alamein in October 1942 reached some 54,000 troops, while during that same period, the Italians had a high of some 150,000 troops. It should be borne in mind that during much of the campaign in Libya after February 1941 the Italian non-motorized infantry divisions were used mainly as static units laying siege to Tobruk at the behest of Rommel who was understandably obsessed with capturing that fortress. Furthermore, the Italians were responsible for providing and delivering most of the supplies needed by both the German and the Italian forces, allowing the Germans to concentrate on fighting rather than being burdened with the considerable logistics difficulties that were part and parcel of fighting in the desert.

Aside from the formal command and operational relationships between the Italians and the Germans, other relationships were often conditioned by personal feelings between individuals of the two nationalities. These feelings could encompass the gamut from sincere respect and admiration to downright disdain and animosity. Unfortunately, the preponderance of anecdotal evidence points to much more negative than positive feelings between the two nationalities, which is not surprising given the long history of strife between the two cultures and the German conviction, fostered by Nazi propaganda, that as an ethnic group they were superior to all other forms of human life on earth. In 1942 there were Italians fighting in the desert who still nurtured a deep and abiding personal animosity towards the Germans based on the loss of family members to them during the First World War. This is exemplified by an incident that occurred on the Alamein front in October 1942. During an awards ceremony being held at the 'Bologna' division headquarters during which General Stumme was to give out Iron Crosses to a number of Italian soldiers, two soldiers from the XXXI Sapper Battalion objected to taking part in the ceremony. One of the two had lost his father

Rommel consulting a map and discussing strategy with high-ranking Italian officers in June 1941.
The officer on the extreme left is General Italo Gariboldi, who in theory outranked Rommel and who
seldom agreed with Rommel's proposals. The bearded officer is Minister of Italian Africa Attlio Teruzzi.
(Massimiliano Afiero)

to the Germans in the First World War, and the other a brother. None of the Italian higher-ups
wished to offend the Germans, so the two soldiers were forcefully invited, grudgingly, to accept their
medals. Although there were instances of individual Germans showing great respect for the performance of the Italians, especially as regards that of the 'Folgore' parachute division at El Alamein,
and of Italians appreciating the professionalism of individual Germans with whom they operated,
when it came to the overall attitudes of each nationality with respect to the other, the picture was
not always so rosy. This attitude, at least on the part of the Germans, seemed to filter down from the
highest levels. According to Caccia Dominioni, three of Rommel's top officers – Gause, Bayerlein
and Westphal – hated and despised the Italians. Rommel himself seemed to alternate between
praise for certain Italian units and despair over their performance. Desmond Young, who generally
is uncharitable and critical of the Italians, quotes Rommel as follows:

> The duty of comradeship obliges me to make clear, particularly as I was supreme commander
> also of the Italians, that the defeats the Italian forces suffered in early July before El Alamein,
> were in no way the fault of the Italian soldiers. The Italian soldier was willing, unselfish and a
> good comrade and, considering his circumstances, his achievement was far above the average.

Overall, there was a stark contrast between the Italians and the Germans in the way they viewed
each other's national characteristics and stereotypes: the Germans viewed the Italians as lazy, disorganized, unreliable and cowardly, while the Italians viewed the Germans as arrogant, pampered,

ruthless, untrustworthy, lacking in compassion and slaves to orders. One incident that illustrates German attitudes and challenges the negative characterization of the Italians relates to a joint Italo–German patrol in late September 1942, the purpose of which was to inspect an enemy mine-field. The patrol consisted of a German lieutenant and sergeant and eight paratroopers, two of whom were Italians from the 'Folgore'. Having reached the minefield, the German lieutenant trig-gered a mine that had not been there the night before and was seriously wounded; the sergeant, reasoning with implacable Teutonic logic that the mission had been accomplished, decided to leave the lieutenant there rather than risk losing any additional lives and to return to friendly lines. When the two 'Folgore' paratroopers were safely back, the Italian way of thinking kicked in: 'The German lieutenant has to be brought back, dead or alive, to our own lines', so the two Italians set out on their own, prepared to deal with whatever might face them. Having found the lieutenant, they slowly and patiently dragged his bleeding body back to their own lines in the hopes that the doctors would be able to save him. The two paratroopers then returned to their own foxholes for some well-earned sleep but were soon rousted out and told to report to General Ramcke, who with a minimum of fuss, awarded Iron Crosses to both men on the spot. Perhaps as a result of this incident, in October 1942, General Georg Stumme, who had replaced Rommel as commander of *Panzerarmee Afrika*, gave orders to all German and Italian divisions that they should study the type of patrols carried out by the 'Folgore' and adopt similar practices.

The Germans, who lost no occasion to complain about not being properly supported by the Italians from time to time, were not themselves innocent of leaving the Italians in the lurch by pulling out of positions without alerting nearby Italian units. On 23 October 1942, while under attack, a group of 'Folgore' paratroopers of V Battalion attempted to request fire from a German artillery unit that was supposed to be supporting them, but there was no answer on the phone. A runner was sent back to the Germans only to find that they were pulling out, with no thought

An example of Italo–German fraternization in the winter of 1942. Two or three Italian 'Giovani Fascisti' are visiting with the crew of a German 37mm Flak 36 position in the desert. Although the German crew are wearing sidecaps, there are at least two steel helmets close to hand on the sandbagged parapet. (USSME)

of informing the Italians of their departure. About a week later, on 2 November, the gunners of 5th Battery, III Group, 22nd Motorized Artillery Regiment of the 'Trieste' division, who had been given orders to fight to the last, became aware that a nearby German battery and the tanks supporting it pulled out without warning, leaving the Italian flanks exposed. On one occasion, when the Australians attacked a position that they believed to be held by the Germans but found that the occupants were Italians instead, their opinion was that the Germans 'were up to their old trick of putting the Italians out in front to take the edge off the attack while they had time to prepare in the second and stronger line'. These incidents expose the irony of the oft-quoted use of 'corseting' that was adopted by the Germans in July 1942 during the First Battle of El Alamein. Corseting consisted of interspersing German infantry units among Italian formations so that the better armed Germans could support the relatively weak Italian units as well as reinforce their morale. In practice, however, it seems that the Italians stayed the course more often than their German counterparts.

On occasion, friction and animosity developed to the point that the two sides exchanged gunfire, and although instances of actual firefights between the Italians and Germans may have been infrequent, they were not rare. During the retreat from El Alamein, a group of Italians, exasperated because the Germans had reserved use of the road for themselves and the German *Felpolizei* refused to let the Italians share the road, opened fire on the Germans, who responded in kind; a number of soldiers were killed and wounded during the incident. A few days later, Caccia Dominioni, traveling in a truck whose muffler was missing, was overtaken by two Germans on a motorcycle and sidecar. When the driver of the motorcycle made an obscene remark about the Italians while passing, Caccia Dominioni, who spoke fluent German, parried with another obscenity in German, whereupon the sidecar occupant leveled his rifle at the Italians. Caccia Dominioni countered by aiming his war-booty Thompson submachine gun at the Germans, who quickly darted into the space between two other vehicles, avoiding a probably deadly showdown.

In addition to these occurrences of willful confrontation, there were also instances of mistaken identity and 'friendly fire'. Caccia Dominioni recounts the tale of two units, one Italian and one German, which on the night of 31 August 1942 became disoriented; the German platoon found an abandoned position and occupied it, while a platoon of paratroopers from 'Folgore', similarly disoriented, ran into the now occupied strongpoint, assuming that it was manned by the British. The Italians fixed bayonets and charged, guns blazing. The Germans, who despite being on amphetamines, did not return fire, but instead raised their hands in surrender. Once the two sides had sorted out the mistake, they both went on their way, on the correct bearings.

These kinds of confrontations and encounters were counterbalanced to a small degree by genuinely cordial relations enjoyed occasionally between individuals or small units. One such instance was the relationship between Caccia Dominioni's XXXI Sapper Battalion and the *Stabskompanie* of the German 115th Schützen Regiment of *15.Panzer-Division*, which happened to be adjacent to the XXXI. The two units developed a close and cordial working relationship, possibly due partly to the fact that Caccia Dominioni spoke German well. The 115th had continuous contact with both 'Ariete' and 'Trieste' and as a result seems to have become somewhat 'Italianized', sporting Italian Sahariana jackets, many of which bore Italian medals and ribbons that had been awarded to them. Their cooperation with the XXXI Sapper Battalion included joint training and exchange of ideas on tactical procedures, as well as sharing dinners. Caccia Dominioni was most impressed by the German grenadiers, characterizing them as humane, romantic, Goethian and sentimental, in clear contrast to the Hitlerian society that Germany had become, as exemplified by the German paratroopers who were Wagnerian, unsettling, grandiose and tempestuous.

Broadly speaking, the Germans acted in a high-handed manner towards the Italians and placed their own interests for survival first. Whether it was appropriating vehicles or reserving roads for their exclusive use, the Germans seemed to believe that it was their natural right to dictate to the

A column of German PzKpfw III tanks on the move in a verdant part of Libya, possibly in the Tripoli area. (Massimiliano Afiero)

A German *Kubelwagen* and an Italian *bersagliere* riding a Guzzi Trialce motorcycle with the *Arco dei Fileni* (referred to by the British as the 'Marble Arch') in the background, erected by the Italians to mark the boundary between Tripolitania and Cyrenaica. The upper distance notation on the signpost on the left, in German, reads: 'To Berlin 3557 km' while the lower notation appears to read 'To Kirkenes 6321 km'. Kirkenes, in Norway, was the furthest point from Libya under German occupation. (Daniele Guglielmi)

The German freighter *Ankara* in 1942, as part of a convoy bound for Africa. Although most convoys to North Africa consisted of Italian vessels, some supplies were also carried on German bottoms. (Maurizio Brescia)

Italians and often behaved arrogantly towards them. The Germans had refined to a science the practice of looting conquered territories of anything of value, including food, fuel, armament and vehicles. Whatever fed the German war machine was fair game, in German eyes, for appropriation. In North Africa, understandably enough, both the Germans and Italians took advantage of food, fuel, weapons and transport assets captured from the British.

The Germans were not averse to appropriating equipment that the Italians had captured, such as they did at El Mechili after the Italians had done the fighting and captured a significant booty of vehicles and other equipment. Some Italian units managed to avoid German 'requisition' of captured vehicles simply by lying about whether they had any such vehicles on hand. A case in point is that of the XXXI Sapper Battalion: half of its assigned vehicles were dead-lined due to lack of parts, or being totally worn out, or having been shot up by the enemy, and despite cannibalization to keep the remaining vehicles running, there was still a shortage of trucks. This was in part offset through the use of captured British vehicles, but higher German headquarters had decreed that all captured vehicles be reported and turned over to the Germans. In order to avoid losing the vehicles, the Italians simply reported that they had no war booty vehicles on hand. The Germans also managed to 'requisition' at least a thousand trucks from the Italian high command in North Africa, which meekly submitted to the German request, thus depriving the Italian frontline troops of already scarce transportation assets. Stripping the Italians of their already limited transportation assets effectively condemned them to fight in place and be destroyed, or to surrender, while covering the hasty retreat of the Germans, who chose to save their own hides rather than stand and fight alongside the Italians. Perhaps such behavior can be justified on the basis of military expediency, saving the 'best' troops for the next fight while sacrificing other 'lower value' troops, but the morality of such a choice is debatable.

When it became clear to Rommel in November 1942 that he could no longer stave off the Eighth Army, ultimately, he chose to save his German forces at the expense of the Italians. All four of the

German divisions at the time (*15.* and *21.Panzer*, and the two light divisions, *90.* and *164.*) were able to disengage and run to the west faster and further than the Italians were able. In contrast, of the nine Italian divisions that took part in the Alamein battles ('Ariete', 'Littorio', 'Trieste', 'Trento', 'Brescia', 'Bologna', 'Pavia', 'Pistoia' and 'Folgore'), only two ('Trieste' and 'Pistoia') survived as identifiable division entities able to fight on into Tunisia. The respective division survival rates were 100 percent for the Germans compared to a paltry 22 percent survival rate for the Italians. These figures are not a reflection of any superior combat capability on the part of the Germans, but rather, of the fact that the Germans had the mobility (sometimes achieved by hijacking Italian transport) to run first and faster from the fighting, while the Italians were left to stave off and delay the British, buying even more time for the Germans to distance themselves from danger. In a 16 November 1942 magazine article, an American journalist observed that: 'When it became obvious to Rommel that there would be little chance to hold anything between El Daba and the frontier, his panzers dissolved, disintegrated and turned tail, leaving the Italians to fight a rear-guard action.' It is not surprising then that the Italians felt embittered, resentful and ill-used by the Germans.

7

Preparation for War and the Italian Advance to Sidi Barrani

The North African campaign can be divided into three broad time periods or phases. The first phase began on 10 June 1940 with Italy's declaration of war against Britain, and four days later hostilities began when the British 11th Hussars crossed the border from Egypt into Libya and captured Fort Capuzzo. This was followed by an Italian counteroffensive (*Operazione E*, Operation E) beginning on 13 September 1940 when the Italian 10th Army under Marshal Rodolfo Graziani consisting of some 150,000 men in seven divisions attacked from Libya into Egypt, breaking through weakly held British frontier posts and quickly driving east past Sid Barrani, stopping at Maktila. There they established defensive positions prior to continuing their offensive, which was tentatively scheduled to resume in December. Typically, the Italian engineers were also put to work extending the coastal road, laying a 120-kilometer stretch from Bardia to Sidi Barrani. The British, meanwhile, had prepared their own counteroffensive which began on 9 December pre-empting the planned Italian move. British forces consisted of the British 7th Armoured Division, two Commonwealth infantry divisions and a Polish brigade. This offensive (Operation Compass) by the highly mobile Western Desert Force of 36,000 men under Wavell and O'Connor against the numerically superior Italian forces was a resounding success for the British and a stunning defeat for the Italians, who had adopted static defensive positions and who were defeated in detail, ultimately losing a total of ten divisions as a result. The offensive was concluded on 7 February 1941 with the capture of Beda Fomm. Because of these developments, Germany sent

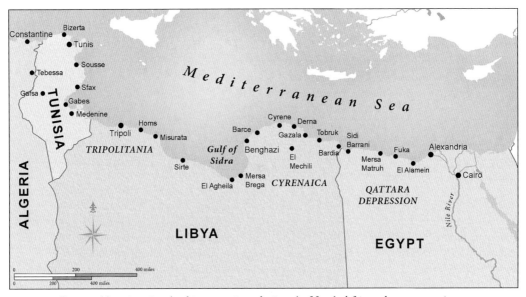

Principal locations involved in operations during the North African desert campaigns.

a small expeditionary force to North Africa to assist the Italians. This led to the second phase of the North African campaign, which lasted from the arrival of the first German contingent in Tripoli on 11 February until the Axis defeat at El Alamein in November 1942. The final phase of the North African campaign began in November 1942 with the Anglo–American forces that had landed in French North Africa (Operation Torch) advancing eastwards from Algeria while Montgomery's Eighth Army advanced north and west against the Italo–German forces, ending with the surrender of all Axis forces in Tunisia in May 1943.

Operazione E (13–16 September 1940)

The Italian military situation in North Africa became more favorable following the defeat of France by the Axis as the demilitarization of French forces in Tunisia allowed the bulk of Italian troops in Libya to be shifted to the Egyptian border. The conquest of Egypt and the Suez Canal would have allowed Italy to link up its colonies in North Africa and East Africa and eliminate British Royal Navy support facilities in the Mediterranean. In North Africa the governor of Libya, Italo Balbo, had the 5th Army under General Italo Gariboldi and the 10th Army under General Mario Berti.

The 5th Army, with 500 artillery pieces and 2,200 trucks, consisted of three army corps: *X Corpo d'Armata* under General Alberto Barbieri and consisting of the 25th Infantry Division 'Bologna', 55th Infantry Division 'Savona' and 60th Infantry Division 'Sabratha'; *XX Corpo d'Armata* under General Francesco Cona with the 17th Infantry Division 'Pavia', 27th Infantry Division 'Brescia' and 61st Infantry Division 'Sirte'; *XXIII Corpo d'Armata* under General Annibale Bergonzoli, with the 1st Blackshirt Division '23 marzo', 2nd Blackshirt Division '28 ottobre' and the 2nd Libyan Division 'Pescatori'.

The 10th Army, with about 200,000 men (plus 30,000 Libyan troops) had 339 L3 light tanks organized into seven independent battalions, 1,600 artillery pieces and 1,000 trucks, and consisted of two army corps: *XXI Corpo d'Armata* under General Lorenzo Dalmazzo with the 62nd Infantry Division 'Marmarica' and 63rd Infantry Division 'Cirene'; and the *XXII Corpo d'Armata* under General Enrico Pitassi Mannella with the 64th Infantry Division 'Catanzaro', 4th Blackshirt Division '3 gennaio' and the 1st Libyan Division 'Sibille'.

Also available were the forces under General Sebastiano Gallina (Sahara Sector) divided into the *Comando Fronte Sud* (Southern Front Command) with two Libyan battalions, one machine gun company, 1 camel-borne battery with 65/17 guns and two 20mm cannon sections; and the *Comando Truppe Sahara* (Sahara Troop Command) with one Saharan battalion, one motorized machine gun company, four *meharisti* companies and ten machine gun companies.

In Egypt, the British had the Western Desert Force commanded by General Richard N. O'Connor, with about 36,000 men comprising the 7th Armoured Division, 4th Indian Division and 6th Australian Division. British equipment included 134 Mark VI light tanks, 114 cruiser medium tanks, a battalion of Matilda infantry tanks and 38 armoured cars. Aircraft numbers were somewhat less than those of the Italians. The British armoured force worried Balbo who, aware of the superiority of the enemy tanks, urgently asked Rome for more powerful new medium tanks. On 20 June the governor of Libya sent the following message to Marshal Badoglio:

> Our assault tanks are old and armed only with old machine guns; the British machine guns mounted on their tanks have bullets that are able to penetrate the thin armour of our tanks. We have no tanks, the antitank guns are old and are not effective against the British tanks.

Following the defeat of France, Balbo had hoped to make up for the lack of supplies and equipment by collecting French materiel in Tunisia, but he was prevented from doing so by the terms of the

Italo–French armistice. He was able only to get a promise from Rome to send 72 M11/39 medium tanks by early July.

Initial Encounters

Following the declaration of war on 10 June 1940 it was the British who took the initiative and were the first to attack the Italian positions along the Libyan border. On 11 June armoured cars of the 11th Hussars of the 7th Armoured Division crossed the border and attacked an Italian column escorted by 17 light tanks; all the Italian tanks were destroyed or captured. During the fighting Colonel Lorenzo D'Avanzo was killed, earning the first Gold Medal for Valor in North Africa.

On 12 and 13 June British attacks continued against isolated border posts at Ridotta Maddalena and Sidi Omar. Furthest to the north was Ridotta Capuzzo, manned by about 200 soldiers, armed with three very old ex-Austrian Schwarzlose machine guns. Some 20 kilometers south of Capuzzo was Sidi Omar, with a garrison of about 60 soldiers. Still further to the south was Ridotta Maddalena, also with a garrison of 60 men. The stronghold at Giarabub, with 800 men, two artillery pieces and 56 machine guns, was 150 kilometers south of Maddalena. Between Giarabub and Maddalena were two platoons of Libyan *ascaris*, at Ueschechet el Heira and Garn el Grein. On 14 June the Italian units defending Ridotta Capuzzo were wiped out, while the *1o Raggruppamento Libico* (1st Libyan Group) had to abandon the positions at Sidi Azeiz and pull back to Bardia. The Italians planned counteroffensive moves which, however, had no effect because the enemy units had already withdrawn. On 17 June the outposts at Ueschechet and Garn el Grein were occupied by the British. Thus, in seven days, all the frontier posts along the Egyptian border fell to the British.

It was not until 28 June, after signing the armistice with France, that the Italian high command decided to pass onto the offensive in Egypt; Badoglio sent Balbo a telegram to advise him to shift all available forces to the Egyptian border and to prepare for action by 15 July. However, on 28 June at 1740 hours, an Italian SM.79 trimotor aircraft aboard which Balbo was approaching Tobruk from Derna was mistakenly shot down by antiaircraft guns of the old Italian armoured cruiser *San Giorgio*, employed as a fixed battery. At the time an enemy air attack was under way over the city and the antiaircraft gunners could not tell the Italian aircraft from the attacking British aircraft. General Rodolfo Graziani took command of the Italian forces in North Africa; he had previously been Governor of Tripolitania and taken an active part in its reconquest following the First World War. Graziani arrived in Tripoli on 30 June.

In early July the 72 M11/39 medium tanks that had been promised to Balbo arrived, along with another 500 motor vehicles. The M11/39 medium tank had a 105HP motor and was armed with a 37/40 gun and two Breda 8mm machine guns. The M11/39 tanks were organized into two battalions, the I and II, which were soon sent to the border with Egypt to challenge the British offensive raids that had continued to be carried out in July. However, because the trailers designated for transporting them turned out not to be able to bear their weight, they had to make a five-day road march to the front under their own power after they had been offloaded in Benghazi. On 5 August near Sidi Azeiz, the M11/39 medium tanks had their first encounter with British tanks and had the better of them; the British lost four tanks in the engagement. On 29 August the I and II battalions were integrated into the newly formed *Comando carri armati della Libia* (Libya Tank Command), which consisted of two *raggruppamenti*, each with three light tank (L3/35) battalions and one medium (M11/39) battalion. The *1o raggruppamento carri* was commanded by Colonel Pietro Aresca, being assigned to the XXIII Army Corps, and the *2o raggruppamento carri* by Colonel Antonio Trivioli, being assigned to the Group of Libyan Divisions. In addition, a mixed tank battalion was formed consisting of one company each of L3/35 and M11/39 tanks, assigned to the *Raggruppamento Maletti*.

General Italo Balbo (saluting). As Governor-General of Libya and Commander-in-Chief of North Africa, Balbo was competent and effective as a leader. His untimely death on 28 June 1940 proved to be a grave setback to Italian operations in North Africa. (Courtesy Giancarlo Garello)

M11/39 tanks near Sidi Barrani, late 1940. The M11/39 was a stop-gap tank prior to the introduction of the M13/40. Its 37mm sponson-mounted gun was only marginally effective against most of the British armour it faced. (Massimiliano Afiero)

Marshal Rodolfo Graziani assumed command in North Africa following the death of Balbo. (Courtesy Giancarlo Garello)

Armourers loading bombs onto a Savoia SM.79 tri-motor bomber in Libya on 2 August 1940. The SM.79 was an effective bomber for the time. (USSME)

A pair of Savoia SM.79 bombers of the 10th Squadriglia approaching a target in Libya, 2 August 1940. The SM.79 was well liked by its crews, who nicknamed it the 'gobbo maledetto' ('damned hunchback') because of its distinctive fuselage dorsal 'hump' that housed a machine gun position. (USSME)

Lieutenant Mario Garello of the *Regia Aeronautica*, on the left, at Sollum in 1940. Garello was a signals officer who was responsible for organizing the RA's telecommunications network in the eastern part of Libya, between Barce and Bardia. There was an obvious lack of adherence to normal uniform regulations; soldiers and officers tended to dress as comfortably as possible to deal with the heat. Garello seems to have attempted to add an element of style with his combination of boots, cap, jacket and sand goggles. (Courtesy Giancarlo Garello)

A column of trucks on the march between Tripoli and Benghazi on 2 August 1940, during the Italian advance towards Egypt. Note the presence of at least three 20mm Breda antiaircraft guns mounted on the leading vehicles. (USSME)

At the end of August after several arguments between Mussolini and Badoglio, Graziani, though not fully convinced of the wisdom of the operation, began to plan an Italian offensive against Egypt. The plan called for an advance on Sidi Barrani along two axes: one in the north along the coast, and one in the south along the Bir er Rabia-Bir er Enba track. In order to carry all the troops with the available trucks, it was decided to limit the forces to be employed in the offensive to five divisions, plus the Special Group under General Pietro Maletti. The three divisions of General Bergonzoli's XXIII Army Corps were to advance along the coast road, while to the south the two Libyan divisions under General Gallina would make their advance. The *Raggruppamento Maletti*, completely motorized and with a wide radius of action, was to remain in reserve. Graziani asked for 600 trucks from Rome in order to completely motorize the attack force. At 1530 on 7 September 1940 Mussolini ordered that the offensive begin on 9 September without the trucks Graziani had requested.

Sidi Barrani

Unable to transport all the units by truck, Graziani had to modify his plans for the offensive, leading to the decision to have the bulk of the troops advance along the coast road. On 8 September orders were issued for the advance. The Libyan divisions would take the lead, followed by the XXIII Army Corps. The '23 marzo' Blackshirt Division under General Antonelli was kept in reserve, while the *Raggruppamento Maletti* was to be ready for any move on the flank of the British deployment. Graziani could also count on the *5a Squadra Aerea* of Libya to support the ground troops with 300 aircraft.

From the beginning, the advance of the Italian troops in Egyptian territory was hampered by bad weather: a *ghibli* (hot Saharan wind) arose, reducing visibility as well as air support, and the temperature was 45 degrees Celsius (113 Fahrenheit) in the shade. The *Raggruppamento Maletti* advanced too far forward, and the XXIII Corps units advanced too quickly, getting entangled

M11/39 tanks advancing towards Sidi Barrani in September 1940. The tank in the center appears to have a water bottle hanging from the forward opening turret hatch. (USSME)

with the Libyan divisions, creating chaos and overcrowding the coastal highway. At dawn on 12 September Graziani was forced to call a 24-hour halt to straighten out the troop deployments. Some changes were also made to the invasion plans: the flanking move from the desert was abandoned and priority instead given to a frontal advance against Sidi Barrani.

Members of the 4th Blackshirt Division's 204th Artillery Regiment manning a First World War booty Austro–Hungarian 105/17 howitzer in September 1940. Artillery and other specialist personnel in the Blackshirt divisions were regular army personnel, not Blackshirt militia. (Massimiliano Afiero)

A column of Italian trucks loaded with infantry advancing in the desert near Sidi Barrani in September 1940. (Massimiliano Afiero)

The attack towards Sollum, the first town across the border, began at dawn on Friday, 13 September, after a heavy artillery barrage and an air bombardment. By 0830 the 1st Libyan Division occupied the outskirts of Sollum, forcing the British to withdraw, and the 2nd Libyan Division had taken Halfaya Pass. The advance resumed the following day, slowed down by strong British resistance who, thanks to their mobile artillery, were able to inflict heavy losses. Portions of the coast road were destroyed by the British, who had enough time to lay several minefields before falling back. These actions caused further delays to the Italian advance; forced to avoid the main road, many Italian vehicles ended up bogging down on the sandy desert tracks or were damaged by mines. Despite these problems, at 1445 on 16 September, the '23 marzo' Blackshirts made their entry into Sidi Barrani, which had by then been abandoned by the British. The following day the Italians occupied Maktila after the British had withdrawn from there. A series of reconnaissance patrols were made in all directions, without finding any signs of the enemy. Italian losses during these first five days of fighting amounted to 120 killed and 410 wounded; a third of the losses were Libyans. The *Regia Aeronautica* lost six aircraft. The British claimed a loss of 50 men.

Mersa Matruh

With the fall of Sidi el Barrani, British forces dug in 120 kilometers further east at Mersa Matruh. General O'Connor had planned to conduct a defensive battle with the few tanks he had left, but for the moment, the British forces could not undertake any offensive action. However, Graziani did not press his advance and again asked Rome for more trucks to be able to continue the offensive. Instead of attacking the remaining British forces and destroying them, he busied himself with improving his supply lines and deployed his troops in a series of fortified camps.

Between 7 and 8 October a flying column of the 'Cirene' division engaged a British motorized column at Gabr bu Raydan. Once again Mussolini was forced to order Graziani to go on the offensive against Mersa Matruh between 10 and 15 October. Graziani responded to the Duce by saying that he would not be ready until the end of October; in order to attack the fortified positions at Mersa Matruh he needed two groups of artillery with 149/13 guns, trucks to move the units and trailers to tow the 37 new M13/40 medium tanks that had arrived in Africa in early October. These tanks were superior to the M11s and were equipped with a 47/32 gun and four Breda 8mm machine guns. The M13s were all assigned to the III tank battalion.

With the start of the Greek campaign on 28 October 1940, Graziani lost all hope of receiving the reinforcements he had requested and began to plan an attack against Mersa Matruh with the forces he had available to him. The British, in the face of Italian passivity (except for a brief clash east of Maktila on 5 November), resumed harassing attacks against the Italian outposts.

On the night of 18 November enemy armoured vehicles infiltrated the Italian defensive positions around Sidi el Barrani. In order to throw them back, the medium tank battalion of the I Armoured Group, a flying column of the 2nd Libyan Division and a column from the *Raggruppamento Maletti* were called into action. The following day, the two Italian columns pushed back the British units, which, however, resumed their attack soon after, hitting the Italian units while they were withdrawing. The rear-guard actions that ensued were resolved by the Italian air force, which strafed the British troops, forcing them to retire. At the same time a group of Italian CR.42 fighter planes faced off against an enemy air squadron, downing six planes without incurring any losses. The Italian units remained at Sidi Barrani until December, despite an avalanche of telegrams by Mussolini to Graziani urging him to resume the offensive. In one of the dispatches the Duce was most eloquent about the wait-and-see attitude of the commander of troops in Africa: 'Who benefited most from this long pause, us or the enemy? I don't hesitate even a moment to answer that, it has benefited the enemy not only more but also exclusively.' In fact, Mussolini was right, and the British had all

Two Italian officers in colonial uniform consulting a map, September 1940. (Massimiliano Afiero)

A platoon of M11/39 tanks of the II Tank Battalion on their way to the front along the Via Balbia during Marshal Graziani's offensive in September 1940. The truck convoy going in the opposite direction is a heterogenous mix of various Italian makes. (USSME)

Captain Antonio Fichera, a company commander in the VII Battalion, 3rd Regiment, 2nd Libyan Division, in September 1940. The tent behind him camouflaged with branches hardly speaks of luxurious officer accommodations. Captain Fichera was captured during the fighting at Alam Tummar on 9 December 1940 and spent six years at a POW camp in India. (Giancarlo Garello)

Members of the 4th Blackshirt Division advancing in the Libyan desert in September 1940. The trucks seem to be well equipped with 20mm Breda guns. The truck in the left foreground is a FIAT 634 N, while the truck in the right foreground is a Lancia 3Ro. (USSME)

Late 1940, a flamethrower version L3 light tank in action near Sollum. (USSME)

A 100/17 howitzer in action in late 1940. A trench has been dug so that the trail can be better anchored in the desert soil. (USSME)

Italian military personnel walking past badly damaged buildings in Sollum following the fighting between the Italians and British in September 1940. (USSME)

Two Libyan *ascari* manning a Breda Model 37 heavy machine gun mounted on the roof of a vehicle's cab. (Ralph Riccio)

A mixed group of Italian and Libyan soldiers handling ammunition for a field piece, September 1940.
(USSME)

the time they needed to reorganize and prepare for a counteroffensive against the Italian forces in early December.

Parenthetically, it should be noted that as a colonel, Babini had commanded all the Italian armoured forces that had been sent to Spain to support Francisco Franco's Nationalist forces during the Spanish Civil War. Although the total armoured force sent to Spain was relatively small (roughly a regiment in size at its height), it did provide some lessons to the Italians, and especially to Babini, with respect to the use of armour. Babini, who by virtue of his relatively recent service in Spain, was probably the most knowledgeable Italian officer, on a practical level, when it came to armour operations. One of the lessons learned by the Italians in Spain was that the main task of tank units was to drive a wedge into enemy forces, with quick and risky actions, to break the heart of the enemy's defense. Unfortunately, although Babini understood this concept, he proved unable to implement it against the British – largely because the Italians were themselves on the defensive and it was the British who were driving wedges into the Italian positions with quick actions and breaking the heart of their defenses.

8

The First British offensive in North Africa
Operation Compass (9 December 1940–7 February 1941)

The British, taking advantage of the inaction on the part of the Italians, took measures to retake the territory they had lost, bringing in men and equipment to North Africa. On the night of 6 December, the British Western Desert Force kicked off Operation Compass, the objective of which was to reoccupy Sidi Barrani, and if that move was successful, extend the offensive to conquer Tobruk. The first Italian positions to be attacked were the fortified camps east of Sidi Barrani. The British 7th Armoured Division moved behind them, attacking from the rear, cutting the coast road at Buq Buq, while at dawn on 9 December the 4th Indian Division and the 7th Royal Tank Regiment attacked the camp at Nibeiwa, where the Italian troops were caught by surprise as they were eating their breakfast. After having destroyed 23 Italian M11/39 tanks parked outside the camp, a force of 48 British Matilda tanks ran unopposed through the tents of the camp itself. The Italian commander of the camp, General Pietro Maletti, barely had time to grab a light machine gun when exiting his tent before he was mortally wounded. The Italians attempted to react, but their antitank guns proved impotent against the British tanks: the shells bounced off the thick armour of the Matildas, making any resistance useless. After a few hours of fierce fighting during which the Italian artillery, as usual, stuck to their guns firing as best they could against the Matildas, the Italian forces were overrun. Following the camp at Nibeiwa, it was the turn of the camp at Tummar West, where the same scene was repeated; the Italians attempted to defend themselves, but the British had tanks and the Italians had no adequate weapons to be used against them. During the fighting at Tummar, the *2a Divisione Libica 'Pescatori'*, under General Armando Pescatori, was destroyed.

On 10 December another independent British motorized column, Selby Force, supported by Matildas, conquered Sidi Barrani, destroying the *4a Divisione Camicie Nere '3 gennaio'*, and on 11 December the *1a Divisione Libica 'Sibille'*, under General Luigi Sibille, was destroyed at Maktila. The 63rd 'Cirene' division avoided engagement as it was in the Halfaya Pass area, while the 64th 'Catanzaro' was in the Bir Tishida area, about 50 kilometers east of the pass. By 14 December, less than a week into the offensive, the British had destroyed the two Libyan divisions, one of the Blackshirt divisions and captured Generals Gallina, Cerio (who had just recently assumed command of the *1a Libica*), Pescatori and Mesari.

Following a brief pause to allow the 6th Australian Division to replace the 4th Indian Division, General Wavell resumed the offensive. On 16 December the remaining Italian forces under General Annibale Bergonzoli pulled back to Bardia whose defensive works were hurriedly strengthened. On 4 January 1941 following a powerful air attack, the defenders of Bardia had to face the onslaught of the Matildas of the 7th Royal Tank Regiment. Two days of bloody fighting ensued, ending in the surrender of two Italian Blackshirt divisions (*1a Divisione Camicie Nere '23 marzo'* and *2a Divisione Camicie Nere '28 ottobre'*) and three infantry divisions (62nd 'Marmarica', 63rd 'Cirene' and 64th 'Catanzaro'), netting another 36,000 prisoners as well as 275 guns, 13 medium and 150 light tanks

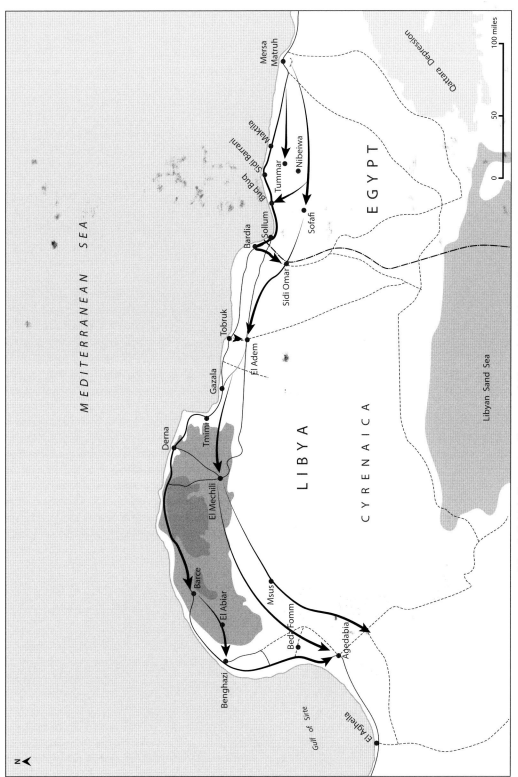

Map 1 British Operation Compass, 9 December 1940–7 February 1941.

A British Matilda infantry tank. During O'Connor's early desert offensive, despite its slow speed and rather small gun, the Matilda's thick armour enabled it to run rampant against Italian defenses. (Ralph Riccio)

General Armando Pescatori, commander of the 2nd Libyan Division, in November 1940. (USSME)

A *bersagliere* patiently repairing a captured Dodge truck. (Luca Massacci)

and 700 trucks for the British. The Italians had suffered 1,703 killed and 3,740 wounded against a British loss of 130 killed and 336 wounded in action.

Once Bardia had fallen, the British headed towards Tobruk, which although it enjoyed an effective system of defensive fortifications, lacked sufficient troops to cover the entire defensive perimeter, which was guarded by only the 61st Infantry Division 'Sirte' and some smaller units (4th Tank Regiment, three artillery groups, one divisional artillery regiment and two infantry battalions). The British attack began on 21 January with the Matildas easily breaking through the defensive perimeter because of poor communications between the Italian forward positions. Bitter fighting ensued and lasted until the following day, when the last Italian forces surrendered. Italian losses at Tobruk amounted to 25,000 prisoners, 87 tanks and 208 guns. Some 8,000 Italian prisoners were moved to a compound at El Adem where, at night, they made small fires to heat themselves. The *Regia Aeronautica*, which had been absent during the daylight hours despite desperate pleas from the ground troops for air support, ventured out at night to bomb presumed enemy positions; seeing the fires and assuming they were British, they unloaded the bombs into the midst of their fellow countrymen, causing numerous deaths and injuries.

On 30 January, Derna fell. By now the situation had degenerated into a rout. The remaining Italian forces attempted to quit all of Cyrenaica, but the small but still effective British motorized forces cut off their retreat. Between 6 and 7 February 1941, between Sceleidima and Agedabia, the remnants of the Italian 10th Army suffered a battle of annihilation. The British called it the 'Battle of Beda Fomm', where the most decisive battle was fought.

A captured British Crusader tank being inspected by a group of curious Italians. Note the missing second and fourth outer road wheels. (Luca Massacci)

A revetted artillery position covered by a net and sparse vegetation. Note the large stock of 75mm ammunition neatly stacked on the left of the position. (USSME)

An antiaircraft crew manning a 20mm Breda Model 35 gun in a revetted position. Their uniforms are a mix of khaki and the older grey-green pattern. (Daniele Guglielmi)

On 9 February the British reached El Agheila where they halted. The troops were by now exhausted and 80 percent of their vehicles had either been destroyed or needed repairs. In addition, some forces had to be transferred to the Greek–Albanian front, where the situation was becoming critical. The Italian defeat had been complete: the British had almost gotten as far as Tripoli. Had they reached that city it would have meant the end of the Italian presence in North Africa. Of the two Italian armies in Libya, there remained only four weak divisions of the 5th Army with no artillery, while the 10th Army had been completely destroyed. Partially redeeming the honor of Italian forces in North Africa were a few outposts that fought to the last, including the fort at Giarabub (commanded by Colonel Salvatore Castagna), deep in the Libyan desert about 250 kilometers (155 miles) south of Bardia, which had continued to hold out despite being cut off and under siege since December 1940.

9

The First Italo–German Counteroffensive in North Africa
Unternehmen Sonnenblume (6 February–25 May 1941)

Concerned about the difficult Italian military situation in Greece and North Africa, Hitler wanted to meet with Mussolini to plan to send men and equipment to the fronts where his ally was in trouble. The meeting between the Duce and the Führer took place between 19 and 20 January at Berchtesgaden and sanctioned German military intervention in North Africa in support of Italian forces. The dispatch of a *Sperrverband*, a military force to block the British offensive, was authorized. The initial force selected was the *5.leichte-Division* (5th Light Division) commanded by General Johannes Streich, based on a detached unit of the *3.Panzer-Division*. In addition, in mid-January, aircraft of the *X Fliegerkorps* of the *Luftwaffe* began to arrive in Italy, including 100 bombers and 20 fighter escorts, tasked with protecting the Italian convoys and attacking British convoys bound for Egypt.

Between 2 and 8 February, precisely at the time that the British were completing their rout of Italian forces in Cyrenaica, convoys bearing the heavy equipment of the 132nd 'Ariete' armoured division commanded by General Ettore Baldassare reached Tripoli. At that time, the division was still equipped with the L3 light tank, which in the recent fighting had proven to be utterly inadequate against British armour. It would take about another five weeks before the first M13/40 medium tanks assigned to the division arrived in Tripoli. The division was organized with three regiments, the 32nd Tank, the 132nd Armoured Artillery and the 8th *Bersaglieri*.

The Italian *Comando Supremo* in Rome had adopted an operational concept for North Africa that was strictly tied to the defense of Tripoli, leaving the eastern part of Tripolitania completely unde-fended. An impressive antitank ditch formed the outer perimeter of Tripoli's defense, while behind the ditch were strongholds manned by the 17th 'Pavia', 25th 'Bologna', 27th 'Brescia' and 55th 'Savona' infantry divisions – all of which lacked adequate artillery. 'Ariete' was held as a maneuver force to support the infantry divisions or to be available to repel any attempts by the British to land between Misurata and Tripoli.

On 10 February, following the debacle at Beda Fomm, no Italian units were in contact with British units. Between El Agheila and Tripoli (736km), the only Italian force was an *articelere* (mobile artillery) regiment that included the *Colonna Santamaria*, which was a motley assortment of stragglers and units that had halted at Sirte (450 kilometers east of Tripoli) and organized into the semblance of a cohesive unit consisting of light tanks, artillery, infantry and engineers led by Lieutenant Colonel Camillo Santamaria Nicolini. This small force dug in at Sirte was determined to resist to the last and on 16 February, less than a week after the initial elements of the *Deutsches Afrika Korps* (DAK) landed at Tripoli, the German 3rd Reconnaissance Battalion under Rüdiger von Wechmar reached Santamaria at Sirte.

Marshal Graziani was replaced as commander in Africa by General Italo Gariboldi. On 11 February 1941 new directives were agreed upon between the Italian and German military commands regarding the employment of German troops in North Africa. Given the deterioration

M13/40 tanks of the VII Tank Battalion, 132nd Armoured Regiment parade through Tripoli, 12 March 1941. These were among the first M13/40s of the 'Ariete' division to arrive in North Africa. (Daniele Guglielmi)

An Italian armourer preparing a bomb for a ground attack mission by one of the Italian JU-87s. The Italian JU-87s were heavily engaged in attacks against Tobruk. (Courtesy Giancarlo Garello)

A patrol led by Colonel De Meo at Bir el Gobi in autumn 1941. Readily identifiable vehicles include a FIAT 508 CM staff car, an AB41 armoured car and, behind it, a SPA 35 Dovunque all-terrain truck. (USSME)

Rommel and General Gastone Gambara exiting Rommel's tactical headquarters in Marmarica in autumn 1941. (USSME)

of the situation in North Africa with the British only a few kilometers from Tripoli, Hitler decided to increase the size of the military forces being sent to support *Unternehmen Sonnenblume* (Operation Sunflower), the codename for the campaign in North Africa. In addition to the *5.leichte-Division*, which was completely motorized and strengthened by a panzer regiment, the Germans decided to send a complete armoured division, the *15.Panzer-Division*. The two divisions were formed as an armoured corps designated the '*Deutsches Afrika Korps*', under the command of *Generalleutnant* Erwin Rommel. Command of the Italo–German forces in North Africa remained in Italian hands, but Rommel was granted freedom of action with respect to both Gariboldi and Marshal Kesselring, who was the commander of German forces in the Mediterranean.

On 12 February Rommel arrived in Tripoli and wasted no time at all in quickly visiting the operational area where the most forward Italian units were deployed. Upon returning from his reconnaissance accompanied by Major Santamaria, Rommel, in agreement with Italian head-quarters, decided to establish a defensive line at the coastal village of Sirte, 450 kilometers (280 miles) east of Tripoli by using units that were available: the 'Pavia' infantry division commanded by General Emilio Giglioli was at Sirte; the 'Ariete' armoured division, the leading elements of which had arrived in Tripoli on 24 January, was at Buerat; along the coast road between Buerat and Sirte was the 'Bologna' infantry division under General Mario Marchinotti; and further to the rear was the 'Brescia' infantry division commanded by General Bortolo Zambon. On 15 February the first German units – the 3rd Reconnaissance Battalion and the 39th *Panzerjäger* Battalion of the *5.leichte-Division* – disembarked at the port in Tripoli. In light of the serious military situation on 17 February, this first contingent was sent to reinforce Italian units in the front line, especially the small force commanded by Lieutenant Colonel Santamaria at Sirte. On 19 February the joint Italo–German combat group pushed as far as Neofilia (An Nawfaliyah), 130 kilometers (81 miles) east of Sirte. On 24 February one of the forward units, the *Vorausabteilung Wechmar* (the group led by Rüdiger von Wechmar), supported by at least part of the *Colonna Santamaria*, clashed with a column of British armoured cars and antitank guns, forcing it to retire after having destroyed three armoured cars and taking three prisoners, among whom was an officer, without having sustained any losses. This was indeed an auspicious baptism of fire for the *Afrika Korps*.

Meanwhile, the enemy forces remained inactive, limiting themselves to replacing the worn-out 7th Armoured Division with the 2nd Armoured Division and the 6th Australian Division with the 9th Australian Division. The British also had to send units to the Greek front and the 4th Indian Division had been sent to Ethiopia. On 4 March Rommel, ignoring orders but aware of the temporary weakness of the enemy forces, decided to go on the offensive, pushing his units to El Agheila, another 120 kilometers (75 miles) further east. Instead of reacting, the British forces opted to pull back to Agedabia. On 9 March units of the 'Ariete' armoured division, as yet incomplete (two M13 tank battalions had yet to arrive) linked up with the *5.leichte-Division*, reaching the front line. In the ensuing days other units of the *5.leichte* landed in Libya – most importantly the 5th Panzer Regiment under Lieutenant Colonel Olbrich on 11 March with its 150 tanks (of which 80 were PzKpfw III and IV). These were quickly sent to Neofilia. Before sending them to the front, however, Rommel had the tanks parade through the streets of Tripoli several times in order to make them seem more numerous and deceive enemy intelligence. On 11 March, 56 M13/40 tanks of the VII Battalion of 'Ariete' under Major Andreani arrived in Tripoli. The arrival of those 136 medium tanks (80 German and 56 Italian) led Rommel to believe that the time was right to go on the offensive against the British, who he rightly assessed as being overextended and weak, ultimately leading him to attack El Agheila and Mersa el Brega.

On 13 March the oasis at Marada was occupied by Italo–German forces to prevent the enemy from making a flanking move from the south. In order to better lead his troops in the desert and be able to personally assess the true combat situation, Rommel moved his headquarters to Sirte. Thus the Rommel myth was born, not only because of his shrewdness and daring in conducting military

A 65/17 gun in Libya, in summer 1941, ready to fire from behind a series of improvised shields. (USSME)

A column of M13/40 tanks of the 'Ariete' division on the move in the desert. (Ralph Riccio)

operations, but also for his humble ability to share the sacrifices and privations alongside his troops. He earned the nickname of 'The Desert Fox' thanks to having employed several stratagems, such as disguising Volkswagen cars as dummy tanks so that the enemy overestimated his strength. These dummy tanks were scattered over the desert, confusing enemy air reconnaissance, which reported the presence of enemy armoured forces where none existed.

On 17 March the 'Brescia' infantry division was subordinated to the DAK for operations. On 19 March 'Brescia' began to relieve the *5.leichte-Division*'s defensive positions and on 23 March it took command of defensive positions in the Sebcha narrows west of El Agheila and on the southern edge of Dor Lanuf.

At dawn on 21 March, in the midst of the Axis counteroffensive, covered by a strong sandstorm, the Australians attacked the stronghold of Giarabub, and at 1000 its commander, Colonel

A column of British prisoners being escorted by what appears to be a native Libyan soldier while truckloads of *Bersaglieri* move towards the front, autumn 1941 (USSME)

A pair of Matildas knocked out in summer 1941 being examined by Italian soldiers. The Matilda's thick armour proved to be almost impervious to most Italian weapons during the early phase of the desert campaign. (USSME)

Salvatore Castagna, sent the following message via radio: 'Since 0400 the enemy launched a strong attack with many mechanized vehicles. Many enemy also dead. I am wounded. Viva l'Italia.' It was the commander's last communication, then the radio was silent until 1700, when a final message reached the *Comando Supremo* in Rome: 'At 1207 strongpoint Number 1 and others overwhelmed after strong defense. The tricolor is still flying over the tower of the redoubt. Captain Brocolini, Lieutenant Ceccani.'

A 105/28 gun in North Africa in October 1941. A total of 12 batteries of these obsolete guns, normally assigned to corps-level artillery groups, saw service in North Africa. (Enrico Finazzer)

A rather well-attired Major Alessandro Menchiori being briefed by a tanker of the 'Ariete' division, 17 October 1941. (USSME)

Thus, the stronghold at Giarabub finally capitulated after having held out for four months, after having rationed food and ammunition and after having always answered 'No' to offers by the enemy to surrender. In the words of Colonel Castagna:

> For about three months, the enemy [mainly the Australian 8th Infantry Brigade] persistently continued to push in all directions to remove the sharp thorn of Giarabub. Two requests to surrender were made, followed by strong attacks, which were completely repulsed. Thus, neither the attacks nor the continuous hammering by artillery and by air aimed at paralyzing all movement on our part, nor the continuous shooting down of resupply aircraft, nor the dire hunger and shortage of ammunition lowered the morale of the defenders who were determined to resist and to make the ultimate sacrifice. At the end of the second half of March the British intensified their attacks, employing increasingly stronger forces supported by a mass of field artillery. It was not until 21 March 1941 that they were able to break through the defensive ring, and after having made it past the many dead and wounded of one strongpoint they overwhelmed the next strongpoint. It was a bitter fight, with no letup, a stream of attacks and counterattacks, an intertwined mix of men, or rather, of living skeletons who stayed on their feet motivated by a burning spirit and by an unshakeable faith, against well-fed Australians who were supplied with much equipment. The flag that waved on the tower of Ridotta Marcucci was burned in sight of the enemy to the shouts of 'Viva l'Italia'.

The attacks against Giarabub had cost the Australians about 100 casualties; the Italians lost 250 killed and 1,030 (including 30 Libyan *ascari*) taken prisoner.

An aerial view of the fortress complex of Giarabub. The Italian garrison held out against Australian attacks for about three months. (Courtesy Giancarlo Garello)

Rommel Strikes

On 24 March despite the misgivings of higher headquarters, Rommel was convinced that he could take advantage of the favorable situation and pushed his forces towards El Agheila, seizing the local airfield there. On 29 March following a meeting with General Gariboldi, it was decided to push the troops even further forward to Mersa el Brega. The Italo–German forces to be employed in the offensive consisted of the *5.leichte-Division*, the 'Ariete' armoured division and the 'Brescia' infantry division with a total of 25,000 men, 231 medium tanks, 117 light tanks, 27 armoured cars, 72 guns and 220 antitank guns. The ground forces were supported by 200 operational aircraft.

Rommel, being the ardent proponent of movement warfare that he was, divided his forces into a series of tactical groups (along *Kampfgruppe* lines) of varying size depending on the situation on the ground. The desert was like the sea, and thus the most important factor affecting the outcome of operations was movement. There would be no massed infantry attacks, but rather, small rapidly moving motorized groups that were able to cause chaos in the ranks of the enemy.

The initial moves towards Mersa Brega by a tactical group consisting of a panzer company, an antitank company and an 88mm battery began on 31 March. To the right of this group were the German 3rd Reconnaissance Battalion and the *Santamaria* column consisting of a machine gun company, a company of L3 light tanks, two platoons of 47/32 antitank guns and two 75/27 gun batteries. Supported by air sorties, the Italo–German units reached Mersa Brega that evening and continued their march, reaching Agedabia on 2 April, taking the British 3rd Armoured Brigade by surprise and putting them to flight. Also on 31 March, 'Pavia' drove Australian rear guard elements back to Mechili. The speed of the Italo–German offensive led the British to believe that they were facing an entire corps, as reported in their bulletins.

Rommel, however, was not yet satisfied and wished to continue the advance to overrun the British. When he was notified that the British had pulled out of Benghazi, he immediately ordered a move in an attempt to cut off the retreating enemy. Rommel decided to attack with part of his troops along the coast towards Benghazi and to use his armoured forces to move across the desert towards El Mechili. Thus, between 3 and 13 April four Italo–German motorized columns headed towards El Mechili and the Gulf of Bomba, reconquering Cyrenaica and once again crossing the Egyptian border as far as Sollum.

In late March 'Ariete' had been earmarked by Rommel to take part in the advance towards the Tobruk–Bardia–Sollum area. The division accordingly was organized into three mixed columns (*colonne miste*), which in concept corresponded roughly to the German *Kampfgruppe* or to the US task force organization. The first column, *Colonna Fabris*, staging out of the Giof el Mataar–Ben Gania area, was led by Lieutenant Colonel Gino Fabris and consisted of III *Bersaglieri* Battalion, two batteries of 75/27 guns from I/132 Artillery, the 142nd Antitank Company with 47/32 guns, and two sections of 20mm guns from the 132nd Artillery Regiment, plus engineer and service elements, as well as a German radio detachment. The second column, *Colonna Montemurro*, located some 13km south of Agedabia and led by Colonel Ugo Montemurro (who, ironically, during the Battle of Caporetto in the First World War was captured by then-lieutenant Erwin Rommel, but managed to escape), commander of the 8th *Bersaglieri* Regiment, consisted of the XII *Bersaglieri* Battalion, one battery of 75/27 guns, the 72nd Antitank Company, and two sections of 20mm guns, plus engineer and service elements. The third column, designated simply as the 'divisional column', was a reserve held by the division commander, General Ettore Baldassare, and consisted of the V *Bersaglieri* Battalion (motorized), one battalion of L3 tanks, the II/132 artillery with 75/27 guns, the 132nd Antitank Company with 47/32 guns, two companies of 37/45 antitank guns, three sections of 20mm guns, and elements of the 132nd Mixed Engineer Company. Its mission was to be ready to move on El Mechili and Tobruk, via Agedabia–Sceleidima–Msus–Ben Gania–Bir Tengedir–Gadd el Ahmar and to cut off escaping enemy forces.

A FIAT-SPA 38R truck loaded with *Bersaglieri* on the way to the front lines in autumn 1941. The 38R was only one of many truck types used by the Italians, who never achieved the kind of motor transport standardization achieved by the Americans and British. (USSME)

On 3 April Rommel ordered a mixed Italo–German detachment, *Gruppe Schwerin*, which included the *Colonna Santamaria*, to advance along Trig el Abd to Ben Gania before advancing still further to Mechili. This column was then followed by the *Colonna Fabris*, which was in turn followed on 4 April by the *Colonna Montemurro*. On 5 April 'Ariete' also attached the recently arrived VII Battalion of M13 tanks to the German 5th Panzer Regiment, *5.leichte-Division* (Lieutenant Colonel Olbrich), for action against El Mechili. Most of the 50 tanks broke down on the sandy track between Agedabia and Msus because they were new and not yet broken in, did not have proper oil filters for the desert conditions and the crews were inexperienced. Only seven of the 50 tanks ultimately made it as far as Tobruk without breaking down. The Italians did, however, quickly adopt measures to remedy this embarrassing performance, and by 19 April, all the tanks were again operational. Throughout the rest of the campaigning in North Africa, the M13s (and later the M14s) suffered from the abnormal wear and tear due to the harsh conditions of desert operations, but the in-service rate for M13s for tanks that were not outright combat losses allowed the Italians to conduct sustained operations in concert with the Germans whenever required.

Meanwhile, Benghazi was occupied on 4 April by von Wechmar, leading the 3rd Reconnaissance Battalion, supported by an artillery battalion from 'Brescia' commanded by Major Ferruccio Cenci. On 4 April Rommel further ordered 'Brescia' to garrison Benghazi and to mount a reconnaissance towards Barce, which was taken on 5 April. Rommel, however, considered El Mechili, the principal caravan hub in Cyrenaica, a priority and continued to insist that it be taken as soon as possible. On 6 April he ordered Santamaria, whose column was closest to that location, to attack. Santamaria,

An M13/40 of the 'Ariete' division at a halt while its commander surveys a desert track. The size of the commander compared to the overall size of the tank provides a good perspective as to the relatively small size of the Italian medium tanks. (USSME)

who knew that El Mechili's defenses were formidable and that the Indian defenders far outnumbered his force, in deference to Rommel's adamant attitude nevertheless on 6 April deployed two batteries of 75/27 guns and two machine gun platoons about a kilometer from El Mechili. When the attacking infantry got to within about 200 meters, the Indians brought withering fire to bear, and the attack force suffered extremely high losses and had to withdraw. Later that day Rommel ordered Streich to seize Mechili, but Streich said that his division was scattered over a wide area due to breakdowns and lack of fuel and would be unable to form up as a cohesive unit.

At about 1500 on 7 April, Fabris, whose column was down to one motorcycle company, two 75/27 batteries, one 47/32 battery and two 20mm sections, reached the outskirts of El Mechili, and by nightfall Montemurro's column, likewise at reduced strength, also reached the area. Late that evening there were a few skirmishes with the defending troops, as well as some exchange of artillery fire. A few small German units also arrived, among them Streich with his forward command post with two tanks and two antiaircraft guns, and by 8 April the combined forces had invested El Mechili. The *Colonna Fabris*, which by now had also picked up the *Santamaria* column, was to the northeast of the town; Montemurro's column was to the south, *Gruppe Schwerin* was to the north, and Olbrich's 5th Panzer Regiment, which had gotten lost along the way, was still far to the west.

The Italians began their attack on El Mechili by subjecting it to an artillery bombardment. The garrison, consisting of 3rd Indian Motor Brigade, sought desperately to find a way out of the encirclement; at 0530 an Indian tactical group attacked the XII *Bersaglieri* Battalion but was met by point-blank fire from the guns of Major Giuseppe Romano's I/132 Artillery, and another Indian attack to the north ran up against *Gruppe Schwerin* and was likewise stopped in its tracks. Continued Indian probing to the south found a gap between the *Fabris* and *Montemurro* columns; while seeking to exploit this corridor, a large motorized column was spotted attempting to escape and immediately came under fire from a combination of 75/27 guns and 47/32 antitank guns firing as fast as the loaders could ram fresh shells into the breeches, and from rapid-firing 20mm Breda antiaircraft guns used in the ground fire role. Montemurro's XII *Bersaglieri* Battalion also joined in attacking the column with all guns blazing, and the commander of the column, Brigadier E.W.D. Vaughan (3rd Indian Motor Brigade) raised the white flag and surrendered to Colonel Montemurro, along with about 1,500 of his men. Italian losses were especially heavy among the artillery crews, who often had to defend their guns in hand-to-hand fighting with the enemy infantry desperately seeking to break out. Total Italian losses amounted to 22 killed, 52 wounded and 19 missing in action. Also surrendering to Montemurro later was Major-General Michael Gambier-Parry of the British 2nd Armoured Division and another 2,000 or so British, Indian and Australian troops as well as large quantities of food, fuel, equipment and vehicles.

In their typical style, the Germans who were on the scene but who contributed little or nothing to the fighting itself, claimed most of the booty for themselves. Among the vehicles seized were two AEC Dorchester armoured command vehicles, which were appropriated by the Germans and named 'Max' and 'Moritz'. 'Max' was subsequently used by Rommel as his mobile headquarters, and 'Moritz' was used by General Ludwig Crüwell.

Although German forces were on the scene, El Mechili developed essentially into a fight between the Italians and the surrounded garrison; as such, it was the first significant encounter between the resurgent Italian forces and the British and its outcome presaged increasing problems and defeats the British and Commonwealth forces were to suffer at the hands of the Italians and Germans for the next year and a half, until the Axis defeat at El Alamein. At least one German account of the engagement goes so far as to paint it as a minor action in which only the Germans were involved, making no mention of the Italians, and claiming credit for the capture of 2,000 British soldiers. The DAK war diary entry for 8 April reflects Major Bolbrinker as having taken Mechili, and although it also refers to the capture of an English general, 60 officers and 1,700 men in addition to much booty, makes absolutely no mention of any Italian participation in the battle. As a result of the engagement at Mechili, Rommel awarded Montemurro the Iron Cross, First Class; this was the first German award bestowed upon an Italian in North Africa.

Siege of Tobruk (10 April–10 December 1941)

Having chased the British forces more than 500 kilometers (311 miles) back across Cyrenaica as far as Tobruk, Rommel was determined to capture the city and its port, but to his dismay found that the British were able to make excellent use of the extensive defensive system the Italians had previously constructed. Beginning on 11 April the Italo–German forces launched a series of abortive attacks against positions along the rather extensive Tobruk perimeter, finally settling down to a siege of the fortress. Throughout the period of the siege, which lasted for 241 days from 10 April to 7 December 1941, the besieging forces consisted almost entirely of Italian infantry divisions better suited to conduct static warfare than they were to conducting mobile operations. The Italian divisions consisted of the 'Brescia', 'Bologna', 'Pavia', 'Trento' and 'Sabratha' divisions; while those divisions ringed the forces in Tobruk and prevented their escape, the three German divisions of the DAK (the *15.* and *21.Panzer-Divisions* and the *90.leichte-Division*) and the two Italian mobile divisions (132nd 'Ariete' armoured division and 101st 'Trieste' motorized division) were free to conduct mobile operations against the British and Commonwealth forces.

On 11 April a combined Italo–German tank attack was made against Redoubt 33 of the Tobruk perimeter by 25 panzers from *5.leichte-Division* and a mix of M13 medium and L3 light tanks from 'Ariete'. The attack was thrown back by Australian antitank fire (using captured Italian 47/32 guns) and cruiser tanks. To make matters worse, the Axis tanks then ran into a minefield and turned back, but then were engaged by British cruiser tanks. The upshot of the sortie was the loss of one panzer, three L3s and one M13, while the British lost two cruisers.

On 11 and 12 April 'Brescia' was moved by German trucks and deployed to the west between the sea and north of Acroma, assuming blocking positions to the west of Tobruk. On the evening of 12 April, the *Colonna Fabris* dug in to the east of Acroma, and the 132nd Artillery Regiment was deployed in an area south of Bir Sceriff to prevent the enemy from being able to sortie out from Tobruk towards El Adem–Giarabub, and the bulk of 'Ariete' took up positions at El Adem. Meanwhile, the *Colonna Montemurro*, swinging further to the east, had been able to gain a certain degree of independence by using supplies found at Bardia left by the retreating Italians during the Operation Compass offensive. On 13 April Montemurro occupied Ridotta Capuzzo, and on 16 April the recently arrived *15.Panzer-Division* reached Capuzzo and Colonel Von Herff took command of all Italian and German forces in the operational sector. Montemurro was ordered by Von Herff to deploy his troops between Sollum and Halfaya Pass.

On 15 April Rommel committed elements of 'Ariete' and the 62nd Infantry Regiment of the 102nd 'Trento' motorized division to attack Ras el Medauar; although the attackers penetrated between Redoubts 13 and 17, the defending Australians fended off the attack and took about 75 Italian prisoners.

On 16 April Rommel again threw the Italians into an attack on Ras el Medauar. This time, a somewhat stronger force consisted of an under-strength composite armoured battalion of six M13 and 12 L3 tanks supported by the 62nd Infantry Regiment, with the objective being Point 187. The attack against the Australians was successful, with the Italian tanks reaching the summit of the hill, but the accompanying infantry had in the meantime been pinned down by Australian artillery fire. The Australians then counterattacked the Italian infantry and captured over 800 officers and men of the 'Trento' division. Bereft of infantry support, before nightfall the 'Ariete' tanks gave up the hill they had occupied.

On 17 April Rommel ordered 'Ariete' to mount yet another attack against the external fortifications of the Tobruk defensive belt to determine the strength of defenses. 'Ariete' formed a force with four M13 and three L3 tanks to test defenses at Ras el Medauar; the tanks were to be supported by a German heavy machine gun company and German infantry, but the MG unit did not show up and the infantry showed up late. The tank force advanced from Acroma in combat formation with Lieutenant Vittorio Bulgarelli's tank sporting highly visible female underwear flying on an antenna and got past Ras el Medauar when the tanks drove into Australian reserve positions and came under heavy fire. The British then sent in seven cruiser tanks to engage the Italian tanks; only one of the M13s (presumably Bulgarelli's) managed to make it back to the Italian lines. Four lieutenants were killed during the engagement and another two were wounded.

On 18 April the *Colonna Santamaria* was deployed between *Gruppe Schwerin* and the bulk of the *5.leichte-Division* on the southeastern front of Tobruk and subordinated to *5.leichte-Division*.

On 19 April the *Colonna Fabris* attacked and seized Point 201 east of Acroma in accordance with Rommel's orders. Three days later, on 22 April, the III *Bersaglieri* Battalion and the I/132 Artillery on Point 201 were violently attacked by Australian infantry supported by tanks and armoured cars and the position was overrun. During the action, Fabris was killed, and the Australians captured 368 *Bersaglieri* and four 20mm guns.

On 1 May the 'Ariete' divisional column consisting of the V *Bersaglieri* Battalion, one battalion of L3 tanks, a 47/32 antitank company, two 37mm antitank companies, three 20mm sections and the II/132 Artillery, supported by German 88mm guns, took up positions near Ras el Medauar. Forts R4, 5, 6 and 7 were all taken by the Italian force (the Germans previously had been unable to take Forts R4 and R5). On the night of 3 May the Australians counterattacked, but the Italian positions held despite heavy losses among the *Bersaglieri* and artillery crews. For the 1 May attack against Tobruk, 'Trento' relieved the German *5.leichte-Division* east of Bir Sceriff. On 4 May V *Bersaglieri* Battalion was counterattacked by the Australians around redoubts 6, 7 and 8. The Australians captured Redoubt 7, but the *Bersaglieri* counterattacked and retook the redoubt. The

A flight of Savoia SM.79 tri-motor bombers in flight over the Mediterranean. These aircraft belong to the 192nd Squadriglia, which operated against Malta, Port Said, Alexandria and Tobruk, as well as conducting day and night attacks on shipping in the Eastern Mediterranean. Aside from the different camouflage schemes, the two aircraft in the foreground have the unit's badge painted on the fuselage, although they are rendered in slightly different versions. (USSME)

Italians lost 150 men in the engagement but held their positions and dissuaded the Australians from mounting any further attacks.

In mid-May, the British launched Operation Brevity, a limited offensive designed to set the stage to relieve the siege of Tobruk. Aside from seizing Halfaya Pass, the operation, which lasted only two days, was a complete failure and Halfaya was retaken by the Axis on 26 May. A period of relative calm around Tobruk ensued; from 15 to 17 June the British launched another attack, Operation Battleaxe, whose aim likewise was to lift the siege of Tobruk, but like the earlier Operation Brevity, it was also essentially a failure.

Following Operation Battleaxe, there was little activity directed against Tobruk until mid-November. In the intervening period, Rommel planned an offensive to recapture Tobruk and thus remove the thorn from his side. Generals Bastico and Gambara disagreed with him, but Rommel, who had ignored Hitler and the German high command when it came to his reconquest of Cyrenaica, intended to do the same with respect to attacking Tobruk. In this regard, he ordered the repositioning of the forces besieging Tobruk. The 'Trento' division replaced the 'Pavia' division, which was placed in reserve; the VII *Bersaglieri* relieved a German regiment at Ras el Medauar; and part of the *90.leichte-Division* was inserted between the 'Trento' and 'Bologna' divisions, with the latter being reinforced by a battalion from 'Sabratha'. A headquarters for the siege of Tobruk was formed, designated 'XXI Corps', under General Enea Navarini. The DAK and XXI Corps together formed *Panzergruppe Afrika*.

On 15 November despite supply problems, Rommel's preparations were complete for the offensive against Tobruk. However, the British had also been planning an offensive (Operation Crusader),

Tanks of the 'Ariete' division in open formation in the vicinity of Bir el Gobi, October or November 1941.
(USSME)

which completely upset Rommel's plans. The Italian infantry divisions besieging Tobruk became embroiled in actions to fend off British forces seeking to link up with the forces inside Tobruk, which at the same time attempted to sally forth to meet the external forces.

On 19 November Crusader tanks of 6th Royal Tank Regiment, on the track between Bir el Gobi and El Adem, ran into dug-in infantry of 'Pavia' division and were forced to turn back. Also, a battalion of infantry from the 'Bologna' division and some 100mm guns were rushed down from Bardia on the coast to Sidi Rezegh as reinforcements. By 20 November 7th Armoured Brigade had reached the Sidi Rezegh–Belhamed area, only to find that the track down the escarpment had been blocked by the I/39 of 'Bologna' along with the 73rd Antitank Company. The next day the British attempted to break out from Tobruk, first using 100 guns to shell the positions held by 'Bologna', 'Brescia' and 'Pavia'. The Italians were initially stunned by this barrage and a company of 'Pavia' was overrun in the predawn darkness, but resistance from 'Bologna' gradually stiffened and the Italians could not be dislodged so the attack was held off all day. Strong opposition by 'Bologna' and 'Pavia' was part of the reason the British breakout attempt was abandoned.

On 22 and 23 November the frontier garrisons of Omar Nuovo, Libyan Omar and Fort Capuzzo fell to 42 and 44 Royal Tank regiments and the New Zealanders cut off Bardia's water supply. About 1,500 Italian prisoners were taken, most of whom were from the 'Savona' Infantry Division and who had fought well and tenaciously. In the meantime, fighting continued in the 'Bologna' sector and strongpoint 'Lion' was taken by 2nd Battalion, York and Lancaster Regiment on 22 November but efforts to clear 'Tugun' and 'Darby Square' of the Italians were repelled. Devastating Italian fire reduced one attacking British company to just 33 men. On 23 November the British 70th Division, supported by 60 tanks, launched a major attack against 'Bologna' in an attempt to reach Sidi Rezegh. 'Bologna' was forced to abandon a number of strongpoints, but providentially, elements of 'Pavia' soon arrived and sealed off the British breakthrough.

On 25 November fighting flared up in the 'Trento' sector, where 2nd Battalion, The Queen's Royal Regiment attacked the 'Bondi' strongpoint but were repelled by heavy fighting. 'Bondi' was not evacuated by 'Trento' until two weeks later during the general withdrawal. While the German *Böttcher Gruppe* was desperately fighting to stave off British tank attacks in the 'Bologna' sector,

Navarini and Gotti scraped together a battalion of *Bersaglieri* from 'Trieste' and used them to repulse the British breakout from Tobruk.

On 26 November British forces occupied El Duda; 'Trieste' ordered a battalion of its 65th Infantry Regiment under Major Reverberi and a battalion of the 66th Infantry Regiment under Lieutenant Colonel Odorici, supported by an artillery group commanded by Major Salerno to reoccupy El Duda. That night, the position was retaken by Odorici's battalion and at dawn on 27 November the British attacked with artillery and tanks, but the Italians held firm. Then, in a completely illogical and unexplained turn of events, the Italians at El Duda were ordered by the commander of 'Trieste', General Piazzoni, to pull out of the position the 66th had taken with a loss of only ten killed and 27 wounded. The battalion's withdrawal on 28 November allowed the New Zealanders to link up with the 32nd Tank Brigade at El Duda. Meanwhile, on 27 November 6th New Zealand Brigade fought a pitched battle with the 9th *Bersaglieri* Regiment who had dug themselves in at the Prophet's Tomb. By 28 November 'Bologna' had regrouped largely in the Bu Amud and Belhamed areas, making the division now stretched out about eight miles from the Via Balbia coast road to the Tobruk bypass road with fighting in several different places. The following day an armoured attack was beaten back in the 'Trento' sector.

On 4 December 'Pavia' and 'Trento' launched a counterattack against the British 70th Division in an attempt to contain it within the Tobruk perimeter. On 6 December one battalion of 'Pavia' division made a stand at Point 157, inflicting heavy casualties on 2nd Durham Light Infantry before being overrun and losing 130 as prisoners. On 6 December Rommel ordered his divisions to retreat westwards, leaving 'Savona' to hold out for as long as possible in the Sollum–Halfaya–Bardia area; they did not surrender until 17 January 1942. The Italian retreat towards the Gazala Line then began. On 8 December after 20 days of heavy fighting, 'Bologna' was ordered to withdraw after having suffered 30 percent casualties. By 10 December 'Brescia' and 'Trento' had withdrawn from the perimeter around the western side of Tobruk and on that day the British 70th Division finally managed to break out of Tobruk, effectively lifting the siege that had been in place since 11 April.

Operation Brevity (15–16 May 1941)

On 15 May the British initiated Operation Brevity designed as a preliminary move to raise the siege of Tobruk. The operation was aptly named, as it lasted only two days before being called off. On the eve of the operation, German and Italian forces were well positioned to challenge it. Between Sollum and Capuzzo were a *Bersaglieri* company plus two *Bersaglieri* platoons from 'Ariete', one antitank company from 'Trento', one 75/27 battery, and one 20mm section, plus the headquarters of 8th *Bersaglieri* Regiment and HQ XII *Bersaglieri* Battalion. At Halfaya were three 47/32 antitank platoons manned by *Bersaglieri*, one 47/32 antitank company, also manned by *Bersaglieri*, and one German company. In the center of the position at Halfaya, in addition to an Italian strongpoint supported by a 75/27 battery of the I/132 Artillery was a German company from the 115 Motorcycle Battalion. At dawn on 15 May the Halfaya positions were taken under artillery fire and the *Bersaglieri* in the central strongpoint were overwhelmed by armour and infantry; 1 Battery/I/132 Artillery was forced to withdraw and was left with only two operational guns. Prior to being overrun, the *Bersaglieri* had managed to knock out seven of the attacking Matildas. The enemy tried surrounding upper Sollum and Point 186 at Capuzzo, but Colonel Montemurro held fast for eight hours; Stukas showed up to bomb the enemy and a German unit arrived to assist the Italians and protect their withdrawal to Bardia, but Montemurro said he was not pulling back. The remaining strongpoints hung on doggedly. Von Herff then counterattacked, restoring the positions at Sollum and Capuzzo, but Halfaya Pass itself remained in British hands. The Montemurro column suffered heavy losses of more than 300 killed. On 26–27 May the Germans (*Kampfgruppe von Herff*), supported by *I Gruppo, 2a Articelere 'Emanuele Filiberto Testa di Ferro'* under Major Leopoldo Pardi, attacked and retook Halfaya Pass from the British.

Operation Battleaxe (15–17 June 1941)

Operation Battleaxe was designed to raise the siege of Tobruk but failed completely in its objectives. Although Fort Capuzzo was captured by the British on 15 June, attacks against Halfaya Pass and Hafid Ridge failed to take their objectives. Halfaya was held by a joint Italo–German force consisting of elements of the Italian 55th 'Savona' division and German elements under the command of Major Wilhelm Bach, known famously as 'Padre Bach' in reference to his peacetime occupation as a Lutheran minister. A major Italian contribution to the defense was a group of 100/17 guns under Major Pardi. The Italian guns, in concert with a German 88mm battery, inflicted a heavy toll on the attackers; at one point, Pardi himself took the place of one of his wounded gunners. A subsequent attack against Halfaya on 16 June met with similarly disastrous results for the British attackers. Pardi and Bach got along famously with each other and developed the teamwork between the Italians and Germans to an enviable degree. Pardi and Bach were almost total opposites in physical appearance and demeanor. Pardi was huge and about six feet tall, whereas Bach was small of stature and humble; Pardi commanded while Bach led his men in a friendly manner like a caring father. The pair challenged the stereotypes of Teutonic and Latin appearance and temperament; their men revered both of them.

On 17 June Rommel used 'Ariete' to act as an anvil for *5.leichte-Division* and *15.Panzer-Division* which engaged and defeated the British armour. During the course of the three-day operation, British tank losses were staggering: 98 out of 104 tanks engaged in the operation were damaged or destroyed, while the combined Axis tank losses amounted to only 12 written off after damaged tanks had been retrieved and repaired.

Post Operation Battleaxe

In July 1941 the 'Ariete' armoured division began to reorganize in the Villaggio Giovanni Berta area. Its 32nd Tank Regiment, consisting of the V, VI and XI tank battalions equipped with machine-gun-armed L3 light tanks was being replaced by a new tank regiment, the 132nd, equipped with M13/40 medium tanks. The first of the battalions, the VII (which was the same battalion most of whose tanks had broken down during the march between Agedabia and El Mechili in early April), arrived in March and the VIII Battalion had arrived around 19 April. A special tactical unit consisting of tanks, *Bersaglieri* and artillery was also created to provide security for division headquarters. By early September the 132nd Tank Regiment, with Lieutenant Colonel Enrico Maretti as its commander, had been formed with a headquarters company and three medium tank battalions, the VII, VIII and IX. The three battalions were brought up to establishment by diverting tanks originally intended for its sister armoured division, the 133rd ('Littorio'). 'Ariete' now had 146 medium tanks, 16 105/28 guns, 32 75/27 guns, eight 47/32 guns and eight 20mm guns. Replacement of the 32nd Regiment by the 132nd Regiment with its medium tanks marked a quantum improvement in the strength and capabilities of the division.

On 10 September 1941 the *Corpo d'Armata di Manovra* (CAM) was established. The CAM comprised 'Ariete', 'Trieste' and the *Reparto Esplorante del Corpo d'Armata di Manovra* (RECAM) – all of which were directly subordinate to *Supercomando Africa Settentrionale*. The RECAM (Mobile Army Corps Reconnaissance Group) consisted of a battalion of the *Polizia dell'Africa Italiana* (PAI,) with armoured cars, an M13 tank company, an L3 tank battalion, a group of two 'Giovani Fascisti'

A 100/17 howitzer mounted on a Lancia 3Ro truck, in action near Bir el
Gobi in 1941. The upper portion of the truck cab has been cut away to lower
the vehicle's silhouette. Four batteries of this type were assigned to the
'flying batteries' subordinate to the RECAM. (Ralph Riccio)

battalions, and a '*batterie volanti*' mobile artillery force consisting of various caliber Italian artillery
pieces mounted on Italian or war booty British and Canadian trucks. The CAM reported directly
to Bastico at *Comando Superiore AS* and was not in Rommel's chain of command. Commander
of the CAM was General Gastone Gambara, who was contemporaneously the Chief of Staff of
Comando Superiore AS. The role of the CAM was to protect Rommel's rear against any British
diversionary attacks coming from Egypt.

On 2 November 'Ariete' was informed by Gambara that it would be redeployed to Bir el Gobi,
and that 'Trieste' would take over the Bir Hacheim positions. 'Ariete' began its move to Bir El
Gobi on the night of 9 November. Bir el Gobi was a crossroads lying on the Trig el Abd and the
Tobruk–Giarabub road; a cement platform with four arrows stood at the crossroads, with the four
arrows indicating the distances to Giarabub, Bir Hacheim, Tobruk and Sidi Omar. Nearby were a
well and an abandoned barracks, but otherwise there was nothing but desert. The Italians judged
that Bir el Gobi was a key position, the door to Tripolitania, which should be held at all costs
against any British initiative during the planned upcoming offensive. Accordingly, when 'Ariete'
arrived, the men began immediately to determine fields of fire, taking advantage of slight undula-
tions in the terrain, and to dig pits and emplacements for everything from individual weapons to
crew-served-weapons to antitank and artillery positions; even the trucks were revetted. The soldiers
and engineers dug, and then dug deeper. Because the Italians attached so much importance to Bir
el Gobi, 'Ariete' was reinforced by a 75/27 artillery group from the 'Pavia' division, a 105/28 group
from army-level artillery, and a truck-mounted battery of 102/35 guns manned by MILMART
(naval militia) personnel.

10

The Second British Offensive in North Africa
Operation Crusader (18 November–30 December 1941)

Operation Crusader was yet another initiative designed to enable the British 8th Army to relieve the siege of Tobruk. The plan was to have XXX Corps, under General Willoughby-Norrie, swing around the right flank of the Italo–German frontier defenses that extended from Bardia to Sollum and Sidi Omar and occupy Gabr Saleh, where presumably Rommel's armoured forces would meet with the British 7th Armoured Division and be defeated. British XIII Corps under General Godwin-Austen would tie down the Axis frontier defenses, and after the tank battle had been won, join with XXX Corps and eliminate the Axis infantry forces along the frontier and around Tobruk.

The British had the equivalent of seven divisions and 770 tanks facing the Axis forces, which consisted of three armoured divisions (two German and one Italian), two motorized divisions (one Italian and one German) and five Italian infantry divisions (although 'Trento' was listed as a motorized division, in effect it was used as a static infantry division). Axis tank strength was 410, of which 272 were German and 138 Italian.

The night before the start of the offensive was marked by a violent rainstorm, which prevented the planned-for British air attacks against the Axis positions prior to the beginning of the offensive. Despite warnings, especially by the Italian intelligence services, Rommel was caught by surprise when on 18 November the British offensive kicked off.

The Italian intelligence service in North Africa at the *Comando Superiore AS* level was headed by Major Mario Revetria, assisted by Captain Giacomo Giuglia, Captain Malatesta and Lieutenant Barnato, and included a signals intercept company under Captain Maderni, whose achievements deserve much more credit than they have been accorded. This intelligence detachment had issued warnings based on signal intercepts, other intelligence, and shrewd analysis that the British were preparing their own offensive and would launch an attack, probably on 20 November. Rommel was unimpressed by the assessment, judging the Italian claim to be a manifestation of 'excessive Latin nervousness', and on the morning of 18 November ordered 'Ariete' to displace to Gueret en Nadura, about 20 kilometers (12 miles) southeast of Bir el Gobi. The Italian corps commander, General Gastone Gambara, who believed the Italian intelligence estimate, was adamantly opposed to the move and, taking a leaf from Rommel's own playbook, simply ignored Rommel's orders to pull out of Bir el Gobi. This refusal was made somewhat easier because at the time the CAM was not yet under Rommel's command but answered directly to the *Comando Superiore AS* under Bastico. At any rate, the Italian decision to initially deploy to and then to remain at Bir el Gobi turned out to be extremely fortuitous for Rommel, as it completely upset the timetable of the British offensive and would cost them dearly.

On the afternoon of 18 November initial contact was made between a platoon from 3rd Company, VII Tank Battalion of 'Ariete' and British armoured cars of the 11th Hussars. Based upon this contact, the 132nd Tank Regiment was then deployed to the rear of the Bir el Gobi positions as a maneuver element. On the morning of 19 November, the British 22nd Armoured Brigade moved

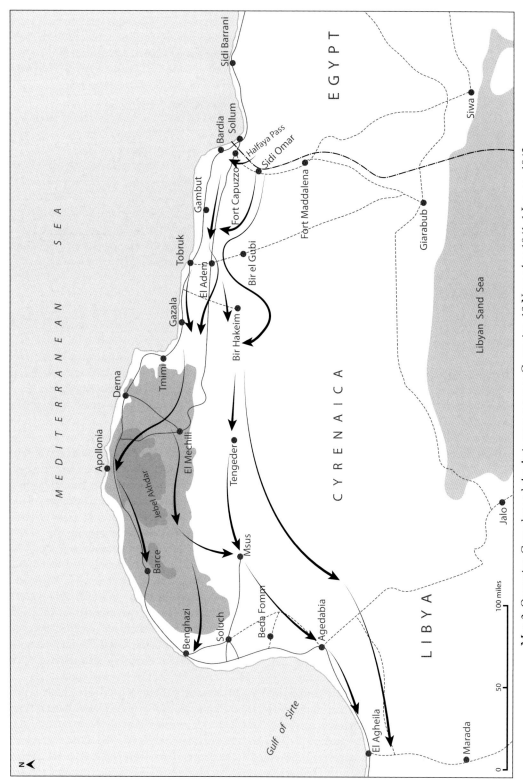

Map 2 Operation Crusader and the Axis retreat across Cyrenaica, 18 November 1941–1 January 1942.

An M3 Stuart light tank of the 8th Hussars wearing the Caunter camouflage scheme, December 1941. This tank has been hit in the turret and suffered an internal fire. The US-supplied Stuart, which made its debut in the desert in November 1941, was nicknamed 'the Honey' by the British. In terms of its size, weight, armour and armament the Stuart was roughly equivalent to the Italian medium tanks in the theater. Powered by a radial aircraft engine, it was much faster than all other tanks in the desert but consumed prodigious amounts of aviation fuel. (TMB 0208.B1)

towards Bir el Gobi. The leading armoured cars, again of the 11th Hussars, were engaged at Got el Dleua by the 3rd Company VII Battalion under Lieutenant Sobrero and a section of 75/27 guns under Lieutenant Vlach. After having driven off the Hussars, the Italian tanks came under fire from 25-pdrs followed by an attack from the rear by a battalion-equivalent of Crusaders of the Royal Gloucestershire Hussars, who knocked out three of the M13s, while losing eight of their own. This encounter was the baptism of fire for 'Ariete' in a tank-versus-tank engagement.

The Italians had prepared their defense of Bir el Gobi based upon three battalion strongpoints: in the center were V *Bersaglieri* Battalion of the 8th *Bersaglieri* Regiment, reinforced by a divisional antitank company with 47/32 guns, and the II/132 Artillery; on the left was III *Bersaglieri* Battalion, also reinforced with a divisional artillery antitank company, and a 75/27 group from 'Pavia' and on the right was XII *Bersaglieri* Battalion reinforced with two companies of 37/45 antitank guns from division and the I/132 Artillery. To the north were deployed the 105/28 group under Major Pasquali and seven truck-mounted 102/35 guns of the MILMART under Captain Priore. All the positions had been skillfully dug in and camouflaged. Further yet to the rear were the bulk of the 138 tanks of the 132nd Tank Regiment.

British forces consisted of the 22nd Armoured Brigade (2nd Royal Gloucestershire Hussars, 3rd and 4th County of London Yeomanry) with a total of 158 of the new Mark VI Crusaders, after which Operation Crusader was named. The brigade lacked adequate artillery, antitank and infantry support (one 25-pdr battery, one antitank battery and one infantry company). The 22nd Armoured Brigade, insufficiently trained and yet to be tested in battle, perhaps were victims of their own propaganda, as they believed that the Italians would offer little resistance before surrendering or turning tail and running. The British proceeded to mount a cavalry-style charge, which as gallant as it may have been, failed to dislodge the Italians. The initial charge by the Royal Gloucestershire Hussars against the center of the Italian defenses was met with fire from 47/32 antitank guns and from the 75/27 guns of the II group, 132nd Artillery Regiment, causing the British tanks to move to their left, into the Italian right wing occupied by VI *Bersaglieri* Battalion. At that point, the British tanks overwhelmed the Italian position, and although many of the Italians indicated their intention to surrender, the lack of British infantry prevented them from being taken prisoner. The British tanks continued to advance with little concern, but the Italians then returned to their guns and the tanks were once again under fire. When 3 and 4 County of London Yeomanry entered the fray, they in turn ran into a minefield as well as coming under concentrated antitank and artillery fire. Up to that point, General Mario Balotta, commanding 'Ariete', had kept the 132nd Tank Regiment to the rear, but he then unleashed the VIII, IX and one company of the VII Battalion under Lieutenant Colonel Maretti against the British tanks. In the wild fighting that ensued, the British tanks came under fire from aggressively and skillfully handled Italian tanks as well as from the truck-mounted 102mm naval guns using armour-piercing rounds which, much like the dreaded German 88, made shambles of the British tanks they engaged. The Italian artillery lived up to its reputation for delivering devastating fire, in spades. Of particular note was the behavior of Captain (Count) Oderisio Piscicelli, commander of I Group, 132nd Artillery Regiment, who had a ladder mounted on a TL37 light artillery tractor, and from that perch directed the fire of his battery's guns. At one point, infuriated at seeing one particular tank escape the fire of his guns, he gave chase to it with the tractor in the hopes of ramming it, but the tank was soon hit by one of his guns. His initiative earned him the sobriquet of '*Duca della Scala*' ('Duke of the Ladder') by his men. By late afternoon the British had had enough, broke off their attack and limped painfully from the battlefield.

Many British accounts of this battle tend to downplay its importance and, in some cases, cite significantly low figures for their tank losses, variously describing the action as a 'bloody nose' for the 22nd Armoured Brigade or as 'a slight brush with the enemy', trivializing what might be considered a pivotal engagement at the time. The brigade had been severely mauled, and although loss estimates vary significantly depending on the source, the most reliable estimates are that the British lost something on the order of 50 Crusaders, while the Italians lost 12 guns and 34 tanks not capable of being repaired. The 132nd Tank Regiment suffered 11 killed, 45 wounded and 65 missing. With respect to the tank losses suffered by each side, it is not clear just how many were lost to enemy tank fire and how many can be attributed to antitank and artillery fire. It would seem reasonable to assume that most of the Italian tanks were knocked out by British Crusaders, given that British artillery was rather limited in numbers and seems not to have played any significant role in the battle. It is somewhat more difficult to determine how many Crusaders were lost in the tank-versus-tank engagement and how many were lost to the guns under Piscicelli, Pasquali and Priore. Regardless, the Italians showed their ability to act as a well-coordinated combined arms team – a capability that was completely lacking on the British side.

The Battle of Bir el Gobi marks a watershed for the Italians in North Africa in several respects. First, even before the battle began, it became clear that the Italian signal intercept and analysis capabilities were considerably better than those of their German counterparts. Second, it reflected the fact that Italian commanders at the army, corps and division level had matured considerably since February of the same year and were now capable of making well-reasoned decisions on their own, to the point that they challenged and ignored German advice and even orders. Third, it provided indisputable proof that Italian training in combined arms operations was effective, much more so than that of the British on this occasion, and that the Italians were henceforth a force to be reckoned with. Somewhat obliquely, it also casts significant doubt as to the inferiority of the Italian medium tanks when matched against roughly equal numbers of the best cruiser tank the British

A 102/35 gun on a FIAT 634N chassis, the cab of which has been totally destroyed. This captured vehicle is of the type used by the Fascist MILMART battery under Captain Priore during the battle of Bir el Gobi in November 1942. (USSME)

fielded at the time, the then brand-new Mark VI Crusader, which was notoriously unreliable and was still armed with the inadequate 2-pdr gun. Finally, as is generally acknowledged in some relatively recent works, the prescience of the Italians in identifying Bir el Gobi as a key position in the anticipated battle and their impressive defense of the position completely upset the timetable of Operation Crusader, throwing British plans into total disarray. It also caused the British, who by many accounts seem to have believed that the Italians would either flee from Bir el Gobi at their approach or would be easily brushed aside, to regard the Italians in a different light and adopt a somewhat more cautious approach in future operations.

On 20 November, 1 South African Brigade made a half-hearted and ill-advised attack against the comfortably ensconced Italians at Bir el Gobi and was easily fended off. The South Africans then were content to simply maintain a watchful eye on the Italians, who had no intention of moving. Later that morning and early in the afternoon, 'Ariete' tanks, which had ventured out on two separate occasions, clashed briefly with South African and British forces, losing two or three tanks in these skirmishes. On 21 November the CAM assigned a motorized battalion of the 'Trieste' to reinforce 'Ariete', which was to be held in reserve for any eventual counterattack, or to assist the Germans if necessary. 'Trieste', meanwhile, still had the mission of holding Bir Hacheim.

On 21 November a British supply column consisting of some 200 trucks escorted by a few light tanks and armoured cars of the 11th Hussars seemed to be headed towards the *bir*. To the Italians this appeared to be a new attack in force, and they accordingly sent out the headquarters security element consisting of a tank platoon, a *Bersaglieri* motorcycle platoon and a mixed artillery battery under Lieutenant Emilio Lo Cicero to deal with the threat. The British attempted to flee but got bogged down in a muddy area at Bir el Sabi, where four of the Italian tanks also bogged down and had to be retrieved. Several hundred prisoners were taken, along with an armoured command truck which was subsequently used by 'Ariete' as its mobile division headquarters.

A Valentine II, A Squadron, 8th Royal Tank Regiment. The Valentine began to replace the earlier Matilda in the desert in November 1941as the standard British infantry tank there but was still armed with the outdated 2-pdr gun. This Valentine II shows the riveted construction that is characteristic of it. (TMB 8674.E1)

On 22 November the CAM ordered 'Ariete' to send a strong armoured column along the Bir el Gobi–Gambut road to support the attack of German armoured forces against positions at Bir bu Cremisa. CAM assigned two motorized battalions and an artillery group from 'Trieste' and a 65/17 flying battery from the RECAM as reinforcements. The column, under General Ismaele Di Nisio, consisted of VIII and IX tank battalions (each minus one company), V *Bersaglieri* Battalion, a 75/27 artillery group, a 65/17 flying battery, a 105/28 battery and a 102/35 MILMART battery. On 23 November the column linked up with *21.Panzer-Division*, and then continued to move north in order to meet up with *15.Panzer-Division*. The three divisions had all linked up by early afternoon on 23 November. At about 1600, Crüwell launched the three divisions against the British at Sid Rezegh and a bitter battle ensued. The South African 5th Brigade was practically destroyed, and the British 22nd Armoured Brigade was down to about 22 tanks, leaving it with only minimal combat capability.

On 24 November the CAM was subordinated to Rommel and became part of *Panzergruppe Afrika*. 'Ariete' was ordered to proceed along with the two German armoured divisions along the Trig el Abd to the Bir Ghirba–Sidi Omar positions. The following morning, one tank battalion was sent out on a reconnaissance patrol; the Italian tanks soon ran into enemy strongpoints overlooking the Trig el Abd. A fight rapidly developed, and the British sent out several light tanks to draw the Italians onto their antitank positions. The Italians responded with artillery fire in support of the tanks and the action ended. That same day 'Trieste' was transferred from Bir Hacheim to El Adem, and the RECAM displaced from El Adem to Bir el Gobi.

On 25 November the 9th *Bersaglieri* Regiment under Colonel Umberto Bordoni occupied Sidi Rezegh, and for three days was subjected to violent attacks by the 2nd New Zealand Division, which it withstood.

On 27 November 'Ariete' was ready to attack enemy forces surrounding the 'Savona' division's positions at Bir Ghirba but was called back urgently by Rommel and ordered to move to El Adem. However, before the move could be made, Rommel changed the order to proceed to Sidi Rezegh. 'Ariete' had to halt during the night of 27 November to resupply at Bir Grasa, and did not reach

Sidi Rezegh until 0800 on 29 November, when it linked up with the German panzers that were already in action there.

Meanwhile, the forward element of 'Ariete', the VII Battalion, approached Point 175, which it believed was now held by *21.Panzer-Division*. The position was in fact still held by the 21st New Zealand Battalion, who mistakenly believed that the approaching Italians were a relief element of the 1st South African Brigade. Because of this double dose of mistaken identity, the Italian tanks and truck-mounted *Bersaglieri* were able to quite serenely drive into the midst of the New Zealanders who had come out to greet what they believed to be their relief force. The Italians were the first to realize the situation for what it was, reacted quickly, and overran the New Zealanders, taking some 200 prisoners as well as large quantities of equipment and supplies. This was the action about which New Zealand General Howard Kippenberger wrote that: 'About 5:30 damned 132nd Armoured Division 'Ariete' turned up … and rolled straight over our infantry at Pt. 175.' The same day the III and V *Bersaglieri* Motorcycle Battalions under Majors Cantella and Gastaldi also helped to overrun the New Zealanders as well as capturing a New Zealand field hospital at El Abiar. In addition to the patients and medical personnel of the hospital, about 300 German prisoners being held there were freed by the Italians. The 21st New Zealand Battalion suffered some 450 killed, wounded and captured.

At dawn on 30 November British artillery opened up on Point 163, where VII Tank Battalion was located, and on Point 162, where VIII and IX battalions were deployed, inflicting some losses. 'Ariete' then fended off several counterattacks, losing 16 tanks while claiming 25 British tanks knocked out. The Italo–German tank forces had achieved a tactical victory over 2nd New Zealand Division and 1st South African Division, which were pushed back to the south of Tobruk, isolating it once again. However, despite their battlefield successes, the Axis supply situation had become very dire.

A column of Mk VI Crusader tanks, with a Mk II CS in the lead, at El Alamein, October 1942. The Crusader, after which Operation Crusader was named, was a rather elegant-looking tank whose reliability did not match its aesthetically pleasing appearance. It suffered from excessive mechanical breakdowns and consequent high deadline rates. (TMB 7781.C4)

At 0700 on 1 December Rommel met with Alessandro Piazzoni, the commander of 'Trieste', and ordered him to get his division moving from Bir bu Cremisa at 0730, to be relieved by 'Pavia'. 'Trieste', along with 'Ariete', was supposed to move along the Trig Capuzzo, and was to block any enemy escape. Piazzoni, however, did not pass on the order to move and allowed his division to have a rather leisurely breakfast. At 1100, when Rommel checked on the progress that 'Trieste' was making and found that it had not yet begun to move, he was livid. An hour later, at around 1200, four and a half hours later than Rommel had planned on, the 66th Infantry Regiment, followed by the 9th *Bersaglieri* Regiment, finally began to move. Rommel was understandably and justifiably furious at the delay. Between 1430 and 1500, the leading elements of 'Trieste' had a brief skirmish with the British who promptly withdrew.

The bulk of 'Ariete' had pulled out of Bir el Gobi by 24 November, leaving behind only a company of L3 tankettes, a few deadlined M13 tanks, two 20mm gun sections, two 47/32 antitank sections, what remained of the 102mm MILMART battery, and the division's field hospital. On 1 December the 136th 'Giovani Fascisti' Regiment moved into Bir el Gobi; their forces consisted of two battalions of well-trained and somewhat fanatical Fascist university students led by regular army officers and NCOs. The 'Giovani Fascisti' force consisted of 1,454 men, armed with 24 Breda mod. 30 6.5mm light machine guns, 12 Breda mod. 37 8mm heavy machine guns, half a dozen 20mm Solothurn antitank rifles, eight 47/32 antitank guns, eight 81mm mortars and a couple of cases of hand grenades in addition to their individual weapons. The ten L3/35 light tanks left behind by 'Ariete' from the November fighting were dug in as static bunkers.

On 2 December Rommel ordered the CAM to withdraw the 'Giovani Fascisti' from Bir el Gobi, move 'Ariete' to Gasr el Arid and that 'Trieste' to follow 'Ariete'. The first part of the order was not carried out, fortunately as it turned out, as the 'Giovani Fascisti' remained and held out against British attacks.

On 3 December British artillery began to shell the Bir el Gobi positions, inflicting some casualties. During the night outlying Italian posts were captured, and on 4 December the positions of I and II battalions were attacked by the 11th Indian Brigade supported by the 4th Armoured Brigade, but the Italian defenders successfully repelled both attacks. Later that day a third attack was mounted which, despite stiff resistance, succeeded in causing one Italian company to fall back to Point 184.

On the night between 4 and 5 December the CAM was ordered to return to Bir el Gobi to assist the 'Giovani Fascisti'; 'Trieste' was also ordered by Gambara of the CAM to move from Bir bu Cremisa and attack Bir el Gobi at 0830 on 6 December with 'Ariete' to follow. 'Ariete', located at Gasr el Arid per Rommel's previous orders, was unable to reach Bir el Gobi by 1300 on 5 December as Rommel wished and did not arrive until the afternoon of 6 December. The British, Indians and South Africans continued to launch attacks until 7 December but could not overcome the stubborn resistance being put up by the Italians, and eventually withdrew. The Italians lost all ten L3 light tanks and suffered some 60 killed, while the British sustained some 300 killed and lost a dozen tanks during the attacks.

On 7 December Rommel ordered 'Ariete' to withdraw and it had to pull out while still engaged, moving from Bir el Gobi to Hagfet Sciaaban–Hagfet en Noza, with 'Trieste' to its left (having replaced 'Pavia') and the DAK to its right. The 'Giovani Fascisti' had no organic transport of their own, so 'Ariete' loaded everyone on board tanks, tractors, limbers and the guns themselves in order to evacuate them.

Meanwhile, on 5 December at El Duda, the VIII Tank Battalion suffered heavy losses because 2 Company had pulled back while under artillery fire, leaving the flank of 1 Company exposed and causing 3 Company to be badly battered, resulting in the loss of a total of 22 tanks.

Also on 5 December Rommel made the decision that it would be necessary and prudent to withdraw back as far as Gazala. The troops were exhausted by the continual moves and fighting and

A 'Giovani Fascisti' light machine gun team seemingly ready for action. This is likely a staged photograph, as other photos of this same team of soldiers show the Breda Model 30 light machine gun without its ammunition magazine. (USSME)

needed rest. Morale was still high, but the troops lacked sleep, food was insufficient and erratic, water was scarce and rationed; bathing or washing clothes was out of the question. At this point, the Italo–German mobile forces were at the end of their tether, and the British, although also sorely tested, were in relatively better shape.

On 6 December 'Ariete' reached the area east of Sidi Rezegh at 0300, but there was no sign of 'Trieste'. At 0700, British artillery fired from the direction of Belhamed, and then artillery from El Duda opened fire. 'Ariete' was caught in a trap, cut off from El Adem and Tobruk. At 0830, tanks and armoured cars coming from the east attacked the 'Ariete' column but were fended off by V *Bersaglieri* and I/132 Artillery. The III *Bersaglieri* made contact with the El Duda position, attacking the New Zealanders there. The V and III *Bersaglieri* then moved southwest, and the battle raged for about an hour. The 'Ariete' rear guard reached El Adem on the afternoon of 6 December, rejoining the division.

On the night of 7 December, following Rommel's orders, all units were to fall back on El Adem and take on as much food, fuel and ammunition possible prior to withdrawing and destroy what was left. 'Trieste' was on the left, DAK on the right and 'Ariete' in reserve. The latter was down to 20 percent strength after 25 days of fighting, and after protecting the infantry withdrawal, reached Mersa el Brega–Uadi Faregh. At this point it was still acting as rear guard, protecting the withdrawing infantry.

During the night of 10/11 December all the divisions had been topped up and continued their withdrawal. 'Bologna', 'Brescia', 'Pavia', 'Trieste', 'Trento' and the DAK held Gazala from 10 to 13 December. At this point, Rommel decided to pull his 'seasoned' (that is, German) troops back to Mersa Brega and El Agheila. On 14 December the Italians woke up to find that they had been abandoned by the Germans. The previous night, there were instances of Germans taking Italian vehicles at gunpoint so that they could make their escape, while the Italians had to begin their retreat on foot.

A second or third series M13/40, as evidenced by the lack of full-length fenders, moving in the desert. The marking on the rear of the turret identifies it as the 4th tank of the 1st Platoon. (USSME)

On the morning of 14 December 'Ariete' was ordered to take Point 204 and make contact with the extreme southern outposts of 'Trieste'. Around 1000, the attack was begun by one battalion of M13 tanks (consisting of all the running tanks of the 132nd Tank Regiment) supported by all available artillery. The attack continued until about 1400, when an agreement was reached with the DAK to continue the attack the following morning. German armour was delayed until about 1400, and then approached from the northwest. The enemy tried to break out with nine Valentine tanks threatening the right flank of XII *Bersaglieri* Battalion; this threat was met by a platoon of M13 tanks, a platoon of 47/32 antitank guns manned by *Bersaglieri*, and fire from the I/132 Artillery. At the same time the positions held by III and V *Bersaglieri* battalions were being attacked by enemy forces from the southeast, but these were rebuffed by antitank and automatic weapons fire. The British finally broke off and retired to the east and contact was reestablished with 'Trieste'. More than 300 prisoners were taken, including the general commanding a South African brigade, 40 guns and many vehicles and much equipment. 'Ariete' had lost more than 50 killed, but the British had failed to threaten 'Brescia', 'Trento' and 'Pavia' from the rear.

As a result of the unannounced German withdrawal, an infantry battalion of 'Pavia' was overrun on 14 December, and on 15 December 'Brescia', 'Pavia' and 'Trento' repelled a strong Polish–New Zealand attack, while 'Trieste' continued to ward off 5th Indian Brigade's attack on Point 208. By mid-afternoon a British III Corps attack had been fought to a standstill, and in the afternoon 'Ariete', with about 30 M13s and *Bersaglieri* motorcycle troops in close support, counterattacked along with the 23 remaining tanks of *15.Panzer-Division*. The attack was successful, and the 1st Battalion, The Buffs (Royal East Kent Regiment) and other troops of the 5th Indian Brigade lost over 1,000 men killed, wounded or taken prisoner.

On 15 December the remaining Italian tanks along with 23 German tanks attacked the rear of the British formation and were able to make progress on the right of Point 204, opening a gap and destroying several dozen guns and capturing 2,000 soldiers, 40 guns and about a hundred vehicles. Two days later 'Ariete' moved to El Mechili, deploying with 'Trieste' to block the tracks coming from the east. The VIII Tank Battalion was down to eight tanks running. On the afternoon of 30 December 'Ariete' and 'Trieste' in the center, with German forces on both sides, hit the enemy right flank at Belandah. At dusk, the British withdrew leaving several tanks, armoured cars and other destroyed vehicles behind.

Although a defensive line had been established at Gazala, Rommel feared that the British would be able to effect an armoured thrust to his south and thus trap his forces. Around this time, *15.Panzer* was at Beda Fomm; *21.Panzer* was at Ghemines; 'Ariete', 'Trieste' and 'Pavia' were near El Abiar; 'Trento' and 'Brescia' were near Barce and Tocra; and *90.leichte* and 'Bologna' were at Agedabia. Consequently, against the wishes of Bastico and the *Comando Supremo* in Rome, Rommel elected to continue withdrawing his forces except for a few isolated garrisons on the coast, further to the west. During this prolonged withdrawal, while the British covered much of the same ground they had during Wavell's offensive a year earlier, the Germans and Italians carried out a fighting withdrawal and 'Ariete' and 'Trieste' continued to cover the retreat of the Italian infantry divisions.

On 24 December 'Ariete' was ordered to move to 18 kilometers (11 miles) south of Agedabia, but at 24 kilometers (15 miles) north of Agedabia it was attacked by pursuing British tanks and armoured cars which were driven off by artillery fire. By 27 December 'Brescia', 'Trento' and 'Pavia' were deployed around Agedabia behind minefields and were at less than half strength. Southeast of Agedabia, 'Ariete', 'Trieste' and the German armoured divisions were ready to attack the enemy towards Gialo. 'Ariete' was severely depleted, down to only six tanks left of the 138 it had at Bir el Gobi on 19 November. The *Bersaglieri* regiment was down to one battalion strength, and the artillery had only two groups with five or six guns each and the 105/28 battery was down to two worn-out guns. This phase of the campaigning had cost the Germans just as dearly as it had the Italians. Rommel's two panzer divisions had been battered and mauled, and were in similarly dire straits, down to only 70 tanks between them.

This *carro commando* (command vehicle) of a self-propelled gun battery has been fitted with a jury-rigged pole ladder to enable long-range observation of targets in the desert. The British also used a similar arrangement mounted on a light truck. In the background are an M13/40 tank and a captured British truck. (USSME)

Further to the east along the coast, the 'Savona' infantry division under General Fedele Di Giorgis had been left to hold out as best it could in Sollum, Bardia and Naqb el Halfaya (the Halfaya Pass) and cover the Axis withdrawal insofar as it was able by tying down Commonwealth forces in that area. During the remainder of December, the 'Savona's supply situation deteriorated and despite attempts to resupply it with food, water and ammunition via air, Bardia fell to enemy forces on 12 January 1942. The mixed force at Bardia, commanded by German General Artur Schmitt, consisted of 2,442 Italians and 2,143 Germans; a similar mixed force in Sollum consisting of 3,819 soldiers of the 'Savona' division and a small number of Germans also fell to the enemy. The remnants of 'Savona' that had managed to hold out at Halfaya, without food and water, finally surrendered on 17 January along with a battalion of the German 104th Schützen Regiment commanded by the inimitable Major Wilhelm 'Padre' Bach.

At the end of December 1941, the Italian forces were at a pathetically low ebb in terms of manning levels. 'Ariete' was hardest hit, down to 1,500 men and only three running tanks; 'Bologna' was not much better off with about 1,800 effectives; 'Trieste' had 2,200; 'Pavia' numbered 3,400; and 'Brescia' and 'Trento' fared relatively well with 3,800 and 4,200, respectively. The lull in the fighting in January enabled these numbers to be improved dramatically: by 1 January the 'Ariete' field repair depot had managed to get another 18 tanks running, and a month later, on 1 February 'Ariete' was up to about 5,700 men and 138 tanks, 'Trieste' was up to about 6,800, 'Brescia' and 'Bologna' were up to about 4,000 each, 'Pavia' was at about 4,650, 'Trento' was at about 4,500 and 'Sabratha' was relatively comfortable at 5,000.

By 1 January 1942 *Panzerarmee Afrika* had been pushed back to El Agheila. Both the Italo–German forces and the British were exhausted, and a period of inactivity ensued. The Italians and Germans, now benefiting from shorter supply lines from Tripoli, took advantage of the respite to replace both troops and equipment, dramatically increasing their posture. The equipment situation for the Italians improved with the delivery of four heavy artillery groups with 149mm and 152mm guns which were used to equip the army-level 8th Artillery *Raggruppamento*, and two new medium tank battalions and two 75/18 self-propelled groups (under Major Giuseppe Pasqualini and Captain Riccardo Viglietti) for 'Ariete'. At the same time, all the X and XXI Corps infantry regiments were reorganized with two battalions, each consisting of only two companies, until sufficient replacements were available to bring the battalions up to full strength.

11

The Second Italo–German Counteroffensive
and British Retreat to Gazala, 21 January–4 February 1942

In January 1942 the 133rd 'Littorio' armoured division under General Gervasio Bitossi arrived in theater and began to familiarize itself with its new surroundings. 'Ariete' now had 138 mostly M14/41 tanks and 'Littorio' had 90 M14s. The latter had only two tank battalions instead of three because it had been forced to provide its other battalion to 'Ariete' in order to bring it up to strength; what would have been its third tank battalion, the XII, with 52 M14/41 tanks, was aboard the *Filzi* when it was sunk on 14 December 1941. To add further to Littorio's misery was the fact that, in order to replace the personnel in those battalions that had been ceded to 'Ariete' and 'Trieste', replacement personnel came from second-line units and were not qualified as armoured crewmen. In January, command of 'Ariete' passed from Mario Balotta to General Giuseppe De Stefanis, who would prove to be a very capable commander.

Meanwhile, 'Trieste' reorganized. Both the 65th and 66th infantry regiments were equipped with two battalions and an 81mm mortar company; the 9th *Bersaglieri* had two battalions, the XXVII and XXXII, and for a brief period the XL as well; the 21st Artillery Regiment had two 75/27 groups, a 100/17 group and a 20mm battery. On 10 November the division took up positions at Uadi Faregh, with 'Ariete' on its left and 'Brescia' on its right.

With his newfound strength and in his characteristically aggressive, optimistic and exuberant fashion, Rommel, to the surprise of the British, once again decided to go on the offensive. On 19 January 'Ariete' and 'Trieste' reached a point 15 kilometers east of El Agheila (Sidi Hmuda). On the night of 20 January, the CAM assumed attack positions; the plan was to trap British forces in a pincer movement between Bir el Ginn and Uadi Faregh, with the CAM operating on the left and DAK on the right. At this point, 'Ariete' had 89 operational medium tanks, and the Germans had 111 PzKpfw III and PzKpfw IV tanks, with another 23 in transit. Following a brief clash with enemy units, 'Ariete' tanks changed direction to the southeast, while DAK was delayed, and the British were able to escape to the northeast.

On 21 January the 66th Infantry Regiment was heavily shelled by enemy artillery; counterbattery fire was provided by a 149/40 group. Several other minor skirmishes occurred between 20 and 23 January. On the afternoon of 23 January 'Ariete' deployed north of 'Trieste' and to the right of DAK; the enemy forces were completely encircled. On 24 January 'Ariete' was to move southeast towards Giof el Mataar, parallel to the German units, in a wide sweep that aimed at destroying the enemy forces. All these moves were made without encountering any opposition.

On 25 January an 'Ariete' tank column occupied Antelat, while 'Trieste' and 'Sabratha' were reinforced by 8th Artillery *Raggruppamento* and remained between Agedabia, Antelat and the road junction for Saunnu.

On 28 January 'Ariete' was ordered to attack Sceleidima from the south along with 'Trieste' attacking from southeast. At about 1200, 'Trieste' units faced the eastern hills of the strong position at Sceleidima, held by troops of 4 Indian Division, and were met with heavy artillery

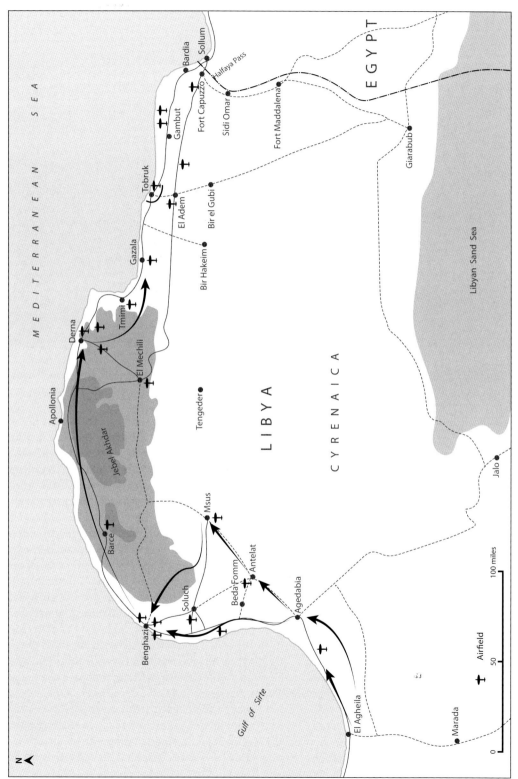

Map 3 The Italo–German advance to Gazala, 21 January–4 February 1942.

The command tank of a self-propelled gun battery being used as a platform for range-finding equipment. The command vehicle was essentially an M13/40 or M14/41 tank with its turret removed and a steel plate added as top covering. (USSME)

fire. Shortly thereafter 'Ariete' arrived, and also came under enemy artillery fire. Elements of the 8th *Bersaglieri* Regiment and of the *'Granatieri di Sardegna'* (IV Antitank Battalion) from 'Ariete' deployed to attack the enemy positions along with infantry from 'Trieste', supported by divisional artillery from both divisions, while the VIII Battalion of the 132nd Tank Regiment under Captain Casale made a flanking move from the north, supported by the 75/18 SP guns under Captain Viglietti. As the M14s supported by artillery fire made their way up the slope towards the enemy positions the defenders reacted violently, attempting to stop the tanks with antitank and artillery fire. Following a brief but sharp firefight, the tanks overran the defenders and attempted to prevent any of them from escaping towards Soluch; however, some enemy motorized forces managed to escape before the ring was closed. At 1445, the remnants of the garrison of the fort at Sceleidima raised the white flag. A number of Indians and three 25-pdr guns were captured. Three of Casale's tanks had been damaged but were repairable. At 1700, the CAM units regrouped and set off towards Soluch, about 15 miles to the northwest, which was reached and occupied at around 1900.

At dawn on 29 January 'Ariete' sent a detachment of *Bersaglieri* along with the VIII Tank Battalion to Ghemines, where it arrived at 0730, capturing the town and several prisoners who offered no resistance. At 1200, CAM ordered 'Ariete' and 'Trieste' to advance to Benghazi, and at 1530, 'Ariete' entered it behind *Kampfgruppe Marcks*. At the same time, 'Trieste' reached the Soluch area ready to support 'Ariete', while 'Sabratha' deployed in the Antelat area.

On 30 January 'Ariete' units relieved German troops at Coefia, cleared the area along the Via Balbia and occupied the main passes between Er Regima and Sceleidima, capturing about a thousand prisoners in the process. 'Trieste' was now deployed between Sceleidima and Ghemines, while 'Sabratha', at Antelat, detached two battalions to Saunnu. On 31 January the Italo–German tank

A truck-mounted 90/53 in battery position in the antiaircraft mode in the desert. Note the impressive size of the 90mm shell. (Nicola Pignato)

totals were down slightly from the numbers a week or so earlier and now stood at 80 Italian and 106 German, plus 46 Italian and 51 German in transit and expected to arrive shortly.

By 3 February the Axis offensive, which had pushed the British into headlong retreat across the territory they had recently won, cost the British 377 tanks, 192 guns and 1,200 vehicles. On 4 February the British halted their retreat and established a defensive line that ran from Gazala on the coast south to Bir Hacheim.

On 8 February the CAM was ordered to move immediately to El Mechili, while DAK moved to Martuba-Tmimi. On the same day the enemy attacked El Mechili with artillery and armour, but the attack was countered and repulsed by Italian artillery. Two days later, on 10 February 'Trieste' at El Mechili was subjected to attacks from the east, south and southeast, while 'Ariete' remained northeast of El Mechili. The XXI Corps deployed 'Pavia' around Benghazi, 'Sabratha' between Antelat and Sceleidima, 'Trento' between Giof el Mataar-Saunnu and corps-level troops around Agedabia.

On 14 February 'Ariete' sent a detachment consisting of IV Antitank Battalion '*Granatieri di Sardegna*' and a detachment of tanks from VIII Battalion to Garet Mereim (Segnali Nord) to protect German paratroopers who were laying a minefield. At 1030, the 'Ariete' detachment ran into an enemy motorized column 30 kilometers (19 miles) east of El Mechili, but following a brief clash, the enemy withdrew to the northeast. A British counterattack from the southeast was quickly beaten back.

On 18 March, Headquarters 133rd Tank Regiment 'Littorio' and 1 Company of the XII Battalion arrived in North Africa; the tanks moved to Homs, while the reserve tank detachments of XI and XII battalions, also originally belonging to the 'Littorio' division, were assigned to VIII Battalion ('Ariete'). Around Easter (5 April), the 132nd was reinforced with new tanks and IX Battalion was up to full strength.

On 15 March 'Trieste', which was responsible for defending the Mechili area, had a strength of 7,087. Although its infantry and *Bersaglieri* regiments were down to only two battalions each, its

Members of the 'Giovani Fascisti' manning a 20mm Breda Model 35 gun in spring 1942. Although in a revetted position, the gun is still on its wheeled carriage. (USSME)

artillery component at the time was quite strong, with 11 149/40 guns, eight 105/28, ten 100/17, 18 75/27 field artillery pieces and four 75/50 antiaircraft guns; it also had 54 47/32 antitank guns and 30 20mm Breda antiaircraft guns. However, on 29 March the 9th *Bersaglieri* Regiment was subordinated to X Corps, thus depriving 'Trieste' of its highly mobile light infantry element. This loss was offset in early May by the addition of the VIII *Bersaglieri* Armoured Battalion with AB41 armoured cars and the XI medium tank battalion which did yeoman service until it was destroyed in the Alamein battles.

On 21 March 'Bologna' was authorized to move forward from its Mersa Brega–Marada positions, but it and another XXI Corps division had to be available in the Agedabia area in order to guarantee protection of Agedabia–Benghazi area by two divisions. 'Littorio' and the *Raggruppamento Celere* had to be held back for defense of Tripolitania.

On 6 April Rommel ordered an offensive with its objectives being Segnali, Bir Temrad and Gasr el Hambar. 'Trieste' and 'Ariete' reached Segnali Sud and Segnali Nord, respectively, pushing as far as Er Cerima. The following day the deployment was as follows: on the left, XXI Corps and *90.leichte* on Via Balbia and 'Trento' at Bir Temrad; on the right, X Corps with 'Pavia' north of Segnali Nord, 'Brescia' at Segnali Nord and 288th Special Group of *90.leichte-Division* at Bir Tengeder; DAK and XX Corps (the CAM had been redesignated XX Corps on 10 March) were deployed north and south of Bir Temrad as maneuver elements.

In early May, Italian divisional artillery regiments were reorganized and standardized on five groups, each of three batteries: two 100/17 howitzer groups, two 75/27 gun groups, one antitank/antiaircraft group with 88/55 guns (the German Flak guns) and two 20mm batteries. The 'Ariete's 132nd Artillery Regiment was an anomaly, with six groups: two 75/27, one 105/28, two 75/18 SP, one mixed with four 90/53 gun batteries and 20mm guns.

A battery of M40 self-propelled guns just disembarked in Tripoli on 31 December 1941.
These SP guns were originally assigned to 'Littorio', but in January 1942 were ceded to
'Ariete'. The foremost vehicle is a command vehicle, armed with twin 8mm machine guns.
Note the difference in the configuration of the superstructure compared to those of the gun
vehicles behind it. (USSME)

Operation Venezia (26 May–30 June 1942): 'The Gazala Gallop'

As of 26 May, at the start of Gazala, DAK had 332 tanks, of which 50 were PzKpfw II, 242
PzKpfw III (including 19 Ausf. IIIJ 'Specials' with the longer 50mm gun) and 40 PzKpfw IV,
with 77 tanks of various marks in reserve. The Italians had 189 M13/14 mediums and 39 L6 light
tanks, plus 20 75/18 self-propelled guns, giving the combined Italo–German forces an overall
total of 560 tanks and 20 SP guns. During the same timeframe, on the British side the 1st and 7th
Armoured divisions could muster 167 Grants, 149 Stuarts and 257 Crusaders; 1st and 32nd Army
Tank brigades together had 166 Valentines and 110 Matildas; 1st Armoured Brigade later had 75
Grants and 70 Stuarts. The British total, including reserves, was 994 tanks, almost twice that of
the Axis, and a further 300 were in transit for delivery.

On 26 May at 1400, the Axis offensive codenamed Operation Venezia began. The northern
segment of the Axis forces, *Gruppe Crüwell*, commanded by *General der Panzertruppen* Ludwig
Crüwell, consisted of the German 115th Schützen Regiment and the Italian XXI Corps ('Sabratha'
and 'Trento' infantry divisions) and X Corps ('Brescia' and 'Pavia' infantry divisions) deployed from
north to south, from the sea to the area west of Sidra Ridge. The southern group consisted of the

'Trieste' motorized division, the 'Ariete' armoured division and the German *15.* and *21.Panzer-Divisions* and the *90.leichte-Division*. The initial attack made by *Gruppe Crüwell* was a feint; 'Sabratha' and 'Trento' engaged the 1st South African Division, while 'Brescia' and 'Pavia' engaged the British 50th Division to prevent those forces from being shifted elsewhere. Meanwhile, the main attack was to consist of a sweeping move in the south made by the mobile forces.

The British defensive line at Gazala consisted of several fortified positions, known as 'boxes', each manned by a brigade and protected by minefields, with the spaces intervening between the boxes covered by patrols. In the north, facing *Gruppe Crüwell*, positions were held by the 1st South African Division (3rd, 2nd and 1st South African brigades), and by the 151st Brigade and the 69th Brigade. Further to the south, where Rommel intended to make his main attack, were the 150th Infantry Brigade box and the box held by the Free French at Bir Hacheim. To the west of El Adem was the box famously known as 'Knightsbridge', held by the 201st Guards Brigade. A small box south of Bir Hacheim was occupied by 3rd Indian Motor Brigade, and further to the south and east was a box at Retma held by 7th Motor Brigade. The 1st and 7th Armoured divisions were stationed behind these boxes to act as a mobile counterattack force.

On 27 May at 0600, 'Ariete', the first Axis force to engage in action, reached enemy positions at Rugbet el Atasc (also known as 'Point 171'), 6 kilometers (4 miles) south of Bir Hacheim, which was held by 3rd Indian Motor Brigade, who laid down heavy artillery fire inflicting losses on the Italians. The German *21.Panzer-Division* was slated to support the attack, but was delayed. Artillery fire from the 2nd Field Regiment continued to inflict heavy losses, while the 90/53 and 88/55 groups of the 132nd Artillery Regiment engaged in counterbattery fire. The 132nd Tank Regiment with IX Battalion on the left and VIII in the leading echelon with companies in line and X Battalion under Major Luigi Pinna in the second echelon, reinforced by the two 75/18 SP groups (DLI and DLII), began their attack at 0630. The sight of this imposing force led the 3rd Brigade's commander, Brigadier A.A.E. Filose, to radio that 'a whole bloody German armoured division' (in fact, 'Ariete') was descending upon him. The Indian brigade's antitank and artillery response was very strong, especially against the left wing of VIII Battalion under Captain Casale, consisting of Lieutenant Boggia's 2nd Company. The lay of the terrain caused the interval between VIII and IX battalions to increase during the attack; realizing this, Lieutenant Colonel Maretti, commanding 132nd Tank Regiment, while ordering Lieutenant Colonel Pasquale Prestisimone to move his IX Battalion to the right, inserted the 7th Company of X Battalion under Second Lieutenant Bazzocchi between the first echelon units, reinforcing the attacking line.

At around 0715, the enemy's outpost line was overrun and the tanks, supported by the self-propelled guns which provided a decisive edge to the action, penetrated deep into the enemy position. The enemy reacted violently, counterattacking continuously. The enemy troops fought stubbornly and had to be rooted out of their holes. They were finally overcome and forced to surrender or flee; the 8th *Bersaglieri* subsequently conducted a mop-up operation. At the conclusion of the fighting, the Indians had suffered some 495 killed and wounded, and over a thousand prisoners consisting of Indians and French colonial forces from Senegal, Madagascar and Equatorial Africa had been taken, plus a large quantity of weapons, artillery, trucks and Bren carriers. Admiral Sir Walter Cowan was among the prisoners taken. Italian losses amounted to 42 dead, 49 wounded, six missing, and 45 tanks destroyed or damaged. The regimental commander, Lieutenant Colonel Maretti, was wounded while herding a group of prisoners, pistol in hand; he was attacked by a very large British officer who immobilized his arms while an Indian soldier hit him on the head with a helmet, knocking him out. Two Italian lieutenants quickly came to his rescue. Maretti was out of action for a few days, returning to action with his head wrapped in a bandage.

While the engagement at Rugbet el Atasc was under way, the second echelon tank force, consisting of Lieutenant Colonel Prestisimone's IX Tank Battalion had lost radio contact with the rest of the regiment and set off in the direction of Bir Hacheim; at 0800 it found itself on the

Italian medium tanks at a halt in February 1942, during the Gazala counteroffensive. (Massimiliano Afiero)

eastern side of Bir Hacheim's defensive perimeter. Bir Hacheim proved to be a much harder nut to crack than Rugbet el Atasc. It had been occupied on 14 February by the Free French, who had taken advantage of the time to prepare strong defensive positions. The French force of 3,800 men consisted of the 1st Demi-Brigade of the Foreign Legion, the 2nd Colonial Demi-Brigade and the 1st Field Artillery Regiment; this force had 16 75mm guns, 60 various caliber antitank guns, 30 40mm antiaircraft guns and 40 81mm mortars. The Italians were unaware of the minefield in front of the French defensive line. Prestisimone launched a frontal attack against the French but only six tanks managed to break into the French positions, and these were also soon immobilized. Prestisimone's tank suffered a broken track; although a competent Italian tank crew could fix a track blown by a mine in about ten minutes, Prestisimone did not have the patience to wait for the track to be repaired, so he took a swig of acquavit and commandeered another tank, which was also soon disabled by a mine. Fortifying himself with yet another gulp of acquavit, he climbed aboard the bow of a third tank and holding onto the tank's gun, began to direct a charge from his precarious perch. This third mount of his also hit a mine and Prestisimone was wounded and captured. The Italians lost 31 tanks and one 75/18 SP gun in the fruitless attacks against unexpectedly strong French opposition – personnel losses were relatively light, consisting of four dead and 87 Italians taken prisoner – and withdrew to consider their next move. All told, the engagements at Rugbet el Atasc and Bir Hacheim on 27 May had cost the 132nd Tank Regiment the loss of 45 tanks, 34 killed, 49 wounded and 102 missing in action. Having assessed the situation, De Stefanis, now commanding 'Ariete', gave orders to link up with DAK to the north. 'Ariete' reached Bir el Harmat before settling down for the night.

'Trieste' motorized division, which had been marching to the left of 'Ariete', had not kept pace or moved far enough south; at 0200 on 27 May it lost contact with 'Ariete' and XX Corps headquarters. It continued to advance according to the initial plan and when daylight dawned, found itself completely isolated in the area of Bir Belafarit, north of Bir Hacheim. Meanwhile, its 52nd Motorized Engineer Battalion spent most of the day patiently and methodically working its way through the British minefields while under fire from the 150th Brigade box, and by 28 May had established a corridor through the minefield. Contemporaneously, the engineers of 'Brescia's 24th Engineer Battalion were also busy clearing another path through the minefields north of the 150th Brigade's box. These corridors cleared by the Italians, although under fire from the British box, allowed Rommel to resupply his beleaguered armoured forces.

At 0800 on 28 May 'Ariete' pushed the 8th *Bersaglieri* Regiment towards El Cherua. The first echelon consisting of V Battalion reinforced with armoured cars, the X Tank Battalion, a 75/27

A battery of 75/27 mod. 06 guns in action against enemy tanks at El Mechili in early February 1942. The 75/27 was the standard division-level artillery piece in North Africa. (Enrico Finazzer)

group under Captain Marino and a 75/18 SP group under Captain Viglietti moved to attack, skirting the eastern edge of the minefield. The second echelon at Bir Harmat consisted of XIII *Bersaglieri* Battalion and a 47/32 antitank company. The advance met with considerable difficulty because of heavy artillery fire and the presence of three belts of mines that hampered movement. The battle continued to develop with tanks from both sides entering the fray. The V *Bersaglieri* Battalion advanced rapidly on foot preventing the enemy, who had resisted doggedly, from pulling back to a secondary defensive line. While clearing the area, the Italians were attacked on their left flank by a large motorized force supported by intense artillery fire. A spirited counterattack by XII Battalion caused the enemy to flee to the northeast in disorder. The Italians later linked up with DAK and *90.leichte-Division* at Rigel Ridge.

On 28 May, and despite a shortage of fuel and ammunition caused by the tempo of operations as well as by attacks on divisional transportation units causing the Axis armoured units to halt, 'Pavia' reconnaissance elements made contact with armoured elements stalled east of the minefields, and 'Trieste', after having thrown back an attack by tanks south of Trig el Abd, made contact with the 'Nizza' cavalry group armoured cars of 'Ariete'. Following bitter fighting, X Corps was able to meet up with XX Corps in the evening, while XXI Corps made no progress due to stiff resistance by 1st South African Division. On 29 May, 'Pavia' and 'Trieste' began to close the ring around the 150th Brigade box.

On 29 May Rommel ordered X Corps to continue to attack until it could link up with XX Corps and pressed 'Trieste' to link up with 'Ariete'. However, by the evening of 29 May the situation had not improved. The X Corps had been attacked by strong armoured forces and although it had beaten them back, had made no forward progress. The XXI Corps had been violently attacked in the central sector and 'Sabratha' division, which had attacked the South Africans south of Gazala but come under tremendous artillery fire, was forced to withdraw with heavy losses. At Got el

Ualeb, 'Trieste' encountered strong resistance which prevented it from advancing to the north, despite the courageous attack made by its XI Tank Battalion led by Major Verri, which consisted largely of southern Italians who had been recruited from the ranks of taxi drivers and truck drivers.

'Ariete', meanwhile, began to advance towards the intersection of Trig Capuzzo and Trig el Abd at Mteifel el Chebir, but strong winds limited visibility. At around 1100, weather conditions improved and VII and IX tank battalions in the leading echelon made contact with the British 2nd Armoured Brigade's Crusaders, joined later by the 22nd Armoured Brigade attacking from the west with 44 tanks. There was fierce fighting throughout the day both at Deir el Aslagh (Aslagh Ridge), which had been taken by the Italians including the 66th regiment of 'Trieste' under Lieutenant Colonel Chiapusso, and at Hagias es Sidra (Sidra Ridge), held by the 8th *Bersaglieri* Regiment, which dominated Trig Capuzzo. The VII, IX and X tank battalions, supported by two 75/18 SP groups under Major Giuseppe Pasqualini and Captain Riccardo Viglietti, supported by divisional artillery, faced off against the British, whose attempts to break through were thwarted. 'Ariete', supported by armour from the German *15.Panzer-Division* forced the British, after having suffered heavy losses, to withdraw in disorder. 'Ariete' suffered no losses during this engagement.

With Aslagh Ridge in the hands of 'Ariete', and an obvious target for the British, De Stefanis set about preparing his division to face a British counterattack by 4th Armoured Brigade. He made maximum use of all the artillery he had at hand. His first line of defense consisted of the 47/32 antitank guns that were still marginally effective against some of the British armour, manned by *Bersaglieri* along the ridge itself; these were backed by the lethal Italian-crewed 88mm guns and the devastatingly effective Italian truck-mounted 90mm antiaircraft guns used in the antitank role. All these guns faced to the east, the presumed direction from which an attack would emanate. The 132nd Tank Regiment was kept behind the ridge ready to maneuver against any armour that might break through the antitank screen.

On 30 May 'Ariete', *15.Panzer-Division* and *90.leichte-Division*, with 'Trieste' to their south, were bunched together in a relatively constricted area between the Trig Capuzzo, Trig el Abd and Acroma–Bir Hacheim tracks. This area soon earned the rather apt nickname of 'The Cauldron' as it was marked by a great deal of confused and violent fighting, with units often intermixed. Within this area was the British box at Sidi Muftah (referred to by the Italians as 'Got el Ualeb') manned by the 50th Infantry Division's 150th Brigade; the 1st Army Tank Brigade was also in the area. The 150th Brigade box was a very strong defensive position consisting of 2,000 men and 80 tanks. German and Italian forces attacked it on 30 May but were repulsed. On 31 May the attack was resumed with both German and Italian forces participating; 'Trieste' repulsed an attack supported by armour emanating from the box.

While *15.Panzer-Division* and *90.leichte-Divison* and the Italian 'Trieste' and 'Pavia' divisions were busy attacking the 150th Brigade box, to the southeast the British attacked the 'Ariete' positions on Aslagh Ridge at 0730 on 30 May. The 132nd Tank Regiment's VIII and IX tank battalions deployed to face the attacking armour. Behind the Italian tanks, on the right wing of the deployment, were two artillery batteries (one 75/18 SP and one 75/27). At 1030, a strong attack by armour consisting mainly of M3 Grants bore down on the right flank. The IX Battalion met the advancing British tanks and a furious clash ensued; after about half an hour the British withdrew. Another attack at about 1730, preceded by smoke and artillery was made against the front held by VIII Battalion, but this attack was also repulsed and at 1830, the British, badly battered, ceased all efforts to break through the line held by 'Ariete'. A night attack against 'Trieste' fared no better. The British lost 57 tanks in the encounters on 30 May. On 31 May, X and XXI Corps cleared the 6-kilometer area between them of British motorized elements.

On 1 June the 150th Brigade box at Got el Ualeb was finally captured by the combined Italo–German forces ('Pavia', 'Trieste' and *15.Panzer-Division*). The 150th Brigade was destroyed, and several Matilda and Valentine tanks were destroyed or captured.

An O.M. Taurus truck mounting a 20mm Breda cannon bypassing a group of British prisoners in the desert in autumn 1941. (USSME)

British Operation Aberdeen began on 5 June but British attempts in the north to break contact between Italian X and XXI Corps failed, following initial negligible success in the 'Brescia' sector. The Italian units pulled back gradually, almost to their own artillery lines, while some truck-mounted 90/53 guns carried out intense shelling against the British attacks, which cost the British the loss of about 50 tanks. The same day, further to the south at Aslagh Ridge, the 9th and 10th Indian brigades attacked and managed to push the 8th *Bersaglieri* off part of the ridge but were then halted by intense artillery fire. The Indians were supposed to have been supported by the 22nd Armoured Brigade, which, however, failed to show up, ultimately causing the attack to fail and the Indians to withdraw. On 11 June 'Ariete' remained on Aslagh Ridge in a position to protect the Axis supply lines.

On 8 June the attack against Bir Hacheim resumed. Rommel committed *90.leichte-Division*, the 115th Schützen Regiment, 'Trieste' and a 75/18 SP battery from 'Ariete' to the attack. French resistance was very strong and determined, but Rommel remained insistent that Bir Hacheim be taken. After bitter fighting, at dawn on 11 June the German and Italian units broke through major resistance points. Bir Hacheim fell, and although a large portion of the garrison managed to escape, 1,500 prisoners, 44 guns and 450 vehicles were captured.

On the same day Rommel reassessed the situation and decided to stick to the same basic plan he had developed for Operation Venezia. This called for *90.leichte Division* to take the right flank, pass south of El Adem and strike towards the tempting target posed by the large British supply center at Belhamed. Meanwhile, *15.Panzer*, teamed up with 'Trieste' further north on the left flank, would aim for Tobruk by attacking between El Adem and Knightsbridge. The remaining pair of armoured divisions – *21.Panzer* and 'Ariete' – were between the northern and southern flanks, still in the Cauldron area, and would keep open the supply corridors that 'Brescia' and 'Trieste' had previously established, as well as deal with British armour in the Knightsbridge area.

At 0840 on 12 June British armoured forces under the cover of a smokescreen launched an attack against 'Ariete' from Point 158, east of Trig Hacheim, attempting to envelop the V/8 *Bersaglieri* and VIII/132 Tank Regiment. The British formation consisted of M3 Grants at the center of the formation, with Mk VI Crusaders on the flanks. Italian tanks and SP guns working in concert broke up the formation of Grants. At around 1130, after bitter fighting, the British quit the field after having suffered heavy losses, withdrawing to the east of Point 158.

On 14 June Rommel sensing a complete victory, pushed his units forward in order to cut off the retreating British units and wipe them out. Eighth Army decided to make a stand at Acroma, 20 kilometers (12 miles) from Tobruk, protected by a vast minefield. That afternoon, Italo–German forces attacked and although they were slowed down by minefields and enemy artillery, finally broke through and the enemy troops surrendered in ever increasing numbers. The XX Corps had advanced in the Trigh Capuzzo area, clearing it of disorganized enemy units. On 16 June 'Trieste' was straddling the Acroma–El Adem road and 'Ariete' had cut the El Adem–Bir el Gobi road. With the Eighth Army in disarray, the Italo–German forces were now in a position to deliver a fatal blow to Tobruk. The Italian XXI and X Corps were given the task of holding the western and southern sides of the boundary, forming a continuous ring around the defended area of the perimeter. 'Ariete' held the southeast corner and DAK, the eastern side. 'Trieste' was deployed to Sidi Rezegh, facing south.

On 17 June Rommel ordered DAK and 'Ariete' to attack Gambut, which was taken on 18 June. The same day 'Trieste' completed the isolation of Tobruk by cutting the coast road to the east of the port. On 19 June the now-isolated Tobruk garrison consisted of the 2nd South African Infantry Division, 11th Indian Brigade, two battalions of the 201st Guards Brigade, 32 Army Tank Brigade and the 4th Antiaircraft Brigade with a total of 35,000 men, plus 61 tanks, about 100 field pieces and 70 antitank guns. 'Ariete' reached its attack position 3 kilometers (2 miles) east of El Adem, facing forts 50 through 53, while 'Trieste' was southwest of El Adem, but on the night of 19/20 June it changed direction and arrived at assigned positions near the fortress. 'Trieste', however, had to be pulled from the attack because 7th Motor Brigade and part of the 4th Armoured Brigade had made a wide move to the south of El Adem and hit the El Hatiam and Bu Cremisa positions with artillery fire.

'Littorio', which had been in Tripolitania since January becoming acclimatized, now arrived at the front and would be stationed southeast of Tobruk near El Adem. At this stage 'Littorio' was still understrength, with only two tank battalions (XII and LI), its 12th *Bersaglieri* Regiment with only two motorized battalions, and the 133rd Artillery Regiment short of its normal complement of guns. The division was in this condition because it had continued to cede its equipment piecemeal to 'Ariete' and 'Trieste' in order to bring those divisions up to their establishment strengths. 'Littorio' had also had to give up much of its motor transport to the central motor pool that was used to move the non-motorized Italian infantry divisions. Realizing that the division was not fully capable, the Italians committed it only at the insistence of Rommel, who as usual got his way.

On 20 June perimeter forts 48, 49, 50, 51 and 53 were captured by Italian sappers of the XXXI Sapper Battalion. The 7th Company, on the right, led by Lieutenant Lino Leonardi, was the first to break into the Tobruk defenses, along with the 8th Company under Captain Renato Amoretti. In the 'Ariete' sector, a battalion of the 8th *Bersaglieri* Regiment, reinforced by 2nd Company, VIII Tank Battalion under Lieutenant Boggia, and a battalion of the 65th Infantry Regiment 'Trieste' reinforced by 1st Company, IX Tank Battalion under Lieutenant Roberti, followed in the wake of the sappers, but were stopped by fierce fire from antitank guns and automatic weapons. At 0730, the division was ordered to advance through the gap created by the DAK, striking the rear of forts 50 and 53. Around dusk, 'Ariete' aimed west to attack the defenses between Bir el Giaser and Sidi Cheralla, and then surrounded Fort Pilastrino, which it occupied by nightfall. Meanwhile, 'Littorio' was blocking British relief attempts to the southeast; the division and 7th Motor Brigade traded artillery fire, but there was no attack as such by the British.

A large group of prisoners, presumably French colonial forces from Madagascar, Senegal and Equatorial Africa captured at Point 171 in May 1942. (USSME)

At dawn on 21 June 'Ariete' organized two mixed columns. The first, led by Lieutenant Colonel Gherardini, commander of the 8th *Bersaglieri*, consisted of the 8th *Bersaglieri*, two tank companies (led by Lieutenants Boggia and Fassone), and a 75/27 group, whose mission was to approach the enemy positions from the north and attack the South Africans at Ras el Medauar from the rear. The second column, consisting of a battalion of the 65th Infantry Regiment, 'Trieste', a tank company (Lieutenant Moscatelli), and a 75/27 group under division command, was tasked with clearing the area southeast of Bir esc Sciausc. These columns bagged a total of 700 prisoners as well as numerous weapons and supplies.

At 0700 on 21 June a British *parlamentaire* presented himself to XXI Corps headquarters to discuss surrender terms. Because of the fast-moving situation, the surrender was not accepted. At 0900, XXI Corps was ordered to cease artillery fire because of the danger to friendly troops. At 0930, Rommel met with General Klopper, commander of 2nd South African Division and of the Tobruk garrison, to discuss capitulation. Despite Klopper's surrender, the 2nd Cameron Highlanders continued to hold out and knocked out seven M14s from 'Ariete', finally surrendering on 22 June. The booty at Tobruk was enormous, consisting of some 32,200 prisoners, including six generals, about 2,000 tons of fuel, 5,000 tons of food, large stores of ammunition, 2,000 vehicles and a number of guns. Despite this huge windfall, the Germans were not willing to share much with the Italians. German guards were posted 'to ensure proper distribution' according to German headquarters, while the Italians griped that the Germans were 'keeping everything for themselves, as usual'. It is ironic that in a campaign that was often characterized as a 'gentleman's war' where both sides generally treated each other's prisoners with respect, the Germans on occasion treated the Italians somewhat worse than they treated enemy prisoners.

A 47/32 antitank gun manned by a Libyan crew, May 1942. Their Italian officer is scanning the horizon for targets. (Enrico Finazzer)

With the fall of Tobruk, the Italo–German forces set about chasing the remaining British and Commonwealth forces out of Libya and across the border into Egypt. Even though the Axis had scored a notable victory by capturing Tobruk and had the British on the run, by about 25 June they had also suffered significant combat losses and general attrition due to the sustained and intense operational tempo since the beginning of Operation Venezia. Although sources differ, the Italians were in somewhat sorry shape. On 25 June Italian forces consisted of the following: in XX Corps, 'Ariete' had ten running M14 tanks, 15 artillery pieces and 600 *Bersaglieri*; 'Trieste' was down to four M13 tanks, 15 armoured cars, 24 guns and 1,500 men total in three regiments (65th, 66th, 9th *Bersaglieri*); 'Littorio' had 30 M14 tanks, 11 guns, 1,000 *Bersaglieri* (12th Regiment). In X Corps, 'Brescia' had only one battalion (II/20) and 'Pavia' was down to one as well (II/27); the Corps also had seven artillery groups and 2,000 *Bersaglieri*. The XXI Corps was designated the '*gruppo d'inseguimento Navarini*' (Navarini Pursuit Group), with IV 'Granatieri' Antitank Battalion, two battalions of the 7th *Bersaglieri*, four battalions of the 'Trento' division and eight artillery groups (totaling 3,000 men and 100 guns). All other forces were left behind between Tobruk and Bardia–Capuzzo, awaiting the transport needed to get them forward.

Despite the depleted status of the Italian divisions, on 24 June, X and XXI Corps units advanced past Buq-Buq without meeting any opposition and by nightfall had occupied Sidi Barrani, the first troops to enter being the 7th and 9th *Bersaglieri* (from 'Trento' and 'Trieste', respectively). El Maktila and Alam el Nibeiwa were also occupied. On 25 June Italo–German units deployed to attack the fortified positions of Mersa Matruh as follows: XXI Corps north of the coast road at Abar el Da'fa-Point 135, X Corps south of the road east of Bir Abu Tunis, DAK at Bir Sidi Ali and XX Corps south of the DAK. Because of a shortage of fuel, 'Littorio', even with its reduced complement of tanks, was stalled and could not keep up with the advancing forces. However, by 26 June, XXI Corps had reached the edge of the minefield protecting Mersa Matruh and X Corps took positions at the fork in the trail for Siwa. DAK and XX Corps clashed with British forces north of Bir Khalda and fighting ended at nightfall with the destruction of 20 Grant tanks. The ring around Mersa Matruh became tighter on 27 June although there were still gaps between units; 'Brescia' and 'Pavia' had arrived in the meantime aboard supply trucks and were deployed south of

Part of the booty taken when Tobruk was recaptured from the British on 21 June 1942. The wide variety of vehicles includes staff cars, light trucks and armoured cars. (Daniele Guglielmi)

the fortress. 'Littorio' was sandwiched in between those divisions and *90.leichte-Division*. The XX Corps was down to 44 tanks due to breakdowns and air attacks.

On 26 June the Italians had suffered a particularly devastating loss. At 1100, Allied fighter-bombers spotted two isolated vehicles and attacked; in those vehicles were the XX Corps commander General Ettore Baldassare, the corps artillery commander General Guido Piacenza, the corps engineer commander Colonel Vittorio Raffaelli, Captain Erculiani, Lieutenant Pierfrancesco Nistri, and their drivers Sergeant De Cian and Tinti. The aircraft dropped three bombs: Piacenza, Erculiani and De Cian died on the spot, while Baldassare and Raffaelli were badly wounded, with Nistri and Tinti suffering only minor injuries. Nistri managed to get Baldassare to a 'Trieste' aid station. Baldassare was distraught over the loss of the other men in the party, and implored Nistri to not lose a minute on his account, stressing the fact that the Italians had reached their assembly area four hours ahead of schedule and that Rommel would be proud of his divisions. At 1345, he was brought to the 'Ariete' medical facility, where he turned the corps over to De Stefanis before expiring at 1400.

That same day, 'Trento', 'Brescia', 'Pavia' and 'Littorio' – all of which were severely depleted and with little artillery – threw a cordon of rickety and emaciated battalions strung out around Mersa Matruh. Many men and small units of 10 Indian Brigade managed to escape at night through the gaps in the Italian net. A few days later, on the morning of 29 June the 7th *Bersaglieri* Regiment and the 4th Company of the XXXII Sapper Battalion entered Mersa Matruh. In addition to taking 6,000 prisoners, there was a considerable amount of booty, including 40 tanks, a number of artillery pieces, and warehouses full of supplies of all sorts, which were soon taken over by the Italians.

During the late-night hours of 29 June 'Littorio' advanced with two columns, one consisting of the LI Tank Battalion to the northeast led by Lieutenant Colonel Salvatore Zappalà, the other to the southeast with 12th *Bersaglieri* Regiment under Colonel Amoroso and the armoured cars of *III Gruppo 'Lancieri di Novara'*. At dawn the next day (30 June), Zappalà's column came under attack from 4th Armoured Brigade, losing several tanks. Zappalà was killed in the action and Lieutenant Musolino (a *carabinieri* officer) assumed command and led a desperate counterattack with 11 tanks, closing to a range of 600 meters before his tank was also hit. Soon after, at Khor el Bayat, the Italians counterattacked and dislodged the enemy. However, as a result of this action 'Littorio'

The crew of this US-supplied M3 Grant medium tank of the 2nd Royal Gloucestershire Hussars photographed in September 1942 looks confident, no doubt because at the time of its arrival in May 1942 the Grant, with its 75mm gun outranged the guns of most of the Axis armour in the desert at the time and was a game changer for the British and Commonwealth forces. The Grant was a stopgap tank until the arrival of the M4 Sherman, also supplied by the US. (TMB 6951.B6)

was down to only ten operational tanks and 133rd Artillery Regiment was down to six guns, with ammunition running low even for those remaining guns.

The *90.leichte-Division*, followed by 'Trento', advanced past the El Qattara road and made for the El Adem track. It engaged enemy units to the south and southeast throughout the morning, making little headway. Italian XXI Corps, with 'Trento', 7th *Bersaglieri* and IV Grenadier Battalion, the XXXII Sapper Battalion, and X Corps with 'Brescia' division came up to join the attack. Around 1300, a column of *90.leichte* headed northeast to reach the coast and thus cut off the El Alamein defenses. XX Corps ('Trieste', with 'Ariete' on the right) advanced past Sanyet el Miteirya in the afternoon and approached the Alam el Dihmaniya area. The *90.leichte* had been stopped southwest of El Qasaba el Gharbiya (south of El Alamein) while XXI Corps, pushing from the west, was checked east of the Qatttara road at positions north of Sanyet el Miteirya. XX Corps was moving to reach a position east of Alam el Dihmaniya, followed by X Corps, which in the meantime, had been ordered to move to southeast of Deir el Abyad.

30 June 1942 marked the high-water point for the Axis forces; it was on that day that the 7th *Bersaglieri* Regiment reached kilometer 111 along the Alexandria–Mersa Matruh section of the coast road, now commemorated by a marble plaque marking the furthest point of the Italo–German penetration into Egypt. By 30 June the British had pulled back from Mersa Matruh to more defensible positions that lay between the sea at El Alamein in the north and the virtually impassable Quattara Depression to the south.

Both sides had suffered staggeringly high tank losses from the beginning of Operation Venezia on 26 May until 30 June–1 July. The British, Germans and Italians were all effectively emasculated in terms of operational readiness rates at the end of the operation. According to one source, on 26 May the Italians had 240 tanks and only about 80 were available on 1 July (a loss rate of almost

Members of the 7th *Bersaglieri* Regiment advancing near Tobruk in June 1942. This photograph highlights the lack of motor transport available to the Italian infantry, as these soldiers have resorted to the use of a somewhat overloaded hand-drawn cart to carry much of their impedimenta. (Massimiliano Afiero)

67 percent); German tank strength on 26 May was 295, and by 1 July was down to an appalling low of 37 for the two panzer divisions combined (a loss rate of 87 percent). Figures for the British holdings at the beginning of the operation are somewhat less precise but appear to have been in the range of 1,300–1,375 tanks, either in units or in transit, and one estimate has put British losses at 1,188 tanks in the 17 days of fighting. Thus, the British losses were very close to those of the German in terms of percentage of tanks lost (about 86 percent). On 1 July Eighth Army stood on the Alamein line with 137 tanks in units and 42 in transit from base workshops to the front. On the same day, there were more than 902 tanks sitting in base workshops, of which only 34 were serviceable. Personnel losses for the Axis for the period amounted to 12,994 Italians and 11,934 Germans killed, wounded or missing.

First Battle of El Alamein (1 July–27 July 1942)

The battles of El Alamein were not fought exclusively, or even preponderantly, at or in the immediate vicinity of that named locality, but rather in the zone that stretched from El Alamein itself, on the coast, south as far as the Qattara Depression. Qattara, site of an ancient sea, covers about 19,605 square kilometers (7,570 square miles) and lies 133 meters (436 feet) below sea level; it is largely covered with salt pans and is basically impassible. Within the El Alamein–Quattara Depression area, noteworthy features, from north to south, are: Alam Halfa, Tell el Mansfra, Tell el Aqqaqir, Deir el Murra, Kidney Ridge, Tell el Eisa, Miteirya Redge, Deir el Dhib, Deir el Shein, Ruweisat Ridge, Alam Nayil, Naqb abu Dweis, Deir Munassib and Qaret el Himeimat.

On 1 July the Italo–German forces consisted of two large groupings: the XXI Corps and the X and XX Corps, and the DAK. XXI Corps, also designated the *'gruppo d'inseguimento Navarini'*, consisted of 'Trento' with four battalions and three artillery groups, the 7th *Bersaglieri* Regiment with two battalions, the IV 'Granatieri' Antitank Battalion, and four artillery groups, totaling 3,000 men and 100 guns. XX Corps consisted of the 'Trieste' motorized division with five battalions (1,500 men), five artillery groups and 30 tanks; the 'Ariete' armoured division with two truck-borne battalions and one antitank battalion of the 8th *Bersaglieri* Regiment (600 men), six artillery groups and 40 tanks; and the 'Littorio' with three battalions of its 12th *Bersaglieri* Regiment (1,000 men) and one 100/17 battery in addition to about 32 tanks. X Corps consisted of the 'Brescia' infantry division with two battalions (one of which was actually from 'Pavia') supported by three artillery groups; the 'Pavia' division with only its artillery regiment with three groups and the 9th *Bersaglieri* Regiment with two battalions and an artillery group. Overall strength of the corps was 2,000 men and 90 guns. Overall Italian strength was 20 infantry battalions, 26 artillery groups and 82 tanks. The DAK consisted of the *15.* and *21.Panzer-Divisions* and the *90.leichte-Division*, making a total of 58 tanks, 15 armoured cars, 77 guns and 65 antitank guns; infantry totaled about 2,000 in 12 battalions. There were thus 32 Axis infantry battalions, 34 artillery groups and 160 tanks (102 Italian plus 58 German). On the British side, there were about 70 infantry battalions, about 600 guns in 25 field artillery regiments and 150 tanks, including the 75mm-gunned Grants.

When the battle began, the ferocity of the fighting affected the Germans as well as the Italians. As the *90.leichte-Division* was attempting to drive to the coast road, it ran into the defensive positions of the 3rd South African Brigade. The South Africans were able to call in fire from seven artillery batteries, which unleashed a catastrophic rain of fire upon the Germans. Subjected to this intense artillery fire, the Germans refused to advance further. Rommel himself then drove to the position, along with members of his combat staff in an attempt to urge his troops forward. However, by this time, many of the German infantry had run to the rear for safety. Rommel was able to prevent a rout by his presence and eventually managed to drag the panicked troops back to the line. Despite the numerous references in various works to the unreliability of Italian infantry units and their lack of will to fight, there seem to have been no comparable instances of Italian units fleeing in panic under intense shelling.

On the night of 2 July Italo–German units reached positions along the line Qattara Boring Works–El Ruweisat ridge–El Mireir depression. On the morning of 3 July 'Ariete' reached a position at Deep Well, but without the support of 'Trieste', which had been delayed by the enemy. 'Trieste' had labored hard to work its way south and southeast to cover the flank of the attacking German panzer divisions, which were making a desperate attempt to reach the coast behind the El Alamein positions. 'Trieste' found itself isolated at Alam Nayil. At 0930, 'Ariete', surrounded by forces four times its own strength, was subjected to an attack from the east, southeast and south by 2nd Brigade, British 1st Armoured Division, supported by artillery from 2nd New Zealand Division and 4th Armoured Division. Furious fighting ensued, with the Italian tanks being hammered relentlessly by artillery and tank fire from all sides. An attempt was made to rally against an infantry attack made by the 4th New Zealand Brigade, but enemy fire was incessant and overwhelming. The fighting lasted for about ten hours. For miles around, the desert was littered with the remains of shattered tanks. 'Ariete' had fought stubbornly and courageously; its artillery had held out until it ran out of ammunition and removed the breechblocks from the guns. What was left of the command pulled back after nightfall to positions held by the 'Pavia' division, protected by violent fire from the guns of the 'Brescia' division. The New Zealanders attempted to cut off the remaining 'Ariete' elements, but at El Mireir were themselves attacked by 'Brescia' and thus failed to do further damage to 'Ariete'.

The action on 3 July during which the division was decimated marked the beginning of the painful and bloody road to El Alamein for 'Ariete'. It had suffered very heavy losses: the 8th *Bersaglieri* Regiment lost 12 officers and 281 other ranks; XII Battalion was particularly hard hit. The 132nd Artillery Regiment lost 11 officers and 225 other ranks killed or captured, while the 132nd Tank

Regiment lost about a hundred men. Equipment losses included 28 guns, 22 M14 tanks out of the 30 that had taken the field, and about a hundred or so other vehicles. The battered survivors managed to scrape together a tank platoon, a 90/53 gun section and a *Bersaglieri* company, which would later form the nucleus of a reconstituted division. This rump command was attached to the *15.Panzer-Division*, which remained in place to protect the 'Pavia' and 'Trieste' positions. Things were not much better that same day for the XII Battalion of 'Littorio' at Ruweisat Ridge. Some 20 M14s under Major dell'Uva ran up against some Grants of the British 1st Armoured Division. Not surprisingly, the 47mm guns of the Italian tanks were no match for the Grants, leading to heavy losses for 'Littorio'.

On 8 July a joint force consisting of *21.Panzer-Division*, 'Littorio' and one battalion from 'Trieste' attacked the position at Bab el Qattara they believed was being held by the New Zealanders. However, unbeknownst to Rommel, the day before, the New Zealanders had very quietly evacuated the position. Following a heavy preparatory artillery barrage, the Italo–German force attacked the position, only to find that it was empty and that their planning and efforts were nothing more than a waste of time and ammunition.

The continued operational activity and its attendant losses resulted in a severely depleted Italian force structure. By 8 July the two Italian armoured divisions and the 'Trieste' motorized division were down to a total of 54 tanks instead of the 430 called for at full establishment, six light gun batteries and 40 antitank guns. Overall, the Italo–German forces were down to about 30 percent of establishment strength, with only 1,200–1,500 combatants left per division.

On 9 July 'Littorio' suffered an early morning surprise attack by the 4th New Zealand Brigade at Mungar Wahla and the Italians managed to fend off the New Zealanders. During the action 3 Group of the 'Lancieri di Novara' Regiment under Captain Ferruccio Dardi, equipped with L6/40 light tanks, was particularly hard hit. Dardi, a cavalryman, stuck his head and torso out of the turret hatch in order to better direct his other tanks and was killed as a result. The next day, along with *Kampfgruppe Kiel*, 'Littorio' occupied Point 78 southeast of Mungar Wahla, which the New Zealanders had been using as an observation point.

Late in the afternoon of 9 July, *21.Panzer*, reinforced by II Group of the 1st Articelere 'Eugenio di Savoia', with 100/17 guns under Major Leopoldo Pardi, was suddenly shifted to Deir el Anqar to stem strong pressure from the 2nd New Zealand Division against 'Brescia'. Major Pardi was killed in action; the loss of this gallant and capable officer was mourned by the Germans as well as the Italians.

At 0500, on 10 July a strong attack was made between the railway line and the sea against the front lines of XXI Corps held by two infantry battalions (II/85 and II/86) of the 'Sabratha' division and XI Battalion of the 7th *Bersaglieri* Regiment. The 9th Australian Division, supported by tanks, broke through as far as the positions of 3rd Articelere 'Duca D'Aosta', threatening Army-level artillery positions. The II/86 infantry and I and IV groups of the *articelere* and the LII 152/37 heavy artillery group under Major Renzo Rastrelli on Hill 33 were overrun, and the enemy captured Point 25 as well as the headquarters of 7th *Bersaglieri* Regiment. Heavy artillery fire prevented 'Trento' to the south from being able to come to their aid.

Meanwhile, the 99th Battery of the XXXIII Group of 149/40 guns under Captain Comi found itself astride the coast road, devoid of any infantry support, facing an attack by the Australians. This battery was an army-level artillery asset and the guns were the most modern and effective of their type in North Africa. Furthermore, its gunners were accustomed to operating far behind the front lines. However, as events were rapidly unfolding, the battery found itself virtually on the front line. In yet another example of the Italian gunners sticking by their guns even when about to be overrun, they leveled their barrels as close to the ground as possible and fired over open sights. All the reduced charge ammunition had been expended, and the battery was left with 400 rounds of shells set calibrated at maximum charge and set to fire at distances up to 23 kilometers (14 miles).

Benito Mussolini reviewing 'Folgore' paratroopers in June 1942, prior to their deployment to North Africa. (USSME)

A 149/40 gun being readied for action. Guns of this type were instrumental in breaking up an Australian attack at almost point-blank range in July 1942. (Enrico Finazzer)

The gunners fired at a feverish pace, ramming the 101-pound shells into the breeches as quickly as they could and sustaining burns from the overheated steel of the guns and glycerine spraying from their recoil mechanisms as every round was fired. Between rounds, the gun layers adjusted the traverse in order to increase the arcs covered by fire. The horizontal barrels were so low that the muzzle blasts furrowed the ground for about 20 meters in front of the guns, raising a huge amount of smoke, dust and flying rocks. The frenetic pace of firing by the four-gun battery lasted between 20 and 30 minutes; after the last of the 400 rounds had been fired, the scene opposite the battery was one of devastation and carnage, presenting a mass of burning vehicles and Australian corpses.

Providentially, the German 352 Infantry Regiment of the *164.leichte-Division* and a reserve battalion of the *90.leichte* showed up to form a provisional defensive line to protect the gunners from the remaining Australian infantry. The decisive action taken by Comi's 99th Battery was a key factor in disrupting the Australian attack, although the situation remained fluid because II/85 regiment, XI *Bersaglieri* Battalion and II Group of the *articelere* were surrounded and cut off, breaking the line between the 'Trento' division and the X *Bersaglieri* Battalion.

Around 1200, the enemy attack slacked off and Rommel pulled units from the south to throw them into the fight for the positions near the coast. At around 1700, those units began a counterattack against the enemy's flank, against Hill 33. Taking part in the attack were *Kampfgruppe Kiel*, X *Bersaglieri* Battalion, elements of *15.Panzer-Division*, and a battalion from 'Trieste' reinforced by 19 tanks (3rd Company of XI Tank Battalion under the somewhat flamboyant Captain Vittorio Bulgarelli, who wore a monocle and pronounced his letter 'r' as a soft or 'French r'). The attack made some initial progress, reaching the railway line, but then was stopped by heavy artillery fire. The 'Trieste' column suffered a loss of 16 of the 20 tanks that had either been hit or bogged down in the salt marsh, but nevertheless managed to reach the area of Bir Abu Khatwa, closing the gap between the German 382 Regiment and the left flank of the 'Trento' division, which was holding its positions.

On the morning of 11 July, the British made another attack, supported by air, with strong motorized and armoured forces and artillery which had been brought up to the salient during the night. The jump-off point was between kilometer 125 and kilometer 130 of the railway line, aimed at the Axis positions at Tell el Eisa (Hill of Jesus). II Battalion of 'Trieste' was surprised and overwhelmed, as were the other units that had been surrounded the previous day (XI *Bersaglieri* Battalion, II/85 infantry 'Sabratha', III/4 Articelere) despite the intervention of all the artillery of the 46th Artillery Regiment of 'Trento'. A total of 1,024 Italians were taken prisoner. In the X Corps sector, 'Pavia' and 'Brescia' divisional artillery repulsed a strong infantry and tank attack.

On 13 July *21.Panzer* attacked enemy positions with the objective of reaching the coast and pushing the enemy back to its old positions. The attack was supported by Stukas and army-level artillery, and after some initial progress, was stopped at Point 13, southwest of El Alamein. The attack resumed on 14 July with 'Trieste', *Kampfgruppe Kiel* and German reconnaissance elements that made it as far as Point 25, west of Bir Abu Khatwa and the kilometer 130 marker on the coast road. During this phase, I Battalion of the 85th Regiment, 'Sabratha' division, led by Lieutenant Colonel Angelozzi, recaptured Tell el Eisa in a bold push. Although accounts are somewhat confusing, it appears that the 3rd Company of XI Tank Battalion, commanded by Captain Bulgarelli, attacked in the vicinity of Marsa el Hamra; its 19 tanks charged against enemy 6-pdrs and 25-pdrs and, except for one, were knocked out before they reached the British gun line. The single remaining tank, license plate RE 3700, which now forms part of the commemorative display at the Italian war memorial at El Alamein, made it past the guns but was subsequently also destroyed along with its crew. That same afternoon (14 July), 'Littorio', reinforced by the German 288th Special Unit with a number of tanks from *15.Panzer-Division*, reached the area of Deir el Anqar while combat elements of the 'Ariete' Division aggressively reoccupied the Deep Well area, four kilometers (2.5 miles) south of Alam Nayil.

On 15 July the central front of X Corps was attacked by the 2nd New Zealand Division and elements of 5th Indian Division supported by the 22nd Armoured Brigade with El Ruweisat (Ruweisat Ridge) as their objective. The area was defended by understrength elements of the 'Brescia' and 'Pavia' divisions. 'Brescia' could muster only two infantry battalions, the II/20th and the III/20th, as well as the III/19th which was a battalion of reservists, some of whom had never even fired a weapon and had arrived on line less than a week before. 'Pavia' was also understrength. Some 'Brescia' positions were overrun, and the division headquarters, along with its commanding general, Giacomo Lombardi, was captured. The understrength 'Pavia' infantry division put up stiff resistance with its 28th Infantry Regiment and 26th Artillery Regiment preventing enemy forces from widening the breach they had made. The British had already taken the Deir el Shein position from the 9th *Bersaglieri*, and their penetration threatened to compromise the entire central sector of the Axis positions. Rommel accordingly transferred *21.Panzer-Division* and the 3rd Reconnaissance Battalion and inserted them between 'Brescia' and 'Pavia', reinforcing the front to the east. On the evening of 15 July Deir el Shein and Ruweisat positions were retaken by Axis forces. The New Zealanders had lost some 205 men killed or wounded, plus another 1,200 taken prisoner by the Germans. On the Italian side, 'Brescia' and 'Pavia' lost 2,000 men taken prisoner.

On the day of his capture, General Lombardi, along with several of his staff officers were loaded aboard his own command truck to be brought back to the British rear area. The light truck, which was a captured British war-booty vehicle that had the Italian tricolor flag painted on its hood, was hit by machine gun fire from other British forces who believed the truck to be Italian. Several British soldiers and an Italian major were killed. Taking advantage of the confusion, Lombardi suggested to the British driver a route to safety, which in fact was a route back to Italian lines. The general and his officers then overcame the remaining British soldiers in the truck and made it to Italian lines, where Lombardi resumed command of what was left of his division. Lombardi's reprieve was short-lived, however, as he was badly wounded by an enemy bomb shortly thereafter.

At dawn on 17 July the Australian 24th and 6th brigades launched an attack against Miteirya Ridge that focused on the boundary between the 'Trieste' and 'Trento' divisions. The remnants of XXXII Sapper Battalion were surrounded and put up a stubborn resistance against the Australians but were overrun and wiped out. The Australians took 736 prisoners. The same day, while leading his troops, the

A pair of M40 self-propelled guns in the desert, May 1942. Note the dust raised by firing. These would have belonged to either the recently arrived DLI or DLII SP groups, both assigned to the 'Ariete' division. (Massimiliano Afiero)

commander of the 65th Regiment, Colonel Gherardo Vaiaraini, was mortally wounded. What was left of the 'Sabratha' division's 85th and 86th infantry regiments were badly mauled and lost their positions at Tell el Eisa. Enemy forces then sought to enlarge their breakthrough to the south but came under heavy artillery fire from the 46th Artillery Regiment and 81mm mortar fire from the 'Trento' division. Particularly distinguishing itself was the III Battalion, 61st Infantry Regiment which, although surrounded, bore the brunt of the fighting and held the line in the sector. Rommel cited the battalion in his order of the day, while the Italian higher command itself ignored its accomplishment. The Australian advance was definitively halted by fire from XXI Corps artillery and attack by the German 382 Infantry Regiment which reoccupied Points 23 and 25 at Tell el Eisa. Although the situation had generally stabilized by the evening of 17 July, some parts of the line had been pushed back.

On 18 July reinforcements to the front consisted of three groups (two 75/27 and one 100/17) of the 205th Artillery Regiment of the 'Bologna' division, deployed to the right of the 'Trieste' division where there was the greatest threat of an enemy breakthrough. The rest of the 'Bologna' division was making the 620-kilometer (385-mile) march from Ain el Gazala to El Alamein, on foot, under the blazing sun, suffering from dysentery, heat, exhaustion and lack of proper sleep, and another 11 artillery groups were on their way from Tripolitania. On 18/19 July *Comando Supremo* in Rome, having finally grasped the seriousness of the situation after heated disagreements with Rommel, began to take measures to shift or send additional units. Scheduled to be sent from Italy were the 'Folgore' parachute division and the 'Pistoia' motorized division as well as reserve units to flesh out 'Brescia' and an additional 14 artillery groups. In order to deny its use by the British, Rommel decided to occupy Siwa Oasis, and on 20 July it was reached and occupied by Italian forces that were reinforced a few days later by the 'Giovani Fascisti' division.

On 21 July British and Commonwealth forces launched a strong attack against the Italian positions on Ruweisat Ridge. The attacking forces consisted of 2nd New Zealand Division, 5th Indian Division, 1st Armoured Division and 22nd Armoured Brigade. The Italians at Deir el Mireir had observed the attack preparations, and 'Ariete' artillery put the New Zealanders under fire. One company of New Zealanders managed to make it through the minefield but was met by intense fire from the defending *Bersaglieri*, as well as fire from tanks further to the rear. The battered New Zealanders had no choice but to abandon the attack.

On 22 July the Italian line at Deir el Shein was attacked, but all the Italian positions held fast against the attackers. Particularly distinguishing themselves were the 132nd Artillery Regiment ('Ariete'), III/61st and III/62nd battalions of 'Trento', the 28th Infantry Regiment and 26th

An AB41 armoured car and a FIAT 626 cargo truck halted along the Via Balbia in spring of 1942. The armoured car belonged to a *Bersaglieri* reconnaissance unit. (Ralph Riccio)

Artillery Regiment of 'Pavia', and the 19th Infantry Regiment and 1st Articelere Regiment of the 'Brescia' division.

On 22 July while leading an ad hoc formation counterattacking an Australian breakthrough, the commander of the 66th Regiment, Colonel Umberto Zanetti, was killed in action. He was the second 'Trieste' regimental commander to be killed in less than a week.

On 27 July the British launched a new offensive. The British 69th Brigade was able to break through to Deir el Dhib, where it overcame resistance by the I/61 Infantry Regiment, 'Trento' and overwhelmed it. The 69th Brigade was forced to withdraw under protection of tanks of the 1st Armoured Division, which lost 21 tanks to artillery fire from 'Trento' divisional artillery. At about 1500, the British launched a fresh attack, aiming for the boundary between 'Pavia' and 'Trento' divisions, with the objective of breaking through between Sanyet el Miteirya and Deir el Dhib. By nightfall, however, the British had lost 70 tanks due to stubborn Italian resistance, largely assisted by the 'Trieste' reconnaissance battalion. The integrated resistance of Italian armour, artillery and infantry repulsed repeated enemy attacks.

The Italian defensive posture was improving, especially in the central sector, at Qaret el Abd and in the extreme south at Naq Abu Dweis, where extensive defensive works were being built. Minefields were being laid at the rate of 150,000 mines per month. However, Italian divisions were at severely reduced strength, sometimes lacking entire battalions and artillery groups. *Comando Superiore AS* requested 6,500 infantry and 6,000 artillery replacements to be sent via air, and equipment by sea, in addition to another 24,000 men for security and operational needs in Libya. The available aircraft personnel lift capacity was 300 men per day, meaning that more than 40 days would be needed to airlift the minimum number of infantry and artillery replacements of 12,500 men. In practice, very little of this requirement could be or actually was met.

A battery of 75/18 self-propelled guns being unloaded from a ship convoy newly arrived in Tripoli. The first vehicle is a command vehicle, while the others are M41 75/18 SP gun vehicles. (Daniele Guglielmi)

12

The Third British Offensive: El Alamein and the Italo–German Retreat to the West
Battle of Alam Halfa (30 August–5 September 1942)

In mid-August, Rommel was fully aware that time was against him and that the British were able to replace and add men and equipment on a much larger scale than he could hope for. Accordingly, in his characteristically aggressive and optimistic style, despite facing a lack of fuel for his mobile forces, he nevertheless set about planning another offensive, codenamed Operation Caballo. The offensive was to develop in two phases: the first consisted of the transfer of a strike group (DAK and XX Corps) to an assembly area in the south but simulating a concentration in the north by using logistics vehicles to raise clouds of dust, with the move to be completed by 29 August. The second, or attack, phase was to consist of the Italo–German infantry breaking through the minefields and seizing the frontline British positions, while in the south the mobile forces would strike quickly to the north-northeast. Italian XX Corps (with the 'Ariete' and 'Littorio' armoured divisions and the workhorse 'Trieste' motorized division) in the El Karita area and German *90.leichte-Division* to its north would provide cover to the DAK flank on the left (from El Alamein) and the Italo–German reconnaissance units would cover the extreme southern flank.

On 30 August the first-echelon Italo–German forces consisted, in the north, between the sea and the El Mireir depression, of Italian XXI Corps (7th *Bersaglieri* Regiment, and 'Trento' and 'Bologna' infantry divisions), plus the German *164.leichte-Division* and the Ramcke parachute brigade. South of that, between Er Mireir and the Qattara Depression, was Italian X Corps ('Brescia' infantry division, XII Battalion of the 8th *Bersaglieri* Regiment, XXXVI Battalion of the 12th *Bersaglieri* Regiment, and the 'Folgore' parachute division). Behind X Corps was a maneuver force consisting of the 'Ariete' and 'Littorio' armoured divisions, the 'Trieste' motorized division, the DAK with its *15.* and *21.Panzer-Divisions*, the German *90.leichte-Division*, and a mixed force of Italian and German reconnaissance units. These forces amounted to 39 Italian and 28 German infantry battalions, 536 guns (336 Italian, 200 German) and 510 tanks (229 German and 281 Italian, of which 29 were German PzKpfw II and 38 Italian L 6/40 light tanks which were almost useless). Facing them were Eighth Army's 1,038 tanks which included 170 M3 Grants and 252 M4 Shermans mounting 75mm guns and 884 guns plus slightly more than 1,400 antitank guns. The only German tank capable of effectively challenging the Grants and Shermans was the new Panzer IV Special mounting the long 75mm gun.

Late in the day on 30 August the Italo–German forces formed up in the south and began their advance. However, due to Allied foreknowledge of Rommel's plans, air strikes, and a delayed start by XX Corps which then went off on a wrong heading and ran into a minefield, the enterprise was off to an inauspicious beginning. By dawn of 31 August 'Ariete' and 'Trieste' were bogged down in minefields; 'Littorio', whose IV Tank Battalion, *III Gruppo 'Lancieri di Novara'* and a self-propelled 75/18 battery were the foremost elements of the attack, had made progress through the minefields but was somewhat behind schedule, and only the RECAM and the 185th 'Folgore' parachute division reached their assigned objectives on time.

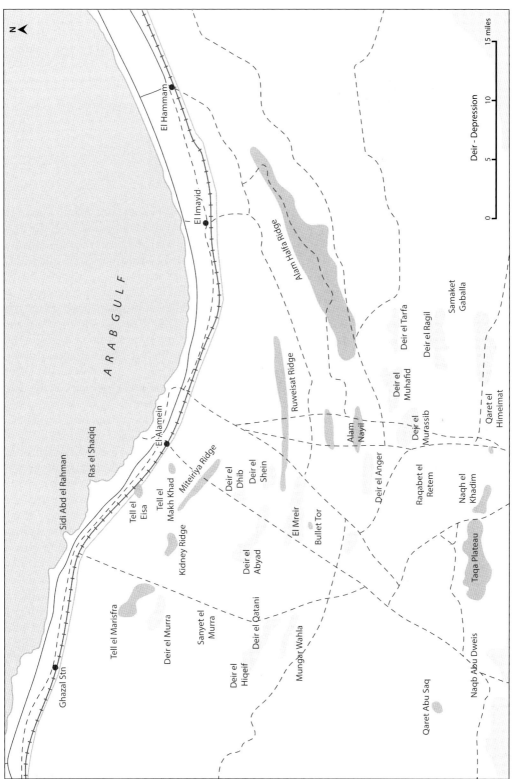

Map 4 The Alam Halfa and El Alamein battles, 30 August–11 November 1942.

The size and weight of the 47/32 gun enabled it to be displaced easily by its crew, as seen here with unusual, mottled camouflage scheme in March 1942. The truck in the background is a FIAT 626. (Enrico Finazzer)

As of 0830 on 31 August the northern feint (the *164.leichte-Division* and 'Trento') and the German Ramcke parachute brigade had pushed as far as Deep Well. By nightfall of 31 August, DAK had reached Manaqir el Taiyora, XX Corps was at Deir Muhafid and *90.leichte-Division* made it to Deep Well. 'Ariete' and 'Trieste' had been slowed down by British defenses and mine-fields, and enemy resistance was stronger than had been expected. The attack was suspended on the night of 31 August. Fuel was in short supply and the supplies that had been so glibly promised by *Comando Supremo* in Rome had not reached Africa. The only Italian unit still in decent shape was the 'Littorio', with its leading column consisting of 1st battery, *DLIV Gruppo* (self-propelled) and a company of the IV Tank Battalion, along with the *90.leichte-Division*, managing to reach Alam Halfa, but were unable to exploit their success due to a lack of fuel. The XI Tank Battalion also was able to reach a forward position at Managir el Taijira but was soon forced to fall back. The *DLIV Gruppo* had arrived in early August and had done well in its baptism of fire, knocking out about 20 enemy tanks for a loss of two of its own 14 self-propelled guns.

On 1 and 2 September the British continued to hammer the Axis forces, and on 2 September Rommel ordered his forces to withdraw in stages, using the Italians to hold the British at bay so the Germans could begin their withdrawal: 'Littorio' was ordered to hold its present position while DAK fell back first, while 'Littorio', 'Trieste' and *90.leichte* were to fall back later in sequence. On 3 September counterattacks by 6th New Zealand Brigade and 1st Indian Division were repulsed by 'Brescia' and 187th Regiment, 'Folgore' parachute division who inflicted heavy casualties and captured the New Zealand 6th Brigade commander, Brigadier Clifton. Preceding one attack carried out by the 187th Regiment, a reserve officer, Major Aurelio Rossi, who had been a *bersagliere* before joining the paratroopers, produced a trumpet and sounded the charge rather than wait for the red signal flare that was supposed to indicate the start of the attack. Upon hearing the trumpet, the headquarters staff immediately concluded that it must be Rossi *'quel matto'* ('that madman') and did not know whether to laugh or get angry at his antics. Rossi was one of 14 officers and 112 NCOs and other ranks of the 'Folgore' who met their deaths that day.

On 3 September the Axis offensive was suspended, with its units pulling back to positions at El Taqa-Bab el Qattara. By 6 September the withdrawal was complete, and the Germans and Italians rested and refitted, accomplishing miracles of repair, reaching a total of 306 German and 191 Italian tanks. As encouraging as those numbers were, on the other side, the British had amassed an astounding 1,351 tanks, including the US-supplied M3 Grant and 300 of the newly arrived M4 Shermans, both mounting 75mm guns.

On 8 September the fighting at Alam Halfa came to an end. The Italians referred to the Alam Halfa battles as the *'sei giorni'* ('six days') as well as the 'Battle of Santa Rosa', in recognition of the 3 September feast day of Santa Rosa. Axis personnel losses were 1,859 German and 1,051 Italian and about 45 German and 11 Italian tanks, 53 guns and 400 vehicles of various types.

The British lost 1,600–1,750 men plus 350 taken prisoner, 150 tanks and 18–30 guns. Between 24 and 31 August the Axis forces had received only 13,000 tons of supplies, while the British had amassed at least 300,000 tons – a recipe for disaster for Rommel and a windfall for the exceedingly cautious Montgomery who had taken over command of Eighth Army some three weeks earlier on 15 August.

On 13 September, less than a month after the abortive 19 August Operation Jubilee raid on Dieppe, the British launched an attack codenamed Operation Agreement (sometimes mistakenly referred to as Operation Daffodil) against Tobruk, which was very ineptly executed and ended up being an unmitigated disaster. The attacking amphibious forces consisted of about 400 Royal Marines of the 11th Battalion and 180 Argyll and Sutherland Highlanders, supported by about 150 Special Air Service soldiers attacking from the landward desert side. These forces were supported by one cruiser, two destroyers, 17 motor torpedo boats (MTBs), one submarine and a number of motor launches and landing craft. During the early morning hours of 14 September, the destroyers HMS *Zulu* and HMS *Sikh* landed their troops in the wrong place, and although the British managed to capture one of the Italian 152mm coastal gun positions during the initial phase of the attack, the position was soon retaken by counterattacking Italian marines of the San Marco battalion. German forces engaged the northern and western landing parties, while the Italians dealt with the British who landed further south and east. At the same time German shore batteries attacked and sank HMS *Sikh* in the harbor; HMS *Zulu* was also subsequently sunk. The light antiaircraft cruiser HMS *Coventry*, also supporting the action, was badly damaged by German JU-87 dive bombers and later sank. Several of the MTBs and launches were sunk by German and Italian aircraft as well as Italian MTBs. The British had badly underestimated the capabilities of the defending Italian and German forces, who reacted swiftly, violently and very effectively. Like the earlier raid on Dieppe in which almost 60 percent of the landing forces and one destroyer and some 550 naval personnel were lost, British losses incurred during the failed Tobruk raid were painfully high, amounting to almost 300 killed and 576 captured, against very light Italian and German losses.

A group of British/ Commonwealth prisoners, reflecting the varied composition of British forces in the desert. The man sitting in the foreground is likely from the French colonial forces and the soldier facing the camera in the upper right of the photo may be Indian. (USSME)

In a related engagement codenamed Operation Nicety on 16 September a British column staging out of Kufra Oasis attacked the 500-man Italian garrison at Gialo. The Italians had been fore-warned of the attack through captured enemy documents and were prepared to meet the attacking force, which consisted of some 200 men aboard several vehicles and who nevertheless managed to penetrate some of the defenses. The British failed to occupy the oasis completely, but surrounded it and brought it under artillery fire, although they were themselves were under heavy attack by Italian and German aircraft.

The next day, Marshal Ugo Cavallero arrived in Libya and ordered that the oasis be cleared of the British, but it took until 19 September for a relief force to be properly organized. The force, which left from Agedabia, consisted of the 'Pavia's 35th Infantry Regiment, two artillery groups and a self-propelled battery, three 20mm batteries, a platoon of M14/41 tanks, a squadron of the 'Monferrato' with 21 armoured cars, 138 trucks, four ambulances and four water tankers. By 21 September the column had covered the 220 kilometers (137 miles) to Gialo and, as it neared the oasis, the British force disengaged without further action.

Another brief action occurred on 30 September when, as part of Operation Braganza three battalions of the 131st Brigade, of the Queen's Royal Regiment, 44th Infantry Division attacked the 'Folgore' positions near Deir el Munassib. The British had trained extensively for the attack, including a dry run, and believed the positions were held by elements of 'Trieste', unaware that they would face the 'Folgore' instead. At 0415, while an earth-shattering barrage was being laid down upon the Italian positions by nine artillery regiments, the British infantry began to advance. The barrage fell upon the trenches of the IX Battalion, destroying some of the gun positions. However,

An M13/40 tank in the desert in March 1942. The crew are wearing the leather coat issued to tank crews. The crew have also piled some of their kit, rather than the oft-seen sandbags, on the front glacis. (Massimiliano Afiero)

the Italian paratroopers, who had come through the barrage, horrific as it was, relatively unscathed, reacted energetically with machine gun and mortar fire and, along with the Ramcke' brigade's Hübner battalion, broke up the British attack. 'Folgore' claims to have lost 45 men in the engagement, including six officers, while accounts vary as to the number of British casualties, but there seem to have been about 200 British dead and wounded and 150 prisoners.

For the rest of September and most of October, both sides took time to reorganize and improve their respective supply situations. This was manifestly easier for the British than it was for the Axis who had to contend with an overextended supply line and a precarious replacement situation, while the British had no lengthy supply line to concern them and were receiving ever-increasing amounts of supplies from the Americans.

In late October the Germans had 249 tanks and the Italian XX Corps had a total of 278 M13/M14 tanks and 20 L6/40 light tanks; 'Ariete' had 129 mediums, 'Littorio' had 115 mediums and 20 light, and 'Trieste' had a battalion with 34 medium tanks. Facing them were 1,029 tanks, among them 252 Shermans and 170 Grants. Overall strength of *Panzerarmee Afrika* was about 54,000 Italian and 54,000 German troops, while the British could muster about 220,500 men.

Second Battle of El Alamein (23 October–11 November 1942)

Operation Lightfoot (23 October–29 October 1942)
On the eve of the second battle of El Alamein, the northern sector from the sea to El Mireir consisted of the Italian XXI Corps, which was comprised of the 7th *Bersaglieri* Regiment, the 'Trento' infantry division, the 'Bologna' infantry division, the German *164.leichte-Division* and two battalions of the Ramcke parachute brigade. The second echelon consisted of the Italian 'Littorio' armoured division with the LI Tank Battalion (with M13/40 tanks), the IV and XII medium tank battalions (with M14/41 tanks), the DLIV and DLVI self-propelled groups, the XXI, XXII and XXXVI *Bersaglieri* battalions, a 75/27 group, a 100/17 group, an antiaircraft/antitank group with German 88mm guns (a total of 116 medium tanks, 18 75/18 SP guns, ten German 88mm guns, two war booty 25-pdrs, 12 75/27 guns, eight 100/17 howitzers and ten 20mm guns) and the German *15.Panzer-Division*. To the south, between El Mireir and Qaret el Himeimat, was the Italian X Corps, which was comprised of the 'Brescia' infantry division (interestingly, the commander's name was Brunetto Brunetti and his chief of staff was named Bruno Bruno), the 'Folgore' parachute division, the 'Pavia' infantry division and two battalions of the German Ramcke parachute brigade. Corps troops consisted of two battalions of the 9th *Bersaglieri* Regiment, the XXXI Sapper Battalion and two artillery groups. The second echelon consisted of the Italian 'Ariete' armoured division and the German *21.Panzer-Division*. Army reserve was comprised of the German *90.leichte-Division* and the Italian 'Trieste' infantry division as well as a few smaller Italian and German units.

Facing the Italo–German forces were, from north to south, British XXX Corps, with the 9th Australian Infantry Division, 51st Highland Division, 2nd New Zealand Division, 1st South African Division and 4th Indian Division; south of El Ruweisat was British XIII Corps, with the 50th Division, 44th Division and a Free French Brigade. In second echelon, in the XXX Corps sector were the 1st Armoured Brigade and the 10th Armoured Brigade, and in the southern sector, behind XIII Corps was the 7th Armoured Division.

It was at this point that Montgomery decided that, rather than attacking in the south and against the Italo–German armoured forces as had normally been the case in the past, he would concentrate his effort in the north, focusing primarily on the weaker Italian infantry divisions, depriving the Axis of their static defense divisions, thus leaving the mobile divisions open to attack. This was the indirect approach suggested earlier by Auchinleck and Dorman-Smith.

These M4A1 Shermans belong to C Squadron, Queen's Bays. The M4A1 made its initial appearance in British hands in the desert just in time for the final battle of El Alamein. The M4A1 supplied by the US was characterized by its one-piece cast upper hull, three-piece bolted transmission housing and early-style M3 bogie truck. Its 75mm gun mounted in a turret was a significant improvement over the earlier M3 Grant medium and provided a decisive edge over most of the German and Italian armour during the October/November battles. (TMB 3240.B2)

On 23 October British Operation Lightfoot kicked off. In the northern sector, the positions held by the German *164.leichte-Division* and the Italian infantry divisions of X and XXI Corps came under heavy attack. The sector defended by the 12,000 men of 'Trento' and the German *164.leichte-Division* was attacked by a British force numbering some 70,000 men supported by 600 tanks. The 51st Highland Division advanced against 'Trento' north of Kidney Ridge but was stopped by heavy fire from 'Trento's 46th Artillery Regiment, although some infantry elements of 'Trento' were overrun and fell back. From 23 to 30 October the 'Trento' field hospital, which had been to the rear of the lines that had been hit so hard, suddenly found itself in the heart of the battle, and for eight days managed to continue to function efficiently and effectively as a hospital, tending to not only Italians and Germans, but also caring for British, Australians, New Zealanders, Indians, and whoever else happened to be swept along by the fighting in the area. It was in constant danger, as artillery had been dug in close to it and counterbattery fire, apparently unaware of the hospital's existence despite the large red crosses emblazoned on the tents, came uncomfortably close to the hospital tents. Likewise, at one point, a tank duel occurred in the immediate vicinity, but the overworked and exhausted medical staff still were able to work professionally and imperturbably amid the chaos and danger.

Further south, in the Ruweisat Ridge area, 'Bologna' and 'Brescia' were attacked by the 2nd New Zealand, 1st South African and 4th Indian divisions, but the Italian positions held against the onslaught. Between 23 and 25 October, 'Littorio', operating in concert with *15.Panzer-Division*, was also heavily engaged, losing 13 medium tanks, one 75/18 SP, two 100/17 howitzers, two 75/27 guns and three 88mm guns. Still further south were the 'Pavia' infantry division and the 'Folgore' parachute division. The latter was particularly well prepared along the Deir Alinda–Deir el Munassib–Qaret el Himeimat–Naqb Rala line, occupying a front of about 15 kilometers (9 miles). The total force of about 5,000, of which about 4,000 were paratroopers, organized the defense as a series of strongpoints surrounded by minefields. The strongpoints were mutually supporting, and each had the capability to cover a 360-degree field of fire. The right flank of the line butted up against the Qattara Depression. The 'Folgore' dispositions from north to south consisted of the 187th Regiment (Lieutenant Colonel Alberto Bechi Luserna), the two-battalion *Raggruppamento Ruspoli* (Lieutenant Colonel Marescotti Ruspoli), and the 186th Regiment (Lieutenant Colonel Pietro Tantillo).

Luserna, the commander of the 187th, was somewhat of a Renaissance man: he came from a distinguished family, spoke perfect English, was a charismatic leader well-liked by his men, and was described as: 'A man who is good in the assault, good with beautiful women, good at a gala court event, and good at working on volumes in a library.' In a somewhat bizarre quirk of history, Marescotti Ruspoli and his older brother Costantino, both officers serving with 'Folgore' and who would be killed in action only two days apart, were both born in New York City where they lived for some years before setting foot in Italy with their parents, who had decided to return to Italy.

Reinforcing the division, which had only two 47/32 groups of its own, were one 75/27 group of 1 Articelere 'Brescia', one 100/17 group of 'Trieste', one 88/55 group and one 90/53 group from 'Ariete', one mixed German group, and two groups from 'Pavia'. Facing them were the British 55th Division, 4th Armoured Brigade, 44th Division, 7th Armoured Division and the Free French brigade.

The main British attack on the night of 23 October, beginning with an intense artillery barrage, was directed against the 'Folgore' positions between Deir el Munassib to the north and Qaret el Himemat to the south. However, at about 2230, Italian artillery zeroed in on the British 7th Queen's Battalion in its assembly area and wrought havoc upon the troops. Nevertheless, the British rallied and began to move forward. The first of the 'Folgore's companies to be attacked on 23 October were the 6th/II under Marengo di Moriondo, the VIII/185 sappers and the 19th/VII under Alfonso Salerno. They defended themselves furiously, although suffering heavy losses. Some positions were overrun by tanks, and some were abandoned after heavy fighting. The 12th/V led by Captain Marco Cristofori, attacked following a massive artillery preparation and repulsed the attackers. Of the 90 men of Moriondo's company, only 15 survived the onslaught, and of those,

Two tanks of the 'Littorio' division prior to the Alamein battles in 1942. Although barely legible in the photograph, the lead tank has the 'Littorio' division's motto '*a colpo sicuro*' ('One shot, one kill') painted on the upper portion of the gun mantlet. (USSME)

most were wounded and led back to safer positions by Lieutenant De Tura. The 'Folgore' positions held despite their light armament and the odds against them, while the Queen's Battalion suffered 76 killed or missing and 104 wounded. Among the 'Folgore' officers killed was Lieutenant Colonel Marescotti Ruspoli, the *raggruppamento* commander, who fell while leading a counterattack.

Meanwhile, down at the southern end of the line, at the Naqb Rala plateau, the V Battalion of 'Folgore', under Major Giuseppe Izzo, was holding a 7-kilometer (4-mile) stretch of the line with about 300 paratroopers. V Battalion consisted mainly of men who formerly had been *alpini* – the tough, no-nonsense alpine troops recruited from the mountain folk along Italy's northern alpine arc. Guessing that the enemy would attack from the south, Izzo put together a rag-tag quick reaction force of about 90 clerks, cooks and assorted other personnel 'borrowed' from his three line companies, which he somewhat tongue-in-cheek designated as his '*massa di manovra*' ('maneuver mass'). Shortly after midnight, these positions were attacked by Free French forces.

[Parenthetically, the Free French, who were tough and accustomed to hard fighting, had serious misgivings about the feasibility of the operation: French General Pierre-Marie Koenig had voiced his well-founded and well-reasoned misgivings to British Lieutenant General Brian Horrocks, who in September 1944 would ignore similar warnings from another foreign general, the Pole Sosabowski, but was overruled.]

The French accordingly attacked and made some initial progress, but overall, their attack was uncoordinated and not properly supported by artillery once it had begun. The paratroopers engaged in one of their somewhat unusual tactics, letting the French get into their positions, whereupon they rallied in small groups of three or four men, assaulting the French with automatic weapons, bayonets and prodigious numbers of hand grenades. At the end of furious fighting, the French withdrew somewhat precipitously, having suffered some 190 casualties killed or taken prisoner, as well as having lost several vehicles and antitank guns to Italian mortar and artillery fire. This had also cost the Italians dearly; of Izzo's quick-reaction force of 90, 70 lay dead or wounded on the sand, with Izzo himself being wounded by a bullet in the knee.

On 25 October 'Littorio' and 'Trento' engaged in bloody fighting against the 2nd Armoured Brigade and the 9th Australian Division, supported by 7 British Motor Brigade. Major Giuseppe Beja of 'Trento' proved to be a particularly stubborn infantry officer who rallied as many survivors as he could in order to continue fighting despite the odds. German armour, which was supposed to act in concert with 'Littorio', showed up late, enabling the British to concentrate their fire on 'Littorio', including the use of phosphorous shells, which came as a disconcerting surprise to the Italians. The attacking enemy forces were thrown back, due more to the bravery of the Italian tankers than to the effectiveness of their 47/32 guns. 'Ariete's X Battalion along with DLII self-propelled group were transferred north while 'Littorio' threw itself against the enemy. 'Littorio's IV Battalion fought doggedly and valiantly against the 10th Armoured Division, and lost two company commanders, 40 M14/41 tanks, three 75/18 SP guns, one 88mm gun and one 100/17 howitzer as well as sustaining a high casualty rate; the DLVI Gruppo claimed the destruction of 12 enemy tanks and 19 trucks. The XII Battalion helped stabilize the situation at Kidney Ridge and on the morning of 26 October it and *15.Panzer-Division* launched a counterattack, with support of all of the army-level artillery assets, slowly regaining territory and salvaging the situation at Kidney Ridge, but at the price of 20 M14s (some of which were retrieved and subsequently repaired), six 75/18 SP guns and 60 personnel lost. The British lost 24 Sherman tanks, mainly to fire from antitank guns. *DLIV Gruppo* took part in several counterattacks on 26 October supporting first the XII and then the IV tank battalions against the 1st South African Infantry Division and 2nd New Zealand Division. In a separate action, the Italians fended off an attack against the German 382 Battalion; the 2nd Battery of the DLVI SP group destroyed five enemy tanks, 11 trucks and three antitank guns. During the night, an understrength company of the German 115th Schützen Regiment was overrun and two platoons of IV Tank Battalion intervened, pushing past the trenches that had been held by the 'Trento' infantry division, losing two tanks to mines.

A company of M13/40 tanks on the move around the time of the battle of Alam Halfa, August 1942.
(Massimiliano Afiero)

On 26 October Australian forces occupied Point 28, some ten miles from the coast, giving the British the opportunity to move towards the mosque at Sidi el Rahman and turn the Italo–German lines. It was thus a key point in the battle. Accordingly, Italian XXI Corps ordered the 7th *Bersaglieri* Regiment's Colonel Nicola Straziota to retake the hill. Straziota was known as a resourceful officer who asked few questions and was used to resolving problems rather than complaining about them. The order from corps headquarters for Straziota to personally lead the attack was superfluous: he knew his job, his place and his duty. The battalion chosen for the action was the XI, led by Captain Bernardo Pasqualini, a recalled officer who was more than 50 years old, but described as morally and physically in his 20s.

The next day, the battalion began its attack against stiff resistance as well as artillery fire and air attack, resulting in many killed and wounded. As night fell the decimated battalion resumed its attack and managed to take the western side of Point 28, all at a cost of 50 killed and 150 wounded out of the initial force of 450 men. These losses added further to the horrific casualty toll suffered by the 7th *Bersaglieri* since its landing in North Africa some 16 months earlier; only eight of the 77 officers and about 130 of the 1,400 NCOs and *Bersaglieri* who had begun the campaign were left of the original group. The remnants of the battalion, along with the *IV Gruppo* of 'Trento's 46th Artillery Regiment, assumed defensive positions. Point 28 was never completely retaken, even though the German *90.leichte-Division* mounted its own attack from the south.

During the night of 26 October, the British focused their efforts against the 'Folgore' salient at Deir el Munassib. Following the usual heavy preparatory artillery fire, at 2200, British infantry attacked in three columns, the first consisting of the Green Howards supported by armoured cars, the second by Free French forces and the third by the Queen's Own Royal West Kent Regiment supported by a battalion of tanks from the 4th Hussars. By 2300, the Italians were facing threats from all sides, but a series of counterattacks stabilized the situation in the areas held by the companies under Cristofori and Simoni, but the positions held by 67 paratroopers in the center,

Ammunition exploding inside this M13/40 of the 'Littorio' division blew the turret top off and dislocated it. (Nicola Pignato)

under Captain Ruspoli, was overwhelmed at around 0400, on 27 October. Captain Ruspoli was killed, two days after the death of his younger brother Marescotti Ruspoli. At around 0500, concentrated Italian artillery fire enabled the few survivors from that position to withdraw and the British attack was stalled. British bodies littered the area in front of the positions held by the II, IV, VII and VIII parachute battalions. One isolated outpost under Lieutenant Renato Mascarin continued to hold out against British tanks. When invited to surrender by the British, Mascarin replied in the Milanese dialect, '*Andè sulla forca*' ('Go hang yourself') and in an act of sheer desperation, armed only with a paratrooper's fighting knife, jumped on the glacis of a tank; he slipped from the glacis and was run over by the tank. During the period of the initial British onslaught from 23 to 26 October the Italians lost 1,599 killed, wounded or missing, while the Germans lost 1,664.

On 27 October fighting further intensified and in the late afternoon the two German panzer divisions, along with 'Littorio' and the IX Tank Battalion and DLII self-propelled group of 'Ariete' counterattacked the strongly held enemy positions at Deir el Murra, between minefields L and J, which caused heavy Italian losses and the subsequent Italian withdrawal. In front of Point 34, 2 Battery/DLIV Group of 'Littorio', while supporting XII Tank Battalion, destroyed eight Shermans but lost two vehicles and the battery's commander. During the night 2 Battery managed to disengage along with the tanks of IV Battalion, and at dawn came upon positions held by the 88/55 group of 'Littorio', freeing the artillerymen from encirclement. The paired German *164.leichte-Division* and Italian 'Trento' had also suffered heavily; III Battalion of the German 382 Infantry Regiment was down to one officer and ten men, while the 62nd Infantry Regiment of 'Trento' could muster only 150 men. That same day the Axis command decided to shift *21.Panzer* and 'Ariete' from the northern part of the front, but it was too late to change the course of the battle. At the beginning of the battle, 'Ariete' had fielded 111 tanks and 12 self-propelled guns in three formations, the strongest of which defended the rear of the 'Brescia' infantry division, and which

Despite heavy Axis losses during the winter battles of 1942, the fighting was not all one-sided, as witnessed by this group of British prisoners. (USSME)

A pair of M13/40 tanks in November 1942, at the time of Second Alamein. The tank in the foreground is second or third series version, as evidenced by the abbreviated fender, while the tank in the background appears to have the full-length fender of the earlier model M13/40 and later M14/41. The open side hatch door appears to be painted in grey-green. Normally this door was painted to match the exterior color of the tank, indicating that the tank's original color had been grey-green. (Massimiliano Afiero)

ended up being the last obstacle between Deir el Murra and Bir el Abd. On 27 and 28 October 'Littorio', which had remained engaged in furious fighting, lost a total of another 30 tanks, two 75/18 SP guns and six 88mm guns and on 1 November, it was down to 30 tanks, 15 75/18 SP guns, ten 75/27 guns, seven 100/17 howitzers, two 88mm guns and five 20mm guns.

On 28 October IX Battalion and DLII Group of 'Ariete', as well as IV Battalion of 'Littorio', were wiped out. At El Whiska, the DLIV Group destroyed about 20 enemy tanks, but at the end of the fighting was left with only four operational SPs. That same day, the 1st Battery of 'Littorio's *DLVI Gruppo* under Captain Filippo Sciortino, supported by German infantry, destroyed several enemy vehicles and took about 350 British prisoners. Also on the same day, in order to alleviate the shortage of water, water bowsers from 'Littorio' made it to Uadi Nagamish, a small oasis with good water about 22 kilometers (14 miles) west of Mersa Matruh. A few trucks had been filled with water when a patrol of ten British armed trucks showed up and captured the Italians. As soon as he learned of this, General Bitossi called the chief of the 'Littorio' division's 85th Royal Carabinieri detachment, Lieutenant Umberto Musolino (a native of Calabria in southern Italy, a region known for its particularly stubborn people) and said: 'Fix this situation straightaway. Take half a company of tanks.' Musolino left with the tanks, freed the Italians and took some British prisoners, putting the rest to flight.

By 29 October after repeated attacks against the positions held by the 'Folgore' paratroopers, the British ceased further action against the Italians in that sector. The attacks had cost the British the loss of 69 tanks, about 600 dead and 197 prisoners. The Italians reported losses of about 375 killed and 225 wounded. Of the 12 'Folgore' infantry battalion and artillery group commanders that were on the line in July, by late October, eight had been killed and two wounded. The 'Folgore' had given the British a hard time, and its reputation was such, that several prisoners confessed that all things considered, it was preferable to fight against the Germans.

After having buried their own dead, in an act of human compassion an Italian chaplain, along with four paratroopers, ventured out in the evening to collect and bury the enemy dead that were close by. This group was spotted by the British, who sent out an armed patrol to determine what the movement on the Italian side was about. The patrol approached the Italian party cautiously and asked the chaplain what they were doing. The chaplain responded that they were burying the British dead, and that he had collected their identity discs to turn over to the British so that the families of the deceased could be informed. The chaplain then told the officer that he intended to resume his work the next night; the officer said that he would report the activity to his higher headquarters. Allegedly, when Montgomery heard of the incident, he gave orders that the Italians should not be permitted to resume their work, thus leaving the remaining British bodies to be left where they were, eventually to be covered by the desert sand.

On the morning of 29 October, after assessing the progression of the battle, Rommel decided to pull back to the position at Fuqa before British pressure became too great to counter. Accordingly, on 30 October Rommel made an explicit request to *Comando Supremo* for the temporary loan of 1,500 trucks and the necessary fuel for them in order to withdraw the Italian infantry of X Corps, as well as the Ramcke parachute brigade, from the southern end of the line. Rather predictably, the request was not acted upon because the Italian high command, which wanted Rommel to hold the line at El Alamein, feared that if it gave Rommel the trucks, he would not stop at Fuqa but would keep on retreating.

On the night of 30 October *21.Panzer-Division* began to be relieved by 'Trieste' motorized division in the Kidney Ridge area. This move was a reflection of Rommel's desire to save as many of his German tank forces as possible, sacrificing the Italian infantry in the process. On 31 October the remnants of the 61st Infantry Regiment under Captain Ruggierio and the 62nd Infantry Regiment under the redoubtable Major Beja of the 'Trento' division, organized themselves as best they could and continued to fight.

A captured British 25-pdr being put to good use against its former owners. The 'Trento' division formed a 12-gun battalion equipped with 25-pdrs. (Damiele Guglielmi)

Operation Supercharge (2 November–11 November 1942)

British Operation Supercharge began on 2 November. The British had about 900 tanks, many of them Shermans and Grants, while the Germans had 90, and the Italians, surprisingly in better shape, had 189, making an Axis total of about 280 tanks, or less than a third of the British number.

In some respects, Operation Supercharge was a repeat of Wavell's Operation Compass some 23 months earlier: in both instances, the British staged out of Egypt and pushed the Italians (as well as the Germans in the latter operation) unrelentingly to the west. The similarity ends there, however, as there were significant differences between the two operations. Whereas Compass had pitted a small, highly mobile British force against a vastly superior Italo–German force that was almost completely immobile, Supercharge saw a much larger and incomparably better equipped force face off against German and Italian forces, which this time included a fair proportion of experienced Italian mobile forces. Once the Germans had taken the lead in extricating their own forces, all of which were mobile, they left the abandoned Italians even more greatly outnumbered to face the British onslaught. The end-result for the Italians was just as catastrophic as Compass had been: seven divisions ('Ariete' and 'Littorio' armoured, 'Trento' motorized, 'Folgore' parachute, and 'Brescia', 'Bologna' and 'Pavia' infantry) were either completely destroyed, captured, or rendered combat ineffective, but this time, although some fresh divisions were being shipped in from Italy, there were no other divisions in situ in Libya to deploy against the British.

The morning of 2 November brought with it the Battle of Tel el Aqqaqir, which would become the last great tank battle in the Egyptian desert. The Italo–German tank force of 100 tanks (35 German and on the Italian side 38, scraped together from the remnants of 'Littorio's XII and LI tank battalions, and the 27 remaining tanks of XI Tank Battalion of 'Trieste') was attacked by the British 9th Armoured Brigade, which had a mix of 130 Sherman, Grant and Crusader tanks. Both sides suffered heavily during the engagement. Unable to stand up against the 75mm guns that armed the Shermans and Grants they were pitted against, the 'Littorio' and 'Trieste' tanks were knocked out one by one. Among the tank commanders who were killed during the fighting

Part of a battery of M41 75/18 self-propelled guns at the time of the Second Battle of El Alamein in November 1942. By this time, the SP groups were severely depleted from losses suffered during combat operations. One Italian SP battery commander likened the Italian SP guns to fleas compared to the size of the Shermans but added that they were fleas with a terrible bite that gave no quarter. (Massimiliano Afiero)

was Captain Vittorio Bulgarelli of the XI Tank Battalion, the same officer who as a lieutenant in April 1941 had gone into an attack against Tobruk with his tank sporting female undergarments from its antenna. On the evening of 2 November all that remained of 'Littorio' were two motorized *Bersaglieri* companies and about 20 tanks. Its IV Battalion was reduced to only two tanks which, under Lieutenant Fazio Marchegiani, were sent off to join the one remaining tank company of *15.Panzer-Division*. The same day, the 65th Infantry Regiment of 'Trieste' was surrounded and overwhelmed by the 133rd Motor Brigade, while its sister regiment, the 66th, at the southern end of the line, barely managed to hold on. The British were reported to have lost 75 of their 94 Shermans, mainly to the Axis antitank screen.

On the afternoon of 2 November Rommel decided to begin to withdraw the Italian infantry divisions and the German *164.leichte-Division* to Fuqa, about 90 kilometers (56 miles) to the rear of the present line, and move 'Ariete', once again subordinate to XX Corps, to the north. This left the southern sector with 'Folgore', 'Brescia' and 'Pavia' divisions, with a reserve consisting of the *Gruppo Squadroni 'Nizza Cavalleria'*, V *Bersaglieri* Battalion (truck-borne) and II Antitank Battalion of 8th *Bersaglieri* Regiment and two batteries of the 132nd Artillery Regiment (one 75/27 and one 105/28). The Italian and German motorized and armoured divisions were to contain and absorb British pressure, allowing the infantry divisions to break contact and withdraw on foot or aboard any trucks that could be spared. The motorized and armoured forces were to subsequently pull back as well, but very slowly.

At 1445 on 2 November 'Ariete' was ordered to move north and to assemble by 0600 on 3 November in the Deir el Murra area in order to participate in the decisive battle. Up until that time, during the first part of the British offensive, 'Ariete' had not been heavily committed. In the south its artillery groups (90/53, 88/55 and 105/28) had provided effective fire support against the British 7th Armoured Division. Only one tactical group consisting of the IX Tank Battalion and DLII 75/18 self-propelled group had been engaged on 27 and 28 October, in furious fighting alongside German armoured units which were counterattacking. The division was thus essentially intact with 111 tanks of the 132nd Tank Regiment and 12 75/18 SP guns of the 132nd Artillery Regiment. The order of battle at the time was: 8th *Bersaglieri* Regiment (HQ and XII truck-borne battalion); 132nd Tank Regiment (HQ, IX, X and XII tank battalions with 111 medium tanks); 132nd Artillery Regiment (HQ, two 75/18 SP groups with 12 guns, I and II *Gruppi* 75/27

The torpedo boat *Partenope* in summer of 1942. *Partenope* was part of the escort for the tanker *Proserpina* and freighter *Tergestea*, both of which were carrying supplies desperately needed by *Panzerarmee Afrika* but were sunk by British air attacks on 26 October 1942. (Erminio Bagnasco collection via Maurizio Brescia)

totaling three batteries, and a mixed group with one 105/28 battery, two 90/53 batteries and one 88/55 battery) and service units. From its rear echelon positions in the south between Qaret el Khadim and Hiviset Busala, on the evening of 2 November 'Ariete', in combat formation with XIII Battalion leading, followed by IX and X battalions, began its march to the north to meet the enemy. Morale within the division was very high. 'Ariete' was to take up positions on the right flank of what was left of 'Littorio' and 'Trieste' at Tel el Aqqaqir; the reconstituted Italian XX Corps would represent the center of the Axis line, with DAK and X Corps to the north and XXI Corps to the south. Axis infantry would then pull back to Fuqa.

During the night of 2/3 November the infantry divisions broke off contact and began to withdraw to the west as far as the area 15 kilometers (9 miles) east of El Daba. The withdrawal, especially in the central and southern sectors went unnoticed by the British. Unfortunately, however, it was proceeding very slowly because of the lack of trucks, forcing the soldiers to pull back on foot and haul their heavy weapons and ammunition themselves by hand. Despite these problems, on the morning of 3 November the divisions had established new positions.

On the night of 3 November 'Ariete' reached the Pass for Cars position. Orders from De Stefanis, the XX Corps commander, were to 'advance north-northeast for about 35 kilometers (22 miles), establish a defensive barrier facing east between Alam Burt Sabai el Gherbi and Deir el Beida to protect our infantry divisions as they withdraw'. 'Ariete' reached the assigned positions and deployed in a defensive posture: 8th *Bersaglieri* organized forward defensive strongpoints, while the armoured maneuver element was behind them and the 132nd Artillery Regiment was in the area east of Deir el Murra.

At 2300 on 2 November 'Folgore' received orders to fall back to Gebel Kalakh, some 25 kilometers (15.5 miles) to the rear. This was a bitter pill to swallow for the paratroopers who had managed to stave off greatly superior enemy forces and still retained their will to fight. They were obliged to pull out of their positions as quietly as possible before dawn. All equipment that might be useful to the enemy but that could not be taken with them because of a lack of transport assets was destroyed; everything else, including antitank guns, was carried on their shoulders or dragged across the sandy ground. By daylight on 3 November the 3,000 or so remaining paratroopers had reached their new positions and begun to dig in. Providentially, three water bowsers showed up,

A battery of captured British 25-pdrs, complete with their prime movers and limbers, being employed by the 'Folgore' division in late 1942. (Luca Massacci)

which were able to provide enough water for at least another day. However, 'Folgore' was now isolated from the rest of the army. The emaciated, exhausted and thirsty men cleaned their weapons and prepared to hold out to the end. For the next few days, the paratroopers continued to bear the brunt of heavy shelling, unable to respond in kind

As of 1300 on 3 November German infantry units were assembling at positions at Sidi Abd el Rahman–Tell el Mansfra–Deir el Murra. XXI Corps and 'Trieste' division (now down to only its 66th Infantry Regiment and three groups of the 21st Artillery Regiment) completed their withdrawal to Qaret el Aguwat–Sid Aqaba. X Corps, not pressed by the enemy, had completed its initial withdrawal move and was resuming its retirement to Gebel Kalakh–Red Track (Pista Rossa)–Ariete Track–Tonnen Pista–Deir el Harra. Meanwhile, DAK was deployed in a concave semicircle in front of enemy positions at Tell el Aqqaqir and 'Ariete' was further to the southeast with its left flank in contact with *15.Panzer-Division* elements. 'Bologna' pulled out of its positions ahead of schedule, obliging 'Ariete' to plug the gap north of Deir el Qatani.

At 1330 on 3 November Hitler ordered all forces to stand fast and not to pull back. This order threw everything into confusion and 30 hours of disorientation and inactivity followed. Most units stopped where they were and tried to establish contact with adjacent units and patch together a rudimentary defense, but some, like 'Bologna', which had already managed to make its way somewhat to the west, attempted to turn back in their tracks in order to reach the defensive positions that were being organized. It is arguable if Hitler's order to stand fast, while possibly applicable to the Germans, should have been paid any heed to by the Italians, who were not bound by any clear chain of command that had Hitler overriding the Italian Supreme Command. The irony is that, despite Hitler's order, it was the German divisions that disengaged from combat before the Italians did, while the Italians, as ordered by Rommel, were the ones who stood, fought, sacrificed themselves or were forced to surrender because they were overrun by the British, paying a much higher price than the Germans

On the evening of 3 November Rommel ordered XX Corps to redeploy by dawn on 4 November immediately west and southwest of Deir el Murra. 'Ariete', deploying between that location and Bir el Abd was to maintain contact with *15.Panzer-Division* on its left (at Tell el Mansfra) and on its right with XXI Corps ('Trento' and 'Bologna' divisions). The order specified that 'the line must be held and defended to the last and could not be abandoned without explicit orders from Rommel'.

This 75/18 self-propelled gun has just been offloaded from a trailer in late 1942. Note the inverted triangle tactical sign on the right rear of the hull and on the casemate, which identifies it as belonging to the 1st Battery. A couple of FIAT 508 CM staff cars are in the background. (USSME)

At 0230 on 4 November the British attacked along three axes: Sidi Abd el Rahman, Tell el Aqqaqir and Alam Burt Sabai and Gergi-Bir el Abd. The Axis antitank screen initially held the attacking forces in check, but the Italo–German armour force by this time was severely depleted, consisting of only 24 German panzers and 17 M14s for 'Littorio', while 'Ariete' was able to muster about 100 M14s. Rommel pulled the German armour back on the plain of Tell el Mansfra.

During this general timeframe, in response to pleas from Rommel and from the Italians who needed transportation in order to be able to disengage effectively, Delease (*Delegazione Africa Settentionale*, the liaison element between the *Armata Corazzata Italo–Tedesca* and the *Comando Supremo* in Rome) promised to send 1,000 trucks, which according to one source was later scaled down to 195, of which only 19 and their trailers reached the front. The Delease diary, however, reflects the promise of 500 heavy trucks, but was able to scrape up only 150, a number capable of transporting 3,000 troops and their equipment. The column set off for X Corps from El Daba on the afternoon of 3 November but was reduced to about 100 trucks by enemy air attacks, with only around 15 ultimately reaching their destination. This did nothing to alleviate the plight of the non-motorized divisions.

A battery of M40 75/18 self-propelled guns of the V (later renamed '*DLI Gruppo*') of the 132nd Artillery Regiment, 'Ariete' division, deployed in the desert. (USSME)

'Ariete' sought to reestablish a solid front by linking up with *15.Panzer*, but because of enemy infiltration on its left, it was cut off from the forces to its north. There was also a serious threat of being cut off from XXI Corps to the south. To prevent the British from seizing the ridge that dominated Deir el Murra, on the morning of 4 November the bulk of the armour was shifted to the east-northeast. Facing east, IX Tank Battalion and *DLI Gruppo* were on the left, X Tank Battalion and *DLII Gruppo* were in the center and the XII *Bersaglieri* Battalion with I and II artillery groups were on the right; the XIII Tank Battalion was in the second echelon, approaching Point 65 (Bir el Abd) and a mixed artillery group consisting of one 105/28 battery, two 90/53 batteries and one 88/55 battery were in a central sector that could cover all of the divisional sector by fire.

The battle soon began with 'Ariete' facing the British 22nd Armoured Brigade and 4th Light Armoured Brigade, and no one gave way. It was a battle of M14s against Shermans and British artillery. The Italians fought bravely and stubbornly, but the British tanks and defiladed artillery took an inexorable toll. British armour moved to the south, threatening the right flank of 'Ariete's deployment. The British move was briefly halted by a counterattack by X Battalion and *DLI Gruppo*, supported by desperate fire from 75/27, 88/55 and 105/28 groups.

Around 1200, the full fury of British artillery fell upon 'Ariete'; the RAF joined in, bombing and strafing the Italians. Lieutenant Colonel Renzo Baldini's XIII Battalion was ordered to join in with X Battalion to parry the envelopment of the right flank. Unfortunately, Baldini, who was moving with the 4th and 6th companies, had chosen to advance along a route that was completely exposed to enemy artillery fire. Lieutenant Antonio Covajes, commanding the 5th Company, which was in reserve, realizing his battalion commander's mistake, tried to radio him to warn him, but his radio malfunctioned. Shortly after, a horrific artillery barrage destroyed a great number of the battalion's tanks. Lieutenant De Luca, commander of the 6th Company, assumed command

An Italian defensive position in Egypt, October 1942. The crew is manning a notoriously unreliable Breda Model 30 light machine gun, prone to jamming because its delicate mechanism suffered readily from the ever-present sand. (Massimiliano Afiero)

of what was left of the battalion and changed its route of advance. Meanwhile, Lieutenant Covajes gathered his five remaining tanks together, but soon the jerrycans on one of the tanks were hit and the tank began to burn and had to be abandoned. The British began to lay smoke to mask the movement of their tanks, which broke in between the Italian artillery and the maneuvering Italian tanks, threatening 'Ariete's flanks and rear. Once the British tanks had made it past the *Bersaglieri* they came up against the artillery groups including I and II 75/27 groups, XXXI 88/55 group, DI 90/53 group and XV 105/28 group, all of which kept firing at point-blank range until the Shermans gunned down the crews and overran the guns.

Around 1400, the British succeeded in infiltrating between XX Corps and XXI Corps to its south, cutting off 'Ariete' from the rest of the defensive line. Virtually the entire division, except for the XIII Tank Battalion, was surrounded and out of ammunition for its remaining guns. At about 1530, a final radio message was sent by 'Ariete': *'Carri armati nemici fatta irruzione a sud dell'Ariete. Con ciò Ariete accerchiata. Trovasi a 5 km. nord-ovest Bir el Abd. Carri Ariete combattano'* ('Enemy tanks have broken through south of 'Ariete'. With that 'Ariete' is surrounded. We are 5 kilometers northwest of Bir el Abd. 'Ariete' tanks are still in action). 'Ariete's two self-propelled groups, DLI and DLII, although suffering heavy losses, managed to hang on, fighting until nightfall. Of the battalions that had been destroyed, the butcher's bill was 268 officers and men killed, wounded and missing. Rommel had ordered 'Ariete' to hold its positions; it had done so, and in so doing, had given the Italian infantry divisions of X and XXI Corps a very brief respite and allowed the DAK and *90.leichte-Division* to withdraw to the west, thus saving the day for the Germans. As Barr notes: 'The often unjustly maligned Italian XX Corps had sacrificed itself and prevented the encirclement of the Afrika Korps.'

All that remained of the three XX Corps divisions on the evening of 4 November were the shattered remnants of the three divisions. 'Ariete' could muster its division headquarters, two motorized *Bersaglieri* companies and a few artillery pieces, which were scraped together to form two batteries, a 75/27 battery under Captain Rossetti and a 90/53 battery under Captain D'Angelo. The XIII Battalion of 'Ariete', having escaped destruction at Bir el Abd, was destroyed two days later, on 6 November, at Fuqa. 'Trieste' had its division headquarters, and the 66th Infantry Regiment with two battalions, each of only two companies. 'Littorio' was left with its division headquarters, two motorized *Bersaglieri* companies, two 100/17 guns and 20 M14 tanks.

While 'Ariete' was desperately fighting for survival, 'Bologna', on its flank, valiantly sought to provide it some protection, but soon became embroiled in trying to save its own skin, even going so far as to form up in the classic defensive square on the afternoon of 4 November, to deal with the enemy attacks. What was left of its 40th Infantry Regiment, pursued by British tanks, pulled back with all its weapons, but without a drop of water.

The commander of the 40th Regiment was 52-year-old Lieutenant Colonel Arrigo Dall'Olio, a native of Bologna, who was the quintessential 'wounded warrior'. He had suffered many serious wounds in battles during the First World War and as a result was missing one eye, which was covered by a black monocle, and had a deeply scarred and disfigured face, one arm that was intact but useless, and a leg that was held together by a metal brace. When Dall'Olio first reported to the rear area headquarters prior to assuming command of the 40th, someone asked him how he was going to manage. His answer was: 'That's my business. If I don't make the grade, they'll replace me, but I want to be judged by my actions on the front lines, not here, 700 kilometers from the front.' He was as tough and as principled as they come and remained combative until the very end.

The 40th, along with two battalions of the sister 39th Regiment, held out doggedly until 5 November; that morning, the Italians were completely surrounded by enemy tanks, which began to fire into their midst. The rank-and-file Neapolitan soldiers, who had marched for 50 hours without water and sleep, maintained their unit cohesion and did not question their orders. These were the same soldiers who a few months earlier had endured a grueling march on foot of over 600 kilometers (373 miles) from Ain el Gazala to El Alamein. In terms of sheer physical stamina, they could probably teach their much-better trained paratrooper cousins of the 'Folgore', as well as the Germans, a few lessons. Their will to resist was also undiminished, firing until their ammunition ran out completely late that afternoon. At that point, Dall'Olio sent his aide, Captain Gianni Giacolone and another officer, Captain Emilio Casalgrandi, across the lines in a captured British truck to discuss surrender terms. To the British colonel to whom he reported, Giacalone, a Sicilian who was normally known for his carefree attitude, said with a sulky glare: 'I would like to make it clear that we are no longer firing because we have run out of ammunition. It is for this reason only that we have ceased firing. However, we would still like to fight more than ever.' This battered, exhausted, starving group of swarthy southern Italians, led by what appeared to be the physical wreck of an officer, remained proud and defiant despite, or more likely because of, everything they had been through up to that point and, much like the 'Folgore' paratroopers, refused to raise their hands to acknowledge their defeat to the well-rested, well-fed, splendidly equipped and provisioned troops who faced them.

Shortly after Giacalone had delivered the message to the British, Dall'Olio met with the British colonel who had accepted his surrender. Taking notice of more than a dozen decorations on Dall'Olio's jacket, the British officer asked where he had earned them; his answer was: 'I earned most of them during the First World War, when you and I fought alongside each other.' The Brit then asked: 'And why then are you now my enemy?' Dall'Olio's answer, tinged with a bit of irony, was as follows:

> Right, and I would ask you the same question: Why are you my enemy? Look, I'm a soldier like you, so you should be able to understand me perfectly. I don't really care who is my ally and who is my enemy. I know only one thing: orders that I receive from above and that I have to pass on to those below me, as I did this morning, as long as I had a cartridge left.

On 5 November, General Brunetti, the 'Brescia' commander, tried to salvage what he could of his division by ordering his motorized elements (the artillery and supply sections) to pull back while the foot-borne infantry held fast, but at around 1500, the infantry was attacked by armoured forces and had to surrender. The motorized elements were caught about an hour later, meeting the same fate as the infantry.

Further south, on the evening of 4 November 'Folgore' and 'Pavia' began their retreat, making their way through the night with little difficulty. At 0900 the next morning, enemy armour struck the positions of IV and IX battalions of the 187th Parachute Regiment and II artillery group, acting as the rear guard, but the attack was beaten back by Italian artillery fire. Around 1100, the 'Folgore' divisional column reached Alam Gaballa, where they were attacked by British armoured cars, which were again driven back by Italian artillery. Meanwhile 'Pavia', following in the footsteps of the 'Folgore', ran into difficulty maintaining control over its units that were scattered over a rather large area of rough terrain. Causing even further trouble and confusion was the inadvertent intermingling of 'Folgore' units with those of 'Pavia'; it was not until 0230 at night on 5 November that the latter managed to muster most of its remaining men and begin its withdrawal in an orderly fashion.

Early on the morning of that day, the motorized elements of the division (basically, its artillery) reached Alam Gaballa, but at about 0800, the trailing elements and rear guard, consisting largely of the 27th Infantry Regiment and an artillery group, were attacked by armoured units at Deir el Nuss and forced to surrender. 'Pavia' then established contact with 'Folgore' to its south and began to set up a temporary defensive line prior to attempting to continue onward to Fuqa, which was 50 kilometers (31 miles) distant, by late 6 or early 7 November. 'Folgore' set out with some 3,000 men, mostly on foot (it had a total of about 20 vehicles at its disposal), while 'Pavia', slightly north of 'Folgore', divided its 1,500 men and 26 trucks into two columns. The motorized column, consisting of the division headquarters, artillery, antitank guns and ammunition, set off first, while the infantry regiments continued to plod along on foot. The pitiful remnants of the 'Folgore' para-troopers, many barefoot and all of them without water, continued to drag their heavy weapons by hand across the sand and shale. 'Folgore' made excruciatingly slow progress during the night, and by dawn on 6 November found that it was behind and further to the north of 'Pavia'.

Also at dawn on the 6th, the IV Battalion of 'Folgore', down to a few dozen men and acting as rear guard, was wiped out in the Deir el Serir area. The remnants of the division closed ranks around the 187th Regiment, but by 1400, there was no ammunition left. Lieutenant Colonel Luigi Camosso ordered the weapons to be destroyed and the division to surrender. There was no white flag, nor did the paratroopers raise their hands. At 1435 the same day, the British accorded the honor of arms to the 304 prisoners of the 'Folgore'. According to one Italian author, the British are said to have remarked that: 'The Italians fought very well, especially the 'Folgore' which held out beyond all possible hope.' On 7 November the British general commanding the 44th Division, Major General Ivor Hughes, located General Enrico Frattini, the commander of the 'Folgore' who had been taken prisoner. Hughes arranged a meeting with Frattini, in which he told him that he had heard that Frattini had been killed, but he was glad that that was not indeed the case. He then added that: 'In my long military career I have never encountered soldiers like those of the 'Folgore'.' Frattini answered simply by saying 'Grazie' ('Thanks'); the two then saluted and parted ways. Also on 7 November, the remaining decimated units of 'Pavia', which had regrouped at Mersa Matruh, were finally forced to surrender.

On 5 November 20 tanks and six SP guns from 'Ariete' faced off against 8th Armoured Brigade and suffered heavy losses. In a separate action, six tanks of the XIII Tank Battalion attempted to ward off British forward elements in a desperate defense of Fuqa station. The few remaining SP guns of *DLIV Gruppo* were ordered to fall back to Siwa Oasis, southwest of El Qattara, and from there to Bardia, but were lost one by one because of mechanical failure due to the sustained pace of operations without maintenance or because they ran out of fuel.

The Alamein battles had led to the total or near total destruction of seven of the nine Italian divisions that had been committed to the battle: 'Folgore', 'Trento', 'Bologna', 'Brescia' and 'Pavia'

A pair of M13/40 tanks of the 'Littorio' division halted along a desert track in 1942. The cargo truck bypassing them appears to be a German Ford G917T 3-ton truck. (USSME)

ceased to exist. On 21 November 'Ariete' was officially disbanded and its remnants (two *Bersaglieri* companies, a few artillery pieces of the 132nd Artillery Regiment and a few tanks) along with the remnants of 'Littorio', which had also been officially disbanded on 21 November. 'Trieste', the 3rd 'Cavalleggeri di Monferrato' armoured car squadron and 14 armoured cars from the 'Nizza Cavalleria' were designated the *Gruppo Tattico Ariete*, also often referred to as the '*Gruppo Cantaluppi*' in reference to its commander, Colonel Gaetano Cantaluppi, a feisty, profane, stubborn and unorthodox character if ever there was one.

By 9 November the combined German and Italian forces in the area amounted to little more than a full division, if even that, in terms of both personnel and equipment. The Italians and Germans could each muster about 2,000 infantry, 500 Italian and 3,000 German armoured troops, ten Italian and 11 German tanks, 20 antitank guns, about 30 field guns and 24 antiaircraft guns. Between 13 November and 11 December, the initial elements of the 131st Armoured Division 'Centauro' arrived in Libya; these consisted of 16 medium tanks, 28 armoured cars for the 'Cavalleggeri di Lodi' reconnaissance group, 28 75mm guns, 69 47mm guns, 24 20mm guns, 27 81mm mortars, about 275 trucks and 1,200 men. On paper, the division consisted of the 131st Tank Regiment with three tank battalions, the 5th *Bersaglieri* Regiment with three battalions, and the 131st Artillery Regiment, but what was on paper and what was on the ground were two different things. Prior to that, on 1 October, the 80th Infantry Division (air-transportable) 'La Spezia' landed in North Africa. Somewhat surprisingly, between 9 and 29 November the *Regia Marina* was able to deliver 32,370 tons of material, 620 vehicles and 132 tanks to Libya, marking the last supply delivery.

Estimates as to the number of casualties and prisoners resulting from the Alamein battles vary widely depending on the source consulted. The figure for Axis troops killed in action prior to the beginning of its retreat ranges from about 2,100 killed (1,149 German and 971 Italian) to as many as 5,920 Italians alone killed, 7,000–8,000 wounded and between 17,000 and 23,500 captured. During the retreat, losses rose to 9,000, with 15,000 wounded and 35,000 prisoners. Eighth Army casualties amounted to 2,350 killed, 8,950 wounded and 2,260 missing.

On 13 November elements of 'Centauro', 'La Spezia' and the 'Giovani Fascisti' were ordered to hold Mersa Brega, but by 17 November Rommel had decided that Buerat, further to the west, would be better suited to a defensive stance. 'Centauro' was not without combat experience, having campaigned in Albania, Greece and Yugoslavia from 1939 to 1942. Its baptism of fire in North Africa occurred on 18 November when five of its M14s ran into forward units of the 7th Armoured Division which brought them under fire near Sceleidima. The tanks and the *Bersaglieri* accompanying the tanks quickly responded, staving off the British attackers.

On 16 November the Italians reorganized their surviving units: XX Corps was reconstituted with the 'Centauro' armoured division and the 'Giovani Fascisti' pseudo-division; XXI Corps was assigned the 'La Spezia', 'Pistoia' and 'Trieste' divisions. 'Trieste' consisted of the 65th and 66th infantry regiments and the 21st Artillery Regiment. Both infantry regiments were a hodge-podge of surviving units: I Battalion of the 65th consisted largely of survivors of the regiment, II Battalion was made up largely of 'Bologna' personnel, and III Battalion largely of 'Trento' survivors. The 66th regiment's I Battalion was made up of the original regiment's survivors, II Battalion included soldiers from the IV 'Granatieri' and one company of the 'Folgore', and III Battalion was made up of 'Folgore' personnel. The artillery regiment was in relatively good shape with one 105/28 group, one 100/17 group and two 75/27 groups.

The last forces to arrive at Mersa Brega on 24 November were rear guard elements which halted there only temporarily as the Axis forces continued their trek to the west. Between 25 November and 7 December, the front line stabilized at El Agheila, but on 12 December even that position was abandoned and the retreat to the west continued as Eighth Army pressed its attacks. Two 'Ariete' *autoreparti*, the 132nd and 205th, withdrew almost intact and provided fuel, ammunition, water and mines to the retreating units and assisted in evacuating sick and wounded personnel, while *Gruppo Cantaluppi* was engaged in fending off British attempts to flank the tattered Axis forces from the south. Between 6 and 8 December, the surviving Italian infantry units fell back to Buerat, where they dug antitank ditches and laid about 80,000 mines.

On 11 December the *Gruppo Cantaluppi*, on the southern flank of the Axis line, was all that stood between the British and the retreating Italian and German forces. Its force, which was constantly changing in size and structure, now amounted to a battalion of 57 M14 tanks in desperate need of maintenance, the 66th Infantry Regiment from 'Trieste', a 90/53 group, a 75/27 group from 'Pistoia', the 'Monferrato' armoured car group, and 2,000 men including tank crews, *Bersaglieri* and gunners. As was the new norm, fuel was a critical problem. On the night between 12 and 13 December the British assaulted Mersa Brega, forcing *Gruppo Cantaluppi* to withdraw. On 14 December, Cantaluppi's force was finally reached by the cautiously advancing British near Maaten Giofer. A small delaying element consisting of three tanks and four guns came under attack by some 80 Shermans from 8th Armoured Brigade and gave ground under fire, falling back to the *Gruppo*'s main force deployed astride the coast road near El Agheila. The 66th Infantry Regiment commanded by Colonel Ettore Pettinau, a Sardinian and a fearless leader, was Cantaluppi's forward element, deployed facing east-southeast. The British began an artillery barrage at 0830; at 0900, counterbattery fire silenced the British guns. At 1400, British tanks began to advance against the 'Trieste' positions, and at 1630, Pettinau, sensing that the odds were completely against him, pulled his regiment back. Colonel Cantaluppi, in many respects as impetuous and daring as Rommel, then threw a company of 12 outgunned M14s against the British, losing eight of the tanks. The British then overran the Italian antitank screen of 12 47mm antitank guns. This win for the British, however, came at a high price, as they lost 22 Shermans during this engagement. Rommel himself stated that by their action, the Italians had prevented the British from cutting off the *90.leichte-Division*. Once again, it was the Italians who took the risks and incurred the losses in order to save the Germans.

A week later, on 19 December Rommel was ordered by *Comando Supremo* in Rome to fight to the last at Buerat. This was an impossible order that added much confusion and uncertainty to the already chaotic situation. At the time, there were many Italian artillerymen (officers, NCOs and gunners) with no particular assignments as their guns had been destroyed in the course of the fighting. It was decided to send them to the Tarhuna area, where a 'collection center for artillerymen' had been established, in order to patch together batteries and groups with guns that had been salvaged in Tripolitania. This center was headed by a Colonel Sprovietri, an artillery officer, who managed to form two *raggruppamenti* with an assortment of guns. One *raggruppamento* was equipped with the smaller caliber guns, under the command of Lieutenant Colonel Giuseppe Pasqualini (the former commander of 'Ariete's *DLI Gruppo*, consisting of 75/18 SP guns), was immediately sent forward to Tunisia. The other *raggruppamento*, consisted of a two-battery group of 90/53 guns under Captain Grasso and a two-battery group of the old workhorse 75/27 guns under Captain Pericò, also of 'Ariete'. Equipment for these units was in short supply, but they nevertheless began to train as units. Captain Pericò seems to have been a very adept scrounger, as he befriended several rear-echelon supply officers while he was in Tripoli and was able to load several trucks with canned meat, wine, cheese, mineral water and other food items in preparation for the long journey his gunners would have to make to Tunisia.

As the Italo–German forces were retreating, Italian combat engineers did their best to destroy installations, roads and bridges. One platoon of the 23rd Combat Engineer Company under Second Lieutenant Damiano Galante was especially active in using explosives: at Sollum it used 9,000kg of TNT to wreak havoc, as well as planting explosives to delay the advancing enemy forces at Tocra and Derna, while later blowing up a railway bridge at Akikina in Tunisia.

On 31 December after much indecision, *Comando Supremo* decided that the Italo–German forces should not make a stand at Buerat. Rommel was anxious to get his non-motorized troops (that is, what remained of the Italian infantry) on the move towards Homs and Tarhuna before it was too late to extricate them. A line was established with *Gruppo Cantaluppi* at Buerat, *15.Panzer* and *90.leichte* in the center, and the *Gruppo Centauro* in the south. On 15 January 1943 the remnants of *Gruppo Cantaluppi* merged with the *Gruppo Centauro* and moved to center of line with *90.leichte* to the north and *15.Panzer* to the south. The *Gruppo Centauro*, which now included the assets of the *Gruppo Cantaluppi*, had 57 M14 tanks, 98 field guns, 66 antitank guns and 16 armoured cars. On 16 January part of the group – a battalion of 'Trieste' under Captain Mario Leonida Politi – fought an engagement alongside the *15.Panzer-Division* south of Sedada, incurring heavy losses.

On 17 January the British attacked Sedada, south of Misurata; 'Centauro', with 30 tanks and seven self-propelled guns, faced off against the attack but suffered heavy losses (ten tanks and six of the SP guns). That night the group began to pull back, short of fuel and ammunition, to Sidi Ben Ulid and then to the new Homs–Tarhuna line southwest of Tripoli. Along this line were 32 M14/41 tanks, six 75/18 SP guns, supported by five heavy antitank guns (presumably the remaining 90/53 truck-mounted guns of the *DI Gruppo* of the now-defunct 'Ariete') and four AB41 armoured cars of VIII *Bersaglieri* Battalion. On 19 January the 3rd Company of 'Centauro's XIV Tank Battalion joined the force.

13

The Tunisian Campaign

Almost concurrent with the final battle at El Alamein, on 7 November the Allies launched Operation Torch, which involved the landing of 70,000 American and British troops at Casablanca, Oran and Algiers in French North Africa. The Axis reaction to the landings was to send motorized forces to Tunisia to cover the retreat of the forces in Libya and to challenge the Anglo–American advance from the French colonies. In early November, the first Italian units to land in Tunisia were 10th *Bersaglieri* Regiment, one airborne battalion, the DLVII 75/18 SP Group, and the CI and CXXXVI L40 antitank battalions. The Germans sent an airborne regiment, several infantry battalions and advance elements of *10.Panzer-Division*. These reinforcements attempted to expand the bridgehead in Tunisia and establish contact with the troops retreating from Libya as well as rebuff Anglo–American attempts to prevent that linkup.

The 'Centauro' armoured division, which had also arrived in early November, ceded its XV Battalion to the 'Superga' infantry division and then to the 50th Special Brigade. The XIV and XVII tank battalions and the lone company of the XVI Battalion which reached North Africa were assigned to the *Raggruppamento Cantaluppi*, which included what was left of 'Ariete' and which, in early 1943 was redesignated as the 'Centauro' armoured division, reinforced with the 7th *Bersaglieri* Regiment, the 'Lodi' reconnaissance detachment and the 'Volpi' artillery *raggruppamento*. Some of the tank companies had been equipped with 75/18 SP guns in lieu of M14 tanks.

On 11 November the advance elements of the 1st Infantry Division (Mountain) 'Superga' disembarked at Bizerte, Tunisia, reflecting the urgency on the part of *Comando Supremo* to attempt to salvage the situation in North Africa. The division's commander, General Dante Lorenzelli, who had landed by air, quickly established battle groups and defensive positions at Mateur, Sidi bou Zid and Sidi Belkai. On 14 November the 'Centauro' division's XV Battalion, which had been attached to 'Superga', fought off a US formation at Sened, knocking out 24 tanks and capturing a

General Giovanni Messe, commander of the Italian 1st Army in Tunisia. Messe had previously served as commander of all Italian forces in Russia and is considered by many historians to have been the best Italian general of the Second World War. (Massimiliano Afiero)

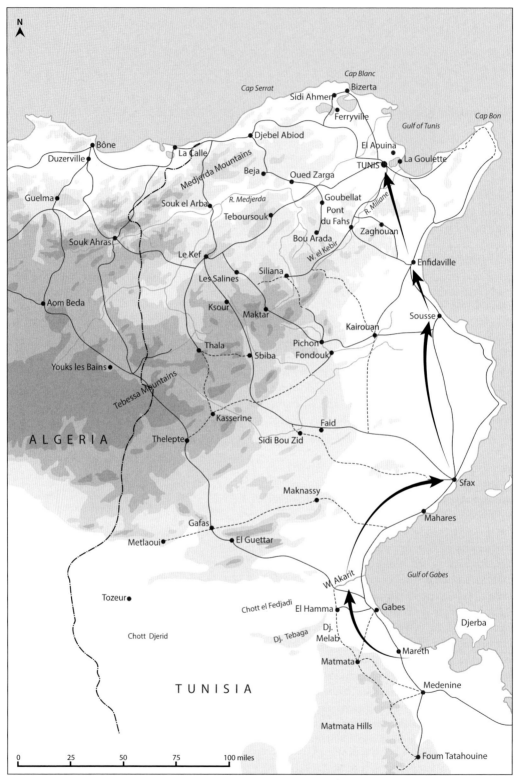

Map 5 Eighth Army advance into Tunisia, December 1942–May 1943.

A pair of M13/40 tanks on a reconnaissance mission in late 1942. (USSME)

number of prisoners. The Italian units that had just arrived in North Africa successfully fought on the night of 24 November blocking – along with other Italo–German units – a strong British attack south of Mateur, losing three SP guns.

On 22 November a tank detachment from Italian 50th Special Brigade heading from Gabes to Gafsa was ambushed by US paratroopers who knocked out five M14s. The 50th Special Brigade (frequently referred to as the 'Imperiali Brigade' after the name of its commander, General Giovanni Imperiali di Francavilla) consisted of the 6th Infantry Battalion, the DLVII 75/18 SP Group and the XV Tank Battalion from 'Centauro'. During a raid against Gafsa on 26 November the US paratroopers again tangled with the XV Battalion but were driven off after having destroyed a fuel dump.

On 10 December the Italians occupied El Guettar and Maknassy, establishing solid defensive positions there. On 24 January 1943 the US 1st Armoured Division engaged elements of the 50th Brigade at Sened Station, inflicting about 100 casualties and taking almost 100 prisoners, for the loss of two American tanks. On 31 January the Americans assaulted Maknassy and ran into determined resistance by 'Centauro'. The following day American forces succeeded in capturing Sened Station from the Italians.

On 2 February command of the *Deutsch–Italienische Panzerarmee*, or *Armata Corazzata Italo–Tedesca*, was assumed by General Giovanni Messe, replacing Rommel, and on 5 February the Italo–German forces were redesignated as the *1a Armata Italiana* (Italian 1st Army). On 10 March Generaloberst Hans-Jürgen von Arnim took command of the *Panzerarmee*, while Rommel took command of the *Heeresgruppe Afrika*. Italian 1st Army consisted of three corps which included the Italian 'Trieste', 'Pistoia', 'La Spezia' and 'Giovani Fascisti' divisions, as well as the German *90.leichte*, *164.leichte* and *15.Panzer-Division*. The German 5th Army consisted of the newly arrived *334.Infanterie-Division*, the *10.Panzer-Division*, the *21.Panzer-Division* and assorted other smaller units, as well as the Italian 'Superga' infantry division. For the first time in North Africa, German troops outnumbered the Italians, 74,000 to 26,000.

The change in designation was accompanied by command changes and on 12 February command of the *Panzerarmee* was assumed by General Giovanni Messe. Also on the 12th, two years to the day after Rommel first arrived in North Africa, the last Italo–German rear guard elements from Libya crossed the border into Tunisia, reaching the Mareth line on 15 February. This ended the

A battery of 65/17 guns of the 'La Spezia' division's 80th Artillery Regiment in Tunisia being towed by Guzzi Trialce motorcycles in early 1943. (Enrico Finazzer)

A Breda Model 35 20mm antiaircraft gun position. The crew are wearing the tropical pith helmet favored by many Italians in the desert, especially artillery crews and *Bersaglieri*. Two of the crew have sand goggles on their helmets. (Massimiliano Afiero)

2,100-kilometer (1,300-mile) retreat of the battered but still dangerous Italian and German forces from El Alamein to Tunisia, plodding along at about 20 kilometers (12 miles) per day for 102 days.

On 13 February the ever-dynamic Rommel assembled his forces for a proposed raid on Gafsa. The attack was to consist of *15.Panzer* with 53 tanks and 'Centauro' with 23 M14s from El Guettar. 'Centauro' consisted of the 5th *Bersaglieri* Regiment (three battalions), two artillery battalions from the 131st Artillery Regiment, one tank battalion and one *semovente* group. The battle of Kasserine Pass began on 14 February. Coordination between German 5th Army and the Italian 1st Army was not good because of the differing views of their commanders, General Hans-Jürgen von Arnim and General Giovanni Messe. On 19 February 'Centauro' (one tank battalion and part of 5th *Bersaglieri* Regiment) was brought up to reinforce *15.Panzer* at Kasserine Pass. The next day, the German assault group resumed its attack against the pass, while 'Centauro's tanks were held in reserve to exploit a possible breakthrough. One battalion of *Bersaglieri* on the right flank took Djebel Semmama after a bloody fight. The Italian action was instrumental in breaking through US positions. 'Centauro' advanced five miles towards Tebessa, encountering no enemy forces. On 21 February, *15.Panzer* and 'Centauro' moved from the Kasserine Pass to seize Djebel el Hamra but came up against US resistance and failed to reach their objective. On 22 February, the 5th *Bersaglieri* Regiment was holding a line against strong US counterattacks from Djebel el Hamra. *15.Panzer* and the DLIV SP Group launched a counterattack, temporarily relieving pressure on the *Bersaglieri*, but were later counterattacked by US forces who drove the *Bersaglieri* back to Kasserine.

A 47/32 antitank gun well camouflaged in a stand of cacti in Tunisia, 1943. Although obsolete, the Italians continued to use this gun throughout the desert campaign to good effect. (USSME)

The attack stalled with not unfavorable results for the Italo–German forces. About 180 American tanks had been destroyed, along with 210 guns, 200 half-tracks and 510 other vehicles. On 23 February, the remnants of 'Centauro' pulled back to El Ank and Bir Marabot in the Gafsa area.

On 6 March following meetings between Rommel and Messe, the Italian 1st Army launched a spoiling attack designated Operation Capri, designed to take Medenine. The forces consisted largely of German units (elements of the three German panzer divisions, two reconnaissance battalions, five infantry battalions, a parachute battalion and seven field artillery batteries); the Italians contributed the 'La Spezia' and 'Trieste' battle groups with two battalions each, plus assorted miscellaneous units. However, Montgomery had been forewarned by ULTRA intercepts of the impending attack and was therefore prepared for it. After a rather brief encounter, the Axis forces abandoned the attack in the evening of the following day, losing about 40 tanks, against a loss of only six British tanks, and a number of other vehicles and guns.

On 17 March General George S. Patton launched the derisively named Operation Wop to capture Gafsa. The attack consisted of 90,000 men against a mixed Italo–German force of 7,100. 'Centauro', acting as a mobile rear guard had 30 M14 tanks, and *10.Panzer-Division* with 50 panzers running, conducted a fighting withdrawal to better positions at El Guettar. At Uadi Mejirda, the I Battalion of 'Trieste' and II Group of the 21st Artillery, commanded by Captain Mario Politi with orders to hold out as long as possible, was heavily engaged. It held in the face of repeated attacks until 26 March when Politi was ordered to withdraw. On 20 March US forces attacked the 'Imperiali' Brigade positions at Maknassy. On 21 March what was left of 'Centauro' fought stubbornly throughout the day and managed to stem the advance of the US 5th Army, which however, resumed its advance at El Hamma towards Gabes on 25 March. 'Centauro' held out for about another week, and finally quit the Mareth Line. On 31 March the Italians suffered a serious breakthrough in the center of their line, but the second-line strongpoints held firm and artillery stopped the attack with heavy losses to the Americans. The remnants of 'Centauro' were reduced to *raggruppamento* strength with 18 tanks and two SP guns of the XVI Battalion and 31st Regiment (an additional 31 tanks and three SP guns were in the regimental repair depot at Rennouch) that continued fighting at El Guettar alongside *10.Panzer-Division*.

Operation Pugilist (20–22 March 1943)

In the 1930s the French had fortified a line that ran roughly from Gabes on the coast inland to Medenine; the line followed the course of the Wadi Zigzaou, a natural antitank ditch between 60 and 200 feet wide and 20 feet deep. It was designed to defend against Italian forces that were stationed in Libya, but in 1940, when the armistice was signed between France and Italy, the fortifications were abandoned by the French. The line took its name from Mareth, which was close to the coast, southeast of Gabes. Italo–German deployments along the line from the sea to the Matmata Hills consisted of the 136th 'Giovani Fascisti' division, the 101st 'Trieste' motorized division, the German *90.leichte-Division*, the 80th 'La Spezia' infantry (air-transportable) division, the 16th 'Pistoia' infantry division and the German *164.leichte-Afrika Division*. Also in the Tebaga Gap area was the *Raggruppamento Sahariano* under General Alberto Mannerini, consisting of one border guard regiment plus another border guard battalion, two machine gun battalions, seven Saharan companies, a squadron group from the 'Lancieri di Novara' Regiment, an artillery group and a mixed engineer battalion. Mobile forces to the rear of the frontline units were the German *15.Panzer* and *21.Panzer* divisions, and the 131st 'Centauro' armoured division; the latter, however, had only 38 tanks and six self-propelled guns at its disposal.

After initial moves and preparations that were carried out beginning as early as 11 March, on 20 March the Eighth Army launched Operation Pugilist against the Mareth Line. The attack began

A patrol of SPA-Viberti mod. 42 Saharianas in Tunisia in March 1943. The Sahariana, purpose-built for desert operations, was based on the AB41 armoured car chassis. The vehicle in the foreground is armed with a 20mm Breda cannon, while the second vehicle mounts a 47/32 antitank gun. (USSME)

An M3 Stuart of the 13th Armoured Regiment outside of Maknassy, Tunisia, in January 1943. The partially obscured name on the sponson appears to be 'Equalizer'. (SC 282399)

with an intense artillery barrage in the coastal sector held by the Italian infantry divisions and was followed by a rather weak infantry assault against the Italo–German positions. Apparently, Montgomery, flushed with his continuous string of victories since El Alamein, was overconfident and believed that the forces opposing him would be easy game. However, when the attack was launched, things did not go well for the British. In the northern section of the line, the British 50th and 51st infantry divisions attacked the positions of the 'Giovani Fascisti' and the 'Trieste' divisions and made it across the main defensive line at Wadi Zigzaou in the face of spirited Italian resistance, especially by the 'Giovani Fascisti'. Durham Light Infantry managed to seize Oerzi and Ksiba Ouest by the middle of the night, but the 50th Royal Tank Regiment was unable to get more than a few of its Valentine tanks across Wadi Zigzaou to support the infantry. The next day, both 50th and 51st divisions, having suffered heavy casualties, were pushed back to the edge of Wadi Zigzaou and withdrew. On 22 March Montgomery acknowledged that the attack had to be called off; his misplaced overconfidence and essentially sloppy planning resulted in an embarrassing failure for Eighth Army.

Meantime, on 19 March General Freyberg's New Zealand Corps had made it through a gap in the Matmata Hills and by 21 March had reached the Tebaga Gap. However, Freyberg's advance had been detected by General Mannerini, who deployed his Saharan Group, numbering about 2,500 assorted troops to defend the Gap. Messe then ordered the German *164.leichte-Division* to pull out of its Mareth Line position and move to support Mannerini, and also redeployed *21.Panzer-Division* to meet the New Zealand threat. The New Zealanders, supported by 8th Armoured Brigade, managed to force a gap during the early morning hours of 22 March but as daylight dawned, the Italians, now reinforced by the German forces that Messe had juggled to send to their aid, blocked any further progress at making it through the Tebaga Gap.

On 24 March General von Arnim, who had replaced Rommel, ordered that the Mareth Line be evacuated beginning the next day. Messe's Italian divisions were to pull back to the Wadi Akarit line, where they would make yet another stand against the rather ponderous and at times stumbling, but ever implacable advance of the Eighth Army. While the units were pulling out of the Mareth positions, Montgomery launched Operation Supercharge II on 26 March which was aimed at engaging the German armour and eventually seizing El Hamma behind the Mareth Line. Messe continued to move the Italian infantry to the Wadi Akarit line, and by 29 March what was left of the German panzers likewise pulled back to Wadi Akarit, which the British reached the next day.

As soon as the Italian divisions reached the Akarit positions they began to dig in and improve their defensive positions. The Wadi Akarit line was shorter than the Mareth Line had been, and like it, was anchored on the coast. Despite the relatively favorable defensive terrain, the Italian and German divisions had suffered from attrition during the fighting along the Mareth Line and the Tebaga Gap and were therefore somewhat weaker in terms of manpower. From the sea inland, the deployment consisted of *90.leichte-Division* and the 'Giovani Fascisti', with 'Pistoia', 'La Spezia' and 'Trieste' divisions in the center, and *164.leichte-Division* and Mannerini's Saharan Group holding the right of the line. These forces were backed by *15.Panzer-Division* as a mobile counterattack force, while *10.Panzer*, *21.Panzer* and 'Centauro' were to the northwest, facing the Americans near El Guettar.

Prospects were not bright for the Italo–German forces. On 6 April, the Eighth Army attacked the Akarit positions; the main attack, made by British 50th and 51st infantry divisions and 4th Indian Division was directed against the Italian infantry divisions ('Pistoia', 'La Spezia' and 'Trieste') in the center of the line. Although the Italians fought stubbornly and fiercely, 'Trieste' was eventually overwhelmed by the sheer numbers of the attacking infantry. By that evening, with the units low on ammunition, Messe gave the order to pull back some 280 kilometers (about 175 miles) to Enfidaville. The mobile units (essentially the German units) began to pull back using their organic transport, while the Italian units, as usual lacking transport assets, once again began their march on foot. It is no wonder that of the 7,000 Axis troops who were captured, the bulk were Italian; they could not pull back fast enough on foot to outrun the pursuing British nor did they

A *Giovane Fascista* with a Fiat Model 1935 machine gun, date unknown, but likely in Tunisia.
(Bruno Benvenuti)

An M14/41 entering the outskirts of a Tunisian village in 1943. The sign on the side of the road indicates distances to Ste Marie du Zit, Bou-Ficha and Zriba – all locations roughly 50–60 kilometers (31–37 miles) south of Tunis. Some attempt at providing camouflage has been made by placing branches on the turret. (USSME)

have the time, the ammunition, or any easily defensible terrain that would allow them to attempt to make another stand on their own.

Averaging about 25 miles per day, shredded remnants of the Italian and German forces almost miraculously managed to maintain some semblance of unit cohesion and reached Enfidaville by 12 and 13 April. Both the German and Italian forces were severely depleted; the worst of the lot was probably the 'La Spezia' division, which was down to less than two companies. Nonetheless, from 13 to 30 April the Italians fended off a series of attacks by British forces. The most noteworthy of these actions for the Italians was the defense of Takrouna by 'Trieste' division, in the center of the Axis line.

Defending Takrouna, which was deemed to be a key point of the defensive system, was the I Battalion of the 66th Regiment and an attached German platoon under the command of the overworked Captain Mario Politi. His father had somewhat prophetically bestowed the middle name of Leonida (Leonidas), the Greek hero of the defense of Thermopylae, upon Politi, who would more than live up to the name in the days to come. Between 16 and 18 April the British artillery pounded Takrouna, which consisted of a small village atop a modest limestone crop hill feature. To the left of Takrouna, at Dj Bir, was a company of the German 47th Regiment. Politi had organized a 360-degree defense and planned to lay mines along the entire perimeter, but the attack prevented that initiative. At dawn on 20 April, enemy infantry supported by tanks began to attack. The German positions at Dj Bir were overcome after putting up fierce resistance. New Zealand Maori infantry infiltrated the southern slopes of the hill and attempted to climb from the southwest, but were stopped by fire from the 4th Company, which took some prisoners. An Italian chaplain later counted 150 enemy dead. The Maoris continued to attack, however, and overwhelmed the positions held by the 2nd Company, which enabled the Maoris to break into the houses in the town. Politi then led the headquarters platoon in a counterattack to relieve pressure on the 1st Company. The battalion infirmary was about to be overrun, but the New Zealanders were driven off at the last moment by hand grenades thrown by the chaplain, Don Giuseppe Maccariello. As the situation grew more serious, 'Trieste' sent two companies of 'Folgore' paratroopers and a company of 'Granatieri' to reinforce the position. The 'Folgore' troopers, in house-to-house fighting, were able to flush the Maoris out of the buildings in Takrouna, and by the night of 20 April Politi had managed to stabilize the situation. On 21 April the positions were once again taken under heavy artillery fire, fresh enemy troops were thrown into the fray, and the Italian positions began to be overwhelmed. At 1445, Politi sent the following message to 'Trieste' headquarters:

> Situation extremely critical, desperate stop. We have fired our last cartridges stop. Losses are very heavy stop. The enemy has occupied almost all of our positions stop. Very many enemy infantry which continues to increase stop. They have a lot of tanks down below stop. Situation desperate stop. Hurry up, hurry up, Politi.

An attempt to send the 103rd 'Arditi' Company as a relief force failed, and at 1705, 'Trieste' received a message that the radio center was under attack; this was followed by silence. By the night of 21 April the 'Trieste' battalion's position at Takrouna had fallen. Of the initial 560 men, subsequently reinforced by a further 300, only about 50 managed to escape unharmed. The action earned Politi his third Silver Medal, as well as a battlefield promotion to major.

On 25 April (Easter Sunday) the 6th New Zealand Brigade attacked the sector held by the 'Giovani Fascisti', particularly Point 141; the Italians suffered 156 killed, wounded and missing, but counted about 150 dead enemy bodies in front of their positions. Point 141 changed hands several times afterwards but was finally taken definitively by the 'Giovani Fascisti's 3rd Company, which was reduced to only 20 men at the end of the fighting. Between 9 and 13 May during the

A battery of M41 SP guns on the march in Tunisia in 1943. The rearmost vehicle displays the name 'Colubrina' on the rear plate, indicating that it belongs to the 2nd Battery of the DLIX Group of the 'Centauro' armoured division. (USSME)

so-called 'Second Battle of Enfidaville', Point 141 continued to be held by the 'Giovani Fascisti'. On 10 May *90.leichte-Division* surrendered, but the 'Giovani Fascisti' continued to hold out until the announcement of surrender on 13 May.

The last relatively noteworthy success scored by Italian armour in North Africa was on 25 April at Gebel bou Kurnine, when the recently arrived DLIX self-propelled gun group, also known as 'Gruppo Piscicelli', with 12 SP guns and 12 M14/41 tanks of the 'Centauro's XIV Battalion, engaged attacking British tanks for two hours and drove them off, knocking out about 28. [Parenthetically, Piscicelli, who had been dubbed *'Duca della Scala'* by his men during Operation Crusader, had left Libya and returned to Italy in early 1942 but in April 1943 was asked by Messe to return to North Africa because of his expertise in artillery employment.] On 26 April 'Centauro's' last ten M14s were integrated into *10.Panzer* and 'Centauro' was officially disbanded.

On 6 May five self-propelled guns from 'Gruppo Piscicelli' ambushed the extreme left flank of an Allied armoured column, but Piscicelli's own vehicle was hit, seriously wounding him. The surviving SP guns held off the attacking tanks for a few hours, protecting the German artillery at Maharine, at the request of *15.Panzer-Division*. The group then managed to reach the Mateur–Tunis road junction. On 8 May the last engagement by the self-propelled guns took place on the road that led to Porto Farina by a group consisting of four SP guns and the lone tank of Second Lieutenant Orlando of XV Battalion, a few panzers and an 88mm gun battery. Two of the SP guns were hit, and a few German tanks were set on fire. A pair of *semoventi* continued to fight, firing their last remaining rounds and knocking out an American tank.

On 9 May the German 5th Army surrendered to US II Corps, while the Italian 1st Army continued to resist until 13 May when Messe surrendered, definitively ending the Axis presence in North Africa.

A 47/32 SP gun in an overwatch position in Tunisia, 1943. The small size of this vehicle made it relatively easy to camouflage, as has been done here by using readily available vegetation. (USSME)

A column of 47/32 SP guns moving in Tunisia in 1943. Five battalions of these guns were deployed to Tunisia. (USSME)

The figures for losses on both sides vary somewhat depending on the source consulted. For the period of the Tunisian campaign on the Axis side, the Italians lost some 3,700 men killed, while the Germans lost about 8,500 killed, and another 40,000–50,000 Italian and German soldiers were wounded. About 90,000 Italians were taken prisoner along with about 102,000 Germans. On the opposing side, the British and Commonwealth forces suffered about 6,200 killed, 21,500 wounded and 10,500 missing. The Free French also lost about 2,150 killed and 10,250 wounded. The Americans, latecomers to the fighting, incurred about 2,700 killed, 9,000 wounded and 6,500 missing.

Conclusion

Viewed objectively, the overall performance of the Italian army and of individual Italian units, officers and soldiers in North Africa was at the very least competent and adequate. Following the initial disastrous performance in late 1940 to early 1941, the Italians learned quickly and developed respectable combat skills. While it would be foolish and unrealistic to ignore the fact that the Germans under Rommel played a crucial role in getting the Italians on their feet in the wake of Wavell's offensive, it would likewise be myopic to ignore the fact that the Italians shouldered a large burden of the fighting against the British and Commonwealth, and later American, forces in North Africa. The German *Afrika Korps* consisting of three divisions fought hard and well, captured the imagination of the Allies and seems to have covered itself with glory, but the *Italian Corpo d'Armata di Manovra* (CAM), later to become XX Corps, from early 1941 to early 1942 consisting of only two divisions, the 'Ariete' armoured and 'Trieste' motorized, was just as active as the *Afrika Korps* which consistently relied upon the Italian corps to support and act in concert with it. The Italian XX Corps was later augmented by the 'Littorio' armoured division and represented the only Italian mobile assets for most of the period of combat operations in Libya and Egypt. Virtually all the other Italian formations consisted of straight leg infantry divisions that lacked adequate mobility, and hence, were used by Rommel in largely static roles such as during the siege of Tobruk, or in defensive positions as determined by Rommel. When attacked, these formations stood their ground and fought well, often doggedly, costing the British time, effort and casualties. Considering the lack of mobility of the Italian infantry divisions and their relative paucity of artillery, their ability to survive for as long as they did against the much more mobile and better equipped British and Commonwealth forces is quite impressive.

Certainly, Allied wartime propaganda tended to cast the Italians as rather passive, lacking in martial spirit and unwilling to fight, ready to surrender at the earliest convenience. If that had indeed been the case, on 4 November 1942 the pitifully small, battered, bruised and exhausted remnants of what had been XX Corps consisting of three divisions and now amounting to less than two infantry battalions, two artillery batteries and 20 (or fewer) tanks, would have surrendered rather than continue to fight. Instead, it seems that the Italians, at least in their own minds, may have been battered but were not beaten, decimated but not destroyed, debilitated but not demoralized, wounded but not whipped. Given what they had already suffered and endured, these survivors were probably the toughest of the tough; they still managed to resist, fighting rear guard actions, hopelessly outnumbered, while retreating towards Tunisia. Indeed, more often than not it was the Italians who were all that stood between the Germans and the pursuing British forces and who fended off vastly superior numbers of overly cautious British forces. If the conventional view of the lackluster performance of the Italians had any merit following the outcome of Alamein in November 1942, the Italians that had survived should have said, 'To hell with it, we fought as best we could, it's time to quit' and marched off willingly into captivity and safety, but in fact, their reaction seems to have been more along the lines of 'To hell with you, we're not done yet, if you want us, come and get us' or, in Italian, something along the lines of '*Vaffanculo*' ('Go get buggered'). That attitude, and their actual performance during the retreat, are indicative of a fighting force that was every bit as tough and resilient as their German partners, if not even more so.

It should also be borne in mind that the Italians were saddled with the vital task of supplying all of the forces, Italian and German alike, with virtually all the supplies that were needed to enable the combatants of both nations to carry out operations in the harsh and unforgiving desert environment. With minor exceptions, it was the Italians who ferried all the needed supplies from Italy to North Africa on Italian ships protected by the Italian navy, and once in theater, provided all the logistics personnel and trucks needed to transport the supplies to the front. This relieved the Germans of the burdens associated with the logistics tail of the forces and enabled the *Afrika Korps* to focus on fighting; it is self-evident that without the Italians, the Germans would never have had enough supplies to fight in the first place.

The leadership qualities on the Italian side are often disparaged or completely ignored in English and German works. Indeed, often the Italians themselves focus on other aspects of operations and devote little analysis to the performance of most of their higher-ranking officers. However, there seems to have been little if any discord among the senior Italian officers who fought the war in North Africa, and as a general rule, the Italian senior and mid-level officer corps performed well in the desert. Company-grade officers often inspired a fierce devotion among their subordinates, but one has to read Italian accounts to find such examples. Although one can pick and choose examples to support one's point of view one way or another, it is legitimate to point out that many British and US accounts of the war furnish examples of less than stellar British and American generals such as O'Moore Creagh, Ritchie and, on the American side, Fredendall, whereas subsequent to the initial moves in the desert in late 1940 and early 1941 it is difficult to find accounts of sheer ineptitude or malfeasance on the part of the Italian generals involved in the fighting, with the possible exception being the questionable actions and behavior of General Piazzoni of 'Trieste' in December 1941. On the German side, the animosity and in-fighting between Rommel and von Arnim in Tunisia is well known, as is the contentious nature of relations between Rommel and Streich.

Thus, if the performance of the Italians from general officer down to the humblest of privates (*soldati semplici*) is to be assessed fairly and objectively, the conclusion should be that, as happens in every other army that the world has ever seen, there were episodes of heroism, courage and abnegation as well as of malfeasance and dereliction of duty. Soldiers of every nation that participated in combat in the desert engaged in acts of spirited attack, dogged defense, surrender and sacrifice to their death. To compound as well as to perpetuate the misconception regarding Italian performance, when Italian forces are mentioned in English-language historiography, it is more often than not in a negative manner. Such a consistently biased, incomplete and misleading portrayal of history does a disservice to the Italians of all ranks who fought and fought well in the desert. Giuseppe Rizzo, who served in North Africa as a major with the 'Ariete' and who chronicled the war there, describes Italian performance in the desert as follows:

> All units of all Italian divisions fought faithfully and with a spirit of sacrifice that was pushed to sublime limits. There was not a single act of weakness, of disloyalty, of faint-heartedness during all of these terrible days of bitter fighting. There were instead many instances of daring, or courage and of heroism. The dead, the wounded, the maimed, the heroes dead and alive, in the tens of thousands, bear witness to the dedication, the loyalty and the discipline of our soldiers in the discharge of their duty. The thousands and thousands of examples of the nobility of the action of our soldiers certainly deserved greater appreciation and recognition by both friends as well as enemies. They spare no ridiculous assertions, offenses or malicious judgments, acting in bad faith or out of a desire to denigrate. However, the truth, which is the pure essence of history, is light that cannot be obfuscated, is indestructible reality.

Whilst Rizzo may have engaged in some hyperbole, his overall thrust has merit, especially when he states that the actions of Italian soldiers 'certainly deserved greater appreciation and recognition by both friends as well as enemies'. Hopefully, this book redresses, at least to some extent, the historical narrative that has been largely accepted up until this time and puts the performance of the Italians in the desert into a more balanced perspective.

Personal Postscript

The American co-author considers himself fortunate enough to have served with or have been acquainted with a few survivors of the fighting in the desert. While serving a tour with the US Army at the NATO headquarters in Verona, Italy, I was very fortunate to have worked for Brigadier General Emilio LoCicero who, as a lieutenant in North Africa, had commanded the 'Ariete' division's headquarters security force and who had one particularly amusing story to tell about an encounter he had with Rommel. LoCicero had driven across a stretch of desert on a motorcycle to deliver a message to Rommel but was unaware that during the ride the seat of his pants had split open, exposing his buttocks, and when he turned away after having delivered his message, Rommel called his attention to the fact that his backside was showing and suggested that he find a new pair of pants. Another former 'Ariete' officer who I had the pleasure of knowing while stationed in Verona, Colonel Ferdinando Martinelli, was full of stories and praise for Colonel Gaetano Cantaluppi, under whom he had served during the retreat to Tunisia.

On another note, an incident that occurred while I was serving with the US Army at NATO headquarters vividly underscores the condescending attitude the Germans often displayed towards the Italians some 35 years earlier in the desert – an attitude apparently undiminished by the passage of time. The occasion was a joint planning session between the Italians and a visiting group of German officers headed by a colonel. The ranking Italian officer, and host, was a colonel named Giovanni De Bartolomeis, an extremely courteous, professional, impeccably dressed and well-groomed officer. De Bartolomeis had commanded the 'Savoia' Cavalry Regiment, and as such, was entitled to wear a crimson red tie with his uniform, commemorating a 'Savoia' messenger who, in 1706, had been wounded by a saber cut to the neck but, although bleeding profusely, had managed to bring the news of a victory against the French to Vittorio Amedeo II. At one point in the discussion with the Germans, the subject came up as to what kind of air defense assets the Italians were planning to include in the force package that was being proposed. The Italian answer was that they had .50 caliber machine guns on their vehicles and would also use individual weapons. The Germans, whose force package included twin 35mm Gepard self-propelled guns, clearly thought that the Italian equipment was inadequate. Perhaps believing that his statement was merely the expression of a self-evident truth that the Italians would accept without comment, the German colonel who headed the delegation then said through an interpreter: 'No wonder you Italians did so badly during the war. You do not know how to organize.' The Italians in the room, however, reacting to this colossal gaffe, looked at each other in amazement, while Colonel De Bartolomeis' face became as red as his crimson tie and the knuckles of his clenched fists visibly whitened. De Bartolomeis very deliberately turned to the interpreter and remarked:

> I want you to repeat what I say exactly as I say it. Please tell our German guests that we Italians know what kind of soldiers the Germans can be. Tell the colonel that after the Italian armistice of 8 September 1943, my father, brother and I, who were all officers in the army, swore allegiance to the king and refused to continue to fight alongside the Germans. The Germans killed my father and brother and beat my mother until she told them where I could be found.

The Germans then put me on a truck bound for a camp in Germany; I jumped out of the truck at the Brenner Pass, joined a band of partisans, and then killed many Germans.

The Germans were shocked and embarrassed beyond words. De Bartolomeis then added: 'This is a good time to break for lunch. Please tell our guests that we will go to the officer's club and that we Italians will do what we do very well and offer them a good meal.' Needless to say, the luncheon, which was excellent, turned out to be a very subdued affair.

Appendix I

Motorization, Mechanization and Modernization of the *Regio Esercito*

Italy went to war in 1940 almost totally unprepared from the standpoint of the numbers and quality of equipment needed by a modern army to conduct effective operations. This unpreparedness was attributable primarily to a lack of natural resources and industrial capacity to produce all the armaments needed by Italy's three services, but other factors included faulty assumptions as to where and in what type of terrain the war would be fought, who would be Italy's enemies and her allies, and when the war would start.

Until about 1938 Italy believed that in any future war it would be able to count on support from its traditional allies, France and Great Britain, who could supply it with many of the resources Italy lacked. Once Italy allied herself with Germany, however, the entire equation changed, as Germany had its own resource problems. Another major mistaken assumption during the interwar years was that Italy would be limited to fighting a defensive war along its Alpine borders; this assumption was very influential in determining the numbers and type of equipment that the *Regio Esercito* adopted prior to the war.

Although as early as 1938 the Italian Army realized that mechanized forces would be essential in the looming conflict, it had to contend with the fact that the civilian economy in Italy had not yet developed into a motorized society, which was a prerequisite for a motorized and mechanized army. In 1939 on the eve of the war, Italy had only about 300,000 cars, or roughly one for every 130 people, while neighboring France had almost two million cars, or one for every 23 people. Germany and Britain had similarly high ratios of cars to people. Motorization in Italy suffered not only because of the lack of large numbers of vehicles, but also because low vehicle numbers meant that most Italians did not know how to drive, and relatively few Italians were trained mechanics, despite their genius for designing and developing high-quality automobiles, many of which were exported. In 1939 shortly after the army had declared its intention to mechanize, Mussolini promulgated a national policy called the '*politica automobilistica in funzione militare*' ('automotive policy and its military function') which was designed to increase motorization of Italian society as a whole. However, this policy was to prove to be too late to enable the country to provide the army with the equipment, knowledge and experience it needed prior to the outset of the war.

In addition to being a resource-poor country lacking raw materials such as iron ore and oil, Italy's industrial base, although capable and impressive in many respects, was not large or extensive enough to be able to cope with all the demands made on it to produce the quantities of equipment needed by its armed forces. Most military production was vested in a handful of firms, including Fiat, Ansaldo–Fossati, Odero–Terni–Orlando and Breda. In addition to being the primary producers of equipment such as tanks, armoured cars, artillery and trucks for the *Regio Esercito*, the same companies were involved in shipbuilding for the navy and producing airframes and aero engines for the air force, as well as producing items such as locomotives and railway cars for the civilian economy. There simply was not enough industrial capacity to produce everything that was needed, even if there had been enough raw materials on hand.

This lack of capacity manifested itself in the inability to produce the numbers of trucks needed to motorize the army and the number of modern tanks needed to mechanize the army. In a somewhat ironic sequence of events, Italy recognized early on that the tank would play an important role in future warfare and developed the largest tank force in the world in the 1930s. The problem, however, was that the 'tanks' in question consisted almost exclusively of the CV33/L3 light tank, or more precisely, a turretless tankette armed with machine guns; the small number of cannon-armed Fiat 3000 tanks were essentially of First World War vintage. The *Regio Esercito* thus found itself with a huge number of very light tanks designed for operations in Italy's mountains, and with little funding to replace them with anything better. The army was stuck with the wrong tank for the mission that later developed, and it took some time for the army to reprioritize industry to meet the challenge of designing and building a medium tank suited to developing requirements.

Italy produced about 3,300 tracked armoured vehicles during the war (excluding the 1,700 or so L3 light tanks produced prior to the war); even accounting for the disparities in the size of other countries and their armed forces, this figure pales in comparison to the UK, which produced about 28,000; Germany, with about 50,000; the US with about 89,000; and the USSR with a staggering 120,000. There was not only a shortfall in numbers, but a relative qualitative deficiency as well. In the case of the most widely produced tanks, the M13/40 and the similar M14/41, while basically competitive with their foreign contemporaries at the time of their introduction, they soon became outclassed, especially in terms of armour and armament. Italian industry was unable to develop a more capable tank in time to be of any use; the P40, which mounted a 75mm gun, was already obsolescent by the time it was produced in small numbers, most of which were appropriated and used by the Germans subsequent to the September 1943 armistice. At one point, the Italians considered producing a direct copy of the excellent Soviet T-34 tank, but that initiative never was acted upon. They did, however, produce a prototype of an almost exact copy of the British Mark VI Crusader, designated the '*carro M celere sahariano*', mounting a slightly improved 47/40 gun and powered by a 250HP engine. There were also several promising self-propelled guns such as the M41 90/53, M42 75/34 and M43 105/25, but none of them were produced in appreciable numbers, and none saw service in the desert.

The lack of production capacity, coupled with competing priorities and financial problems, also resulted in the inability to modernize the army's equipment, especially its artillery and antitank holdings. As a result of its victory over Austria–Hungary in the First World War, Italy had received a huge number of artillery pieces as war reparations. These guns, in addition to the substantial number that the Italians had already captured during the war, were mostly excellent and produced by Škoda, ranging from the 75/13 mountain howitzer to the 100/17 gun and the 149/13 howitzer. Due largely to financial constraints and the belief that these guns were adequate for the next war being waged along Italy's mountain frontier, there was no urgency until 1938 to modernize artillery holdings. At that time, Italy launched an artillery modernization program that was supposed to be far-reaching.

The program envisioned the development and adoption of several modern guns, including the 75/18 howitzer, the 75/32 gun, the 149/19 howitzer, the 149/40 gun and the 210/22 howitzer. However, aside from the 75/18 howitzer, only limited numbers of the other modern types were produced or fielded. As a result, when Italy did enter the war, most of its artillery was antiquated, and to make matters even worse, the army had decided to adopt the 75mm gun as its standard divisional artillery gun rather than adopt a larger caliber like virtually every other major army. Thus, even though there were some of the newer 75/18 and 75/32 guns available, virtually all of the 75mm guns used by the Italians in the desert were the First World War 75/27 Model 1906 guns that had been 'modernized' by being fitted with steel wheels and rubber tires. The 75/27 guns were supplemented in the desert by ex-Austrian 100/17 guns and a very small number of the excellent modern 149/40 gun at army level.

In the area of antitank weapons, the Italians adopted the Austrian Böhler 47/32 antitank gun in 1935. At the time of its introduction, it was able to cope with much of the armour it was expected to face, but by 1941 it was no longer adequate. Unfortunately, developing or adopting a more powerful antitank gun was not a priority, although the Italians did make excellent use of the 90/53 dual-purpose gun in the antitank role, but only to a limited extent. The 90/53, derived from a naval gun, was one of the fruits of the modernization program and proved to be an exceptionally fine weapon, every bit as good as the famous German 88mm.

In terms of antiaircraft artillery, there was the superb 20mm Breda Model 35 and Model 39 light automatic cannon. That weapon was one of the few contemporary weapons generally available in sufficient numbers in the desert and was in fact highly respected by the British, who used captured examples whenever they could.

Appendix II

Italian Divisions in North Africa

Divisions destroyed/disbanded (25 total)
Early campaign: 10
Middle period: 9
Tunisia: 6

The Italians committed a total of 25 divisions in North Africa from June 1940 to May 1943; of these, four were Blackshirt militia divisions (*Milizia Volontaria per la Sicurezza Nazionale*, MVSN) and two were Libyan divisions consisting of native Libyans led by Italian officers. There were five different types of Italian infantry division deployed to North Africa: most of the infantry divisions were the *divisione autotrasportabile tipo AS* (North Africa type semi-motorized divisions), one was a mountain infantry division (*fanteria da montagna*), one was an air-transportable division (*aviotrasportabile*), one was a parachute division (*paracadutista*) and two were motorized (*motorizzata*). There were three armoured divisions (*corazzata*); the 136th 'Giovani Fascisti' Division was an anomaly, because although it was designated as an armoured division, it was actually a light infantry division with no tanks.

Number/name	Dates in North Africa
1a Divisione fanteria 'Superga' (fanteria da montagna)	November 1942–12 May 1943
16a Divisione fanteria 'Pistoia' (autotrasportabile tipo AS)	September 1942–13 May 1943
17a Divisione fanteria 'Pavia' (autotrasportabile tipo AS)	April 1939–25 November 1942
25a Divisione fanteria 'Bologna' (autotrasportabile tipo AS)	September 1939–25 November 1942
27a Divisione fanteria 'Brescia' (autotrasportabile tipo AS)	May 1939–25 November 1942
55a Divisione fanteria 'Savona' (autotrasportabile tipo AS)	April 1939–17 January 1942
60a Divisione fanteria 'Sabratha' (autotrasportabile tipo AS)	May 1937–25 July 1942
61a Divisione fanteria 'Sirte' (autotrasportabile tipo AS)	9 May 1937–23 January 1941
62a Divisione fanteria 'Marmarica' (autotrasportabile tipo AS)	9 May 1937–5 January 1941
63a Divisione fanteria 'Cirene' (autotrasportabile tipo AS)	October 1937–5 January 1941
64a Divisione fanteria 'Catanzaro' (autotrasportabile tipo AS)	June 1940–5 January 1941
80a Divisione fanteria 'La Spezia' (aviotrasportabile)	October 1942–14 May 1943
185a Divisione paracadutisti 'Folgore' (paracadutisti)	August 1942–29 November 1942
101a Divisione motorizzata 'Trieste'	April 1941–13 May 1943
102a Divisione motorizzata 'Trento'	March 1941–25 November 1942

Number/name	Dates in North Africa
131a Divisione corazzata 'Centauro'	November 1942–26 April 1943
132a Divisione corazzata 'Ariete'	January 1941–21 November 1942
133a Divisione corazzata 'Littorio'	December 1941–21 November 1942
136a Divisione corazzata 'Giovani Fascisti'	July 1941–13 May 1943
1a CCNN '23 marzo' (MVSN)	October 1937–5 January 1941
2a CCNN '28 ottobre' (MVSN)	1939–5 January 1941
3a CCNN '21 aprile' (MVSN)	September 1939–May 1940
4a CCNN '3 gennaio' (MVSN)	June 1940–12 December 1940
1a Divisione libica 'Sibille'	March 1940–January 1941
2a Divisione libica 'Pescatori'	March 1940–January 1941

Appendix III

Italian Divisional Histories

Designation and type: *1a Divisione fanteria 'Superga'* (mountain infantry division)

Dates of service in North Africa: November 1942–12 May 1943

Origins: The 'Superga' division was constituted on 5 April 1939, and in 1940 the division participated in the attack against France. In 1942 it was scheduled to be part of the force that was to invade Malta, but that operation never took place. On 11 November 1942 the division was sent to Tunisia, landing at Bizerte. On 20 November it was operational in the Enfidaville area; on 1 December it moved to Sousse and Sfax; and on 26 December it was in position south of Tunis. From late January to February 1943, it fought in the Koukat Depression. On 12 May it surrendered to British forces.

Strength, structure and equipment: Despite its designation as a mountain infantry division, 'Superga' was in fact organized as a standard Type 42 semi-motorized division. Authorized strength was 7,000 men, structured with two infantry regiments (*91o* and *92o reggimento fanteria*), an artillery regiment (*5o reggimento artiglieria*), an engineer battalion and service and support units. Major equipment included 24 75/27 field guns, 12 100/17 guns, eight 65/17 guns, eight 47/32 antitank guns and 16 20mm Breda guns.

Commanders in North Africa: *generale di divisione* Curio Barbasetti di Prun (5 April 1939–10 September 1940); *generale di divisione* Dante Lorenzelli (11 September 1940–23 December 1942); *generale di divisione* Conte Fernando Gelich (24 December 1942–13 May 1943)

Major actions in North Africa: Enfidaville, Koukat

Designation and type: *16a Divisione di fanteria 'Pistoia'* (Type 42 infantry division)

Dates of service in North Africa: September 1942–13 May 1943

Origins: The 'Pistoia' infantry division was formed in 1939, based on the earlier 'Fossalta' infantry division. In 1940 and 1941 it was stationed in Italy, and in July 1942 was sent to Athens, Greece. In September 1942 the division was sent to North Africa and stationed along the Egyptian border; in October it was assigned defensive positions around Sollum, Bardia and Halfaya. On 11 November the division suffered heavy British attacks and was forced to withdraw from its positions and join the Axis forces that were retreating to the west. On 4 March 1943 it reached the Mareth Line; subsequently it fought at Mareth, Wadi Akarit, Enfidaville and Takrouna. The 'Pistoia' was overwhelmed on 13 May and ceased to exist as a division.

Strength, structure and equipment: Authorized strength was 7,000 men, structured with two infantry regiments (*35o* and *36o reggimento fanteria*), an artillery regiment (*3o reggimento artiglieria*), an engineer battalion and service and support units. Major equipment included 24 75/27 field guns, 12 100/17 guns, eight 65/17 guns, eight 47/32 antitank guns and 16 20mm Breda guns.

Commanders in North Africa: *generale di divisione* Mario Priore (1 September 1939–14 July 1940); *generale di brigata* Egidio Levis (15 July–20 November 1940); *generale di divisione* Guglielmo Negro (15 December 1940–19 July 1942); Giuseppe Falugi (20 July 1942–13 May 1943)

Major actions in North Africa: Bardia, Halfaya, Mareth, Medenine, Enfidaville, Takrouna

Designation and type: *17a Divisione di fanteria 'Pavia'* (Type 42 infantry division)

Dates of service in North Africa: April 1939–25 November 1942

Origins: The 'Pavia' infantry division, formed on 27 April 1939, was the successor to the 17th 'Rubicone' infantry division. It was assigned to Libya, where in June 1940 it was stationed on the border with Tunisia, and later transferred to the area west of Tripoli. In March 1941 following the Italian defeat at the hands of the British during Operation Compass, the division was deployed near Benghazi. Subsequently, it operated in the areas of Sirte, Derna and Martuba, and in June 1941 it became part of the force besieging Tobruk. During the December withdrawal from Tobruk, 'Pavia' acted as a rear guard at El Adem, where it put up a spirited defense. It later fought at Tmimi, Mechili and El Agheila. In June 1942, 'Pavia' was used in a mopping-up role, taking charge of 6,000 prisoners. By July the division had advanced as far as Deir el Abiad, south of El Alamein, taking part in the first battle of El Alamein, acting to cover the 132nd 'Ariete' armoured division, and on 14–15 July, participating in the fighting at Ruweisat Ridge. During the Second Battle of El Alamein, 'Pavia' fought alongside the 'Folgore' parachute division on the southern edge of the Axis line. 'Pavia' suffered badly during the fighting, surrendering on 7 November. It was officially disbanded on 25 November 1942.

Strength, structure and equipment: Authorized strength was 7,000 men, structured with two infantry regiments (*27o* and *28o reggimento fanteria*), an artillery regiment (*26o reggimento artiglieria*), an engineer battalion and service and support units. Major equipment included 24 75/27 field guns, 12 100/17 guns, eight 65/17 guns, eight 47/32 antitank guns and 16 20mm Breda guns.

Commanders in North Africa: *generale di brigata* Pietro Zaglio (24 May 1939–1 April 1941); *generale di brigata* Antonio Franceschini (18 May 1941–23 March 1942); *generale di brigata* Arturo Torriano (9 April–19 August 1942); *generale di brigata* Nazzareno Scattaglia (20 August–4 November 1942)

Major actions in North Africa: Benghazi, Seige of Tobruk, First Battle of El Alamein, Second Battle of El Alamein

Designation and type: *25a Divisione di fanteria 'Bologna'* (Type 42 infantry division)

Dates of service in North Africa: April 1939–25 November 1942

Origins: The 'Bologna' infantry division was formed on 27 April 1939 as the successor to the 'Volturno' infantry division. The 'Volturno' had been a territorial division based in Naples; almost all of its personnel were Neapolitans, or from areas surrounding Naples. During the desert campaigning, 'Bologna' was one of the more active and battle-hardened infantry divisions that the Italians fielded. On 10 June 1940 the division was deployed along the Libyan border with Tunisia, and was later transferred to south of Tripoli, at Bir el Ghnem. During Operation Compass, the division fought in the Derna–Mechili area in late January, and subsequently retreated as far as Ghemines, which it reached on 5 February. In March, 'Bologna' advanced to Sirte, and in May it was transferred to the Tobruk front to participate in the siege of that city. On 11 December the division took up defensive positions at Derna, subsequently pulling back to Agedabia and El Agheila. In mid-July 1942 the division was deployed to the El Mireir area southwest of El Alamein and participated in the battle of Alam Halfa. 'Bologna' suffered heavy losses on 4 and 5 November, and its remnants were disbanded on 25 November. Some surviving constituent units joined other Italian units and fought into Tunisia until February 1943.

Strength, structure and equipment: Authorized strength was 7,000 men, structured with two infantry regiments (*39o* and *40o reggimento fanteria*), an artillery regiment (*205o reggimento artiglieria*), an engineer battalion and service and support units. Major equipment included 24 75/27 field guns, 12 100/17 guns, eight 65/17 guns, eight 47/32 antitank guns and 16 20mm Breda guns.

Commanders in North Africa: *generale di brigata* Carlo Gotti (1939–24 August 1941); *generale di divisione* Alessandro Gloria (25 August 1941–November 1942)

Major actions in North Africa: Derna/Mechili, Tobruk, Alam Halfa, Second Battle of El Alamein

Designation and type: *27a Divisione di fanteria 'Brescia'* (Type 42 infantry division)

Dates of service in North Africa: 24 May 1939–25 November 1942

Origins: The 'Brescia' infantry division was formed on 24 May 1939 as the successor to the earlier 27th 'Sila' infantry division. Its recruits were mainly from province of Calabria in southern Italy. As the 'Sila', the division took part in the Second Ethiopian War in 1935–1936. On 24 May 1939 the division was renamed the 'Brescia' and sent to Libya. In June 1940 it fought against French-supported Tunisian irregular forces around Zawiya, Libya. Elements of the division fought at Mechili and Derna during the British desert offensive in December 1940 and although it had to fall back, it avoided being destroyed. In April 1941 'Brescia' participated in the capture of Bardia, and subsequently was part of the force that besieged Tobruk. It fought in the battles of Gazala and Mersa Matruh in June 1942 and later fought in both the First Battle of El Alamein and the Second Battle of El Alamein. The division was destroyed by the British on 7 November 1942 and was officially disbanded on 25 November.

Strength, structure and equipment: Authorized strength was 7,000 men; in 1940 it was structured with two infantry regiments (*19o* and *20o reggimento fanteria*), an artillery regiment (*55o reggimento artiglieria*), an engineer battalion, and service and support units. In 1941 the *55o reggimento artiglieria* was replaced by the *1o Reggimento Artiglieria Celere 'Principe Eugenio di Savoia'*. Major equipment included 24 75/27 field guns, 12 100/17 guns, eight 65/17 guns, eight 47/32 antitank guns and 16 20mm Breda guns.

Commanders in North Africa: *generale di divisione* Giuseppe Cremascoli (1939–1 March 1941); *generale di divisione* Bartolo Zambon (2 March–10 October 1941); *generale di divisione* Benvenuto Gioda (11 October 1941–31 December 1942); *generale di brigata* Giacomo Lombardi (1 January–20 July 1942); *generale* Dino Parri (30 July–15 August 1942); *generale di divisione* Giovanni Battista Oxilia (16 August–8 September 1942); *generale* Alessandro Predieri (9 September–13 October 1942); *generale di divisione* Brunetto Brunetti (19 October–5 November 1942)

Major actions in North Africa: Mechili/Derna, Tobruk, Gazala/Mersa Matruh, First Battle of El Alamein, Second Battle of El Alamein

Designation and type: *55a Divisione di fanteria 'Savona'* (Type 42 infantry division)

Dates of service in North Africa: September 1939–17 January 1942

Origins: The 55th 'Savona' infantry division was formed in Salerno in April 1939; most of its personnel were from the area of Salerno and Naples. The division was sent to Libya in September 1939 where it was stationed on the Libyan border with Tunisia. It remained assigned to the defense of the Tripoli area until April 1941 and thus escaped being caught in the British offensive of late 1940–early 1941. In November 1941 the division was moved to the Egyptian border area, deploying between Ridotta Capuzzo and Sidi Omar. In early December as the *Afrika Korps* began its retreat to the Gazala Line, 'Savona' was ordered to cover the withdrawal by holding Commonwealth forces in the Sollum–Bardia area. The division, short of food and ammunition, managed to hold out until mid-January 1942. 'Savona' was finally forced to capitulate on 17 January and was formally disbanded.

Strength, structure and equipment: Authorized strength was 7,000 men; in 1940 it was structured with two infantry regiments (*15o* and *16o reggimento fanteria*), an artillery regiment (*12o reggimento artiglieria*), an armoured car battalion (*4o 'Genova Cavalleria'*) an engineer battalion, a machine gun battalion, and service and support units. Major equipment included 14 75/27 field guns, 12 105 mm guns, four independent batteries with a total of 16 coast defense guns of varying caliber, and an antitank battalion with eight 37/45 and four 47/32 guns.

Commanders in North Africa: *generale di divisione* Pietro Maggiani (1 September 1939–9 September 1940); *generale di brigata* Ferruccio Paganuzzi (10 September 1940–12 March 1941); *generale di divisione* Pietro Maggiani (14 March–3 November 1941); *generale di divisione* Fedele De Giorgis (4 November 1941–17 January 1942)

Major actions in North Africa: Sollum–Bardia

Designation and type: *60a Divisione di fanteria 'Sabratha'* (Type 42 infantry division)

Dates of service in North Africa: May 1937–25 July 1942

Origins: The 'Sabratha' was established in May 1937 in Gharyan, Libya, and from June to December 1940 was primarily engaged in garrison duty in Tripoli. In December, the division was moved to defensive positions south of Derna. During late January 1941 it fought a series of delaying actions against the advancing British forces during Operation Compass, then falling back towards Benghazi, finally losing contact with British forces. The remnants of the division then retreated to the Agedabia–Sirte area, where it took up defensive positions along the coast. By May 1941 the division had been reformed and was moved to defensive positions inland; in September 1941 it was assigned reserve duties east of Tobruk, and later was assigned to cover the Sollum area, but was soon forced to withdraw from there towards Derna and El Mechili. On 23 December 1941 it made a stand along the coastal road at Mersa Brega, blocking the Allied advance there. A month later, on 23 January 1942, the division advanced to Agedabia. On 16 June 'Sabratha' engaged and defeated enemy forces at Ain el Gazala, participating in the capture of 6,000 prisoners. Following the fall of Tobruk on 21 June the division advanced through Bardia and Sidi Barrani, reaching the line at El Alamein on 1 July. On 10 July the 'Sabratha' positions at Tell el Eisa were attacked by the Australians, losing some 1,500 prisoners. On 14 July the Italians counterattacked, retaking the Tell el Eisa ridge. What was left of the division was incorporated into the 61st Infantry Regiment of the 102nd 'Trento' motorized division. The division was officially disbanded on 25 July 1942.

Strength, structure and equipment: Authorized strength was 7,000 men, structured with two infantry regiments (*85o* and *86o reggimento fanteria*), an artillery regiment (*42o reggimento artiglieria*), an engineer battalion, and service and support units. Major equipment included 24 75/27 field guns, 12 100/17 guns, eight 65/17 guns, eight 47/32 antitank guns and 16 20mm Breda guns.

Commanders in North Africa: *generale di divisione* Guido Della Bona (23 May 1938–1941); *generale di divisione* Riccardo De Cosa (2–24 April 1941); *generale di divisione* Mario Soldarelli (25 April 1941–25 July 1942)

Major actions in North Africa: Operation Compass, Ain el Gazala, Tell el Eisa

Designation and type: *61a Divisione di fanteria 'Sirte'* (Type 42 infantry division)

Dates of service in North Africa: 9 May 1937–23 January 1941

Origins: The 61st 'Sirte' infantry division was formed at Misurata, Libya on 9 May 1937. In June 1940 it was deployed to the Libya–Tunisia border. It was subsequently sent to the Gambut area, where it was engaged in supply route protection. In December part of the division was deployed to the east of Tobruk and part between Ain Gazala and Trig Capuzzo. By January 1941 the entire division was deployed east of Tobruk and on 8 January was engaged in violent combat with British forces. On 23 January the division was destroyed and is considered to have been disbanded on that date.

Strength, structure and equipment: Authorized strength was 7,000 men, structured with two infantry regiments (*69o* and *70o reggimento fanteria*), an artillery regiment (*43o reggimento artiglieria*), an engineer battalion, and service and support units. Major equipment included 24 75/27 field guns, 12 100/17 guns, eight 65/17 guns, eight 47/32 antitank guns and 16 20mm Breda guns.

Commanders in North Africa: *generale di divisione* Alberto Barbieri (1 July 1937–9 June 1940); *generale di divisione* Valentino Babini (10–31 June 1940); *generale di brigata* Vincenzo Della Mura (1 July 1940–23 January 1941)

Major actions in North Africa: Tobruk

Designation and type: *62a Divisione di fanteria 'Marmarica'* (Type 42 infantry division)

Dates of service in North Africa: 9 May 1937–5 January 1941

Origins: The 62nd 'Marmarica' infantry division was formed in Derna, Libya on 9 May 1937. It took part in the Italian invasion of Egypt that began on 13 September 1940. On 11 December the division was in position at Sidi Omar, but after the British unleashed Operation Compass it retreated to Bardia, where it settled in on 16 December. Between 3 and 5 January 1941 the battle of Bardia was fought, ending with the destruction of the 62nd Infantry Division.

Strength, structure and equipment: Authorized strength was 7,000 men, structured with two infantry regiments (*115o* and *116o reggimento fanteria*), an artillery regiment (*44o reggimento artiglieria*), the LXIII light tank battalion, an engineer battalion, and service and support units. Major equipment included 46 L3/35 light tanks, 24 75/27 field guns, 12 100/17 guns, eight 65/17 guns, eight 47/32 antitank guns and 16 20mm Breda guns.

Commanders in North Africa: *generale di divisione* Angelo Rossi (20 May 1937–9 December 1938); *generale di brigata* Armando Pescatori (10 December 1938–9 April 1939); *generale di divisione* Francesco Laviano (10 April 1939–28 May 1940); *generale di divisione* Ruggero Tracchia (29 May 1940–5 January 1941)

Major actions in North Africa: Battle of Bardia

Designation and type: *63a Divisione di fanteria 'Cirene'* (Type 42 infantry division)

Dates of service in North Africa: 1 October 1937–5 January 1941

Origins: The 63rd 'Cirene' infantry division was formed in Libya on 1 October 1937 and from 1937 to 1940 it was essentially engaged in garrison duties. In June 1940 it was deployed near El Adem, south of Tobruk, engaged in security duties, and in August was transferred to the Bardia–Sollum area. On 13 September it took part in the Italian attack towards Egypt, where it advanced as far as Sidi el Barrani. In December the division fell back towards Sollum in the face of the British offensive, suffering heavy losses; it then took up defensive positions in Bardia. The division was destroyed at Bardia on 5 January 1941.

Strength, structure and equipment: Authorized strength was 7,000 men, structured with two infantry regiments (*157o* and *158o reggimento fanteria*), an artillery regiment (*45o reggimento artiglieria*), the LXII light tank battalion, an engineer battalion and service and support units. Major equipment included 46 L3/35 light tanks, 24 75/27 field guns, 12 100/17 guns, eight 65/17 guns, eight 47/32 antitank guns and 16 20mm Breda guns.

Commanders in North Africa: *generale di divisione* Carlo Spatocco (1 October 1937–19 September 1940); *generale di brigata* Alessandro De Guidi (20 September 1940–5 January 1941)

Major actions in North Africa: Side el Barrani, Sollum, Bardia

Designation and type: *64a Divisione di fanteria 'Catanzaro'* (Type 42 infantry division)

Dates of service in North Africa: 3 June 1940–5 January 1941

Origins: The 64th 'Catanzaro' infantry division was formed on 3 June 1940 in Libya and deployed to Acroma as part of the Tobruk defensive perimeter. During the 13 September Italian offensive towards Egypt, the division provided route security along the Via Balbia in the Gambut–Sidi bu Amud area and later in the Sidi Barrani area. In December it was shifted to the Buq Buq sector, and on 9 December the division suffered heavy British attacks which it managed to stave off. Continued attacks forced the division to fall back to Bir Tishdida, thence to Sollum, and finally to Bardia by 15 December. The division continued to hold out in the face of violent attacks until 5 January when it was destroyed and officially disbanded.

Strength, structure and equipment: Authorized strength was 7,000 men, structured with two infantry regiments (*141o* and *142o reggimento fanteria*), an artillery regiment (*203o reggimento artiglieria*), an engineer battalion and service and support units. Major equipment included 24 75/27 field guns, 12 100/17 guns, eight 65/17 guns, eight 47/32 antitank guns and 16 20mm Breda guns.

Commanders in North Africa: *generale di brigata* Nicola Spinelli (3–8 June 1940); *generale di brigata* Giuseppe Stefanelli (9–14 June 1940); *generale di brigata* Lorenzo Mugnai (15 June–26 November 1940); *generale di brigata* Giuseppe Amico (27 November 1940–5 January 1941)

Major actions in North Africa: Buq Buq, Bardia

Designation and type: *80a Divisione di fanteria 'La Spezia'* (air transportable division)

Dates of service in North Africa: October 1942–14 May 1943

Origins: The 'La Spezia' air transportable division was formed on 15 November 1941. It was scheduled to take part in the planned invasion of Malta, but that operation was canceled. On 1 October 1942 the division was airlifted to Libya where it took up positions between Mersa el Brega and El Agheila. In January 1943 it withdrew in the face of the British westward advance, falling back first to the Tarhuna–Homs line, then to Tripoli–Zawiya, and finally to the Mareth Line in Tunisia. Pushed by the British advance, 'La Spezia' fell back to the Wadi Akarit defensive line, then withdrew further to Enfidaville. The division was overrun on 13 May and disbanded on 14 May.

Strength, structure and equipment: The division was structured with two infantry regiments (*125o* and *126o reggimento fanteria*), an artillery regiment (*80o reggimento artiglieria*), a *Bersaglieri* battalion (XXXIX), an additional artillery group (CCCLXIII), the LXXX Antitank Battalion with 47/32 SP guns, a machine gun battalion, engineer battalion, and service and support units. Major equipment included 36 65/17 guns, eight 20mm Breda antiaircraft guns, possibly 24 75/27 guns, and 20 L40 47/32 SP guns.

Commanders in North Africa: *generale di divisione* Quirino Armellini (18 November 1941–31 January 1942); *generale di brigata* Alessandro Maccario (1 February–14 May 1942); *generale di divisione* Gavino Pizzolato (15 May 1942–27 March 1943); *generale di brigata* Arturo Scattini (29 March–13 May 1943)

Major actions in North Africa: Mersa Brega/El Agheila, Tarhuna–Homs, Mareth Line, Wadi Akarit, Enfidaville

Designation and type: *101a Divisione motorizzata 'Trieste'* (motorized division)

Dates of service in North Africa: April 1941–May 1943

Origins: The 'Trieste' motorized division was established on 2 January 1939 as a successor to the 'Po' motorized division. In June 1940 it participated in the Italian attack on France. In August 1941 the division was ordered to Libya and assigned to the *Corpo d'Armata di Manovra* (CAM). Throughout the desert campaign in North Africa, its status as a motorized division allowed 'Trieste' to operate in close conjunction with the 132nd 'Ariete' Armoured Division, first as part of the CAM and then as part of Italian XX Corps. It fought in all major battles of the campaign and distinguished itself on many occasions. Having fought from Egypt and Libya into Tunisia, the division was formally disbanded on 13 May 1943 with its surrender to the Allies in Tunisia.

Strength, structure and equipment: The division had an establishment of 6,700 men and was structured with two motorized infantry regiments (*65o* and *66o reggimento motorizzato*), the *9o reggimento Bersaglieri*, an artillery regiment (*21o reggimento artiglieria motorizzato*), the XI medium tank battalion, an engineer battalion, and service and support units. Major equipment included 24 75/27 guns, 24 100/17 guns, 12 88mm or 90mm dual-purpose guns, 20 20mm Breda antiaircraft guns and 54 M13/40 medium tanks.

Commanders in North Africa: *generaler di divisione* Vito Ferroni (10 August 1939–9 September 1940); *generale di divisione* Alessandro Piazzoni (10 September 1940–10 December 1941); *generale di brigata* Arnaldo Azzi (11 December 1941–29 July 1942); *generale di brigata* Francesco La Ferla (30 July 1942–13 May 1943)

Major actions in North Africa: Operation Crusader, Tobruk, Gazala, First Battle of El Alamein, Second Battle of El Alamein, Mareth Line, Wadi Akarit, Enfidaville

Designation and type: *102a Divisone motorizzata 'Trento'* (motorized division)

Dates of service in North Africa: March 1941–25 November 1942

Origins: The 102nd 'Trento' motorized division was formed on 2 January 1939. It fought briefly during the Italian attack on France in June 1940. In March 1941 the division was transferred to Libya in the Misurata area. It was heavily engaged in most of the fighting between May 1941 and the Second Battle of El Alamein in November 1942. Its 7th *Bersaglieri* Regiment was especially active and was often used to shore up defenses or to counterattack on short notice.

Strength, structure and equipment: The division had an establishment of 6,700 men and was structured with two motorized infantry regiments (*61o* and *62o reggimento motorizzato*), the *7o reggimento Bersaglieri*, an artillery regiment (*44o reggimento artiglieria motorizzato*), an engineer battalion, and service and support units. Major equipment included 24 75/27 guns, 24 100/17 guns, 12 88mm dual-purpose guns and 20 20mm Breda antiaircraft guns. Despite its designation as a motorized division, it was used more frequently as a standard non-motorized division rather than a mobile force operating in close conjunction with the armoured divisions.

Commanders in North Africa: *generale di divisione* Luigi Nuvoloni (1939–24 August 1941); *generale di divisione* Giuseppe De Stefanis (25 August 1941–18 January 1942); *generale di brigata* Carlo Gotti (19 January–16 February 1942); *generale di brigata* Francesco Scotti (17 February–13 October 1942); *generale di brigata* Giorgio Masina (14 October–4 November 1942)

Major actions in North Africa: Operation Brevity, Operation Battleaxe, Operation Crusader, Gazala, Mersa Matruh, First Battle of El Alamein, Second Battle of El Alamein

Designation and type: *131a Divisione corazzata 'Centauro'* (armoured division)

Dates of service in North Africa: November 1942–13 May 1943

Origins: The 131st 'Centauro' ('Centaur') armoured division was formed on 20 April 1939 in Cremona, based on the *1a Brigata Corazzata* (1st Armoured Brigade). At the time, the principal elements of the division were the 31st Tank Regiment, with 163 L3 tanks, the 5th *Bersaglieri* Regiment, and the 131st Armoured Artillery Regiment. After training in the area near Siena, during the summer of 1940 it was deployed to Albania, where it operated until October. On 28 October 'Centauro' was redeployed to the Greek front and was subsequently deployed to Albanian–Yugoslav border from March through May 1941. In November 1942 the division, composed of the 31st Tank Regiment with the XIV, XV and XVII medium tank battalions, the 5th *Bersaglieri* Regiment, and the 131st Armoured Artillery Regiment was sent to Tunisia piecemeal and incomplete. The XIV and XVII tank battalions were assigned to the *Gruppo Tattico Cantaluppi*, which was redesignated the 'Centauro' armoured division in early 1943. After fighting at Kasserine, on 20 March 1943 'Centauro' engaged in combat against the US II Corps at Gafsa and El Guettar and was almost destroyed in 12 days of fighting. Beginning on 4 April its self-propelled groups (DLIII, DLVII and DLIX) fought their final battles. Its few surviving tanks were subordinated to the German 10th Panzer Division, and the remnants of the 5th *Bersaglieri* Regiment were absorbed by the *Kampfgruppe Manteuffel*. 'Centauro' was officially disbanded in April 1943.

Strength, structure and equipment: Because its constituent units continued to be parceled out piecemeal, the division never reached an authorized strength level, which should have been about 9,000 men. Structurally, it consisted of the 31st Tank Regiment, the 5th *Bersaglieri* Regiment and the 131st Artillery Regiment as well as service and support units. Major equipment included 162 M14/41 medium tanks, 24 M41 75/18 self-propelled guns, 24 75/27, 12 105/28 guns and 12 90/53 dual purpose guns.

Commanders in North Africa: *generale di brigata* Giovanni Magli (20 April 1939–22 February 1941); *generale di brigata* Gavino Pizzolato (23 February 1941–28 February 1942); *generale di brigata* Giorgio Carlo Calvi Di Bèrgolo (1 March 1942–7 April 1943)

Major actions in North Africa: Kasserine Pass, Gafsa, El Guettar

Designation and type: *132a Divisione corazzata 'Ariete'* (armoured division)

Dates of service in North Africa: 24 January 1941–15 January 1943. Although to all intents and purposes the division was destroyed as an entity in early November 1942, some remaining elements continued to bear the 'Ariete' name until it was definitively canceled on 1 January 1943.

Origins: The 132nd 'Ariete' (in English: 'Ram') armoured division was formed on 1 February 1939 from the *2a Brigata Corazzata*. It was the first Italian armoured division to be officially established. Until the outbreak of the war, the division was stationed in Italy; in January 1941 it was deployed to Tripoli, reaching full organic strength in February. It began operations on 7 March subordinate to the Italian *Corpo d'Armata di Manovra* (CAM). Its first combat action occurred on 7 April near El Mechili, against the 3rd Indian Motorised Brigade, during which it took almost 2,000 prisoners. It then took part in the siege of Tobruk; some elements also reached Halfaya Pass. In August it stopped to reorganize at Ain el Gazala. September saw the 132nd Tank Regiment added to 'Ariete's organic structure. During November the British launched the Operation Crusader offensive aimed at attacking the Axis positions from the south. When battle was joined at Bir el Gobi on 18 November between 'Ariete' and the British 22nd Armoured Brigade, the Italians emerged as the victors. A number of engagements ensued between November 1941 and October 1942 when 'Ariete' was destroyed as a divisional entity on 4 November at Bir el Abd. During that action, virtually the entire division, except for the XIII Tank Battalion was destroyed. Two days later, on 6 November, the XIII Battalion was overwhelmed by enemy forces in the vicinity of Fuqa and destroyed. The division was formally disbanded on 8 December 1942 although some surviving elements continued to use the 'Ariete' name until 15 January 1943.

Strength, structure and equipment: Strength and structure varied while the division was assigned to North Africa. Authorized strength varied from about 8,600 to 9,887, depending on the timeframe and organizational structure; at its lowest ebb, combat losses brought the division's strength down to about 1,500 men in December 1941. Structurally, the division consisted of the 32nd Tank Regiment, the 132nd Artillery Regiment, the 8th *Bersaglieri* Regiment, and engineer, signal, medical, transportation and other service and support units. The division began its campaigning in North Africa with the 32nd Tank Regiment, equipped with the L3/35 light tank, but in July 1941 it reorganized; the 32nd Tank Regiment was replaced by the 132nd Tank Regiment with the M13/40 medium tank, although the 32nd also continued to be employed in a secondary role. Depending on the timeframe, major equipment items included 188 M13/40 and later, the M14/41 medium tank, 117 L3/35 light tanks, 24 M40 75/18 self-propelled guns, 24 75/27, 12 105/28 guns and 12 90/53 dual purpose guns.

Commanders in North Africa: *generale di divisione* Ettore Baldassare (15 November 1939–21 July 1941); *generale di divisione* Mario Balotta (21 July 1941–19 January 1942); *generale di divisione* Giuseppe De Stefanis (20 January–27 June 1942); *generale* Francesco Antonio Arena (28 June–26 July 1942); *generale* Adolfo Infante (27 July–16 September 1942); *generale* Francesco Antonio Arena (17 September–25 November 1942); *colonnello* Gaetano Cantaluppi (26 November 1942–15 January 1943)

Major actions in North Africa: El Mechili, Tobruk, Operation Brevity, Operation Battleaxe, Bir el Gobi, Operation Crusader, Gazala, Operation Venezia, First Battle of Alamein, Alam Halfa, Second Battle of Alamein

Designation and type: *133a Divisione corazzata 'Littorio'* (armoured division)

Dates of service in North Africa: December 1941–21 November 1942

Origins: The 133rd 'Littorio' armoured division (the name derives from the Fascist symbol of the *fascio littorio*, or lictor's *fasce*, which was a bundle of elm or birch branches bound around an axe symbolizing authority, which was carried by an official known as the '*littore*' or lictor; the name 'Littorio' originally was assigned to an assault division that fought valorously in Spain from 1937 to 1939) was formed in November 1939 and consisted of the 33rd Tank Regiment, the 12th *Bersaglieri* Regiment and the 133rd Artillery Regiment. It participated in action on the Alpine front during the brief campaign waged by Italy against France in June 1940. In 1941 along with 'Centauro', it campaigned successfully in Yugoslavia. From 1942 to 1943 it was engaged in North Africa operating with 'Ariete' and the German armoured elements of the *Afrika Korps* (*15.* and *21.Panzer-Division*), forming *Panzerarmee Afrika*, known in Italian as the '*Armata Corazzata Italo-Tedesca*', or ACIT. In November 1942 after having taken heavy losses at El Alamein, what was left of the division was absorbed into the '*Gruppo Tattico 'Ariete''*, and the division itself was formally disbanded that same month. The 'Littorio' name later was assigned to one of the infantry divisions of Mussolini's Fascist Italian Social Republic.

Strength, structure and equipment: Like the 131st 'Centauro', the 'Littorio' never achieved full manning levels. Its structure varied according to timeframe: in 1941 it consisted of the 133rd Tank Regiment, the 12th *Bersaglieri* Regiment, the 133rd Artillery Regiment, and service and support units; in 1942 its structure was modified with the 133rd Tank Regiment and 12th *Bersaglieri* Regiment remaining, but the 133rd Artillery Regiment being replaced by the *3o Reggimento Artiglieria Celere 'Principe Amadeo Duca d'Aosta'*, and the addition of the *III Gruppo Squadroni* of the *5o Reggimento 'Lancieri di Novara'*. Major equipment items included (theoretically) 162 M14/41 medium tanks, about 40 L6/40 light tanks, 24 75/27 guns, 12 105/28 guns and 24 M41 75/18 self-propelled guns

Commanders in North Africa: *generale di divisione* Gervasio Bitossi (6 November 1939–7 July 1942); *generale di brigata* Emilio Becuzzi (8–24 July 1942); *generale di divisione* Carlo Ceriana-Mayneri (25 July–17 September 1942, temporary assignment while Bitossi was assigned to other duties); *generale di divisione* Gervasio Bitossi (21 September–4 November 1942)

Major actions in North Africa: Operation Venezia, First Battle of Alamein, Alam Halfa, Second Battle of Alamein

Designation and type: *136a Divisione corazzata 'Giovani Fascisti'* (in fact an infantry division despite 'armoured' being in its title)

Dates of service in North Africa: July 1942–13 May 1943

Origins: The origins of the 'Giovani Fascisti' ('Young Fascists') division are somewhat complicated; in 1940 with Italy's entry into the war, the *Gioventù Italiana del Littorio* (GIL), a Fascist paramilitary youth group, organized a huge march of around 20,000 youths provisionally divided into 25 battalions. Following much political maneuvering and posturing, the battalions were disbanded and the youths formed a Blackshirt Assault Legion (the 301st), but it was soon determined that they did not meet required draft standards and the Legion was also disbanded. However, on 18 April 1941 a *Gruppo Battaglioni 'Giovani Fascisti'* was formed, which was to be integrated into the *Regio Esercito*. After more bureaucratic problems had been resolved, in July 1941 the *Gruppo Battaglioni 'Giovani Fascisti'* embarked for Libya where they arrived on 29 July. Initially, the Group was assigned garrison duties in the areas of Homs and Misurata, but after the battalions were issued 47/32 antitank guns and 81mm mortars they were sent to the front lines, taking part in the second battle of Bir el Gobi in December 1941. The 'Giovani Fascisti' force there consisted of 1,454 men whose heaviest armament consisted of eight 47/32 guns and eight 81mm mortars; their defenses were bolstered by 12 L3/35 light tanks that were dug in as bunkers and two M13/40 medium tanks. From 3 to 7 December the 'Giovani Fascisti' held off a vastly superior British force until a German relief force reached Bir el Gobi. On 24 May 1942 the 136th 'Giovani Fascisti' armoured division was established, although in fact it was neither armoured nor a division; the designation was more of an honorific title to recognize the fight put up by the 'Giovani Fascisti' at Bi el Gobi. The 'Giovani Fascisti' also acquitted themselves well in the fighting in Tunisia, being among the last Italian troops to surrender.

Strength, structure and equipment: Despite its rather grandiose designation as an armoured division, it was in fact nothing more than an infantry division with a rather unusual artillery component. Structurally, in 1943 it consisted of the 'Giovani Fascisti' Infantry Regiment, the 8th *Bersaglieri* Regiment, the 136th Artillery Regiment, the *III Gruppo Squadroni Corazzato 'Cavalleggeri di Monferrato'*, an independent infantry battalion, an engineer battalion, an antitank battalion, and service and support units. The artillery regiment was largely based on the old '*batterie volanti*' ('flying batteries') and consisted of two groups armed with 65/17 guns mounted on ex-British Morris CS8 trucks, one group of 75/27 guns mounted on TL37 light tractors, one group of 100/17 guns mounted on Lancia 3Ro trucks, an antiaircraft artillery battery with 20mm Breda mod. 35 guns; the armoured squadron was equipped with AB41 armoured cars and the antitank battalion with the 47/32 antitank gun.

Commanders in North Africa: *generale di brigata* Ismaele Di Nisio (24 May–21 November 1942); *generale di divisione* Nino Sozzani (22 November 1942–12 April 1943); *generale di divisione* Guido Boselli (13 April–13 May 1943)

Major actions in North Africa: Bir el Gobi, El Agheila Mersa Brega, Tarhuna, Wadi Akarit, Enfidaville

Designation and type: *185a Divisione paracadutisti 'Folgore'* (parachute division)

Dates of service in North Africa: August–29 November 1942

Origins: The 185th 'Folgore' ('Lightning') parachute division had its origins in July 1940 when three battalions were formed in Tarquinia; two of the battalions were manned by *Regio Esercito* personnel and one by *carabinieri*. The unit continued to be strengthened, modified and expanded until by 1 September 1941 the *1a Divisione Paracadutisti* was formed. The division was slated to take part in Operation C3, which was the planned invasion of Malta; however, that operation was canceled. The division was then sent to North Africa in August 1942 under the cover designation of 185th '*Cacciatori d'Africa*' division, subsequently altered to the 185th parachute division 'Folgore' later that month. Although it fought in North Africa for only a relatively brief period (about four months), it achieved an enviable reputation based on its combat actions at the southern end or extreme right flank of the Axis deployment at El Alamein. It fought doggedly and valiantly against overwhelming numerical and material odds, and it is part of the division's legend that not one of its paratroopers ever raised their hands in the traditional gesture of surrender. Of the approximately 5,000 'Folgorini', of whom about

4,000 were paratroopers and the rest support and service elements, only some 300 survived either being killed or captured by the time the Second Battle of Alamein was over. The division was formally disbanded on 29 November 1942. The few survivors, along with some replacements later formed the *CLXXV Battaglione Paracadutisti 'Folgore'*, consisting of five companies and integrated into the 66th Infantry Regiment of the 'Trieste' motorized division. The battalion fought in all the major engagements in Tunisia, surrendering with the rest of the Axis forces there on 13 May 1943.

Strength, structure and equipment: The division had a strength of about 5,000 men, of whom about 4,000 were jump-qualified. It was structured with two parachute regiments (*186o* and *187o reggimento fanteria paracadutisti*), an artillery regiment (*185o reggimento artiglieria paracadutisti*), a parachute engineer battalion, a mortar company, and service and support units. In September 1942 the division was organized into tactical groups (*raggruppamenti tattici*, more or less equivalent to the German *Kampfgruppe* concept). These were the *Raggruppamento Tattico 'Ruspoli'* (VII parachute and VIII sapper battalions), the *Raggruppamento Tattico 'Bechi'* (II and IV battalions), the *Raggruppamento Tattico 'Camosso'* (IX and X battalions) and the *Raggruppamento Tattico 'Tantillo'* (V and VI battalions). Having been conceived and organized as a parachute division, it had no heavy armament in the form of field guns or howitzers; its heaviest weapons were the 47/32 antitank gun and the 81mm mortar.

Commanders in North Africa: *generale di brigata* Francesco Sapienza (1 September 1941–early 1942); *generale di divisione* Enrico Frattini (early 1942–November 1942)

Major actions in North Africa: Second Battle of El Alamein

Designation and type: *1a Divisione libica 'Sibille'* (Libyan infantry division)

Dates of service in North Africa: March 1940–January 1941

Origins: This division was originally formed in the 1920s as the Italian Libyan Infantry Division (*Divisione fanteria 'Libia'*). It took part in the occupation of Abyssinia, after which it was disbanded. On the eve of the Second World War, the division was reconstituted as the *1a Divisione libica 'Sibille'*, named after its commanding general, Luigi Sibille. On 13 September 1940 the division, along with the 1st Libyan Parachute Battalion attacked the British position at Sollum. On 10 December the division, along with the paratroopers, was dug in at Maktila; the following day, after having resisted bitterly, the division was wiped out. It was formally disbanded in January 1941. Some survivors of the division were later incorporated into the 'Raggruppamento Sahariano Mannerini'.

Strength, structure and equipment: Division establishment was 7,224 men, structured with two Libyan 'groups' (*1o* and *2o raggruppamento fanteria libica*) with three battalions each, an artillery group (*1o raggruppamento artiglieria libica*), an antitank company, an engineer battalion, and division services. Officers and specialist personnel were Italian, but infantry NCOs and soldiers, who were referred to as 'ascari', were Libyan. Major equipment included 24 77/28 field guns, 16 20mm Breda guns and eight 47/32 antitank guns.

Commanders in North Africa: *generale di divisione* Luigi Sibille (20 April–4 July 1940); *generale di divisione* Giovanni Cerio (5 July–9 December 1940)

Major actions in North Africa: Sollum, Maktila

Designation and type: *2a Divisione libica 'Pescatori'* (Libyan infantry division)

Dates of service in North Africa: March 1940–January 1941

Origins: On the eve of the Second World War the division was established as the *2a Divisione libica 'Pescatori'*, named after its commanding general, Armando Pescatori. Its combat record was rather brief; it was dug in at Alam el Tummar, and on 9 December 1940 it was destroyed by the British 7th Royal Tank Regiment.

Strength, structure and equipment: Division establishment was 7,224 men, structured with two Libyan 'groups' (*3o* and *4o raggruppamento fanteria libica*) with three battalions each, an artillery group (*2o raggruppamento artiglieria libica*), the IX Light Tank Battalion, an antitank company, an engineer battalion, and division services. Officers and specialist personnel were Italian, but infantry NCOs and soldiers who were referred to as '*ascari*' were Libyan. Major equipment included 46 L3/35 light tanks, 24 77/28 field guns, 16 20mm Breda guns and eight 47/32 antitank guns.

Commander in North Africa: *generale di brigata* Armando Pescatori (1 March–10 December 1940)

Major action in North Africa: Alam el Tummar

Designation and type: *1a divisione CCNN '23 marzo'* (Blackshirt division)

Dates of service in North Africa: October 1937–5 January 1941

Origins: Formed for participation in the Second Italo–Abyssinian War, it was reconstituted following that conflict and was sent to Libya. It was destroyed during the British offensive of 1940–1941.

Strength, structure and equipment: In 1940 the division consisted of two CCNN (*Camicie Nere*) legions (219th and 233rd), each with three battalions; these were supported by an antitank company, a machine gun battalion, the 201st Artillery Regiment, a light tank battalion and a mixed engineer battalion. Equipment consisted of eight 47/32 antitank guns, 12 100/17 howitzers, 24 75/27 guns, 16 20mm guns and 46 L3/35 light tanks.

Commander in North Africa: *generale* Francesco Antonelli (1940–6 January 1941)

Major actions in North Africa: Part of the invasion force into Egypt in 1940, the division retreated to Libya in December 1940 and was destroyed at Sidi Barrani, Bardia, in January 1941.

Designation and type: *2a divisione CCNN '28 ottobre'* (Blackshirt division)

Dates of service in North Africa: 1939–5 January 1941

Origins: Formed in 1935 for participation in the Second Italo–Abyssinian War. Disbanded, then reconstituted and sent to Libya. It was destroyed at Bardia in early 1941.

Strength, structure and equipment: In 1940 the division consisted of two CCNN (*Camicie Nere*) legions (231st and 238th), each with three battalions; these were supported by an antitank company, a machine gun battalion, the 202nd Artillery Regiment, a light tank battalion and a mixed engineer battalion. Equipment consisted of eight 47/32 antitank guns, 12 100/17 howitzers, 16 20mm guns and 46 L3/35 light tanks.

Commander in North Africa: *generale* Francesco Argentino (1940–11 January 1941)

Major action in North Africa: Bardia

Designation and type: *4a Divisione CCNN '3 gennaio'* (Blackshirt division)

Dates of service in North Africa: June 1940–12 December 1940

Origins: The *4a Divisione CCNN '3 gennaio'* was formed on 10 May 1935 and stationed in the Formia area in Italy. In late August it was shipped to Italian East Africa. After that campaign it returned to Italy where it was disbanded. It was later reorganized and sent to Libya in June 1940.

Strength, structure and equipment: In 1940 the division consisted of two CCNN (*Camicie Nere*) legions (250th and 270th), each with three battalions; these were supported by an antitank company, a machine gun battalion, the 204th Artillery Regiment and a mixed engineer battalion. Equipment consisted of eight 47/32 antitank guns, 12 100/17 howitzers and 24 75/27 guns.

Commander in North Africa: *generale* Fabio Merzari (1940)

Major action in North Africa: Sidi Barrani

Appendix IV

Comparative Division Structure

132a Divisione Corazzata 'Ariete' (February 1941)

32o reggimento carristi
8o reggimento Bersaglieri
132o reggimento artiglieria
132o compagnia misto del genio
132o autoreparto misto
132a sezione sussistenza
Strength: 5,100

Major equipment items:
117 L3 light tanks
24 75/27 guns
36 47/32 and 37/45 antitank guns
6 20mm guns

132a Divisione Corazzata 'Ariete' (January 1942)

Reparte Esplorante Corazzato (RECO) 'Ariete'
132o reggimento carristi
8o reggimento Bersaglieri
132o reggimento artiglieria corazzata
CXXXII battaglione misto del genio
IV battaglione controcarro 'Granatieri di Sardegna'
132a sezione sanità
132a sezione sussistenza
82o autogruppo misto
Strength: 8,600

Major equipment items:
189 M14/41 medium tanks
24 75/18 self-propelled guns
38 AB41 armoured cars
24 75/27 guns
12 105/28 guns
12 90/53 dual-purpose guns
42 47/32 antitank guns
32 20mm guns

101a Divisione Motorizzata 'Trieste' (October 1942)

65o reggimento fanteria motorizzata 'Valtellina'
66o reggimento fanteria motorizzata 'Trieste'
9o reggimento Bersaglieri
XI battaglione carri medi
21o reggimento artiglieria motorizzata 'Po'
32o battaglione del genio motorizzato
90o sezione sanità
17a sezione sussistenza
80a autosezione pesante
39a unità chirurgica
Strength: 6,700

Major equipment items:
24 75/27 guns
24 100/17 guns
12 88mm or 90mm dual-purpose AA/AT guns
24 20mm AA guns
52 M13/40 medium tanks

27a Divisione Autotrasportabile Tipo AS 'Brescia' (June 1942)

19o reggimento fanteria motorizzata 'Brescia'
20o reggimento fanteria motorizzata 'Brescia'
55o reggimento artiglieria
27o battaglione misto del genio
34a sezione sanità
34a sezione sussistenza
35a unità chirurgica
95o ospedale da campo
Strength: 7,500

Major equipment items:
8 47/32 AT guns
8 65/17 support guns
24 75/27 guns
12 100/17 guns
16 20/65 AA guns

21.Panzer-Division (July 1942)

Panzer Regiment 5
Panzergrenadier Regiment 104
Panzer Aufklärungs Abteilung 3 (mot.)
Panzerjäger Abteilung 39 (mot)
Panzer Pionier Bataillon 200 (mot)

Panzer Artillerie Regiment 155 (mot)
Panzer Nachrichten Abteilung 200 (mot)
Feldersatz Bataillon 200
Division Nachschub Führer 200 (mot)
Fla Bataillon 617 (sfl)
Strength: 12,000

Major equipment items:
15 Pak 35/36 AT guns
37 Pak 38 AT guns
24 LeFH 18 guns
8 FH 18 guns
4 K 18 guns
8 Flak 36/37 88mm dual-purpose AA/AT guns
71 PzKpfw II light tanks
111 PzKpfw III medium tanks
30 PzKpfw IV medium tanks

90.leichte Afrika-Division (August 1942)

Leichte Infanterie Regiment 155 (mot)
Panzergrenadier Regiment 200
Panzergrenadier Regiment 361
Aufklärungs Abteilung 580 (mot.)
Pionier Bataillon 900 (mot)
Panzerjäger Abteilung 190 (mot)
Panzer Nachrichten Abteilung 190 (mot)
Artillerie Regiment 190 (mot)
Panzer Abeilung 190
Feldersatz Bataillon 90/190
Panzerjäger Abteilung 605 (sfl)
Fla Bataillon 606 (sfl)
Sonderveband 288 (mot)
Division Nachschub Führer 190 (mot)
Strength: 14,500

Major equipment items:
18 80mm mortars
27 *Panzerjäger I* self-propelled 47mm antitank guns
4 75mm mountain guns
12 LeFH 18 guns

British Armoured Division (February 1942)

Armoured Brigade Group (x2):
3 x armoured regiments
1 x artillery regiment + AT battery

1 x motor battalion
1 x light AA battery
1 x engineer company

Motor Brigade Group:
3 x motor battalions
1 x artillery regiment
1 x light AA battery
1 x engineer battalion

Armoured Car Regiment
Divisional artillery
Divisional engineers
Strength: 15,000

Major equipment items:
British armoured divisions in early 1942 had somewhat varied equipment holdings. Determining the force structure and equipment holdings of British armoured divisions is not a straightforward affair as their structures were not held to a rigid standard. It should also be borne in mind that British unit echelon designations could be misleading: British brigade groups roughly equated to an Italian regiment, British tank regiments were essentially equivalent to Italian and German battalions and squadrons were equivalent to companies. Depending on whether the regiments were equipped with US supplied tanks or with a mix of British and US tanks, the regiments could have from 45 to 48 tanks; the regiments equipped with US tanks typically had 45 M3 Stuart light tanks and 21 M3 Grant medium tanks. Mixed regiments had 36 British Crusaders and 12 American M3 Grants. A division with two brigade groups would thus have 270–288 tanks. Additional equipment, including that in the division's motor brigade, was 54 25-pdr guns, 48 antitank guns and 54 antiaircraft guns.

British Infantry Division

3 x infantry brigades (each with three infantry battalions)
1 x artillery brigade
1 x reconnaissance regiment
1 x medium machine gun battalion
1 x divisional engineer battalion
1 x divisional signals battalion
1 x Royal Army Service Corps battalion
1 x military police company

Major equipment items:
36 Vickers machine guns
16 4.2-inch mortars
72 25-pdr guns
48 antitank guns
54 40mm Bofors antiaircraft guns

Appendix V

Italian Tank and Armoured Artillery Units and Commanders in North Africa, 1940–1943

Armoured divisions (*divisioni corazzate*)

Unit designation (dates in North Africa) commanders

131a Divisione Corazzata 'Centauro' (13 November 1941–26 April 1943) *generale di divisone* Giovanni Magli (20 April 1939–22 July 1941); *generale di brigata* Gavino Pizzolato (23 February 1941–28 February 1942); *generale di brigata* Giorgio Calvi di Bèrgolo (1 March 1942–7 April 1943)

132a Divisione Corazzata 'Ariete' (24 January 1941–15 January 1943) *generale di divisione* Ettore Baldassare (15 November 1939–21 July 1941); *generale di divisione* Mario Balotta (21 July 1941–19 January 1942); *generale di divisione* Giuseppe De Stefanis (20 January–27 June 1942); *generale di brigata* Francesco Antonio Arena (28 June–27 July 1942); *generale* Adolfo Infante (27 July–16 September 1942); *generale di brigata* Francesco Antonio Arena (17 September–25 November 1942); *col.* Gaetano Cantaluppi (26 November 1942–15 January 1943)

133a Divisone Corazzata 'Littorio' (January–21 November 1942) *generale di divisione* Gervasio Bitossi (6 November 1939–7 July 1942); *generale di brigata* Emilio Becuzzi (8–24 July 1942); *generale di divisione* Carlo Ceriania-Mayneri (25 July–17 September 1942); *generale di divisione* Gervasio Bitossi (21 September–4 November 1942)

Tank regiments (*reggimenti carri*)

Unit designation (dates in North Africa) commanders

31o reggimento carri (13 November 1941–18 April 1943) *col.* Gaspare Raffo (1943)

32o reggimento carri (24 January 1941–8 January 1942) *col.* Alvise Brunetti (April 1941); *ten.col.* Enrico Maretti (until June 1941); *col.* D'Aiello (September 1941)

132o reggimento carri (15 June 1941–November 1942) *ten.col.* Enrico Maretti (15 June 1941–November 1942)

133o reggimento carri (1 June 1941–November 1942) *col.* Pietro Zuco (30 June 1942); *col.* Martinelli (June–September 1942); *col.* Giuseppe Bonini (September 1942)

Tank battalions (*battaglioni carri*)

*Light tank battalions (*battaglioni carri leggeri*) (L3/35 and L6)*
Unit designation (equipment type) (number assigned) (dates in North Africa) parent unit; commanders

I (L3/35) (29) (24 January 1941–1 January 1942) *32o reggimento carri*; *ten.col.* Rispoli

II (L3/35) (40?) (24 January 1941–1 January 1942) *32o reggimento carri*
III (L3/35) (40?) (24 January 1941–1 January 1942) *32o reggimento carri*
IV (L3/35) (40?)
V (L3/35) (40?) (December 1940–1 January 1942) *3o reggimento carri*; *magg.* Zoppolato (December 1940); later *magg.* Miduri; then *magg.* Mattioli
IX (L3/35) (46?) (1939?–11 December 1940) *col.* Lorenzo D'Avanzo (until 16 June 1940)
XI (L3/35) (40?)
XX (L3/35) (50) (1939?–January 1941) *cap.* Russo
XXI (L3/35) (46) (June 1940–22 January 1941)
LX (L3/35) (46) (June 1940–7 February 1941) *cap.* Pasella
LXI (L3/35) (46) (June 1940–7 February 1941) *ten.col.* Sbrocchi
LXII (L3/35) (46) (June 1940–5 January 1941)
LXIII (L3/35) (46) (June 1940–10 December 1940)
VIII (L6/40) (?) (September–October 1942), assigned to 'Trieste' Motorized Division
XXI (L6/40) (?) *15o RECO 'Cavalleggeri di Lodi'*, assigned to 'Centauro' Armoured Division
III Gruppo, 'Lancieri di Novara' (L6/40) (April–October 1942) *132a 'Ariete'*, then *133a 'Littorio'*; *magg.* Valentini; then *magg.* Laricchiuta; (*1o Squadrone cap.* Dardi; *2o Squadrone s.ten.* Oddini; *3o Squadrone* (?) *ten.* Fausto Sartorio)
III Gruppo 'Nizza Cavalleria' (L6/40) (June–November 1942?), assigned to 'Ariete' Armoured Division; *ten.col.* Grignoli
'Cavalleggeri di Lodi' (L6/40) (February 1942–13 May 1943) *15o* RECO; *2o Squadrone cap.* Montessoro

*Medium tank battalions (*battaglioni carri medi*) (M11/39, M13/40, M14/41)*
Unit designation (equipment type) (number assigned) (dates in North Africa) parent unit; commanders
I* (M11/39) (36) (July 1940–February 1941) *32o reggimento carri*
II (M11/39) (36) (July 1940–February 1941) *32o reggimento carri*
III (M13/40) (37) (September 1940–February 1941) *4o reggimento carri*; *ten.col.* Carlo Ghioldi
IV (M13/40) (30) (8 October 1940–February 1941)
IV** (M14/41) (?) (June 1941–November 1942) *33o reggimento carri*; *ten.col.* Rocco Casamassima (July–25 October 1942); then *magg.* Dino Campini; then *cap.* Angelini
V (M13/40) (37) (11 November 1940–February 1941) *32o reggimento carri*; *magg.* Zoppolato; then *ten.col.* Emilio Jezzi
VI (M13/40) (45-47) (December 1940–February 1941) *33o reggimento carri*
VII (M13/40) (50) (January 1941–November 1942) *132o reggimento carri*; *cap.* Ursu (January 1941); *magg.* Andreani (11 March 1941)
VIII (M13/40) (52-56) (September 1941–November 1942) *132o reggimento carri*; *cap.* Casale de Bustis y Figaroa (1941)
IX (M13/40) (41-46) *132o reggimento carri*; *ten.col.* Buttafuochi (until 23 January 1942); *ten.col.* Pasquale Prestisimone (until 27 May 1942); then *magg.* Brucato; then *cap.* Luigi Grata; *ten.col.* Corrado Mazzara (November 1942?)
X (M13/40) (52) *132o reggimento carri*; *magg.* Luigi Pinna (until May 1942); *cap.* Grata (November 1942)
XI (M14/41) (56) (January–November 1942) *133o reggimento carri*; *magg.* Gabriele Verri (January–2 November 1942); *magg.* Giovanni Tumino (2 November 1942–?); subordinate to 'Trieste' Motorized Division

XII (M14/41) (15 June–2 November 1942) *133o reggimento carri*; *magg.* Cesare Lasagna (early 1942); *magg.* Enrico Dell'Uva (15 June–12 July 1942); *magg.* Fabbri (July –17 October 1942); *cap.* Costanzo Preve (17 October–2 November 1942)

XIII (M14/41) (75) (July 1941–November 1942) *132o reggimento carri*; *cap.* Casale (January 1942); *ten.col.* Baldini (November 1942)

XIV (M14/41) (60) (October 1942–April 1943) *31o reggimento carri*; *ten.col.* Giglianelli Fiumi (1941); *magg.* Clementi (April 1943)

XV (M14/41) (40 + 4 75/18 SP guns) (December 1942–May 1943) *31o reggimento carri*

XVII (M14/41) (45) (October 1942–?) *31o reggimento carri*; *ten.col.* Cesare Lasagna

XXI (M13/40) (37) (17 January–February 1941) assigned to *Brigata Corazzata Speciale* in Libya

LI (M14/41) (80) (August 1941–November 1942) *133o reggimento carri*: *ten.col.* Salvatore Zappalà (?–30 June 1942); *magg.* Giuscardi (July 1942); *cap.* Tito Puddu (?–28 October 1942)

LII (M14/41) (?) (October 1941–November 1942) RECO 'Ariete'; *ten.col.* Rossi

*The I and II battalions were structured with only two tank companies each.

**This appears to be a second-generation IV Battalion. The original IV M13/40 battalion was destroyed during the British offensive of 1940–1941.

Self-propelled (SP) gun groups (*gruppi semoventi*) (M40/41 75/18 SP, L40 47/32 SP)

Unit designation (equipment type) (number assigned) (dates in North Africa) parent unit; commanders

DLI (M.40 75/18 SP guns) (12) (14 May–November 1942) *132o reggimento artiglieria*; *ten.col.* Riccardo Viglietti (until 4 November 1942); then *cap.* Folchi

DLII (M.40 75/18 SP guns) (12) (14 May–November 1942) *132o reggimento artiglieria*; *ten.col.* Giuseppe Pasqualini

DLIII Sunk in transit to North Africa

DLIV (M.41 75/18 SP guns) (12) (6 August–30 October 1942) *133o reggimento artiglieria*; *magg.* Tommaso Baronc (until 28 October 1942); then *cap.* Davide Beretta

DLV (?: 'Littorio'??)

DLVI (M.41 75/18 SP guns) (?–November 1942) *133o reggimento artiglieria*; *ten.col.* Francesco Del Duce

DLVII (M.41 75/18 SP guns) (?–April 1943), assigned to 'Centauro' Armoured Division

DLIX (M.41 75/18 SP guns) (?–8 May 1943) *col.* Oderisio Piscicelli

I (L40 SP guns) (20) (?–May 1943?) 'Superga' Infantry Division, Tunisia

XII (L40 SP guns) Tunisia

LXXX (L40 SP guns) 'La Spezia' Air Transportable Division, Tunisia

CI (L40 SP guns) (1943) XXX Corps, Tunisia

CXXXIV (L40 SP guns) (1943) XXX Corps, Tunisia

CXXXVI (L40 SP guns) (1943) XXX Corps, Tunisia

Note: In mid-1942 some Italian medium tank battalions began to include a battery of four 75/18 SP guns as part of the structure.

Appendix VI

Tank Comparisons

	Gun	Armour	Weight	HP	Speed**	Range(km)
Italian:						
L3	2x8mm MG	13mm	3.8 tons	43	42/20	130
L 6/40	20mm	40mm	7.5 tons	68	42/25	200
M 11/39	37mm	30mm	12 tons	105	34/14	200
M 14/41*	47mm	42mm	14 tons	145	35/15	210
British:						
Vickers Mk VI	.50 Caliber	14mm	5 tons	88	56/40	210
Cruiser A9	2-pdr (40mm)	14mm	13 tons	150	40/-	240
Cruiser A10	2-pdr	30mm	14.3 tons	150	26/13	160
Cruiser A13	2-pdr	30mm	15 tons	340	48/23	140
Cruiser A15	2-pdr (later w/6-pdr)	40mmn	20 tons	340	42/24	325
Mk II Matilda	2-pdr	78mm	25 tons	178	26/14	260
Mk III Valentine	2-pdr	65mm	16 tons	138	24/-	140
German:						
PzKpfw IIF	20mm	35mm	9.5 tons	138	40/20	190
PzKpfw IIIF	37 mm	30mm	19.8 tons	296	40/20	155
PzKpfw IIIJ	50mm	50mm	21.6 tons	296	40/20	155
PzKpfw IV E	75mm L/24	50mm	22 tons	296	40/20	210
PzKpfw IV F2	75mm/L43	50mm	23 tons	296	42/20	200
US:						
M3 Stuart	37mm	38mm	12 tons	250	58/25	120
M3 Grant	75mm	51mm	27 tons	400	42/20	195
M4 Sherman	75mm	51mm	30 tons	400	40/20	160

Note: The Italian M13/40 and slightly improved M14/41, although designated medium tanks according to Italian weight categories, were more properly in the light tank category as defined by most other nations at the time. That distinction noted, the M13 and M14 fared relatively well against their British light and medium contemporaries in combat as well as on paper. They were relatively underpowered and consequently somewhat slower than most of the British tanks, and their armour (equal to or better than the early Cruisers) was thin and tended to split or fracture when hit. On the positive side, their range compared favorably with that of most of their British opponents and they were powered by a diesel engine, whose fuel was somewhat less volatile than gasoline and their fuel consumption rate was incomparably better than that of any of the other medium tanks in the desert. This relatively low fuel consumption meant less need for fuel and, consequently, put less of a strain on the supply system than would otherwise have been the case. The 47mm gun, as detailed in a separate Appendix was roughly equal to the British 2-pdr and had the added advantage of being able to fire high explosive (HE) as well as armour piercing (AP) ammunition. One complaint that Italian tankers had was that the third forward gear often failed, an unwelcome inconvenience, especially in a combat situation. The reliability of the Italian medium tanks, though often decried, was no worse than that of most of the British tanks; the much newer A15 Crusader, for example, was still armed with the 2-pdr and was by all accounts notoriously unreliable. Similarly, the M13 and M14, although much lighter, compared favorably with the first versions of the German mediums in terms of armour protection and range, but lacked the firepower of the German tanks. The Italian mediums were roughly equal to the US M3 Stuart light tank, and better in some respects, but were absolutely no match for the 75mm-gunned US Grant and Sherman tanks, which outclassed all others, British and German (apart from the Panzer IV F2) alike, in the desert.

*The M14/41 was a slightly improved version of the M13/40, The most notable improvement was a slightly more powerful diesel engine which was equipped with improved air filters designed to cope with desert conditions, which increased the performance and reliability of the tank. By the end of the fighting in the desert, most Italian medium tanks there were the M14/41s.

**Speeds are in km/h and are for road/cross-country.

Appendix VII

Tank Gun Performance Data

	Gun	Muzzle velocity	Shell weight (kg)	Penetration (mm) 100/500m
Italian:				
Model 35	20mm	840 m/s	0.135	-/30mm
47/32	47mm	630 m/s	1.44	58mm/43mm AP
		250 m/s	2.37	50/50mm HEAT
British:				
OQF 2-pdr	40mm	792 m/s	1.08	49mm/37mm AP/T
		792 m/s	1.22	73mm/65mm APBC
OQF 6-pdr	57mm	846 m/s	2.86	??/APC
Germany:				
KwK 30 L/55	20mm	900 m/s	0.12	31mm/21mm AP
KwK 38 L/42	50mm	685 m/s	2.06	73mm/59mm APCBC
KwK 39 L/60	50mm	835 m/s	2.06	96mm/79mm APCBC
KwK 37 L/24	75mm	385 m/s	6.8	60mm/52mm APCBC
KwK 40 L/43	75mm	740 m/s	6.8	133mm/121mm APCBC
US:				
M3	37mm	884 m/s	0.87	/36mm AP
			0.87	/61mm APBC
M2	75mm	563m/s	6.63	78mm/72mm

Note: Although often described as an inadequate tank weapon, the Italian 47/32 gun mounted on Italian medium tanks proved to be generally satisfactory against a considerable proportion of the British designed and produced armour it faced in the desert. Its armour-piercing round was effective against the armour of the British A9, A10 and A13 cruisers, as well as against the newer-generation A15 Crusader. The 47/32 gun fired a slightly heavier shell than that of the British Ordnance QF 2-pdr, and unlike the 2-pdr was also able to fire a HE round which enabled it to engage and suppress enemy infantry and antitank gun crews. It was, however, outclassed by most of the guns mounted on German tanks, as well as quite obviously the M2 75mm gun mounted on the American Grant and Sherman tanks.

Key to ammunition type abbreviations:
AP: Armour piercing
AP-T: Armour piercing tracer
APBC: Armour piercing, ballistic capped
APCBC: Armour piercing, capped, ballistic cap
APCR: Armour piercing, composite, rigid
HE-T: High explosive tracer
HEAT: High explosive, antitank (hollow charge)

Appendix VIII

Field and Antitank Artillery Data Comparison

Field artillery: Gun	Muzzle velocity	Shell weight (kg)	Range (meters)
Italy:			
75/18	425 m/s	6.4 kg (HE)	9,400
75/27 mod. 06	502 m/s	6.35 kg (HE)	10,240
100/17 mod. 14/16	407 m/s	13.8 kg	9,200
105/28	565 m/s	16.24 kg (HE)	11,425
104/32-105/32	685 m/s	17.5 kg (HE)	16,200
149/35	651 m/s	45.96 kg (HE)	17,500
149/40 mod. 35	800 m/s	46.2 kg	23,700
152/37	692 m/s	54 kg (HE)	21,840
Britain:			
QF 25-pdr Mk II	198-451 m/s	11.4 kg	12,000
BL 4.5 inch	686 m/s	25 kg	18,000
BL 5.5 inch	590 m/s	37.1 kg	16,550
BL 7.2 inch howitzer	517 m/s	92 kg	15,500
Germany			
leFH 18 10,5 cm	470 m/s	14.81 kg	10,675
sFH 18 15cm	520 m/s	43.52 kg	13,325

Antitank artillery: Gun	Muzzle velocity	Shell weight (kg)	Effective range	Penetration
Italy				
37/45	745 m/s	0.68 kg	800	34mm
47/32	630 m/s	1.44 kg	650	40mm
65/17	320-255 m/s	4.23 kg	500	76mm
90/53	830 m/s	11.25 kg	1,000	101mm
Britain				
QF 2-pdr (40mm)	792 m/s	1.08-1.22 kg	914	49mm
QF 6-pdr (57mm)	846 m/s	2.86 kg	1,650	66mm
QF 17-pdr (76.2mm)	880 m/s	7.7 kg	2,000	110mm

Germany

Pak 35/36 3,7 cm	762 m/s	0.368 kg	800	31mm
Pak 38 5 cm	1,130 m/s	2.25 kg	1,000	61mm
FlaK 18	840 m/s	20.71 kg	1,000	119mm

Note: The Italian 75/18 howitzer armed the M40/M41 self-propelled guns in the desert and was used in the antitank role as well as in the artillery support role. When firing the HEAT round, the 75/18 was able to defeat any tank in the desert. The L40 47/32 self-propelled gun was not used until the fighting in Tunisia. The 65/17 gun was originally a pack gun for use in the mountains; pressed into the antitank role in North Africa, its maximum effective range against tanks was 500 meters. The 90/53 gun was a dual-purpose gun employed by the Italians against tanks as well as aircraft, just as the Germans used the very similar 88mm antiaircraft gun in the antitank role.

Appendix IX

Italian Armoured Vehicles Employed in North Africa

Carro Armato Leggero L3

An early series L3/35 light tank. Armed with only two 8mm machine guns, it was outclassed at the beginning of the conflict. (Fiat)

Although commonly referred to as a light tank, this vehicle, could more properly be described as a tankette. In the 1928-29 timeframe, Italian authorities showed an interest in a small, light vehicle that would be suitable for use in mountainous terrain, leading to acquisition of four Carden Loyd Mark VI tankettes from Britain in 1929. Subsequently, Fiat–Ansaldo developed a light tank clearly inspired by the Carden Loyd Mark VI, resulting in the *Carro Veloce* (CV, fast tank) CV33, armed with a single 6.5mm air-cooled weapon. Development continued and in 1935 the CV35 appeared with twin 8mm armament. A number of CVs (later renamed L3s) also underwent field modifications; among these were substitution of the twin 8mm machine guns with a single 12.7mm Breda SAFAT heavy machine gun in Libya in late 1940, and installation of a 45mm Brixia mortar or 20mm Solothurn antitank rifle in Libya in autumn of 1940.

Born as a 'mountain tank', the L3 was not meant to be used in lieu of heavier tanks but was designed according to the Italian doctrine of the period for security and reconnaissance duties and was also to be utilized in the elimination of small pockets of resistance. When Italy entered the war almost all of its armour consisted of L3s; consequently, more than 75 percent of the tank formations encountered by the British in their desert offensive of late 1940 and early 1941 were comprised of the L3, whose armour was not even proof against the weapons of British armoured cars that they met in combat. The L3 was referred to by its crews as the '*scatola di sardine*' ('sardine can'), presumably in reference to its size, its tiny fighting compartment and to its meager armour protection. The L3 continued to be used in North Africa in a secondary role until mid-1942.

Specifications L3/35
Manufacturer: Fiat/Ansaldo–Fossati
Year adopted: 1933
Number produced: Approximately 1,700 of all series combined
Crew: 2 (driver, gunner)
Weight: 3,456kg (7,619lbs)
Main gun: 2 x 8mm Fiat 14/35 machine guns
Elevation: –12 degrees to +15 degrees
Traverse: 12 degrees right/left
Ammunition capacity: 2,320 rounds
Engine: Fiat CV3-005, 4-cylinder in-line gasoline, 2,745cc
Horsepower: 43HP @ 2,400rpm
Fuel capacity: 65 liters (17 US gallons; 14.3 Imperial gallons)
Maximum speed (road): 42km/h (26mph)
Maximum speed (cross country): 15km/h (9.5mph)
Operating radius (road): 130–140km (80–87 miles)
Operating radius (cross-country): 5–6 hours
Armour (hull): 13.5mm front and rear; 8.5mm sides; 6mm floor, deck and roof
Length: 3,150mm (10 feet 4 inches)
Width: 1,400mm (4 feet 7 inches)
Height: 1,280mm (4 feet 2 inches)
Track width: 190mm (7 inches)
Ground pressure: 0.7kg/cm2 (9.96 psi)
Ground clearance: 250mm (10 inches) (L3/35); 280mm (11 inches) (L3/38)
Trench crossing: 2,000mm (6 feet 6 inches)
Vertical obstacle: 650mm (2 feet 1 inch)
Fording depth: 700mm (2 feet 3 inches)
Dates of service in North Africa: 1938–January 1942

Carro Armato Leggero L6/40

The L6/40 was the result of a private initiative by Ansaldo begun in 1935 to develop a tank aimed at the export market. Between 1935 and 1940 more than a dozen different configurations of the vehicle were built, either as complete prototypes or as partial mockups with varying armament fits, hull, turret and suspension configurations. The first prototype, which in reality was an L3 whose hull and suspension had been modified and fitted with a turret mounting a single weapon, weighed about four metric tons, had a hull similar to that of the L3, and a suspension with four large-diameter roadwheels per side (replacing the six smaller roadwheels of the L3). A turret mounting a 6.5mm Fiat Model 28 machine gun was fitted on top of the hull. A number of other variants followed in 1936 and 1937, and in 1938 a version mounting the turret similar to that later installed on the AB40 armoured car with two 8mm Breda Model 38 machine guns, was presented to the Italian Army for consideration, although at the time it was not seeking to adopt any new light tank. During 1939 another version armed with a 37/26 gun and 8mm coaxial machine gun was presented, followed by another version mounting the 20mm Breda Model 35 cannon, resulting in the definitive prototype of the L6/40 which was accepted by the Italian Army in March 1940. Due

The L6/40 light tank, armed with a 20mm gun, proved to be an unsatisfactory design. (Fiat)

to production delays, assignments to cavalry and *Bersaglieri* units did not begin until late 1941. The L6 made its combat debut in North Africa in late December 1941–early January 1942, assigned to reconnaissance units. Overall, the L6 was not a satisfactory tank, even by Italian standards. Due to its height in relationship to its width and length, it was not a very stable vehicle and suffered from torsion bar failure and transmission problems. Armament, armour and performance were all inadequate.

Specifications L6/40
Manufacturer: Fiat/Ansaldo–Fossati
Year adopted: 1940
Number produced: 432–444 (precise figure not available)
Crew: 2 (commander/gunner, driver)
Weight: 6,840kg (15,079lbs)
Main gun: Breda Model 35 20mm gun
Elevation: –12 degrees to +20 degrees
Traverse: 360 degrees
Secondary armament: Breda Model 38 8mm machine gun (coaxial)
Ammunition capacity: 312 20mm rounds; 1,560 8mm rounds
Engine: SPA 18 VT, 4-cylinder in-line gasoline, 4,053cc
Horsepower: 68HP @ 2,500rpm
Power-to-weight ratio: 10HP/ton
Fuel capacity: 165 liters (43.6 US gallons; 32.3 Imperial gallons)

Maximum speed (road): 42km/h (26mph)
Maximum speed (cross country): 20–25km/h (12–16mph)
Operating radius (road): 200km (124 miles)
Operating radius (cross-country): 5–10 hours
Armour (turret): 40mm frontal; 15mm lateral; 6mm top
Armour (hull): 30mm frontal; 15mm sides and rear; 6mm top, deck and floor
Length: 3,820mm (12 feet 6 inches)
Width: 1,860mm (6 feet 1 inch)
Height: 2,175mm (7 feet 1 inch)
Track width: 260mm (10 inches)
Ground pressure: 0.44kg/cm2 (6.26psi)
Ground clearance: 400mm (3 feet 4 inches)
Trench crossing: 1,700m (5 feet 7 inches)
Vertical obstacle: 700mm (2 feet 4 inches)
Fording depth: 800mm (2 feet 8 inches)
Radio: RF1 CA (command tanks also had an RF2 CA)
Dates of service in North Africa: February 1942–May 1943

Carro Armato Medio M11/39

The M11/39, Italy's first medium tank design, suffered from a sponson-mounted 37mm gun and an inadequate engine. (CSEM)

The lineage of all Italian medium tanks that were used in the Second World War can be traced to the first prototype of the M11/39 that was introduced in 1937. The prototype used the basic suspension system of the L3, with six pairs of roadwheels on each side. Its configuration was similar to that of the later US M3 Lee, having a 37mm gun in a right-hand sponson and two 8mm machine guns in a turret. Another prototype that followed in 1938 introduced a new suspension system, with eight pairs of roadwheels in four bogeys per side, which was used on all subsequent production models of Italian medium and heavy tanks. An order was placed for 100 M11/39s in January 1938, with deliveries to begin soon thereafter, but initial delivery did not occur until May 1939. It soon became apparent that it would be preferable to alter the tank's configuration by mounting the main gun in the turret and the machine guns in the hull, leading to development of the M13/40 with a conventional armament layout. In June 1940, 72 M11/39s were sent to Libya, and by February 1941 all of them had been either destroyed or captured by the British during their first desert offensive. The captured tanks that were serviceable were utilized for a time by British Commonwealth forces, which were themselves in need of additional armour from whatever source was available (the Australians formed three squadrons with captured material, designated 'Dingo', 'Wombat' and 'Rabbit', with prominent silhouettes of large white kangaroos painted on the sides and turrets to prevent them from attack by friendly forces).

Specifications M11/39
Manufacturer: Fiat/Ansaldo–Fossati
Year adopted: 1939
Number produced: 100
Crew: 3 (commander/machine gunner, gunner, driver)
Weight: 11,000kg (24,250lbs)
Main gun: Vickers–Terni 37/40 semiautomatic gun
Elevation: –8 degrees to +12 degrees
Traverse: 30 degrees
Secondary armament: 2 x 8mm Breda Model 38 machine guns (2,808 rounds)
Ammunition capacity: 84 37mm rounds; 2,808 8mm rounds
Engine: SPA 8T V8 diesel, 11,140cc
Horsepower: 105HP @ 1,800rpm
Power-to-weight ratio: 9.6HP/ton
Fuel capacity: 145 liters (38.3 US gallons; 39.9 Imperial gallons) plus 37 liters (9.75 US gallons; 8.1 Imperial gallons) reserve
Maximum speed (road): 33.9km/h (25mph)
Maximum speed (cross country): 14km/h (9mph)
Operating radius (road): 200km (124 miles)
Operating radius (cross-country): 10 hours
Armour (turret): 30mm front, 14mm sides, 7mm top
Armour (hull): 30mm frontal, 15mm sides, 8mm top deck, 6mm engine deck
Length: 4,730mm (15 feet 6 inches)
Width: 2,180mm (7 feet 2 inches)
Height: 2,300mm (7 feet 7 inches)
Track width: 260mm (10.23 inches)
Ground pressure: 0.7kg/cm2 (9.96psi)
Ground clearance: 360mm (1 foot 2 inches)
Trench crossing: 2,000mm (6 feet 7 inches)
Vertical obstacle: 800mm (2 feet 8 inches)
Fording depth: 1000mm (3 feet 3 inches)
Radio: None
Dates of service in North Africa: June 1940–February 1941

Carro Armato Medio **M13/40**

An early production version M13/40. Along with the slightly improved M14/41, it formed the backbone of Italian armoured forces in the desert. (RAC 375.50)

Even before the war began – in 1939 to be precise – it became apparent that the M11/39 was not a satisfactory medium tank and development of a suitable successor was initiated. The basic hull of the M11 was utilized as a starting point, but the rest of the vehicle was much revised and took on a conventional appearance with the main gun being mounted in the turret (essentially the same metamorphosis that occurred between the US M3 Grant and M4 Sherman). Armour was improved and horsepower was increased from 105 to 125 resulting in the M13/40. An initial order for 430 M13s (later reduced to 400) was placed in December 1939 with deliveries to begin in August 1940. Subsequent orders brought the total of M13s to 710.

The M13/40 was the best known of the Italian tanks used during the war, and along with its improved version, the M14/41 was the standard medium tank used by Italian armoured divisions. Although designated as a medium tank according to Italian weight criteria, at less than 14 metric tons the M13 was more appropriately a light tank. The M13 initially suffered from frequent mechanical breakdowns in the desert, but in this respect was no worse than British tanks of the period that had not been designed for desert operations. It suffered from a low power-to-weight ratio, resulting in relatively slow speed for its size, and its armour plate had a tendency to split when hit. Most of the mechanical difficulties experienced by the M13 in the desert environment were largely remedied by the adoption of new filters to protect the oil and cooling liquid, and by an improved fuel pump, electrical system, engine lubrication system and inertia starter. A positive point of the M13 was its diesel engine which significantly reduced the incidence of catching fire when hit, as well as being simpler to maintain than comparable gasoline engines and providing better fuel economy. At the time of its introduction into the North African theater of operations in November 1940, its 47mm main armament could be favorably compared to that of the bulk of opposing armour, and it could hold its own against British cruisers and the US supplied M3 Stuart.

However, with the advent of the US built M3 Grant medium tank in May 1942, armed with a 75mm gun, the M13 was outclassed. As with the M11, considerable numbers of these vehicles, when captured, were used by Commonwealth armoured units.

Specifications M13/40
Manufacturer: Fiat/Ansaldo–Fossati
Year adopted: 1940
Number produced: 710 (some sources quote 785–799)
Crew: 4 (commander/gunner, loader, machine gunner, driver)
Weight: 13,700kg (30,203lbs)
Main gun: Ansaldo semi-automatic 47/32 gun modified for tank use
Elevation: –10 degrees to +20 degrees
Traverse: 360 degrees
Secondary armament: 2 x 8mm Breda Model 38 machine guns mounted in hull front; one
    Breda Model 38 coaxially mounted; one Breda Model 38 mounted for antiaircraft defense
Ammunition capacity: 87 47mm rounds; 3,048 8mm rounds
Engine: SPA 8T V8 diesel, 11,140cc
Horsepower: 125HP @ 1,800rpm
Power-to-weight ratio: 8.92HP/ton
Fuel capacity: 145 liters (38.3 US gallons; 39.9 Imperial gallons), plus 35 liters (9.25 US gallons;
    7.7 Imperial gallons) reserve
Maximum speed (road): 31.8km/h (20mph)
Maximum speed (cross country): 14–15km/h (9mph)
Operating radius (road): 210km (130 miles)
Operating radius (cross-country): 10 hours
Armour (turret): 42mm frontal, 25mm sides and rear, 15mm top
Armour (hull): 30mm frontal, 25mm sides and rear, 6mm floor
Length: 4,915mm (16 feet 2 inches)
Width: 2,280mm (7 feet 6 inches)
Height: 2,370mm (7 feet 10 inches)
Track width: 260mm (10 inches)
Ground pressure: 0.92kg/cm2 (13.1psi)
Ground clearance: 410mm (1 foot 4 inches)
Trench crossing: 2,100mm (6 feet 11 inches)
Vertical obstacle: 800mm (2 feet 8 inches)
Fording depth: 1,000mm (3 feet 3 inches)
Radio: None, later RF1 CA
Dates of service in North Africa: September 1940–November 1942

Carro Armato Medio M14/41

Commencing in mid-1941, a SPA diesel engine developing 145 horsepower was installed in the M13/40 and the up-engined vehicle subsequently was designated the M14/41. The new engine, which was equipped with air filters designed to cope with desert conditions, improved both the performance and reliability of the tank. Full-length fenders were also reintroduced on the M14; early fenders were smooth on top, but later production M14s had X-shaped stiffening ribs stamped into the top surface of the forward portion of the fenders. Another feature of the M14 was the mud scraper that was fitted behind the front drive sprocket.

Autoblinda AB41, 8th *Bersaglieri* Regiment, 132nd 'Ariete' Armoured Division, Egypt, May 1942.
(Artwork by and © David Bocquelet)

L6/40, 'Lancieri di Novara' Cavalry Regiment, 133rd 'Littorio' Armoured Division, August 1942.
(Artwork by and © David Bocquelet)

I

L3/35, North Africa, February 1941. (Artwork by and © David Bocquelet)

Ford CMP with 20mm Breda Model 35, *batterie volanti, Reparto Esplorante Corpo d'Armata di Manovra*, Libya, 1941. (Artwork by and © David Bocquelet)

Autocannone 90/53 su Lancia 3Ro, DI Gruppo, 132 Artillery Regiment, 132nd 'Ariete' Armoured Division, Egypt, 1942. (Artwork by and © David Bocquelet)

Autocannone da 100/17 su Lancia 3Ro, *batterie volanti, Reparto Esplorante Corpo d'Armata di Manovra*, Libya, 1941. (Artwork by and © David Bocquelet)

M11/39, II Tank Battalion, *4 Reggimento, Brigata Corazzata Speciale*, Libya, September 1940. (Artwork by and © David Bocquelet)

M13/40, 1st Company, VII Tank Battalion, 132nd Tank Regiment, 132nd 'Ariete' Armoured division, North Africa, November 1941. (Artwork by and © David Bocquelet)

M14/41, Tunisia, XIV Tank Battalion, 31st Tank Regiment, 131st 'Centauro' Armoured division, early 1943. (Artwork by and © David Bocquelet)

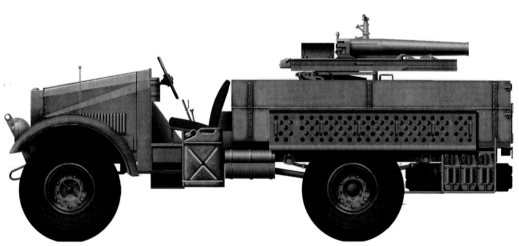

Morris CS8 with 65/17 gun, *batterie volanti, Reparto Esplorante Corpo d'Armata di Manovra*, Libya, 1941. (Artwork by and © David Bocquelet)

Semovente M41 da 75/18, DLIX Gruppo, 131 Artillery Regiment, 131st 'Centauro' Armoured Division, May 1943. (Artwork by and © David Bocquelet)

Semovente da 47/32, CXXXVI Antitank Battalion, Tunisia, January 1943. (Artwork by and © David Bocquelet)

A column of Italian M11/39 tanks in North Africa, 1940. (Open source)

Italian vehicles in the Western Desert. At the front is Fiat Balilla 1100 Furgoncino. A Fiat 666 is in the background. Photograph taken by General Erwin Rommel in 1941. (Open source)

M13/40 tanks of 'Ariete' Division, Libya 1941. (Open source)

M14/41 tanks and other vehicles (Breda 41 recovery tractor on the right; Lancia 3 Ro and Fiat 626 on the left) awaiting transport to North Africa at an Italian port c. 1942. (Open source)

Specifications M14/41
(Except as noted below, specifications and characteristics are identical to those given above for
  the M13/40.)
Year adopted: 1941
Number produced: 695 (some sources refer to figures between 895 to over 1,100)
Weight: 14,000kg (30,864lbs)
Engine: SPA 15T M41, V8 diesel, 11,980cc
Horsepower: 145HP @ 1,900rpm
Power-to-weight ratio: 9.66HP/ton
Fuel capacity: 150 liters (39.6 US gallons; 33 Imperial gallons), plus 40 liters (10.6 US gallons;
  8.8 Imperial gallons) reserve
Maximum speed (road): 35.5km/h (22mph)
Maximum speed (cross country): 15km/h (9mph)
Ground pressure: 0.96kg/cm2 (13.65psi)
Radio: RF1 CA (and RF2 CA on the Centro Radio, or Radio Center tank)
Dates of service in North Africa: June 1941–May 1943

Semovente L40 47/32

The L40 self-propelled gun mounted a 47mm gun on an L6/40 tank chassis. (Fiat)

The Italian Army Staff was interested in equipping the *Bersaglieri* regiments with a self-propelled
antitank gun in lieu of the towed 47/32 gun. During the course of development of the L6 light
tank Ansaldo had examined the possibility of building an SP gun based on its chassis and in the
spring of 1941 a prototype was presented. The vehicle used all of the mechanical and suspension
components of the tank and mounted the 47/32 gun in a closed-topped casemate; the top was soon
eliminated because of ventilation problems. In June 1941 an order for 583 L6 tanks was reduced
to 283 examples, with the remaining 300 chassis being diverted to produce a self-propelled 47/32
antitank gun. It was hoped that eventually all of the *Regio Esercito*'s 47mm antitank guns would
be mounted on this chassis. The vehicle was conceived as a light assault and support vehicle to be

used in conjunction with light tanks and reconnaissance vehicles as well as being used to eliminate strongpoints and generally to support the infantry. Doctrinally, it was not envisaged as a tank destroyer, although it was often pressed into service in that role when more suitable systems were not available. Six battalions equipped with the L40 SP gun saw service in Tunisia.

Specifications L40
Manufacturer: Fiat/Ansaldo–Fossati
Year adopted: 1942
Number produced: 357
Crew: 2 (later 3; commander/loader, gunner, driver)
Weight: 6,700kg (14,783lbs)
Main gun: Ansaldo (Böhler license) mod. 39 47/32 gun
Elevation: –12 degrees to +20 degrees
Traverse: 27 degrees
Ammunition: 70 rounds
Secondary armament: None (apart from individual crew weapons)
Engine: SPA 18 VT, 4-cylinder in-line, 4,053cc
Horsepower: 68HP
Power-to-weight ratio: 10.15HP/ton
Fuel capacity: 160 liters (42.25 US gallons; 35.2 Imperial gallons), plus 20 liters (5.3 US gallons; 4.4 Imperial gallons) reserve
Maximum speed (road): 42km/h (26mph)
Maximum speed (cross-country): 20–25km/h (12–15mph)
Operating radius (road): 200km (124 miles)
Operating radius (cross-country): 5 hours
Armour: 30mm frontal, 15mm sides, 6mm floor and roof
Length: 3,820mm (12 feet 6 inches)
Width: 1,860mm (6 feet 1 inch)
Height: 1,690mm (5 feet 6 inches)
Track width: 260mm (10 inches)
Ground clearance: 400mm (3 feet 4 inches)
Trench crossing: 1,700m (5 feet 7 inches)
Vertical obstacle: 700mm (2 feet 4 inches)
Fording depth: 1,000mm (3 feet 4 inches)
Radio: None, RF1 CA on the platoon command version, the company command version also had an RF2 CA
Dates of service in North Africa: 1941–May 1943

Semovente M40 75/18 & Semovente M41 75/18

This excellent self-propelled gun/howitzer was the first Italian self-propelled gun to be produced in series in the Second World War. A wooden mockup was presented in January 1941 and the proto-type was tested in February. Several modifications were made to the 75/18 Model 1935 howitzer to render it compatible for use as a self-propelled system. Modifications included addition of the characteristic perforated muzzle brake (the first of its kind used on any self-propelled gun) which helped limit the recoil travel of the gun to 350mm (13.8 inches). A series of orders soon followed (for 60 units in May 1941, 144 in December and 200 in May 1942). Production models were assigned to operational units later in 1942.

An M41 75/18 self-propelled gun, built on the M14/41 tank chassis; this system differed slightly from the earlier M40 SP gun, which was built on the M13/40 chassis. (Fiat)

The first vehicles of this type to participate in combat were assigned to two self-propelled artillery groups of the 'Ariete' armoured division and received their baptism of fire in May 1942. These guns were employed in much the same fashion as the German *Jagdpanzer* in an antitank role, although they originally were designed to be utilized in a self-propelled artillery role in the armoured division, as well as for indirect fire. At the time of their introduction in North Africa, their armament (despite the rather short barrel length, low muzzle velocity and consequent relatively short effective range) was formidable in comparison to both British and German tank guns. The effectiveness of their gun was further enhanced by the use of '*effetto pronto*' (HEAT) ammunition. Crews of these vehicles were very confident of their capabilities and found the 75/18 gun to be an extremely reliable weapon. Crews in at least one Group (the DLIV) increased ammunition stowage capacity to about 100 rounds by removing the crew seats and simply sitting on the extra ammunition. To coordinate and control the SPG batteries the M40 and M41 *carro comando per reparti semoventi* (command tank for SPGs units) were produced, based on the hull of the standard medium tank, with the turret removed.

Specifications M40 and M41
Manufacturer: Fiat/Ansaldo–Fossati
Year adopted: 1941
Number produced: 222 (60 on M13 chassis, 162 on M14 chassis)
Crew: 3 (commander/gunner, loader, driver)

Weight: 13,100kg (28,880lbs)
Main gun: Ansaldo mod. 35 75/18 gun/howitzer (modified)
Elevation: –12 degrees to +22 degrees
Traverse: 40 degrees
Secondary armament: One 8mm machine gun with 1,104 rounds
Ammunition capacity: 44 75mm rounds; 1,104 8mm rounds
Engine: SPA 15 TM 41, V8 diesel, 11,980cc
Horsepower: 125HP @ 1,800rpm (145HP @ 1,900rpm M14)
Power-to-weight ratio: 11.1HP/ton
Fuel capacity: 150 liters (39.7 US gallons; 33 Imperial gallons) plus 40 liters (10.6 US gallons;
     8.8 Imperial gallons) reserve
Maximum speed (road): 35km/h (22mph)
Maximum speed (cross-country): 15km/h (9mph)
Operating radius (road): 210km (130 miles)
Armour (hull): 50mm (25 + 25) frontal, 25mm sides and rear, 9-15mm top, 6mm floor
Length: 4,915mm (16 feet 1 inch) (M.15)
Width: 2,200mm (7 feet 2 inches)
Height: 1,850mm (6 feet)
Track width: 260mm (10 inches)
Ground clearance: 380mm (1 foot 3 inches)
Trench crossing: 2,100mm (6 feet 10 inches)
Vertical obstacle: 800mm (2 feet 7 inches)
Fording depth: 1,000mm (3 feet 3 inches)
Ground pressure: 0.96kg/cm2 (13.65psi)
Radio: RF1 CA
Dates of service in North Africa: May 1942–April 1943

Autoblinda AB41

The *autoblinda* (or *autoblindo*, armoured car) AB41, based on the earlier AB40, was the most widely used Italian armoured car during the war. The largest single change compared to the AB40 was the substitution of a 20mm cannon and coaxially mounted machine gun in lieu of the two machine guns in the turret of the AB40. The vehicle had a number of unique features, especially in its steering and suspension systems. It was a 4-wheel drive vehicle, and all four wheels, which were independently sprung, were steerable. Utilizing its dual steering system allowed the vehicle to be driven in either direction without having to turn around and thus expose the vehicle's flank to enemy fire. The spare tires mounted on the hull sides in a free-wheeling fashion prevented bellying when crossing obstacles. Its suspension system allowed the vehicle to achieve relatively high cross-country speeds. It was well-suited to desert operations, even though it suffered from some mechanical problems. The AB41 were assigned to the cavalry and reconnaissance elements of the armoured and motorized divisions in North Africa.

Specifications AB41
Manufacturer: SPA/Ansaldo–Fossati
Year adopted: 1941
Number produced: 624
Crew: 4 (commander/gunner, 2 drivers, rear gunner/radioman)
Weight: 7,400kg (16,314lbs)

The AB41 armoured car was widely used in the desert, largely by *Bersaglieri* reconnaissance units. (Fiat)

Main gun: Breda Model 35 20mm cannon
Elevation: −12 degrees to +20 degrees
Ammunition capacity: 456 20mm rounds
Secondary armament: 2 x 8mm Breda Model 38 machine guns
Ammunition capacity: 456 20mm rounds; 1,992 8mm rounds
Engine: SPA ABM 1 6-cylinder in-line gasoline, 4,995cc
Horsepower: 808HP @ 2,700rpm
Power-to-weight ratio: 10.8HP/ton
Fuel capacity: 118 liters (31.2 US gallons; 26 Imperial gallons), plus 57 liters (15 US gallons;
    12.5 Imperial gallons) auxiliary tank, plus 20 liters (5.25 US gallons; 4.4 Imperial gallons)
    reserve
Maximum speed (road): 78km/h (48mph)
Maximum speed (cross country): 20km/h (12mph)
Operating radius (road): 400km (248 miles)
Operating radius (cross-country): 8 hours
Armour (turret): 18mm frontal, 10mm sides, 6mm top
Armour (hull): 8mm frontal, 8.5mm sides, 6mm top deck and floor
Length: 5,200mm (17 feet 1 inch)
Width: 1,920mm (6 feet 3 inches)
Height: 2,484mm (8 feet 2 inches)
Wheelbase: 3,200mm (10 feet 6 inches)
Track: 1,634mm (5 feet 4 inches)
Ground clearance: 350mm (1 foot)
Vertical obstacle: 350mm (1 foot)
Fording depth: 700mm (2 feet 4 inches)
Radio: RF 3 M mod.1941
Dates of service in North Africa: 1940–1943

Appendix X

Italian Artillery Employed in North Africa

20/65 Breda mod. 35 and mod. 39 antiaircraft gun

The 20mm Breda Model 35 cannon on its three-trail field carriage. (Ralph Riccio)

One of the outstanding Italian achievements in weapons design and production during the 1930s was the Breda Model 35 (and its derivative Model 39) dual-purpose cannon. Designed as an antiaircraft weapon, it also saw extensive use as an antitank and antipersonnel weapon and was mounted on several Italian armoured and non-armoured vehicles as main or heavy armament. The Breda 35 was designed in response to an early 1930s Italian Army requirement for an automatic antiaircraft gun to provide a low altitude air defense capability. In 1932 Breda entered its proposal into competition against several other contenders, including those from Scotti, Oerlikon, Madsen and Lübbe. In 1935 following extensive testing, the Breda was judged the winner.

The Breda was a gas-operated weapon. Ammunition was fed by a 12-round charger plate that collected the spent cartridge cases. The Model 35 mount consisted of a three-legged platform that was carried on a two-wheel trailer; it had a counterbalance system and parallelogram sights that enabled the gunner to stand behind the gun while tracking and firing. As with most Italian light guns, the Breda could be broken down into four loads, in this case, for transport by pack animal in mountain terrain. Normally it was either towed by a light truck or mounted in the bed of a truck for mobility.

The Breda was first employed by the Italians during the Civil War in Spain in 1936 where 138 of the Model 35 guns were sent to support the Italian troop contingent there. Although its effectiveness against enemy aircraft flying at altitudes above 2,000 meters was judged unsatisfactory, as might be expected for a low-level air defense gun, its performance against tanks, armoured vehicles and other ground targets was deemed to be very satisfactory, thus establishing the parameters for future use in the ground role.

Organizationally, during the early period of the Second World War, one battery of eight Breda 20/65 guns was assigned to the artillery regiments of Italian infantry divisions, while the armoured, motorized and cavalry divisions, as well as the Libyan and Militia divisions and the corps-level artillery regiments each had two similar eight-gun batteries. As the war continued and more of the Breda guns became available, some batteries were replaced by companies, notably in the armoured and motorized divisions in North Africa.

Both the Breda Model 35 and Model 39 were mounted aboard captured 15cwt Ford and Chevrolet Canadian Military Pattern (CMP) trucks in North Africa and formed part of the 'batterie volanti' ('flying batteries') that wrote a special chapter in the annals of Italian operations in the desert. The Model 39 stationary mount was preferred over the Model 35 for mounting on wheeled vehicles. Allied fighter pilots soon came to respect the capabilities of the Bredas that routinely provided protection for Italian mobile columns in the desert. British and Commonwealth forces eagerly put to use as many captured Bredas as possible, as they were far superior to the machine guns normally used by the British for air defense and were much more convenient than the excellent but very heavy 40mm Bofors in Commonwealth service.

Specifications
Designation: *Cannone-mitragliera Breda da 20/65, mod. 35* and *mod. 39*
Originator: Società Italiana Ernesto Breda, Brescia
Producers: Breda Meccanica Bresciana (Brescia and Rome); Fabbrica d'Armi Terni
Caliber: 20mm (0.787 inches)
Length of tube: 1,870mm (73.6 inches)
Overall length: 3,302.8mm (130.03 inches)
Overall height: 1,120mm (in firing position) (44.09 inches)
Weight in action: 330kg (726lbs)
Wheel track: 1,000mm (39.4 inches)
Wheel type/diameter: Steel spokes or pressed steel disc wheels with solid tires/600mm (23.62 inches)
Breech type: Gas-operated recoil
Recuperator type: Gas-operated
Elevation: –10 degrees to +80 degrees
Traverse: 360 degrees
Muzzle velocity: 840m/s (2,756fps)
Maximum range: 5,500 meters (6,015 yards) ground targets; 2,700 meters (8,858 feet) anti-aircraft role
Rate of fire: 240 rounds per minute
Ammunition types: AA, AP
Shell weight: 135g (0.297lbs)
Armour penetration: 30mm (1.18 inches) at 500 meters (547 yards)

Solothurn S-18/1000 antitank rifle

A 20mm Solothurn antitank gun being manned by *Bersaglieri*. The Solothurn was effective only against lightly armoured vehicles. (Massimiliano Afiero)

The Italians adopted the German-designed Swiss Solothurn to fill the need for a support weapon that capable of defeating armoured cars, light tracked vehicles and light tanks. At the time of its selection by the *Regio Esercito* in 1939 the Solothurn was an effective weapon for its size and capable of defeating the types of light armour likely to be encountered in many contemporary situations. The gun (technically an antitank rifle) was recoil-operated and fed by a ten-round box magazine mounted on the left-hand side of the weapon. It used the Italian manufactured Breda mod. 35 20mm armour piercing explosive round, whose penetration was comparable to that of the Rheinmetall or Solothurn rounds. The Solothurn could be fitted with different pattern muzzle brakes depending on the type of ammunition used.

The Solothurn was a crew-served weapon with a crew of four and could be carried on and fired from the SO-9 two-wheel cart that could be pulled by the crew. In addition to the gun, the cart carried two ammunition cases, each holding three ten-round magazines for a total of 60 rounds available. The gun could also be fitted with a bipod for firing when not on the cart.

Deliveries to the *Regio Esercito* began in the summer of 1940 and by September the first 100 had been shipped to Libya. The most credible information indicates that in early 1942, 350 Solothurns were on hand in North Africa. In February 1943, 114 were still available with the Italian 1st Army in Tunisia. In 1940, in North Africa, it was planned that the weapon would be assigned on the scale of two per standard infantry, *Bersaglieri* and Libyan battalions. The *divisione tipo AS* (North Africa Type Division) formed in 1941 had a platoon in each company, amounting to 12 per battalion, plus a regimental company of undetermined size; the later *tipo AS42* (North Africa Type 42) divisions were issued 12 per battalion, for a total of 72 per division. *Bersaglieri* battalions of the armoured and motorized divisions in North Africa also had 12 per battalion plus a regimental company with eight more guns. The 'Superga' division had a company of 12 Solothurns incorporated into the divisional antitank battalion. The company consisted of a headquarters squad and three Solothurn platoons of two squads, each with two Solothurns. The 'Folgore' parachute division had assigned an antitank squad with two Solothurns per battalion plus six more weapons in the divisional *guastatori* (sapper) company, and the two battalions of 'Giovani Fascisti' had one platoon of two squads per company, for a total number of 12 per battalion. These numbers reflected requirements specified in organizational tables, but the extent to which the guns were actually issued varied according to unit and timeframe. Some Solothurns were mounted on pickup trucks, L3 tankettes or, later, captured British Universal Carriers and the AS42 light desert truck.

Specifications
Designation: *Fucile anticarro tipo S*
Originator: Rheinmetall–Borsig AG, Düsseldorf
Producer: Waffenfabrik Solothurn, Zurich
Caliber: 20mm (0.787 inches)
Length of tube: 1,420mm (55.9 inches) with flash hider; 1,300mm (51.2 inches) without flash hider/muzzle brake
Overall length: 2,160mm (85 inches)
Overall width: 180mm (7 inches)
Overall height: 413mm (16.3 inches) on bipod
Weight in action: 54.7kg (120.6lbs) without bipod; 58.7kg (129.4lbs) with bipod; 127kg (280lbs) with cart
Wheel track: NA/bipod mounted
Wheel type/diameter: For SO-9 cart, pressed steel/400mm (15.75 inches)
Breech type: Positively locked on firing by rotation of locking lugs
Recuperator type: Spring
Elevation: 0 degrees to +10 degrees
Traverse: 50 degrees
Muzzle velocity: 832m/s (2,730fps)
Maximum range: 3,000 meters (3,281 yards) maximum; 500 meters (547 yards) effective
Rate of fire: 10-20 rounds per minute
Ammunition types: Armour piercing tracer (AP-T); high explosive tracer (HE-T); AP training; HE training
Shell weight: 320g (0.7lbs) for both AP-T and HE-T
Armour penetration: 20–22mm (0.79–0.86 inches) at 100 meters (109 yards)

37/45 antitank gun (3.7 cm PaK 35/36)

During the Second World War, the Italians were furnished with several models of artillery by their German allies. The first of these was the 37/45 antitank gun, or PaK 35/36 in German parlance. Development of the very popular German Rheinmetall–Borsig 3.7 cm Pak 35/36 L45 antitank gun, of which some 15,000 copies were built, dates to 1933 with its initial combat use being in Spain in 1936. The gun was exported to several countries and was also copied; the best example of this perhaps is the US 37mm M3 antitank gun. The PaK 35/36 was a contemporary of the British 2-pdr antitank gun and the Bofors 37mm antitank gun but was somewhat inferior in performance, although in 1940 it was still one of the best antitank guns available. After only a few months into the war, as tank armour increased in thickness, it became inadequate for the role but nevertheless served throughout the war until 1945. The PaK 35/36 had a split trail carriage and was fitted with steel wheels, pneumatic tires and a small sloping shield; the gun itself was semi-automatic in the

A German-supplied 3.7 cm PaK 35/36 antitank gun in late 1941. This gun was only marginally effective against most British armour. It was issued to the 'Ariete', 'Brescia', 'Bologna' and 'Pavia' divisions. (USSME)

sense that the sliding wedge breech closed automatically. The gun could be towed by virtually any kind of tractor or truck, and it could also be moved by the gunners for short distances.

Penetration capabilities varied by AP ammunition type and range, from 64mm at 100 meters falling off to 22.5mm at 600 meters. The Germans also supplied Italy with hollow charge ammunition (the Stielgranate 41) that could penetrate up to 180mm of armour, but the disadvantage to using this ammunition was that it was effective only at relatively close range (about 300 meters), and consequently was somewhat hazardous to the crew who would be exposed to enemy fire from longer ranges. No Stielgranate 41 were employed by the Italians in North Africa.

Italy's first exposure to the gun was in 1935–1936 during the war against Ethiopia; the Ethiopians had 30 of these guns purchased from Germany, some of which were captured by the *Regio Esercito*. During the Spanish Civil War, Germany supplied 40 to Italian forces in Spain in 1936. In 1937 during a visit to Germany the Italian Army Chief of Staff, General Pariani, was shown and possibly offered the weapon for purchase, but he was of the correct opinion that performance of the Ansaldo/Böhler 47/32 antitank gun that had been adopted by Italy was superior to that of the PaK 35/36, aside from its armour-piercing capability at short distances. However, apparently to supplement the 47/32, Italy acquired a batch of 100 PaK 35/36s in 1940, the first of which was sent as a sample sometime in 1940 with the remaining 99 arriving in Naples in December 1940. Of the 100, 87 were sent to Libya and the remainder were held in Italy for possible shipment to Italian East

Africa. The gun saw service in North Africa, particularly during the Axis offensive of spring 1941 when it was assigned as part of the antitank assets to the 'Ariete' armoured division as well as to the 'Bologna', 'Brescia' and 'Pavia' divisions.

Specifications
Designation: *Cannone controcarro da 37/45*; original designation 3.7 cm PaK 35/36 L45
Number acquired: 100
Originator: Rheinmetall–Borsig AG, Düsseldorf
Producer: Rheinmetall–Borsig AG, Düsseldorf
Caliber: 37mm (1.46 inches)
Length of tube: 1,665mm (65.5 inches)
Overall width: 1,650mm (65 inches)
Overall height: 1,220mm (48 inches)
Weight in action: 444kg (979lbs)
Carriage: Split trail
Wheel track: 1,540mm (60.6 inches)
Wheel type/diameter: Steel with pneumatic tires
Breech type: Sliding wedge
Recuperator type: Hydro-spring
Elevation: –8 degrees to +25 degrees
Traverse: 59 degrees with trails open; 4 degrees 30 minutes with trails closed
Muzzle velocity: 745m/s (2,444fps)
Maximum range: 6,800 meters (7,437 yards) maximum; 800 meters (875 yards) effective
Rate of fire: 12–15 rounds per minute
Ammunition types: AP, HE, hollow charge, training
Shell weight: AP 0.68kg (1.5lbs)
Armour penetration: 34mm (1.3 inches) at 100 meters (109 yards) (3.7cm Pzgr Ptr.); 64mm (2.5 inches) at 100 meters (3.7cm Pzgr Patr. 40)

47/32 mod. 35 and mod. 39 gun

The Breda/Böhler 47/32 mod. 35 gun was the most widely used antitank and infantry support gun in the Italian Army during the Second World War. The gun was originally designed and developed by the Austrian firm of Böhler and was adopted by the Italian Army in 1935 to replace the First World War vintage 65/17 infantry support gun. It met the *Regio Esercito*'s need to have a modern piece for direct infantry support and antitank use, a role that in the 1930s was gaining increasing importance as a result of the new theories concerning the use of tanks in modern warfare. The Böhler was an ideal antitank gun for the times as it was small, light, easily transportable, highly accurate and able to penetrate the armour of most contemporary tanks. It used a variety of ammunition, from explosive to armour piercing, and during the war it used HEAT ammunition ('EP' and 'EPS', in Italian parlance) developed by the Italians.

Soon after adoption the gun was licensed to Italian industry and produced locally in several thousand copies. With respect to the original Austrian gun, the Italian model underwent several modifications including improvements designed to make replacing the barrel easier and a stronger suspension system. The 47/32 gun had a split trail carriage; the trails could be positioned separately according to conditions of the ground so as to permit fire on virtually all types of terrain. While in the firing position, the wheels could be removed, giving the gun a very low silhouette. It had a mono-bloc steel barrel with a sliding wedge breech mechanism. The gun was slightly improved

Bersaglieri manning a 47/32 antitank gun in Tunisia. The gun's small size and low silhouette made it easy to conceal and difficult to spot, especially by advancing enemy armour. (Enrico Finazzer)

in the Model 39 variant for motorized units, with new spoked wheels replacing the disc wheels, reinforced suspension and a new optical sight for antitank fire.

According to tables of organization, in June 1940 each infantry regiment was supposed to have eight 47/32 guns for close support fire, and each infantry division likewise was supposed to have an additional divisional company with eight guns as an antitank unit. In 1941 the army began to constitute independent antitank battalions based on 24 pieces, for assignment at the corps and divisional level. Between 1941 and 1942 the infantry battalions of the motorized divisions and *Bersaglieri* and 'Giovani Fascisti' battalions of the armoured and motorized divisions, as well as the 'Superga' and 'La Spezia' divisions were reinforced by the addition of one, two or three platoons of four 47/32 guns. The 47/32 was also the heaviest weapon assigned to the parachute divisions. Each of the three parachute infantry regiments in the 'Folgore' division had a company with six of the 47/32 guns, and the divisional artillery regiments had three battalions with two batteries equipped with the 47/32.

In North Africa the gun was mounted on specially designed rotating platforms on trucks such as the Lancia 3Ro, as well as on the AS37 and AS42 light desert trucks and on the later AS43. The 47/32 was also in the Ansaldo modified version 47/32 *per carro*, the main armament on the Italian M13 and M14 medium tanks as well as on the L40 light self-propelled gun. Although by 1942 the 47/32 was inadequate as a first-line antitank weapon, it nevertheless had acquitted itself well during the initial years of the conflict, outclassing other antitank weapons of the time such as the British 2-pdr and the German 3.7cm PaK 35/36 antitank gun.

Specifications
Designation: *Cannone anticarro e d'accompagnamento 47/32, mod. 35* and *mod. 39*
Adopted by Italy: 1935
Inventory (10 June 1940): 928

Subsequent production: about 3,000
Originator: Böhler, Kapfenberg, Austria
Producer: Breda; Cogne; Ansaldo (Pozzuoli); Arsenali Regio Esercito (Piacenza, Naples and Turin)
Caliber: 47mm (1.85 inches)
Crew: 5
Length of tube: 1,680mm (66.1 inches)
Overall length: 3,920mm (154.3 inches)
Overall width: 1,020mm (40.1 inches)
Overall height: 744mm (29.3 inches)
Weight in action: 277 kg (611lbs)
Carriage: Split trail
Wheel track: 880mm (34.6 inches)
Wheel type/diameter:Model 39 Elektron alloy with seven spokes; semi-pneumatic Celerflex tires/600mm (23.62 inches); Model 35 were fitted with disc wheels instead
Breech type: Horizontal sliding wedge
Recuperator type: Spring
Elevation: –10 degrees to +56 degrees
Traverse: 60 degrees
Muzzle velocity: 630m/s (2,067fps) AP; 250m/s (820fps) HE
Maximum range: 7,000 meters (7,655 yards) maximum; 3,500 meters (3,828 yards) effective
Rate of fire: 7–8 rounds per minute
Ammunition types: AP, HE, hollow charge
Shell weight: AP 1.5kg (3.3lbs); HE 2.45kg (5.4lbs)
Armour penetration: 40mm at 650 meters (1.6 inches at 711 yards)

65/17 gun

Tunisia, spring 1943. The age of some of these 65/17 guns is attested to by the original steel rimmed wooden spoked wheels on all but the gun in the foreground in this battery. (Enrico Finazzer)

The *cannone da 65/17*, first conceived in 1902, was designed by the Turin Arsenal. Originally designated as the *cannone 65A* (that is, '*acciaio*', 'steel') to distinguish it from other pieces made of *bronzo* (bronze, B) or *ghisa* (cast iron, G), it was adopted by the Italian Army in 1910 to equip the mountain artillery regiments. The 65/17 was the first gun to be entirely conceived, developed and built in Italy that incorporated a recoil mechanism, and for its time it was a modern piece, even though so much time had elapsed between its original concept and its adoption that it could no longer be considered the latest word in mountain artillery, especially with respect to its elevation and traverse capabilities. Ammunition types were HE, HEAT, shrapnel and canister.

In the 1920s several batteries of the 65/17 took part in operations to reconquer Libya. On occasion, the gun was carried aboard Fiat 15ter trucks to provide mobility. In the Second World War, the 65/17 was widely used and saw action on all fronts in which the Italians were engaged. In North Africa the 65/17 initially was mounted on Fiat 634 trucks but beginning in spring of 1941 these guns were mounted on captured British Morris CS8 light trucks and formed part of the so-called '*batterie volanti*' ('flying batteries') that were quite effective as mobile artillery attached to Italian reconnaissance units and, later, with the 'Giovani Fascisti' division. Essentially, the shield and wheels were removed from the guns which were then mounted on specially fabricated mounts that could rotate 360° fixed to the truck beds. These improvised truck/gun combinations proved to be fairly successful systems; a total of seven batteries (28 guns) were equipped with these guns, which functioned effectively in the antitank role as well as in the conventional artillery role. Later, the 80th Artillery Regiment of the 'La Spezia' air-transportable division sent to fight in Tunisia had these light pieces adapted for towing with specially modified Guzzi Trialce motor-tricycles. Its regiment was formed of two battalions of two batteries, on four guns and four motor-tricycles each. Despite its age, during the Second World War the 65/17 proved itself to still be an effective weapon. Its larger caliber and EP ammunition provided antitank performance superior to the newer 47/32 gun.

Specifications
Designation: Initially (January 1918) designated as '*65A*' (the 'A' signifying '*acciaio*', or 'steel'); subsequently the designation was changed to '*65 da montagna*', and from 1926 the gun was known as the '*cannone d'accompagnamento da 65/17*'
Adopted: 1913
Inventory (10 June 1940): 700
Originator: Arsenale Regio Esercito Torino
Producer: Westinghouse (Vado Ligure) for slide and cradle; Terni, Naples Arsenal and Turin Arsenal for the guns and carriages; the firm of Franchi–Gregorini was also involved in some aspects of manufacture
Caliber: 65mm (2.56 inches)
Length of tube: 1,150mm (45.275 inches)
Overall length: 3,570mm (140.5 inches)
Overall width: 1,000mm (39.4 inches)
Overall height: 1,250mm (49.2 inches)
Weight in action: 556kg (1,226lbs)
Carriage: Single trail
Wheel track: 960mm (37.7 inches)
Wheel type/diameter: Wood spoke artillery wheels with 12 spokes/700mm (27.5 inches)
Breech type: Eccentric screw
Recuperator type: Spring
Recoil length: 950mm
Elevation: −7 degrees 30 minutes to +20 degrees

Traverse: 8 degrees
Muzzle velocity: 320–355m/s (1,050–1,165fps)
Maximum range: 6,500 meters (7,108 yards); effective antitank range 500 meters (547 yards)
Rate of fire: 6–12 rounds per minute
Ammunition types: HE, shrapnel, canister, AP (1936), EP (1942)
Shell weight: HE 4.23kg (9.33lbs); AP 4,23kg (9.33lbs)
Armour penetration: 76mm

75/27 mod. 06 gun

A 75/27 gun being readied to fire at El Mechili in February 1942. Note the empty shell casings in the foreground. (Enrico Finazzer)

In 1902 the Italian Army realized that the time had come to replace its old model 75A 75mm field guns mounted on rigid carriages with a more modern gun of similar caliber that incorporated a recoil system. Several guns were tested, including a modernized version of the 75A, a 73mm Krupp gun and a 75mm Krupp gun; the 75mm Krupp gun was chosen as a result. In 1906 the gun was accepted for service designated simply as the '75/27', but subsequently it was redesignated as the mod.1906 to distinguish it from the 75/27 French Déport adopted by Italy in 1911 (and designated the '75/27 mod. 11'). In order to meet wartime requirements, between 1916 and 1919 a total of 2,400 were produced and used extensively during the First World War.

The gun was sturdily constructed and reliable; its pole trail, however, restricted its elevation. It had a constant recoil mechanism, a steel outer barrel with a liner and was fitted with a 4mm

(0.16 inch) shield to protect the gunners. Its original configuration featured wooden spoke artillery wheels that were standard on virtually all similar field pieces during the First World War. Prior to the Second World War, the original wheels were replaced by new metal ones with semi-pneumatic rubber tires for direct towing by light artillery tractors, principally the TL37.

The gun could use an optical panoramic sight for direct fire or an elevating arc for indirect fire; open sights consisting of a blade front sight and notched rear sight were fixed to the gun itself. It fired mainly explosive ammunition, but for special purposes, as in the antitank role, it could use armour piercing or HEAT (EP and EPS) rounds. However, its effectiveness as an antitank gun was rather low even with the special ammunition, and effective range was limited to about 700 meters.

On the eve of Italy's entry into the Second World War, about 1,700 guns of this type remained in service, some 101 used as static artillery in fortified bunkers on different mounts. Along with their contemporary, the French-origin 75/27 mod. 11, they formed the backbone of the divisional artillery regiments, with as many as two battalions out of three, and even though unable to match the capabilities of most of the Allied artillery they faced, bore the brunt of the Italian artillery's workload. The 75/27 mod. 06 was used mainly in the North African campaign where it was at a serious disadvantage compared to the excellent, much more modern British 25-pdr. Taking a leaf from the British, in 1943 a circular platform similar to the one used with the 25-pdr was developed that enabled a full 360° traverse for the mod. 06, but this entered service too late to be of any use in North Africa. By May 1941 there were only 75 of these guns left in Africa, of which six still retained the old wood spoke artillery wheels. By October of 1941 the number of mod. 06 guns in North Africa had risen to 263, then being reduced to only 93 guns following the British Operation Crusader. During the campaign in North Africa, some German field batteries had been issued the mod. 06 as a stopgap measure until sufficient German equipment could be furnished.

Specifications
Designation: *Cannone da 75/27 mod. 06*
Adopted by Italy: 1906
Originator: Krupp A.G., Essen
Producer: Krupp (initial production); Italian Army arsenals (Naples and Turin) series production
Caliber: 75mm (2.95 inches)
Length of tube: 2,250mm (88.6 inches)
Weight in action: 1,015kg (2,238lbs) with shield
Carriage: Single pole trail
Wheel track: 1,520mm (59.8 inches)
Wheel type/diameter: Originally 12-spoke wood artillery wheels with steel rims; later about 18 out of 100 of the guns in service received new axles whose wheels were Elektron alloy and later metal spoke wheels with solid or semi-pneumatic tires; 1,300mm (51.2 inches)
Breech type: Horizontal sliding wedge
Recuperator type: Four springs
Elevation: −10 degrees to +16 degrees
Traverse: 7 degrees
Muzzle velocity: 502m/s (1,647fps)
Maximum range: 10,240 meters (11,199 yards)
Rate of fire: 6–8 rounds per minute
Ammunition types: HE, chemical (gas, never used in the Second World War), inert training
Shell weight: HE 6.35kg (14lbs)

75/27 mod. 11 gun

A 75/27 mod. 11 gun mounted on a SPA TL37 tractor chassis in North Africa. (Enrico Finazzer)

The *Regio Esercito* was less than completely happy with the performance of the Krupp 75/27 gun that had been adopted in 1906. The difficulty encountered in moving the Krupp gun over rough terrain coupled with its very limited traverse and elevation capability led the Italians to reconsider their choice and seek a possible alternative. Accordingly, in 1910 they ran a series of tests with a Déport, initially in France and then in Italy. Following the tests, the Italian Army bought two batteries of Déports for operational testing. In order to clearly distinguish between the two guns, the Krupp was designated the '*cannone 75/27 mod. 06*', and the Déport the '*cannone 75/27 mod. 11*', reflecting the respective years of adoption (1906 and 1911). The most significant difference between the two guns was the split trail of the Déport which allowed a much greater elevation than the Krupp. The variable recoil system of the Déport was radically different than that of the Krupp, consisting of two recoil systems that worked in concert with each other, limiting recoil to about a quarter that of the mod. 06. The Déport, which was fitted with a 4mm (0.16 inch) thick gunner's shield similar to that of the mod. 06, was easily recognizable by the prominent box housing above the barrel that contained the recoil mechanism.

During the interwar period, the 75/27 mod. 11 remained as a first-line weapon in the artillery regiments of the infantry divisions, while a number of improvements to increase range and mobility were made. Variable charge ammunition was introduced that increased range by 2,000 meters; ultimately, over a dozen different types of ammunition were provided for the mod. 11, covering a spectrum from the original basic HE round through chemical, smoke and EPS hollow-charge ammunition.

During the Second World War, the 75/27 mod. 11 was employed operationally on all fronts in which the Italians fought, except for Italian East Africa. It served alongside the mod. 06 in North Africa. At the beginning of the war, the armoured divisions in that theater that were to receive the 75/32 instead replaced their 75/27 mod. 11 with the mod. 06 for unknown reasons. Of the 108 mod. 11 guns in North Africa in 1942, by February 1943 only ten remained. The circular firing platform developed for the 75/27 mod. 06, copied from the British, was also suitable for use by the mod. 11. Three batteries of the mod. 11 were mounted on SPA TL37 light tractors in North Africa in 1942 to form a battalion of '*batterie volanti*' ('flying batteries') to provide better mobility; the gun/tractor combination was a local conversion and proved fairly effective.

Specifications
Designation: *Cannone 75/27 mod. 11*
Adopted by Italy: 1911
Originator: Déport (France)
Producer: Italian consortium led by Vickers Terni
Caliber: 75mm (2.95 inches)
Crew: 4
Length of tube: 2,132mm (83.9 inches)
Overall length: 4,160mm (163.8 inches) in battery; 850mm (334.65 inches) traveling
Overall width: 1,900mm (74.8 inches) traveling
Overall height: 1,700mm (66.9 inches)
Weight in action: 1,076kg (2,372lbs)
Carriage: Split trail
Wheel track: 1,595mm (62.8 inches)
Wheel diameter: Originally 12-spoke wood artillery wheels with steel rims; later more than
    300 received new axles whose wheels were of the nine pressed metal spoke type with semi-
    pneumatic tires: 1,300mm (51.2 inches)
Breech type: Automatic breech with eccentric screw
Recoil length: 1,360mm
Elevation: −15 degrees to + 65 degrees
Traverse: 52 degrees 9 minutes
Muzzle velocity: 500m/s (1,640fps)
Maximum range: 10,200 meters (11,555 yds)
Rate of fire: 6–8 rounds per minute
Ammunition types: HE, AP, WP, smoke (semi-fixed)
Shell weight: 6.3kg (14lbs) HE

75/27 C.K. antiaircraft gun

The *cannone da 75/27 C.K.* (*Commissione Krupp*) has its roots in the German 75/27 Krupp gun that the Italians examined for purchase in 1913. The onset of the First World War, which saw Italy and Germany on opposite sides, put an end to dealing with Germany for acquisition of the Krupp guns, but Italy had already begun domestic production and by September 1915 could field a number of mobile air defense batteries. The total number of 75/27 C.K. produced during the war amounted to 165 systems, including reserve stocks. Of these, 72 were *autocannoni*, mounted on trucks, the rest being either mounted on trailers or in fixed installations. Throughout the First World War the 75/27 C.K. gave a good account of itself.

After hostilities ceased in 1918, the surviving 75/27 C.K. systems were the only antiaircraft guns retained in Italian service, even though by then they were obsolete. Additionally, in 1926 the Italian Army ordered another 57 guns in order to form a further 14 batteries that were to be mounted on a more modern truck chassis, the Ceirano 50 CMA, developed specifically for the gun.

Three battalions of the 75/27 CK were in Libya at the beginning of hostilities; some pieces were captured by the British, and subsequently recaptured by the Germans, as seen in this example bearing German insignia. (Ralph Riccio)

By far the largest number of Italian truck-mounted artillery systems employed during the Second World War was comprised of the First World War vintage 75/27 C.K. systems, still mounted on the Ceirano 50 CMA truck chassis. In October 1939 prior to Italy's entry into the Second World War, the *Regio Esercito* still had some 166 75/27 C.K. guns in active service. The system formed the mobile antiaircraft battalions of each army corps. As many as three battalions were deployed in North Africa as early as 1937, although it was widely accepted that the Ceirano was too heavy to move in a desert environment and therefore unable to move outside the few roads of the colony of Libya. The XX Battalion was assigned without great success to the *Brigata Corazzata Speciale*, an armoured brigade formed in 1940 by hastily gathering together all the armoured units deployed in that area. It is questionable whether the pieces could have been better adapted to antitank support as had been demonstrated by the use of antiaircraft guns in the antitank role by the Germans in France, but no one in the Italian Army hierarchy had the thought of using them in this new role at the time. Interestingly, a few of the *autocannone da 75/27 C.K.* that were captured by the British in North Africa subsequently were recaptured by the Germans who used them in the antitank as well as air defense roles.

Specifications
Designation: *Cannone da 75/27 C.K.*
Adopted by Italy: 1915
Originator: Krupp AG
Producer: Arsenale Regio Esercito di Napoli
Caliber: 75mm (2.95 inches)
Length of tube: 2,250mm (88.6 inches)
Overall length: 2,195mm (86.4 inches)
Weight in action: 1,030kg (2,270lbs)
Carriage: Pedestal mount
Wheel track: None (pedestal mount)

Wheel type/diameter: None
Breech type: Horizontal wedge
Elevation: 0 degrees to + 70 degrees
Traverse: 360 degrees
Muzzle velocity: 510m/s (1,673fps)
Maximum range: 6,100 meters (6,671 yards)
Rate of fire: 15 rounds per minute
Ammunition types: AA
Shell weight: 6.1kg (13.5lbs)

77/28 mod. 5 and mod. 5/8 gun

The 77/28 gun was the designation given by the Italians to the First World War Škoda 8cm M5 and M5/8 field gun. The mod. 5 and 5/8 guns captured by the Italians or acquired by Italy after the First World War as war reparations were used in the Italian colonies to a limited extent during the Second World War. The Italian Army decided to deploy the 77/28 in the colonies and equip the local colonial troops with this piece in Italian East Africa and Libya. In this role, it fought during the initial phases of the Second World War. Later, in 1942, dozens of these pieces were assigned to some infantry divisions in North Africa (the 'Brescia', 'Bologna' and 'Pavia' divisions), which used this veteran piece as an antitank gun in the absence of anything better. These divisions took part in the battle of El Alamein using this equipment. Other 77/28 guns were assigned in 1943 in Tunisia to the 'Centauro' armoured division, the 'La Spezia' air-transportable division and the 'Trieste' motorized division as well as the special desert unit called the *Raggruppamento Sahariano* ('Sahara Battlegroup').

Specifications
Designation: *Cannone da 77/28, mod. 5* and *mod. 5/8* – ex-Austro–Hungarian *8cm Feldkanone M5* and *8cm Feldkanone M5/8*
Originator: Škoda, Plzeň (Bohemia, now part of the Czech Republic)
Producer: Škoda; Böhler
User countries: Austria–Hungary, Italy, Hungary, Yugoslavia, Czechoslovakia, Austria, Germany (after September 1943)
Caliber: 76.5mm (3.01 inches)
Length of tube: 2,285mm (89.96 inches)
Weight in action: 1,050kg (2,315lbs)
Carriage: Box trail
Wheel track: 1,610mm (63.39 inches)
Wheel type/diameter: 12-spoke wood wheels with steel rims/1,300mm (51.18 inches)
Breech type: Horizontal sliding wedge
Recuperator type: Hydro-spring
Elevation: –7 degrees to +18 degrees
Traverse: 8 degrees
Muzzle velocity: 536m/s (1,759fps)
Maximum range: 8,500 meters (9,296 yards) HE; 6,100 meters (6,671 yards) shrapnel
Rate of fire: 8–10 rounds per minute
Ammunition types: HE, shrapnel
Shell weight: 6.34kg (13.76lbs) HE; 6.68kg (14.73lbs)

75/46 mod. 34, mod. 34M and mod. 40 antiaircraft gun

A 75/46 antiaircraft gun of the 90th Gruppo in Tunisia. (Enrico Finazzer)

At the end of the 1920s, as the Italian Army was taking stock of its overall artillery inventory and assessing requirements for new weapons, it became apparent that a replacement was needed for the aging 75/27 C.K. and other assorted First World War vintage antiaircraft guns of Italian and Austro–Hungarian manufacture. The results of early attempts by Ansaldo and OTO, which, respectively, developed 75/50 and 75/45 prototypes, were disappointing, leading the army to test some foreign weapons for possible adoption. One of the weapons, the Bofors 75/mm M29, caught the attention of Ansaldo engineers who used it as the basis for their design of the *cannone da 75/46*. It is interesting to note that a clandestine design team from Krupp was working in Sweden at the time of development of the Bofors Model 29, and that many elements of the Bofors design were later incorporated into the German 88mm Flak 18. Thus, the Italian 75/46, which borrowed features from the Bofors Model 29 could be considered either a half-brother or a cousin to the iconic 88. The *cannone da 75/46 mod. 34*, adopted by the *Regio Esercito* in 1934 also proved to be an effective antitank gun.

An initial order for 100 guns was placed in late 1933 or early 1934, and by October 1939, 84 pieces had been delivered; in June 1940 the number of guns on hand had decreased to 76, probably explained by the fact that eight guns sent to Spain remained there. The 75/46 saw its first action in Spain where two test batteries (eight guns) were sent during the civil war. After that, either in the static or in the field version, it took part in every campaign fought by the Italian army in the Second World War. Five field battalions, the XIV, XXXV, XL, XC and XCI, were sent to Tunisia in 1943 taking part in the final battles against the Allies on North African soil; it goes without saying that they could do little to stop the mounting tide of Allied aircraft and armoured vehicles.

Specifications
Designation: *Cannone da 75/46 C.A., mod. 34, mod. 34M* and *mod. 40*
Adopted: 1934
Originator: Ansaldo
Producer: Ansaldo-Pozzuoli, Arsenale Regio Esercito di Piacenza, OTO
Caliber: 75mm (2.95 inches)
Length of barrel: 3,450mm (135.8 inches)
Overall length: 7,400mm (291.34 inches)
Overall width: 1,850mm (72.83 inches)
Overall height: 2,150mm (84.65 inches)
Weight in action: 3,300kg (7,275lbs)
Carriage: Folding cruciform pedestal mount on two-wheeled carriage
Wheel track: 1,300mm (51.2 inches)
Breech type: Horizontal wedge
Recuperator type: Hydro-pneumatic
Recoil length: 1,100mm (43.3 inches) maximum; 610mm (24 inches) minimum
Elevation: 0 degrees to +90 degrees
Traverse: 360 degrees
Muzzle velocity: 800m/s (2,625fps)
Maximum effective ceiling: 8,500 meters (27,887 feet)
Rate of fire: 15 rounds per minute
Ammunition types: AA, AT
Shell weight: AA 10.64kg (23.5lbs)

90/53 mod. 39, mod. 41P, mod. 41C antiaircraft gun

A 90/53 gun mounted on a Lancia 3Ro chassis; this captured gun had belonged to the DII Gruppo
Autocannoni of the 'Centauro' armoured division, as seen by the stylized 'Centauro' stencil on the cab door.
(Ralph Riccio)

The *cannone da 90/53* was very similar in appearance and performance characteristics to the iconic 88mm German Flak 18 and Flak 36 antiaircraft guns. Although the 90/53 never was accorded the same coverage or respect as the German 88 in press accounts and popular lore, the 90/53 was in several respects a better gun than the 88: it was simpler to produce, it fired a heavier shell at a higher muzzle velocity and had a higher effective ceiling than the German guns. Like the 88, it was also highly effective as a tank killer. Reference to this gun has made its way into popular Italian jargon: an important or respected person is often referred to as a *'pezzo da novanta'* ('a 90mm piece') roughly equivalent to 'a big gun' in English.

The 90/53 was based on a 90/50 naval gun that had been developed by Ansaldo; in 1938 the *Regio Esercito* put forth a requirement for an antiaircraft gun to replace the 75/46 gun, and in 1939 the DSSTAM asked Ansaldo to develop a ground version of the naval gun. An order was placed for eight test guns, four of which were static versions designated the mod. 41P (the 'P' standing for *'posizione'*, or 'static') and four of which were field versions, designated the mod. 41C (the 'C' standing for *'campale'*, or 'field/mobile'). Due to delays in delivering the mod. 41C towed version, as a stopgap measure in January 1941 the Army General Staff directed Ansaldo to mount the 90/53 gun on both the 4x2 Lancia 3Ro chassis and the 6x4 Breda Dovunque 52 chassis. The prototype of the *autocannone* on the Lancia 3Ro chassis was ready in February 1941. The first field batteries of 90/53 were deployed in the *autocannone* version at the beginning of 1942 in North Africa, assigned to the 'Ariete' (DI Gruppo) and 'Littorio' (DIII Gruppo) armoured divisions. They fought the 1942 campaign until the Battle of El Alamein. Later, another battalion, the DII, was sent to Tunisia along with the 'Centauro' armoured division.

Specifications
Designation: *Cannone da 90/53, mod. 39, mod. 41P* and *mod. 41C*
Adopted: 1939
Originator: Ansaldo
Producer: Ansaldo, OTO
Caliber: 90mm (3.54 inches)
Crew: 9
Length of tube: 5,039mm (198.4 inches)
Overall length: 7,950mm (313 inches) on trailer; 6,520mm (256.7 inches) in battery
Overall width: 2,000mm (78.7 inches) on trailer; 5,000mm (196.9 inches) in battery
Overall height: 2,930mm (115.4 inches) on trailer; 2,000mm (78.7 inches) in battery
Weight in action: 6,240kg (13,757lbs); 8,950kg (19,731lbs) travel weight
Carriage: Pedestal on cruciform platform
Wheel track: 1,994mm (78.5 inches)
Wheel type/diameter: 8-spoke steel wheels with pneumatic tires/12.75 x 32 inches
Breech type: Horizontal sliding wedge
Recuperator type: Hydro-pneumatic (dual)
Recoil length: 905mm at 0 degrees elevation; 780mm at 85 degrees elevation; the recoil regulator compensated for the elevation angle, preventing the breech mechanism from hitting the firing platform
Elevation: –2 degrees to + 85 degrees
Traverse: 360 degrees
Muzzle velocity: 830m/s (2,723fps)
Maximum range: 17,4700 meters horizontal; 12,000 meters ceiling
Rate of fire: 20 rounds per minute
Ammunition types: AA, AP, HE
Shell weight: 10.1kg (22.3lbs) AA; 11.25kg (24.8lbs) AP

100/17 mod. 14 and mod. 16 howitzer

A Škoda 100/17 howitzer firing during the summer of 1942. Received as war reparations from Austro–Hungary after the First World War, the howitzer served the Italians well in North Africa, supplementing the 75/27 gun in divisional artillery regiments. (Enrico Finazzer)

Prior to the First World War, Škoda developed and produced two modern 10cm mountain howitzers, the M8 and M10, which were the first howitzers of the Austro–Hungarian army to be provided with a hydraulic barrel recoil mechanism using the adjustable recoil principle. Škoda subsequently developed a new 10cm field howitzer, the M14, that with modifications became the M16 mountain howitzer, developed specifically for the mountainous terrain of the Italian theater. The end of the First World War saw Italy furnished with a virtual glut of the two versions of the 100/17: there were 1,339 mod. 14 and 95 mod. 16 howitzers as complete guns; of these 212 were scrapped because they were beyond repair. Although the Italians had obtained a large number of 100/17 howitzers, the corresponding stock of ammunition was low. The Italians undertook to remedy this by producing their own ammunition, the mod. 32 shell, which increased the range of the gun by 500 meters. In 1942 the Italians also developed the EP antitank ammunition followed by the EPS in 1943 for use with the 100/17.

Along with the 75/27 gun, during the Second World War the 100/17 howitzer was the backbone of the Italian army divisional artillery that included a battalion of 100/17 in most of the artillery regiments. As a result, the 100/17 appeared on every front where the Italians fought, although in both North Africa and Russia, the range of the 100/17 was found to be inadequate compared to the artillery it faced. In North Africa four batteries of 100/17 guns were mounted on Lancia 3Ro trucks with modified platforms and the cabs cut to allow 360° traverse, to form a battalion. These local conversions, along with various other types of guns mounted on either Italian or captured Commonwealth trucks, fought alongside the other truck-mounted artillery batteries within reconnaissance units. In 1941 it was later to be assigned to the 'Giovani Fascisti' division and fight until the very end of the African campaign in Tunisia. They were a very effective means of providing mobile artillery to support Italian forces in the desert.

Specifications
Designation: *Obice da 100/17, mod. 14* and *mod. 16* – ex-Austro–Hungarian *10cm Feldkanone M.14* and 10cm *Gebirgshaubitze M.16*

Originator: Škoda, Plzeň (Bohemia, now part of the Czech Republic)
Producers: Škoda; Böhler
Caliber: 100mm (3.94 inches)
Length of tube: 1,930mm (76 inches)
Overall length: 5,300mm (208.7 inches)
Overall width: 1,780mm (70 inches) mod.14; 900mm (35.4 inches) mod.16
Weight in action: 1,417kg (3,124lbs) mod 14; 1,235kg (2,723lbs) mod. 16
Carriage: Box trail
Wheel track: 1,550mm (61 inches) mod. 14; 950mm (37.4 inches) mod. 16
Wheel type/diameter: 10-spoke wood wheels with steel rims; upgraded with Elektron wheels
    and semi-pneumatic tires/1,300mm (51.2 inches) mod. 14; 900mm (35.4 inches) mod. 16
Breech type: Horizontal wedge
Recuperator type: Spring
Recoil length: 1,370mm (53.9 inches) maximum; 500mm (19.7 inches) minimum
Elevation: −8 degrees to +48 degrees mod. 14; +70 degrees maximum for mod. 16
Traverse: 5 degrees
Muzzle velocity: 407m/s (1,335fps)
Maximum range: 9,200 meters (10,061 yards)
Rate of fire: 4−6 rounds per minute
Ammunition types: HE, shrapnel, AT
Shell weight: 13.8kg (30.4lbs) HE

105/28 gun

A 105/28 gun in a semi-revetted position engaged against the Tobruk defenses in the fall of 1941.
(Enrico Finazzer)

The *cannone da 105/28* was an Italian field gun based on the French *canon de 105mm de campagne système Schneider*, which in turn was based on the Russian *Putilov 106.7mm M1910-12* gun. Production of the 105-A, as it was originally designated (the 'A' suffix stood for '*acciaio*', 'steel') began in September 1914 and was first issued to units in June 1916. Production continued until 1919. Originally it was designed for animal traction; later, but as early as 1938 a number of 105/28 guns began to be modified for towing at a higher speed, particularly on desert terrain. The gun was fitted with Elektron wheels with semi-pneumatic Celerflex tires, the brake system was modified and a new type of tow hook was fitted. This arrangement allowed the gun to be towed without a limber by a TM40 tractor at speeds up to 40km/h. During the war the Elektron wheels were replaced by pressed steel wheels. Ammunition included high explosive as well as armour-piercing and hollow charge (EP and EPS) ammunition for use in antitank role.

At the outbreak of the Second World War, the 105/28, with a total of 956 pieces in service, still formed, along with the 149/13 howitzer, the backbone of the *raggruppamenti d'artiglieria di corpo d'armata* (army corps artillery groups), and thus it appeared on every front of the war where Italian units were deployed. In North Africa where the guns were constantly at a disadvantage against the British 25-pdr, during the same period there were eight battalions assigned to the four *raggruppamenti di artiglieria di corpo d'armata* (corps artillery assets), plus four independent batteries equipped with the 105/28, assigned to static artillery duties around the major Libyan cities. All of them were lost during the British counteroffensive of December 1940–January 1941 which almost put an end to the Italian presence in North Africa. Subsequently, an undetermined number of the 105/28 guns were shipped to North Africa along with the new divisions assigned there and took part in all the ensuing phases of the war, from the siege of Tobruk to El Alamein to, finally, the defense of the bridgehead of Tunisia where only 33 of the guns were still available, which was further reduced to 14 at the battle of Enfidaville in April 1943.

Specifications
Designation: *Cannone da 105/28*
Originator: Schneider (France)
Adopted by Italy: 1914
Producer: Ansaldo-Genoa
Caliber 105mm (4.13 inches)
Length of tube: 2,987mm (117.6 inches)
Overall length: 6,925mm (272.6 inches) in battery; 7,079mm (278.7 inches) travel
Overall width: 1,950mm (76.8 inches)
Overall height: 1,828mm (72 inches)
Weight in action: 2,170kg in battery (4,784lbs)
Carriage: Box trail
Wheel track: 1,650mm (65 inches)
Wheel type/diameter: 12-spoke wood wheels with steel rims/1,330mm (52.4 inches);
Elektron or pressed steel wheels with semi-pneumatic Celerflex tires/1,300mm (51.22 inches)
Breech type: Eccentric screw, Schneider pattern
Recuperator type: Hydro-pneumatic
Recoil length: 1,200mm (47.28 inches)
Elevation: –5 degrees to +37 degrees
Traverse: 14 degrees
Muzzle velocity: 565m/s (1,854fps)
Maximum range: 11,425 meters (12,495 yards) with the original ammunition; 12,780 meters
    (13,976 yards) with mod. 32 ammunition
Rate of fire: From 1 round per minute to a maximum of 4 rounds per minute

Ammunition types: HE, AP, smoke

Shell weight: HE ammunition: 16.24kg (35.8lbs); mod. 32 ammunition: 16.3kg (35.95 lbs);
hollow charge ammunition (EP): 14kg (30.87lbs)

104/32–105/32 gun

A 105/32 gun ready to fire in Tunisia, spring 1943. Three battalions of this upgraded First World War
Austro–Hungarian piece were sent to Tunisia in late 1942. (Enrico Finazzer)

The *cannone da 105/32* gun was the Škoda *10.4cm Feldhaubitze M.15* re-bored from 104mm to
105mm. The gun originally was conceived as a heavy flat trajectory siege gun, with requirements
being laid down in 1902. The definitive gun was designated the *M.15 10.4cm Feldkanone* and was
used in the heavy artillery role rather than as a siege gun as originally intended. All factors considered, the gun did not have any innovative features, but was for its time an effective and reliable
piece of artillery. The carriage was a standard box trail with two wooden wheels; the steel barrel
was reinforced with two external rings, one in the rear and another in the mid-section. The breech
mechanism was a horizontal sliding wedge and recoil was constant. As was normal for its era, it was
designed for animal towing, although it was adapted by the Italian army to mechanical towing by
way of the '*carrello elastico*' towed by a Pavesi tractor.

Upon Italy's entry into the war in June 1940 there were 12 corps artillery groups equipped with
the 105/32. The 105/32 saw action on a number of fronts including Russia, Tunisia and Sicily. The
LVII, LVIII and LIX battalions were sent to Tunisia at the end of 1942 within the XXX Army
Corps, when the Axis troops made their last stand against the Allied forces who had landed in
Morocco and Algeria.

Specifications
Designation: *Cannone da 105/32* – ex-Austro–Hungarian *10.4cm Feldhaubitze M.15*
Entry in Italian service: After the First World War (captured, war booty)
Originator: Škoda, Plzeň (Bohemia, now part of the Czech Republic)
Producer: Škoda; Magyar Àgyùgyàr (Győr, Hungary)
Caliber: 104mm originally; re-bored by Italian arsenal to 105mm (4.13 inches)

Length of tube: 3,360mm (132.3 inches)
Overall length: 3,640mm (143.3 inches)
Weight in action: 3,299kg with shield (7,273lbs)
Carriage: Box trail
Wheel track: 1,600mm (63 inches)
Wheel type/diameter: 12-spoke wood wheels with steel rims/1,300mm (51.18 inches)
Breech type: Horizontal wedge
Elevation: –10 degrees to +30 degrees
Traverse: 6 degrees
Muzzle velocity: 685m/s (2,247fps)
Maximum range: 16,200 meters (17,717 yards)
Rate of fire: Up to 10 rounds per minute
Ammunition types: HE, shrapnel
Shell weight: 17.5kg (38.6lbs) HE

149/13 howitzer

The *obice da 149/13* began life as the First World War vintage Austro–Hungarian *15cm schwere Feldhaubitze M.14*, introduced into Austro–Hungarian service in 1914, later followed by a modified version designated the Model 14/16. The gun was a Škoda product and reflected that firm's usual standards of robustness and technical innovation. The M.14 fired separate loading ammunition. Significant numbers of the 149/13 were acquired by Italy as war reparations from Austria at the end of the First World War, and during the interwar years were modernized to some extent. In June 1940 the 149/13 was the standard howitzer for army corps artillery, along with the 105/28 or 105/32 guns, and until early 1942 when the new Italian produced 149/19 howitzer began to enter service. The 149/13 saw action in North Africa where 48 took part in the defense of Tobruk in December 1940.

Specifications
Designation: *Obice da 149/13* – ex-Austro–Hungarian *15cm schwere Feldhaubitze M.14* and *M.14/16*
Originator: Škoda, Plzeň (Bohemia, now part of the Czech Republic)
Producer: Škoda; Magyar Àgyùgyàr (Győr, Hungary)
Caliber: 149.1mm (5.87 inches)
Length of tube: 2,090mm (82.28 inches) M.14; 2,120mm (83.46 inches) M.14/16
Weight in action: 2,344kg (5,168 lbs) M.14; 2,765kg (6,096 lbs) M.14/16
Carriage: Box trail
Wheel track: 1,230mm (48.43 inches)
Wheel type/diameter: 12-spoke wood wheels, replaced by 10-spoke steel wheels/1,000mm
    (39.4 inches)
Breech type: Horizontal wedge
Recuperator type: Hydro-pneumatic
Elevation: –5 degrees to + 43 degrees M.14; –5 degrees to +70 degrees M.14/16
Traverse: 6 degrees
Muzzle velocity: 336m/s (1,102fps)
Maximum range: 6,900 meters (7,546 yards) M.14; 8,800 meters (9,624 yards) M.14/16
Rate of fire: 2–3 rounds per minute
Ammunition types: HE, shrapnel (several versions)
Shell weight: 42.5kg (93.7lbs) HE

149/35 gun

The antiquated 149/35 gun was the oldest gun in the Italian artillery inventory, having been adopted in 1901. Despite their age, 85 of these guns saw service in North Africa. (Enrico Finazzer)

In 1940 the *cannone da 149/35* was an extremely antiquated artillery piece, but in the absence of sufficient quantities of more modern pieces of the same caliber, they constituted the most available army-level artillery piece with 923 in stock on 1 June 1940. Overall, the gun's characteristics reflected the age of its adoption. The main feature that distinguished it from every other piece of artillery deployed by any army during the Second World War was the fact that the barrel was rigidly mounted on the carriage; it had no recoil system and no traverse capability. Once Italy entered the war, the gun, despite its obvious limitations, saw service on several fronts, either in the army artillery regiments or as static artillery. In Libya in early 1940, 48 examples were assigned at army level; by January 1942 the number in North Africa had dropped to 46.

Specifications
Designation: *Cannone da 149/35*
Adopted: 1901
Originator: Arsenale del Regio Esercito di Torino
Producer: Ansaldo
Caliber: 149.1mm (5.87 inches)
Length of tube: 5,464mm (215 inches)
Overall length: 6,825mm (268.7 inches)
Overall width: 1,900mm (74.8 inches)
Overall height: 2,310mm (91 inches)
Weight in action: 8,600kg (18,960lbs)
Carriage: Rigid
Wheel track: 1,480mm (58.3 inches); 1,868mm (73.5 inches) with Bonagente grousers
Wheel type/diameter: Wood spoke wheels/1,560mm (61.4 inches)
Breech type: Cylindrical screw
Recuperator type: None

Elevation: –10 degrees to +35 degrees
Traverse: 0 degrees
Muzzle velocity: 651m/s (2,136fps)
Maximum range: 17,500 meters (19,138 yards)
Rate of fire: One round every six minutes
Ammunition types: HE, shrapnel
Shell weight: 45.96kg (109.35lbs) HE

149/40 mod. 35 gun

A battery of 149/40 guns, XXXII Gruppo, in February 1942. These army-level assets were the most modern gun of their type in North Africa. (Enrico Finazzer)

In the context of Italy's artillery modernization, in 1930 the Italian Army Artillery Inspectorate requested both the *Arsenale Regio Esercito di Napoli* and Ansaldo to submit proposals for a new 149mm cannon to replace the old First World War era 149/35, the 152/37 and 152/45 guns. Both prototypes were presented in 1933; although tests of both entries proved satisfactory, the Ansaldo version was chosen over that of the Naples Arsenal, mainly because the Ansaldo version rested on a platform while firing, whereas the Naples Arsenal version rested on its wheels. In June 1935 the new gun was officially adopted as the *cannone da 149/40, mod. 35*. Ultimately, despite plans to acquire more than 700 of these guns, only 51 149/40 guns were produced for the Italian Army. The slow rate of production of the 149/40 was exacerbated by the fact that there was also a lack of heavy artillery tractors needed to tow the guns, limiting their ability to be employed with motorized elements as well as at the army level.

The Ansaldo engineers deserve credit for designing what was unquestionably a first-rate gun. The 149/40 mod. 35 was state-of-the-art for its time. It had an inner barrel liner that could be removed from the tube and replaced in about an hour, even under field conditions. Its split trail allowed a wide traverse arc; stability was assured both by the fact that the entire carriage was lowered to the ground, the wheels being slightly raised off the ground while firing, and the trail legs were further anchored by driving trail stakes into the ground at the end of each leg. With respect to performance, the 149/40 was as good as or better than any of its contemporaries, including the US 155mm M1A1 Long Tom cannon. The German *15cm Kanone 18* and *15cm Kanone 39*, whose barrels were considerably longer than that of the 149/40, had higher muzzle velocities and greater range, but fired a lighter shell. Unfortunately for the *Regio Esercito*, only a fraction of the guns required were ever produced.

In 1941 three mobile groups were formed, the XXXI, XXXII and XXXIV, while the XXXIII formed earlier, also received its tractors. The XXXIII Gruppo was deployed to North Africa, within the *8o Raggruppamento artiglieria d'armata*, and took part in the Axis offensive of spring–summer 1942 towards Egypt. In autumn of that year, it was deployed at El Alamein. Afterwards, it accompanied the retreat of the Italian troops and fought again in Tunisia with the remaining six pieces.

Specifications
Designation: *Cannone da 149/40 mod. 35*
Adopted: 1935
Originator: Ansaldo
Producer: Ansaldo (Genoa)
Caliber: 149.1mm (5.87 inches)
Crew: 9
Length of tube: 6,360mm (250.4 inches)
Overall length: 6,700mm (263.8 inches) in travel position
Overall width: 2,100mm (86.7 inches) traveling; 6,400mm (252 inches) with split trails extended
Weight: 14,340kg (31,614lbs) traveling; 11,430kg (25,199lbs) in action
Carriage: Split trail
Wheel type/diameter:8-hole steel wheels with semi-pneumatic tires/1,400mm (55.1 inches)
Breech type: Horizontal wedge
Recuperator type: Hydro-pneumatic
Recoil length: 1,400mm maximum; 800mm minimum
Elevation: 0 degrees to +45 degrees
Traverse: 57 degrees
Muzzle velocity: 800m/s (2,625fps)
Maximum range: 23,700 meters (25,928 yards)
Rate of fire: One round per minute normal; 2–3 rounds per minute possible
Ammunition types: HE
Shell weight: 46.2kg (101.4lbs)

152/37 gun

The *cannone da 152/37* was another one of the many Škoda types turned over as reparations to Italy at the end of the First World War and subsequently incorporated into its artillery inventory. The original designation of the gun in Austro–Hungarian service was the *15cm Autokanone M.15/16*, derived directly from the M.15 motorized gun. The M.15/16 was a sturdy and reliable heavy field gun, without particularly remarkable characteristics that distinguished it from other artillery pieces of the period. The gun had to be broken down into two loads for towing by heavy tractors; one load consisted of the gun carriage and weighed 8,440kg (18,607lbs), and the second load, consisting of the gun itself, weighed 9,000kg (19,842lbs). In Italian service during the Second World War towing in two loads was performed by a Breda 32 heavy tractor, although there is some evidence of transport on a truck trailer, at least in North Africa. During the 1920s these guns in Italian service were refurbished by Vickers Terni, and range was increased from 20,000 to 22,000 meters (21,872 to 24,059 yards), while the weight of the two loads decreased to 7,900kg (17,417lbs) for the carriage and 8,500kg (18,739lbs) for the gun.

The 152/37, shown being towed in Libya in November 1941, was another one of the many Škoda guns acquired by Italy as booty or reparations following the First World War that served in North Africa. One battery, the LII, was assigned to army-level artillery. (Enrico Finazzer)

In June 1940 there were four battalions with a total of 29 guns, equipped with 152/37, numbered from LI to LIV, assigned to army artillery regiments. The LII went to North Africa in 1942 and took part in the Axis offensive that ended at El Alamein. By September 1942 only one four-gun battery remained operational in North Africa.

Specifications
Designation: *Cannone da 152/37* – ex-Austro–Hungarian *15cm Autokanone M.15/16*
Adopted: After the First World War (captured, war booty)
Originator Škoda, Plzeň (Bohemia, now part of the Czech Republic)
Producer: Škoda
Caliber: 152.4mm (6 inches)
Length of tube: 6,000mm (236.2 inches)
Overall length: 9,850mm (387.8 inches)
Overall width: 2,300mm (90.6 inches)
Weight in action: 11,900kg (26,235lbs)
Carriage: Box trail
Wheel track: 1,750mm (68.9 inches)
Wheel type/diameter:Steel wheels with two staggered rows with 12 spokes to each
    row/1,500mm (59 inches)
Breech type: Horizontal wedge
Recuperator type: Hydro-pneumatic
Recoil length: 1,800mm maximum; 800mm minimum
Elevation: −6 degrees to +45 degrees
Traverse: 6 degrees
Muzzle velocity: 692m/s (2,270fps)
Maximum range: 21,840 meters (23,885 yards); maximum effective 16,000 meters (17,498 yards)
Rate of fire: 1–2 rounds every two minutes
Ammunition types: HE, shrapnel
Shell weight: HE 54kg (119lbs)

Appendix XI

Italian Motor Transport Employed in North Africa

The Italians employed a wide variety of motorcycles, staff cars, administrative, transport and tactical vehicles in North Africa. The following descriptions are not all-encompassing but represent the vehicles most frequently encountered in written or photographic documentation.

Moto Guzzi 500 Alce

The Moto Guzzi 500 Alce and its three-wheeled version, Trialce, was widely issued to Italian units in North Africa. (USSME)

The Moto Guzzi 500 Alce was widely issued to Italian forces. It was produced from 1939 to 1945. The Alce was issued to the *Polizia dell'Africa Italiana*, as well as to the army itself. In the army it was assigned to each regiment for reconnaissance and liaison duties, and in the armoured and motorized divisions in North Africa it equipped entire *Bersaglieri* motorcycle battalions. It was issued in three versions: a single-seat, a two-seat and a version with a sidecar. Some Alces were fitted with a special support for a Breda Model 30 light machine gun; the gun could not be used while the machine was moving, but the support enabled it to be used while stationary.

Length: 222cm (87.4 inches)
Width: 7.9cm (31 inches)
Height: 106.5cm (42 inches)
Unladen weight: 178kg (392lbs)
Engine: Guzzi one cylinder air-cooled, 498.4cc, 13.2HP
Transmission: 4-speed

Speed: 90km/h (56mph)
Range (on road): 300km (186 miles)

Autovettura **Fiat 508** *militare coloniale*

The Fiat 508 CM 'Balilla', based on the civilian Fiat 1100 car, was a widely used staff car in the desert.
(Fiat)

The Fiat 508 CM was a utilitarian military vehicle based on the civilian Fiat 1100 automobile. It was built in a number of slightly different versions. The vehicle was distributed to motorized and armoured units on a priority basis and gradually extended to battalion headquarters as well. Over 6,000 examples were produced, and the car was very well liked by users. It was fitted with a special oil bath filter to cope with the desert sand and performed well in the desert in spite of its 4x2 traction layout.

Length: 361.5cm (142 inches)
Width: 148.2cm (58 inches)
Height: 148cm (58 inches); 163cm (64 inches) with canvas top raised
Carrying capacity: 300kg (661lbs)
Unladen weight: 890kg (1,962lbs)
Engine: Fiat 108 C, 4-cylinder water cooled gasoline, 1,089cc, 30HP
Transmission: 4 speeds forward, one reverse
Speed: 95km/h (59mph)
Range (on road): 366km (227 miles)

Autovettura **Alfa Romeo 2500 C**

Like the Fiat 508 CM, the Alfa Romeo 2500 C was a militarized version of a civilian vehicle; it was not as suitable or as widely used as the smaller 508 CM. (USSME)

The 2500 C was a militarized version of a civilian vehicle; a 2500 C served as Mussolini's official car. It was developed in 1939 with several modifications to adapt it to military use, including a strengthened frame, shortened wheelbase, larger tires, increased ground clearance, improved lubrication and cooling to cope with high temperatures in the desert, an oil bath filter for the carburetor air intake and placing the batteries under the seats to shield them from the desert heat. The body was also modified in several respects and included ample storage space and attachments for a pick and shovel. The 2500 C entered service in 1941 as a staff vehicle for high-ranking officers but was not enthusiastically received in North Africa where its suspension was judged to be 'rigid' and its tires inadequate. A total of only 150 were produced in 1942–1943.

Length: 470cm (185 inches)
Width: 157cm (62 inches)
Height: 160cm (63 inches)
Carrying capacity: 480kg (1,058lbs)
Unladen weight: 1,650kg (3,638lbs)
Engine: Alfa Romeo 6C 72, 6-cylinder water cooled gasoline, 2,433cc, 90HP
Transmission: 4 speeds forward (3rd and 4th synchronized), one reverse
Speed: 127km/h (79mph)
Range (on road): 850km (528 miles)

Autocarro SPA AS37

The SPA AS37 light desert truck was developed specifically for use in the desert; its large balloon tires enabled it to traverse desert terrain relatively easily. (Fiat)

The SPA AS37 light truck, conceived in 1937, was derived from the TL37 light tractor and was designed specifically for operations in Libya. It was commonly referred to in Italian as the 'Sahariano'. The AS37 could carry a full rifle squad or a 1,200kg (2,646lb) payload. It could also mount a 47mm gun or a 20mm Breda cannon. Its extra-large tires enabled it to move easily over desert sand without bogging down.

Length: 413cm (162.6 inches)
    Width: 183cm (74 inches)
    Height: 218cm (86 inches)
    Carrying capacity: 800kg (1,764lbs)
    Unladen weight 3,650kg (8,047lbs)
    Engine: SPA 18TI, 4-cylinder water-cooled, 4,053cc, 52HP
    Drive layout: 4x2
    Speed: 38.2km/h (23.7mph)
    Range (on road): 170km (106 miles)

Autocarro leggero militare **SPA 38R**

The conventionally configured SPA 38R was replaced by the cab-over-engine Fiat 626 as a general-purpose cargo truck. (Fiat)

The SPA 38R was a light military truck built by the SPA subsidiary of Fiat and was used extensively in North Africa. In addition to the standard cargo body, it was fitted out as an ambulance, a shop van and a refrigerated van. It was a simple, solid truck that had a good load capacity and performed well on roads, and somewhat less so off-road. It was often armed with the 20mm Breda mounted on its bed. A version was also developed, the 36R, which was powered by a 6-cylinder air-cooled gasoline engine and thought to be better suited to operating in the desert environment. The 36R, however, turned out to be a disappointment, its performance having been judged as of limited value.

Length: 578.3cm (228 inches)
Width: 207cm (81 inches)
Height: 255.5cm (101 inches)
Carrying capacity: 3,000kg (6,614lbs)
Unladen weight: 2,500kg (5,512lbs)
Engine: Fiat 18R 4-cylinder water-cooled gasoline, 4,053cc, 56HP
Transmission: 4 speeds forward, one reverse
Drive layout: 4x2
Speed: 52km/h (32mph)
Range (on road): 310km (193 miles)
Range (cross country): 290km (180 miles)

Autocarro SPA CL39

The SPA CL39 was a light truck designed for use primarily by infantry units but was also used to tow artillery up to 75mm. (Fiat)

The SPA L39 was developed in 1938 as a light vehicle for infantry units and was adopted as the CL39 in 1939; the 'colonial' version was adopted in early 1941. The truck was characterized by its extreme simplicity, good handling characteristics and robustness. The version employed in North Africa had an oil bath air filter. The CL39 was used to tow the 20mm Breda cannon, the 47mm antitank gun and the 75/18 howitzer. It was also assigned to the 81mm mortar companies. It could carry ten soldiers in the cargo bed.

Length: 389cm (153 inches)
Width: 152cm (60 inches)
Height: 230cm (91 inches)
Carrying capacity: 1,000kg (2,204lbs)
Unladen weight: 1,630kg (3,594lbs)
Engine: SPA CLF 4-cylinder water-cooled, 25HP
Transmission: 4 speeds forward, one reverse
Drive layout: 4x2
Speed: 38km/h (27mph)
Range (on road): 440km (273 miles)

Autocarro SPA 35 Dovunque

The SPA 35 Dovunque was billed by the Italians as an all-terrain vehicle, hence the name 'Dovunque' ('Anywhere') and served in a variety of roles in North Africa, often mounting a 20mm Breda Model 35 gun. The spare wheel assisted in avoiding bellying. (Fiat)

The SPA was designed to be an all-terrain vehicle (the word '*dovunque*' means 'anywhere'), especially for resupplying artillery units in the desert with ammunition. It could also carry 14 fully equipped troops in addition to the driver and assistant driver. The Dovunque was used extensively in North Africa. It differed from most other trucks used by the Italian Army as it was powered by a gasoline, rather than a diesel, engine.

Length: 503cm (198 inches)
Width: 207cm (81 inches)
Height: 290cm (114 inches)
Carrying capacity: 2,500kg (5,512lbs)
Unladen weight: 4,530kg (9,590lbs)
Engine: Fiat 18T 4-cylinder water-cooled gasoline, 4,053cc, 55HP
Transmission: 8 speeds forward, 2 reverse
Drive layout: 6x2
Speed: 60km/h (37mph)
Range (on road): 1,270km (789 miles)

Autocarro medio **OM Taurus**

The OM Taurus, based on a Swiss Saurer design, was used extensively in North Africa as a troop and cargo carrier. (USSME)

Production of the OM (*Officine Meccaniche*) Taurus began in 1940. It was laid out conventionally with single-axle rear-wheel drive. It proved to be one of the best military trucks used by the Italians in North Africa.

Length: 660cm (260 inches)
Width: 215cm (85 inches)
Height: 266.5cm (105 inches)
Carrying capacity: 3,000kg (6,614lbs)
Unladen weight: 3,500kg (7,716lbs)
Engine: CR 1, 4-cylinder water-cooled diesel, 4,849cc, 65HP
Transmission: 5 speeds forward, one reverse
Drive layout: 4x2
Speed: 62.3km/h (39mph)
Range (on road): 670km (416 miles)

Autocarro **Bianchi Mediolanum 36-68A**

The Bianchi Mediolanum was sent to North Africa in limited numbers, where it proved to be very reliable. (USSME)

The Bianchi Mediolanum ('*Mediolanum*' was the Roman name for Milan) was developed in the mid-1930s, under license from Daimler-Benz. Some 200 examples were sent to North Africa in 1938. It was simple to maintain, easy to drive, gave good fuel mileage and was considered especially suited for service in North Africa. An improved version of the Model 36 was designated the 68A.

Length: 615cm (242 inches)
Width: 206cm (81 inches)
Height: 260cm (102 inches)
Carrying capacity: 3,000kg (6,614lbs)
Engine: MD 4C 4-cylinder water-cooled diesel, 57HP
Transmission: 4 speeds forward, one reverse, with reduction gear
Drive layout: 4x2
Speed: 55km/h (34mph)
Range (on road): 280km (173 miles)

Autocarro medio Bianchi Miles

The Bianchi Miles was essentially a license-built Mercedes truck used by the Italians in Russia as well as North Africa. (USSME)

The Bianchi Miles ('*Miles*' is Latin for 'soldier') was built to the standard of the *autocarro unificato medio* (standard medium truck) by the firm of Edoardo Bianchi of Milan. The Bianchi Miles was designed to be able to accept a number of different types of bodies, including bus and ambulance, in addition to the standard cargo body.

Length: 605.2cm (238 inches)
Width: 220.8cm (86 inches)
Height: 260cm (102 inches)
Carrying capacity: 3,000kg (6,614lbs)
Unladen weight: 3,500kg (7,716lbs)
Engine: CDU 35D 4-cylinder water-cooled diesel, 4,849cc, 65HP
Transmission: 4 speeds forward, one reverse
Drive layout: 4x2
Speed: 64km/h (40mph)
Range (on road): 350km (217 miles)
Range (cross country): 300km (186 miles)

Autocarro medio **Fiat 626 NM**

Fiat 626 was an early Fiat cab-over-engine design. Although as the army's standard medium truck it was used extensively in North Africa, it did not perform or handle as well as several of the other medium trucks used in that theater. (Fiat)

The Fiat 626 was a cab-over-engine type medium truck, based on a civilian model, the 626 N adopted for military use. The military model was designated the 'NM' (*'Nafta Militare'*, 'Diesel Military'). The 626 NM, produced from 1939 to 1945 and later into the postwar period as well, was widely distributed and became the Italian Army's standard medium truck. In North Africa, the 626, as well as its heavier version the 666, was not especially well liked because it was somewhat difficult to drive, especially on unimproved tracks, plus there were problems with engine starting and fuel feed, and the cargo bed did not stand up under hard use in military service. It also suffered from short engine life unless fitted with oil filters for the desert environment.

Length: 621cm (245 inches)
Width: 218cm (86 inches)
Height: 267.5cm (105 inches)
Carrying capacity: 3,000kg (6,614lbs)
Unladen weight: 3,960kg (8,730lbs)
Engine: Fiat Model 326 6-cylinder water-cooled diesel, 5,750cc, 65HP
Transmission: 4 speeds forward, one reverse
Drive layout: 4x2
Speed: 63km/h (40mph)
Range (on road): 400km (249 miles)
Range (cross country): 340km (211 miles)

Autocarro pesante **Fiat 666 NM**

The Fiat 666 was a heavy truck version of the 626 medium and saw extensive service in North Africa. (Fiat)

The Fiat 666 NM was a larger version of the earlier Fiat 626 NM, meeting the requirements of the *autocarro unificato pesante* (standard heavy truck) category. It had the same virtues and vices, broadly speaking, of the smaller 626. Produced beginning in 1940, it had a much higher cargo capacity than the 626; it could also tow a trailer rated at 6,260kg (13,801lbs) which could carry either cargo or 20 soldiers. The 666 NM saw extensive service in North Africa.

Length: 709.5cm (279 inches)
Width: 23.5cm (9 inches)
Height: 285cm (112 inches)
Carrying capacity: 6,000kg (6,614lbs)
Unladen weight: 6,000kg (8,730lbs)
Engine: Fiat Model 365 6-cylinder water-cooled diesel, 9,365cc, 95HP
Transmission: 4 speeds forward, one reverse
Drive layout: 4x2
Speed: 48.3km/h (30mph)
Range (on road): 390km (217 miles)
Range (cross country): 350km (211 miles)

Alfa Romeo 430 RE *militare*

The Alfa Romeo 430 RE entered rather late in the war and saw little service in the North African theatre
(USSME)

The Alfa Romeo 430 RE was a military truck developed as a lighter version of the Alfa Romeo 800 heavy military truck. Production did not begin until 1942 and it was not as widely distributed as the Fiat and Bianchi medium trucks.

Length: 595.5cm (234 inches)
Width: 213cm (84 inches)
Height: 258cm (102 inches)
Carrying capacity: 3,150kg (6,945lbs)
Unladen weight: 3,350kg (7,386lbs)
Engine: 5.8 liter 4-cylinder diesel
Transmission: 4 speeds with 2-speed transfer gearbox
Drive layout: 4x2
Speed: 66km/h (41mph)
Range (on road): 390km (242 miles)
Range (cross country): 350km (217 miles)

Autocarro unificato pesante **Alfa Romeo T.800** *militare*

The Alfa Romeo T.800 heavy truck was widely used in North Africa, although its off-road performance did not match that of several of the other trucks issued in the desert. (USSME)

The Alfa Romeo T.800 was produced from 1940 to 1943 and was widely used in North Africa, although it was designed to operate mainly on paved roads. It was a cab-over-engine design and could carry a heavy payload.

    Length: 684cm (269 inches)
    Width: 235cm (93 inches)
    Height: 285cm (112 inches)
    Carrying capacity: 6,500kg (14,330lbs)
    Unladen weight: 5,500kg (12,125lbs)
    Engine: 6-cylinder water-cooled diesel, 8,725cc, 115HP
    Transmission: 4 speeds with 2-speed transfer gearbox
    Drive layout: 4x2
    Speed: 49km/h (30.5mph)
    Range (on road): 500km (310 miles)

Autocarro pesante Lancia 3RO

A Lancia 3Ro heavy truck, considered to be the most reliable Italian truck in the desert. (Ralph Riccio)

The Lancia 3Ro was powered by a 5-cylinder German Junkers diesel engine, built under license by Lancia and considered to be the Italian Army's most reliable heavy truck. It was used extensively in North Africa in a variety of roles and configurations; in addition to a cargo and troop carrier, it was fitted as a mobile shop truck, water tanker, fuel tanker as well as a variety of armament including the 20mm Breda antiaircraft cannon and the 90/53 dual-purpose gun. As a troop carrier, its ample cargo bed allowed it to carry up to 32 soldiers with their equipment. A report prepared by the *12o autoraggruppamento* in Libya stated that it performed better than any other truck used by the *autoraggruppamento* both on roads and in the desert.

Length: 725cm (285 inches)
Width: 235cm (93 inches)
Height: 300cm (118 inches)
Carrying capacity: 6,390kg (14,088lbs)
Unladen weight: 5,810kg (12,809lbs)
Engine: Junkers 5-cylinder water-cooled diesel, 6,875cc, 64HP
Transmission: 8 speeds forward, 2 reverse
Drive layout: 4x2
Speed: 45km/h (26mph)
Range (on road): 450km (280 miles)

Autocarro pesante **Fiat 634 N**

A Fiat 634 N heavy truck, nicknamed the '*Gigante*' ('Giant') because of its size; the 634 N was used as a platform for the 102/35 naval guns manned by MILMART personnel. (Fiat)

The Fiat 634 N, commonly referred to by the Italians as the '*Gigante*' ('Giant') because of its size and carrying capacity, was a robust heavy truck that saw service in Italian East Africa, and later in Libya, where it was used by the *57o autoreparto pesante* (57th Heavy Transportation Battalion).

Length: 743.5cm (293 inches)
Width: 240cm (95 inches)
Height: 324.5cm (128 inches)
Carrying capacity: 7,640kg (16,843lbs)
Unladen weight: 6,360kg (14,021lbs)
Engine: Fiat 355C, 6-cylinder water-cooled diesel, 8,355cc, 80HP
Transmission: 4 speeds forward
Drive layout: 4x2
Speed: 40km/h (25mph)
Range (on road): 150km (93 miles)

Special purpose vehicles (*veicoli speciali*)

The Italians designed and developed a small number of wheeled vehicles specifically for use in the desert environment. These vehicles were based on modified chassis of existing vehicles – namely the AB42 armoured car chassis and the TL37 light artillery tractor chassis – both of which had in turn been developed or modified for operation in the desert environment. It is interesting to note that during the interwar period the Italians gained considerable experience in desert exploration and in the process had learned some lessons with respect to adapting vehicles to the environment. The large cross-section tires designated as '*Tipo Libia*' used on Italian vehicles (especially the TL37 and its derivatives) reportedly were designed to match the ground pressure exerted by a camel on the sand, and thus avoid bogging down. The *camionetta mod. 42* was a very interesting purpose-built vehicle incorporating many features desirable for desert operations: extremely long range (with supplemental fuel canisters), low silhouette and potent armament for the vehicle class. However, these special-purpose combat vehicles were developed too late and built in too few numbers to influence the outcome of operations to any meaningful degree.

Camionetta desertica SPA-Viberti *mod. 42*

The Sahariana light truck was based on the AB41 armoured car chassis and was developed specially for use in the desert. (Fiat)

Impressed by the success of the British Long Range Desert Group raiding parties, the Italian Army General Staff decided to form a counterpart organization, initially of battalion strength, but later increased to regimental strength (the 10th 'Arditi' Regiment). Ultimately, the regiment had four battalions, each of which had an integral company of *arditi camionettisti* (vehicle-borne raiding parties). The staff further ordered design and production of two special vehicles for this unit: the *camionetta mod. 42* and the *camionetta mod. 43*.

In June 1942 the first prototype of the *camionetta desertica mod. 42* was completed. Although it was not officially adopted until December 1942, deliveries had begun in August. The mod. 42 was based on the chassis of the AB42 armoured car, which was a modified AB41 without the dual-drive feature. Although originally planned to be used for behind the line forays against the Allies, it was used primarily as a reconnaissance vehicle. The vehicle could be equipped with a variety of armament, including the 20mm Breda Model 35 antiaircraft gun, the 20mm Solothurn antitank rifle and the 47mm Model 39 gun. In addition, there were up to three machine gun mountings for the 8mm Breda Model 37 machine gun (one to the right of the driver, and two at the rear corners). Interestingly, the driver's position was just slightly left of the centerline of the vehicle, rather than on the right-hand side common in most Italian military vehicles. The mod. 42 was initially employed operationally in late November 1942 in North Africa and continued to participate in operations until at least May 1943 in Tunisia.

Manufacturer: SPA-Viberti
Year adopted: 1942
Number produced: 100 (various sources quote between 76 and 200)
Crew: 4

Weight: 4,500kg (9,921lbs) (empty weight)
Main gun: Armament fits varied; see text above
Engine: SPA ABM 3, 6-cylinder gasoline
Horsepower: 100HP (some sources quote 80HP)
Power-to-weight ratio: 22.2 HP/ton
Fuel capacity: 145 liters (38.3 US gallons; 31.8 Imperial gallons), plus up to 480 liters (126.8 US gallons; 105.6 Imperial gallons) in fuel canisters
Maximum speed (road): 84km/h (52mph)
Maximum speed (cross country): 50km/h (31mph)
Operating radius (road): 300km (186 miles), plus 1,200km (745 miles) using fuel from on-board fuel canisters
Operating radius (cross-country): 5 hours (25 hours with fuel from additional canisters)
Length: 5,620mm (221.25 inches)
Width: 2,260mm (89 inches)
Height: 1,800mm (70.8 inches)
Wheelbase: 3,200mm (126 inches)
Track width: 1,750mm (69 inches)
Ground clearance: 350mm (13.8 inches)
Fording depth: 700mm (25.5 inches)
Radio: One T.X.O.; one O.C.3
Dates of service in North Africa: November 1942–May 1943

Camionetta desertica SPA-Viberti *mod. 43*

The *camionetta mod. 43* light desert truck, although designed specifically for desert operations, was fielded too late to be sent to North Africa. (Fiat)

In late summer 1942 the prototype of this light desert truck, developed as a result of experience gained from operations in North Africa, was unveiled. The vehicle was based on the chassis of the AS37 light desert truck and was not armoured. The first production model was not ready until January 1943, by which time the Axis forces in North Africa had suffered serious defeats, and the need for the vehicle there was no longer a priority. Although based on the AS37 light truck chassis, the mod. 43 essentially was a completely new vehicle that had few parts in common with the AS37 itself. The body of the mod. 43, built by Viberti, was of a completely different design than that of the AS37; armament consisted of either a 20mm Breda Model 35 cannon or a 47/32 gun on an interchangeable mount, in addition to an 8mm Breda Model 37 machine gun for the vehicle commander, mounted on an integral gooseneck support located on the left front fender. There were no doors to the vehicle, and access to the front seats was through a narrow gap between the front fender and the side storage lockers. In common with most Italian military vehicles, the steering wheel was on the right-hand side. Compared to the AS37, it had a more powerful engine, independent suspension, hydraulic shock absorbers, on-board compressor for tire inflation, hydraulic brakes, four-wheel drive and steerable front wheels only. However, this light truck saw no service in North Africa due to the collapse of the Axis forces there in early 1943.

Designation: *Camionetta desertica* SPA-Viberti *mod. 43*
Manufacturer: SPA/Viberti
Number produced: Uncertain
Crew: 5
Weight: 5,000kg (11,023lbs) (combat loaded)
Armament: Armament first varied
Engine: SPA 18 VT (Variant 4), gasoline, 4,053cc, 73HP
Power-to-weight ratio: 14.6HP/ton
Fuel capacity: 120 liters (31.7 US gallons; 26.4 Imperial gallons) plus 200 liters (52.8 US gallons; 44 Imperial gallons) in fuel containers
Maximum speed (road): 68.5km/h (43mph)
Operating radius (road): 360km (?) (224 miles) (?), plus approximately 600km (373 miles) using fuel from on-board fuel canisters
Length: 4,820mm (15 feet 10 inches)
Width: 2,060mm (6 feet 9 inches)
Height: 2,175mm (7 feet 2 inches)
Wheelbase: 2,500mm (8 feet 2 inches)
Track: 1,600mm (5 feet 3 inches)
Ground clearance: 345mm (1 foot 2 inches)
Fording depth: 700mm (2 feet 4 inches)

SPA TL37 field artillery tractor

The TL37 was a modern artillery tractor widely used in North Africa and the basis for several other specialized desert vehicles. (Nicola Pignato)

In 1935 the Italian Army issued a requirement for a light artillery tractor to tow the suitably modified 75mm and 100mm guns in the inventory. In 1936 SPA engineers in competition with Breda, set to work developing a prototype called the *'trattore di fanteria'* ('infantry tractor') which was further developed into the standard pattern adopted by the Italian Army in 1937 and designated the SPA TL37, with the 'TL' signifying *'trattore leggero'* ('light tractor'). In October 1937, 250 examples were ordered and a test group of 24 TL37s was sent to Libya in 1938 where it was used to tow the 75/27 mod. 06 guns mounted on the *carrello elastico*, as well as towing ammunition trailers for the guns. The results proved to be entirely satisfactory, setting the stage for mechanization of Italian artillery in the desert. At the time it was thought that the TL37 could also fill the need for a light reconnaissance vehicle. The AS37 was a light truck based on the TL37 chassis, while both the *camionetta AS43* and the *camionetta desertica mod. 43* light desert trucks intended for use as a command and reconnaissance vehicle were in turn a development based on the AS37. A local modification of the TL37 tractor in North Africa mounted a 75/27 mod. 11 field gun on the tractor chassis. Three batteries of this unique vehicle were built.

The TL37 artillery tractor was issued to the motorized artillery batteries of infantry, cavalry, motorized and armoured divisions, and saw service in all Italian combat theaters, but its greatest use was in North Africa. Prior to the Axis defeat in Tunisia, on 30 April 1943 there were between 2,150 and 2,267 TL37s of the various versions (excluding the AS37) in service, according to different sources. That the TL37 was a modern, high-quality vehicle well suited for its task as an artillery tractor is attested to by a report by an Australian commission in 1941 which, after having tested the TL37, judged it to be the best artillery tractor available on either side in North Africa.

Designation: TL37 (*trattore leggero 37*)

Manufacturer: Fiat/SPA

Weight (unloaded): 3,181kg (9,076lbs) with pneumatic tires; 3,560kg (748.5lbs) with semi-pneumatic tires

Carrying capacity: 800kg (1,764lbs)

Towing capacity: 2,000kg (4,409lbs)

Length: 4,130mm (162.6 inches)

Width: 1,830mm (72 inches)

Height: 2,180mm with canvas roof (85.8 inches)

Engine: SPA Model 18 TL, 4-cylinder gasoline, 4,053cc (247 cubic inches), 52HP @ 2,000rpm

Transmission: manual transmission with 5 forward speeds and reverse; 4-wheel drive with lockable differential

Fuel capacity: 100 liters (26.5 US gallons; 22 Imperial gallons)

Wheelbase: 2,500mm (98.4 inches)

Track: 1,518mm (59.8 inches) with pneumatic tires; 1,440mm (56.7 inches) with semi-pneumatic tires

Turning radius: 4,500mm (177.2 inches)

Tire size: Artiglio pneumatic 9.00 x 24 and 9.75 x 24; tipo Libia pneumatic 11.25 x 24; Celerflex semi-pneumatic 160 x 881

Maximum speed (road): 38.2km/h (23.7mph) fully loaded

Maximum range: 355km (221 miles) with two supplemental 20-liter (5.3 gallon) canisters

Maximum gradient: 8 percent in 1st gear at 2.4km/h (1.5mph)

Ground clearance: 345mm (13.6 inches)

Fording depth: 700mm (27.6 inches)

SPA TM40 heavy field artillery tractor

The TM40 was a four-wheel drive medium artillery tractor adopted in 1941 that served well in the desert.
(Enrico Finazzer)

The TM40 ('*trattore medio*', 'medium tractor') artillery tractor resulted from a request put forward by the *Regio Esercito* in 1938 for a tractor to replace the old Pavesi tractors. SPA presented its prototype in competition with Breda and Lancia, and after extensive tests it was adopted in 1941. Due to the high degree of satisfaction registered with the earlier TL37, the TM40 followed the same general construction principles. Like the earlier TL37, the TM40 was a four-wheel drive tractor with all four wheels steerable. Unlike the TL37, the TM40 was a cab-over-engine machine. The larger size of the TM40 with respect to the TL37 enabled it to carry a total of eight men (driver and passenger in the front, and six crew in the back seated face to face), as well as ammunition for guns up to 149mm.

Designation: TM40
Manufacturer: Fiat/SPA
Weight (unloaded): 6,575kg (14,495lbs)
Carrying capacity: 1,285kg (2,833lbs)
Towing capacity: 5,000kg (11,023lbs)
Length: 4,680mm (184.3 inches)
Width: 2,200mm (86.6 inches)
Height: 2,800mm (110.2 inches)
Engine: Type 366, 6-cylinder diesel, 9,365cc (572 cubic inches), 105HP @ 2,000rpm
Transmission: manual transmission with 5 forward speeds and reverse; four-wheel drive with lockable differential
Fuel capacity: 140 liters (37 US gallons; 30.8 Imperial gallons)
Wheelbase: 2,500mm (98.4 inches)
Track: 1,630mm (64.2 inches) with pneumatic tires; 1,665mm (65.6 inches) with semi-pneumatic tires
Turning radius: 5,600mm (220.5 inches)
Tire size: Artiglio pneumatic 50 x 9 or 12.75 x 37; semi pneumatic 265 x 980
Maximum speed (road): 43.35km/h (29.96 mph)
Maximum range: 300km (186.4 miles)
Maximum gradient: 45 percent with 5,000kg load
Ground clearance: 330mm (13 inches)
Fording depth: 900mm (35.4 inches)

Breda mod. 32, mod. 33 and mod. 40 heavy tractor

The Breda mod. 32 heavy tractor was the first of a series of Breda heavy artillery tractors used by the *Regio Esercito*. The Breda 32 replaced a number of older prime movers such as the Fiat tipo 20 and Pavesi-Tolotti tipo B tractors and trucks, such as the Fiat 18 BLR to tow army-level heavy artillery. By the outbreak of the Second World War, all Italian heavy artillery regiments had been equipped with this tractor. The Breda mod. 40 was a development, much modernized, of the mod. 32 for use in Italy's African colonies. Although a prototype was ready in 1940 it was not until 1942 that series production began, with the first examples arriving in North Africa during the summer of 1942.

Designation: *Trattrice pesante* Breda 32 and *trattrice pesante* Breda 33
Manufacturer: Breda Meccannica Bresciana
Weight (unloaded): 8,400kg (18,519lbs) mod. 32; 8,500kg (18,739lbs) mod. 33
Carrying capacity: 3,500kg (7,716lbs) on road; 2,500kg (5,512lbs) off road; 2,000kg (4,409lbs) mod. 33

The Breda 40 was an evolution of the earlier Breda 32 heavy artillery tractor. The Italians suffered from a chronic dearth of artillery tractors in North Africa. (Enrico Finazzer)

Towing capacity: Up to 25 tonnes on road at 8 percent grade; 10 tonnes off road
Length: 5,150mm (202.8 inches) mod. 32; 6,320mm (245.7 inches) mod. 33
Width: 2,080mm (81.9 inches) mod. 32; 2,100mm (82.7 inches) mod. 33
Height: 3,000mm (118.1 inches) mod.32; 2,910mm (114.6 inches) mod. 33
Engine: SPA Model T5, 4-cylinder gasoline, 8,150cc (497 cubic inches), 84HP @ 1,450rpm
Transmission: 5 forward speeds, 1 reverse; 4-wheel drive
Fuel capacity: 200 liters (52.8 US gallons; 44 Imperial gallons) mod. 32; 125 liters (33 US gallons; 27.5 Imperial gallons) mod. 33
Wheelbase: 2,650mm (104.3 inches) mod 32; 3,800mm (149.6 inches) mod. 33
Track: 1,680mm (66.1 inches) front and 1,615mm (63.6 inches) rear
Turning radius: 5,750 mm (226.4 inches); 8,000 mm (315 inches) mod. 33
Tire size: Celerflex semi-pneumatic 205 x 980
Maximum speed (road): 30km/h (18.6mph)
Maximum range: 240km (149 miles) unladen on road; 150km (93.2 miles) with towed load on road; 10 hours unladen off-road; six hours with towed load off-road (mod. 32)
Maximum gradient: 35 percent
Ground clearance: 390mm (15.4 inches)
Fording depth: Not applicable
Special notes: 7,500kg (16,535lbs) capacity winch

Designation: *Trattrice pesante Breda 40*
Manufacturer: Breda Meccanica Bresciana
Weight (unloaded): 10,100kg (22,267lbs)
Carrying capacity: 3,500kg (7,716.2lbs) on road; 2,500kg (5,512lbs) off road
Towing capacity: 10,000kg (2204.6lbs)
Length: 5,400mm (212.6 inches)

Width: 2,400mm (94.5 inches)
Height: 2,610mm to top of cab; 2,920mm with canvas cover on rear
Engine: Breda D 11, 6-cylinder diesel, 8,850cc (540 cubic inches), 115HP @ 1,800rpm
Transmission: 5 forward speeds, 1 reverse
Fuel capacity: 200 liters (52.8 US. gallons; 44 Imperial gallons)
Wheelbase: 2,900mm (114.2 inches)
Track: 1,810mm (71.3 inches) front and 1,795mm (70.7 inches) rear
Turning radius: 8,550mm (336.6 inches)
Tire size: 9x50
Maximum speed (road): 41km/h (25.5mph)
Maximum range: 260km (161.6 miles)
Maximum gradient: 48 percent
Ground clearance: 460mm (18.1 inches)
Fording depth: Not applicable

Appendix XII

Italian Vehicle Paint Schemes and Markings

Italian combat vehicles could be encountered in a number of different paint and camouflage schemes, depending on the area of operations, the year of introduction into service and the type of vehicle. Solid colors included gray-green (*grigioverde*), primarily used in Europe, or sand yellow (*kaki sahariano*) used in the desert. Camouflage schemes varied from a gray-green base with relatively broad sand stripes or splotches to a light sand or dark red-brown (*terracotta*) base with irregular random patches of gray-green, or a light sand base with random gray-green and red-brown stripes and patches. Other examples include those with a red-brown base and gray-green stripes.

In a very general sense, combat vehicle camouflage schemes mirrored those, both in color and broadly in pattern, used by the Italian *Regia Aeronautica* (Italian Royal Air Force) of the period. Although the vehicle interiors were painted in gloss white, the inside surfaces of hatch doors were painted to match the exterior surface color scheme so that when the hatch doors were open, they displayed the same color scheme as the outside of the vehicle, rather than presenting a stark white surface contrasting with the exterior scheme.

Italian vehicles in North Africa generally bore a monochrome finish of sand yellow, which was somewhat darker than the British desert sand color. However, there were many exceptions to this general rule: the most prevalent departure from the monochrome scheme was the use of a random pattern of stripes or splotches using a gray-green or red-brown color sprayed over the sand yellow base. This scheme was frequently used on the vehicles belonging to the '*batterie volanti*' ('flying batteries') but could also occasionally be encountered on medium tanks. Another variation was achieved, unintentionally, by the action of dust and sand on the finish of medium tanks whose original livery had been gray-green, then over-sprayed with sand yellow prior to shipment to the desert; the lighter sand color would be abraded by the elements, exposing some of the underlying green scheme with interesting effects. As a field expedient, the tankers sometimes resorted to spraying their vehicle with a coating of used motor oil, then running the tank over the desert terrain in order to coat the oil with dust and sand to achieve a flat, drab finish.

Beginning in the spring of 1942 vehicles belonging to the armoured divisions sported figures or logos denoting the division they belonged to. 'Ariete' armoured division vehicles had a stylized ram's head ('*ariete*' is the Italian word for 'ram') stenciled in black on the vehicle. 'Centauro' vehicles used a black centaur, and 'Littorio' used a bundle of *fasces*, or at times, the emblem of the 'Cavalleggeri Guide' cavalry regiment, in honor of the division commander who was originally from that regiment. The 'Littorio' division's motto, '*A colpo sicuro*' ('A sure shot', or 'One shot, one kill') was painted in red on the mantlet of at least some of the division's medium tanks. Armoured cars belonging to the *Polizia dell'Africa Italiana* had the tricolor Italian flag painted on the hull sides to distinguish them from captured enemy vehicles of the same type.

Army Circular 4400, dated 28 March 1938 amplified by Circular 4640, dated 8 September 1940 specified the size and placement of tactical signs and numbers on tanks and armoured cars. The basic tactical sign consisted of a 20x12 centimeter (approximately 8x5 inch) colored rectangle denoting the company (red for 1st Company, light blue for 2nd Company, yellow for 3rd Company and green for

Bersagliere in Cyrenaica, 1940. 10th *Bersagliere* Regiment.
(Colour artwork by Anderson Subtil © Helion & Company)

Maresciallo d'Italia Ettore Bastico, 1942. Italian Governor-General of Libya.
(Colour artwork by Anderson Subtil © Helion & Company)

Carrista (Tank Crew),
'Ariete' Armoured Division,
1942, Battle of El Alamein.
(Colour artwork by
Anderson Subtil © Helion &
Company)

Paracadutista, 'Folgore' Parachute
Division, 1942, Second Battle of El
Alamein. (Colour artwork by Anderson
Subtil © Helion & Company)

Camicia Nera Scelta (Black Shirt Lance Corporal), 1941, 'Giovani Fascisti' Regiment, Battle of Bir el Gobi.
(Colour artwork by Anderson Subtil © Helion & Company)

XXXI 'Guastatori' Battalion, 1942, Battle of Gazala.
(Colour artwork by Anderson Subtil © Helion & Company)

Soldato, Batteria Volante, 1941, 'Reparto Esplorante Corpo d'Armata'.
(Colour artwork by Anderson Subtil © Helion & Company)

Libyan *Ascari, Compagnia Mitraglieri*, 1940, Sahariano Battalion.
(Colour artwork by Anderson Subtil © Helion & Company)

Mitragliere (Machine Gunner), 1942, 'Pavia' Infantry Division.
(Colour artwork by Anderson Subtil © Helion & Company)

the 4th Company). The company commander's tank had a solid color rectangle, while platoon tanks were identified by vertical white bars within the colored rectangle (one bar for First Platoon, two for Second, three for Third); the white bars were 2x12 centimeters in size (approximately 1 x 5 inches). The number of the tank within the platoon was indicated by an Arabic numeral 10 centimeters high and 1.5 centimeters wide (approximately 4x0.5 inches) placed 2 centimeters (about 0.75 of an inch) above the center of the rectangle, in the same color as the rectangle. The battalion commander's rectangle was a combination of the colors of the companies within the battalion, for example, a battalion with three companies had a rectangle with (from left to right) red, light blue and yellow vertical bands; a battalion consisting of only two companies had red and light blue bands only. Above the battalion commander's rectangle was a Roman numeral in white denoting the battalion number. A black rectangle was used for battalion headquarters tanks, and a white rectangle for the regimental headquarters company. The circulars specified that on the L3 tanks the rectangles were to be placed on the hull sides, and the Roman numerals for the battalions and Arabic numerals for the regiment should be on the rear of the upper hull, on the right and left, respectively. On turreted tanks (the L6 and M series) as well as on the AB series armoured cars, the rectangle was to be applied on the side of the turret as well as on the rear of the turret, and the battalion and regimental numbers were painted in white on the right and left rear corners of the fighting compartment. Notwithstanding the detailed instructions provided by the circulars, in reality the rules were often ignored with respect to both the dimensions and the positioning of the tactical signs.

Self-propelled gun units adopted tactical markings of their own. These included triangles (either normally oriented or inverted) in combinations of black and yellow, bearing either a white vertical stripe or stripes, or a white number above the triangle to denote the battery of assignment. Command vehicles bore a black triangle. Alternately, black or white circles with numbers inside the circles in contrasting colors could be painted on the hull sides, the hull rear or on the front corner of the casemate (as were the triangles). Wide latitude was given to the group commander to choose the type of markings he preferred. The DLIX group's 1st Battery bore the names of historical military leaders (*condottieri*), while those of the 2nd Battery bore names of ancient types of weapons. After December 1942 when the 75/18 SP guns were merged with tank units, the vehicles made use of standard tank unit markings.

Three basic types of marking were used for air recognition. The first was a large white disc 700mm (about 28 inches) in diameter painted on the top of tank turrets or, on the L3's, on the engine deck. The second type, used only at the beginning of the North Africa campaign, was a large white cross (the '*Croce di Savoia*', the Savoy royal family cross), normally on top of the turret or on the sides of captured enemy vehicles. The final type was the rare use of the Italian national colors (red, white and green) painted on either the top or side of the tank turret or on the engine decks of other vehicles, such as the *camionetta desertica mod. 42*. At times, captured vehicles were identified simply by draping an Italian flag over the hood or engine deck of the vehicle.

The Italians used a very structured vehicle license plate system for their combat vehicles. Tanks bore a metal registration plate onto which identifying data was stamped. The plates were white, measuring 23x15 centimeters (approximately 9x6 inches), with the letters '*Ro*' and '*Eto*', signifying '*Regio Esercito*' ('Royal Army') in red. These letters were followed by a flaming bomb symbol, also in red, on the same line. On a line below this data was the registration number in black Arabic numerals. Armoured cars had a similar plate, except that the numbers were followed by the letter B (in red), for '*blindo*' ('armoured car') and did not have the flaming bomb symbol. Some of the older *autocannoni* that originally had been issued registration plates in the First World War may have been encountered with plates that bore the letter 'C' for '*cannone*' ('cannon') in red, following the numbers. The plates normally were affixed to the lower left-hand side of the vehicle's rear. Similar data (using the same colors) was painted directly on the front of the vehicle hull, but not on the older armoured vehicles. *Polizia dell'Africa Italiana* vehicles had the letters 'PAI' on one line, with a four-digit number on the line below.

Appendix XIII

Italian Uniforms in North Africa

The 1931 Baistrocchi reforms called for a redesign of the then current combat uniform, which led to the mod. 40 uniform and its derivatives. The enlisted uniform consisted of a jacket with three buttons and with four pockets with flaps; the jacket could also be buttoned closed at the neck and a cloth belt could be tightened around the waist. Trousers differed depending on the branch of service and could be secured at the bottom by puttees or by socks and boots. The troops were normally issued with brown leather ankle boots that laced, while officers commonly wore riding breeches and high leather pull-on boots.

Italy had a highly regarded textile industry, and Italian uniforms tended to be stylish, innovative, and at least during the early period of the war, well made. North Africa saw the use of a variety of different uniform types and uniform patterns by the Italians, to some extent dependent upon whether they were for officers, NCOs or other ranks. Also, as the war wore on, the quality of the cloth used to make the uniforms worsened, resulting in poor quality uniforms for the enlisted troops. In North Africa, the uniforms were of the same pattern as the continental uniforms but were made of khaki-colored cotton; the basic soldier's uniform was based on the 1935 tropical uniform that had been introduced during the war against Ethiopia, consisting of a khaki jacket and shirt, long trousers tucked into ankle boots, a forage cap (*bustina*) and a M33 steel helmet or a tropical pith helmet. Another cap that became popular was the *bustina 42*, which was a modified sidecap with a visor, vaguely similar to the German M43 field cap. Other headgear that could be encountered were the characteristic *alpino* cap worn by the alpine troops, a red fez with a blue tassel worn by the *Bersaglieri* or a black fez with black tassel worn by the 'Giovani Fascisti'. Although no alpine troops were assigned to North Africa, occasionally an officer or NCO whose basic branch had been the alpine corps would wear his old cap as a source of pride. The *Bersaglieri* also famously wore iridescent cock feathers in their headgear to distinguish themselves from standard infantry units.

A very popular uniform item for officers was the *giacca sahariana* (Sahara jacket), a sort of bush jacket with pleated breast pockets and winged flaps, and ample side pockets; this type of jacket gained some popularity among the Germans in the desert as well. In 1939–1940 a new shirt designed expressly for wear in Libya was introduced, designated the '*camiciotto sahariana*' ('Sahara shirt'), which was similar to but somewhat simpler than the *giacca sahariana*; it was a pullover with a placket that had three buttons. In 1941, shorts or breeches (*pantaloncini*) began to be issued. Because the temperature could drop significantly at night, the troops were also issued a wool great-coat, the colors of which varied from khaki to brown to the continental gray-green. Tankers and armoured artillerymen wore a leather crash helmet and the 1926 pattern blue cotton coveralls or, more commonly, an open-neck shirt, shorts and boots. Tankers were also issued a three-quarter length black leather overcoat.

Throughout the war, almost every conceivable combination of uniform items could be encountered, with officers and other ranks alike using whatever was at hand. The harsh desert environment of sun, sand and dust tended to deteriorate the fabrics at an accelerated rate, and inevitably bleached many of the items. The Italians also made use of captured British uniform items when available. On some occasions, due to the 'borrowing' of uniforms and the aging effects of the weather, it was difficult to determine friend from foe, on either side. Caccia Dominioni relates in a somewhat amusing manner how, during Rommel's offensive in June 1942, a huge percentage of vehicles used by the Axis were captured British vehicles and, to boot, both Germans and Italians were outfitted with captured British uniforms, so that a casual observer would see what was apparently one British army being pursued by another. Another amusing incident also rather pointedly illustrates to what extent captured uniforms were used by the Italians. Whilst chatting with a British officer who had been taken prisoner, an Italian officer, who spoke good English, remarked to the captive that prior to the war he had a London tailor make his suits; the observant British officer, seeing that the Italian was wearing bits of captured British uniform, quipped that apparently the Italian was still doing business with an English tailor.

Most rank insignia consisted of shoulder boards or tabs bearing various emblems and stars denoting rank for officers. NCO shoulder boards were quite simple, with rank denoted by braided stripes. Junior NCOs and other ranks wore chevrons on the upper sleeves of their jackets. Depending on the uniform, after 1940, officer rank could also be displayed on the jacket cuff.

Appendix XIV

Food and Rations

Italian rations generally consisted of foods that were heavy in carbohydrates and fats, but light on meat. What the soldier got to eat in North Africa very much depended on how far to the rear or how close to the front he was. Broadly speaking, garrison or rear-echelon troops could look forward to meals that were heavy in carbohydrates but light on meat. Pasta dishes were prevalent, but potatoes and rice, and vegetable soups or sometimes stews, were also available. Field rations for operational units that were not in an active combat situation tended to duplicate the garrison rations, but there were concessions made to the portability of the food and to making the meals more rapidly consumable. Soup and pasta were cooked in large kettles, with cheese and vegetables added. Items such as canned olives, dried figs and dates were also available in limited quantities. The daily ration was supposed to include 700 grams of bread, 200 grams of pasta or 170 grams of rice (rice was grown extensively in northern Italy and was a staple in that part of the country), 250 grams of meat or canned tuna, 100 grams of potatoes, 10 grams of lard or olive oil, 10 grams of tomato puree, 10 grams of cheese, 4 grams of wine, 10 grams of coffee and 15 grams of sugar; however, it is unlikely that all of these amounts were actually available for consumption on a regular basis. Items such as chocolate, marmalade and similar sweets were not part of the normal issue foods; generally, they were distributed as comfort items ('*generi di conforto*') together with anice or cordiale – two Italian spirits, not very appropriate for the North African theater. Closer to the front, when field kitchens were not available, a '*razione giornaliera*' (daily ration) was issued. This was a group feeding ration meant to be cooked in squad-sized elements as camp food and consisted of large tins of fruit, coffee, sugar, pasta, and so on. This ration was packaged in boxes containing enough food for ten meals, although not specifically broken down into individual meals. Personal rations ('*razione personale*') were issued to troops immediately before combat and were designed to provide basic food items when group or field rations were not practical, or while on the move. This consisted of one can of tuna, one can of prosciutto ham, one pack of soup which consisted of two broth base tablets, two packs of hard bread ('*galletta*') and one pack of sweet biscuits. The processing of canned military rations (canned meats, canned minestrone soup and canned pasta and lentils) was developed by Colonel Ettore Chiarizia in 1929, hence, the occasional reference to '*minestrone Chiarizia*' or '*carne Chiarizia*'. The 'reserve ration' was an emergency ration that was not to be used until authorized. It consisted of a 'brick' of hard bread or hard biscuits, a pack of coffee, milk and sugar, and a pack of sweets. Beginning in January 1942 the canned meat and tuna were replaced by a minestrone (vegetable) soup with pasta and cheese. When tinned meat was available, because of the initials 'AM' (for '*Amministrazione Militare*', 'military administration') stamped on the cans, Italian soldiers in North Africa jokingly referred to it as '*Arabo Morto*' ('dead Arab') or '*Asino Mussolini*' ('Mussolini donkey'), while the Germans who often were supplied with Italian food referred to it as '*Alter Mann*' ('Old Man').

Appendix XV

Select Biographies

The following individuals represent some of the more notable and interesting Italian personalities involved in the North African campaign. It is by no means complete; there were hundreds, if not thousands, of junior officers, NCOs and ordinary soldiers whose deeds and sacrifice were never properly documented or recognized. Generally speaking, the Italians have not been as assiduous or thorough in documenting the lives of many of their notable military figures as have other nations. In many cases, information on the individuals covered below has been scant, incomplete and unreliable. It is also interesting to note how many of the officers who served in North Africa between 1940 and 1943 had served previously in Libya during the Italo–Turkish war there during 1911–12 and who consequently had prior experience operating in the desert.

Francesco Antonio Arena was born in Pizzoni, in Calabria, on 27 March 1889. An officer cadet in 1909, he was commissioned as a second lieutenant in 1911 and as an infantry officer and was sent to Cyrenaica during the Italo–Turkish war, where he earned a Silver Medal for Valor. In 1914 he served in Somalia, where he was promoted to captain. During the First World War he served on the Italo–Austrian front, where he was awarded a second Silver Medal for Valor, promoted to major and awarded a Bronze Medal for Valor for leading his battalion against the Austrians in October 1918. In October 1939 he became chief of staff of IX Army Corps. He served briefly as a paratroop commander, and in February 1942, as a brigadier general, was assigned as deputy commander of the 'Ariete' armoured division in North Africa, assuming command of the division in September 1942. He commanded the division during its epic resistance during the Second Battle of Alamein, subsequently returning to Italy in 1943. In March 1943 he was named commander of the 36th 'Forli' Infantry Division stationed in Athens, Greece. Following the 8 September 1943 armistice and his refusal to collaborate with the Germans, he was sent by the Germans to a prison camp in Poland. While attempting to escape, he was shot by a Russian patrol at Rosko Posen, Poland, on 28 January 1945.

Ettore Baldassare was born in Trani on 27 April 1883. He attended the Military Academy in Turin, and graduated as a lieutenant in the artillery corps. In 1911 he took part in the Italian war against Turkey in Libya and was promoted to captain. During the First World War he rose to the rank of lieutenant colonel and became the 3rd Army's artillery commander. He was promoted to brigadier general in 1936 and major general in 1938. In June 1940 he assumed command of the 'Ariete' armoured division, until July 1941; in May 1942 he assumed command of XX Corps in North Africa. Baldassare had studied and learned from German experience with armour since 1939 and was a strong proponent of the use of combined arms teams. He was killed in action on 25 June 1942, and his loss was said to have been genuinely mourned by Rommel.

Ettore Bastico was born in Bologna on 9 April 1876. In October 1894 he entered the Military Academy at Modena, became a second lieutenant, and in October 1896 was assigned to the 3rd *Bersaglieri* Regiment. Promoted to captain in 1909, he was assigned to the 2nd *Bersaglieri* Regiment and sent to Libya. He served as a colonel during the First World War, and was promoted to general in 1928, subsequently participating in the war in Ethiopia and in the Spanish Civil War. Following those assignments, he returned to Italy where he was appointed commander of the Italian 6th Army (the Army of the Po). He was a personal friend of Mussolini's, and in July 1941 he replaced General Italo Gariboldi as Governor of Libya and commander of Axis troops in Libya. Bastico was Erwin Rommel's nominal superior, but he and Rommel disagreed often and significantly about how the war in North Africa should be conducted. Rommel had a very negative opinion of Bastico and referred to him as '*Bombastico*'. The feuding between the two was a long-running affair, even though at times Rommel's German superior, Field Marshal Albert Kesselring, shared the same views as Bastico and sided with him. On 12 August 1942 Bastico was promoted to the rank of *Maresciallo d'Italia* (Marshal of Italy) to avoid having him being of inferior rank to Rommel. Bastico was recalled to Italy on 5 February 1943 and subsequently retired to private life to write his memoirs. In addition to numerous Italian medals and honorifics, Bastico had been awarded the French *Croix de Guerre* for action in the First World War and the prestigious German Cross in Gold in December 1942. He died in Rome on 2 December 1972.

Alberto Bechi Luserna was born in Spoleto on 21 December 1904. He was from an illustrious family with a long military tradition; one of his relatives, Stanislao Bechi, was an officer who was executed by the Russians in 1863 in Poland because he was fighting for Polish independence. Bechi Luserna attended the Nunziatella Military Academy in Naples and the Military Academy in Modena, becoming a cavalry officer. He participated in the colonial campaigns in Libya and Ethiopia, and later in Italian East Africa, where he commanded native cavalry troops. He was considered to be one of the most promising officers in the *Regio Esercito* and assigned as military attaché to London. During the Second World War he served a brief stint in the military intelligence service and then volunteered to serve with the parachute troops, soon emerging as the charismatic commander of the IV Parachute Battalion of the 'Folgore' division, which was deployed to North Africa on 15 July 1942. In October he was appointed temporary commander of the 187th Parachute Regiment and fought at Deir el Munassib during the battle of El Alamein. Bechi Luserna, with his blonde hair, blue eyes and impeccable English could easily pass as British. In November 1942 he was driving in a recently captured jeep along with his aide, who also happened to be blonde, both wearing captured British kit, heading north trying to reach the coast and rejoin his unit; suddenly they found themselves in the midst of a British column and were not given a second glance by the British; they made their way to the head of the column, and ultimately outdistanced it, catching up with a German rear guard force near El Daba. During the epic retreat to Tunisia, he was recalled to Italy and as a lieutenant colonel was assigned as chief of staff of the 'Nembo' Parachute Division. On 8 September 1943, the date of the armistice with the Allies, Bechi Luserna was in Campidano, Sardinia; the XII Battalion of 'Nembo' had defected to the Germans, and Bechi Luserna, who attempted to dissuade the defectors, was shot by the mutineers on 10 September 1943. He was buried in the sea near Santa Teresa Gallura in the Straits of Bonifacio. He remains known for his writings about the war.

Gervasio Bitossi was born on 2 October 1884; he was a cavalry officer who became one of the leading proponents of armoured warfare in Italy. Bitossi was commissioned on 16 September 1906 and served in 8th Regiment 'Lancieri di Montebello' in 1909. He served as a captain in the First World War in 1915–1918. In 1936, as a colonel, he commanded the *1o Reggimento Misto Motorizzato* (1st Mixed Motorized Regiment) which contained infantry, tank, motorcycle and motorized machine gun units; Bitossi trained all these elements together as part of a combined arms team, the precursor of true mechanized formations in the *Regio Esercito*. Bitossi had a number of high-level command assignments, including leading the 133rd 'Littorio' armoured division in Spain and North Africa, as well as XX Corps in North Africa and II Corps in Italy. He had a reputation for his absolute honesty – a quality which did not always endear him to some of his contemporaries. He became a prisoner of the Germans from September 1943 until the end of the war in 1945. He returned to Italy where he died from an illness he had developed while he was a prisoner in Germany.

Giorgio Calvi de Bèrgolo was born in Athens, Greece, on 15 March 1887. He served in the First World War, earning a number of medals. Following the war, he served as a riding instructor at the Cavalry School. In 1923 he married the eldest daughter of King Vittorio Emanuele III. In 1935 he became Inspector of Cavalry in Libya, and in March 1942, as the liaison officer to *Panzerarmee Afrika*, was promoted to brigadier general, later assuming command of the 131st 'Centauro' armoured division, which he commanded when Italian forces scored their first and only victories against US forces during the battles of the Kasserine Pass and El Guettar. Following the fall of Mussolini, Calvi di Bèrgolo was named commander of the reconstituted 'Centauro II' armoured division, but because of the unit's political unreliability, he was replaced on 7 September, the day prior to the armistice with the Allies. Following announcement of the armistice, Calvi di Bèrgolo acted as an intermediary with Albert Kesselring to secure the status of Rome as an open city. On 23 September he was arrested by the Germans and held as a prisoner until later that year, when he was allowed to go to Switzerland with his family. In 1955 he returned to Italy, where he died on 25 February 1977 in Rome.

Paolo Caccia Dominioni, the 14th Baron of Sillavengo, was born in Nerviano in Lombardy on 14 May 1896. Caccia Dominioni was from a noble Lombard family; his father was a diplomat and Paolo grew up in France, Austria–Hungary, Tunisia and Egypt, becoming fluent in German, French, English and Arabic. During the First World War he served initially as a private soldier and received a commission in March 1916. He was first assigned as a bridging engineer officer, then volunteered for a flamethrower unit. He was transferred to Libya in 1918, contracted the Spanish Flu, and returned to Italy in 1919. He moved to Egypt as an engineer, in 1924, where he was involved in many important building projects. In 1931 he was recalled into the army, where he carried out reconnaissance missions in southern Libya and was promoted to captain. He also served in the war against Ethiopia in 1935 as an intelligence officer. During his prewar sojourn in Egypt, he became the close friend of Vladimir Peniakoff, a Russian engineer and adventurer who would later gain fame as the leader of 'Popski's Private Army'; Caccia Dominioni and Peniakoff faced each other as potential enemies during the desert campaign but renewed their friendship after the war. [In connection with Peniakoff, it is interesting to note that when he commanded the small raiding unit known as 'Popski's Private Army', he adopted a badge for the unit's berets that bore the 'ex libris' design that Caccia Dominioni had created for him before the war.] By 1941 Caccia Dominioni was an officer in the *alpini*, and in July 1942, as a major, was assigned to command the *XXXI Battaglione Guastatori* (31st Assault Engineer Battalion). He fought at El Alamein, evaded capture, and returned to Italy. Following the 8 September 1943 armistice with the Allies, Caccia Dominioni avoided being captured by the Germans and joined the 106th Garibaldi Partisan Brigade. After the war, he returned to Egypt until 1958, where he was instrumental in building the memorial and Italian war cemetery at Hill 33 (usually referred to in Italian as Quota 33; its rather lengthy Arab designation is Tell el Sheikh Fadl Abu Sharshir, Hill of sheik Fadl, father of Sharshir) near El Alamein. He wrote several books chronicling Italian operations in North Africa, as well as some relating to the First World War and to his travels in the Middle East. Caccia Dominioni died on 12 August 1992 at the Celio military hospital in Rome at the age of 96.

Gaetano Cantaluppi was born in Milan in 1890 and began his military career as a volunteer in Libya in 1911, serving in the First World War as a captain. He commanded the 82nd 'Torino' Infantry Regiment in 1938 and was commandant of the Military Academy at Modena in 1939. During the North African campaign, Colonel Cantaluppi, who acted as interim commander of the 'Ariete' armoured division in its final days, may have been one of the most colorful Italian armour officers who served in North Africa. According to an officer who served under him, he was given to much loud cursing, yelling and arm-waving while stubbornly refusing to be intimidated by the overwhelming odds he and his men faced during the retreat from Libya to Tunisia. He was a charismatic character who was able to motivate and inspire his troops to carry on and fight despite the obviously hopelessly situation. Cantaluppi exhibited these characteristics while commanding what was left of 'Ariete' shortly after Bir el Abd, when the remaining elements of 'Ariete', along with remnants of the 'Littorio' armoured division and of the 'Trieste' motorized division were consolidated as the Gruppo Tattico 'Ariete' ('Ariete' Tactical Group), under Cantaluppi; this formation was also at times referred to as the 'Gruppo Tattico Cantaluppi' but was later renamed the Gruppo Tattico 'Centauro'. In December 1942 he was awarded the German Iron Cross First Class by Rommel. Following the September 1943 armistice with the Allies, Cantaluppi was arrested by the SS because he belonged to the *Comitato Nazionale della Liberazione di Verona* (National Liberation Committee of Verona) and sent to a prisoner of war camp at Flossenburg. He survived the war, attained the rank of general, commanded the 'Folgore' motorized division 1948-49 and died in Verona in 1984.

Giuseppe de Stefanis was born on 20 December 1885 in La Spezia. He was an artillery officer who served as a captain and later major in the First World War. From 1932 to 1938 he commanded a number of artillery regiments; in 1940–1941 he commanded the 'Pinerolo' infantry division, then commanded the 'Trento' motorized division in 1941 and the 'Ariete' armoured division in May 1942 in North Africa. In June 1942 he assumed command of XX Corps. From May to September 1943 he was deputy chief of the Army General Staff, and in October 1943 he assumed command of LI Corps. He was considered by the Germans as well as the Italians to be one of the most competent and courageous of the Italian generals; his calmness under fire was legendary. Following the 8 September 1943 armistice with the Allies, De Stefanis became head of a delegation that sought to gain a greater role for Italian combat forces fighting alongside the Allies in Italy. De Stefanis died in Rome on 11 December 1965.

Gino Fabris was born in Vicenza on 7 September 1890. He served in the First World War and as part of the Italian volunteer corps during the Spanish Civil War. As a lieutenant colonel commanding the III *Bersaglieri* Battalion of the 8th *Bersaglieri* Regiment (designated the '*Colonna Fabris*') he was in the vanguard of the attack ordered by Rommel against El Mechili; the 'Fabris' column was part of the force that compelled the surrender of British General Gambier-Parry and some 1,200 prisoners. He was killed in action on 22 April 1941 at Acroma while leading his battalion and was posthumously awarded the Silver Medal for Military Valor for his actions at El Mechili.

Federico Ferrari-Orsi was born on 18 December 1886 in Rivoli in the province of Turin. He was an avid and accomplished soccer player, helping to found the Torino Soccer Club. He attended the Royal Military Academy in Modena, graduating in 1909 as a cavalry second lieutenant. Promoted to first lieutenant, he was sent to Libya from 1913 to 1916. He served in the First World War as a captain, earning several medals. In 1920 he asked to return to Libya, where he organized and commanded a native Spahi unit. Between 1931 and 1936 he continued to be promoted and commanded several schools, and in 1936 was promoted to brigadier general. He was deputy commander of the 102nd 'Trento' Motorized Division and commander of the *1a Divisione Celere*

'*Eugenio di Savoia*'. At the beginning of the Second World War, he was promoted to major general and from April to September 1941 fought in Yugoslavia and the Balkans. In the summer of 1941, he was assigned to North Africa where, as a lieutenant general, he took command of the Italian X Corps. He was awarded numerous Italian medals during both world wars as well as the German Iron Cross First Class. He was killed by a mine at Deir el Munassib on 18 October 1942, shortly before the Second Battle of El Alamein.

Enrico Frattini was born in Naples on 31 May 1891; he became an engineer officer in 1912 and was sent to Libya in 1913. He was promoted to captain in 1915, remaining in Tripolitania. During the First World War he commanded several engineer units on the front lines. Promoted to lieutenant colonel in 1926, he was assigned as military attaché to Tokyo in 1929. Promotions to colonel and brigadier general followed in 1933 and 1938, respectively. In 1941, although still an engineer officer, he was assigned the task of creating an airborne unit after the task had been refused by several other generals. In the summer of 1942, he was sent to North Africa in command of the 'Folgore' parachute division which he had been instrumental in organizing. With the death of General Ferrari-Orsi, Frattini assumed command of the X Corps. The legendary resistance put up by the 'Folgore' earned it the respect of the British, and Frattini, who surrendered to General Hughes of the British 44th Division, was complimented by Hughes on the division's performance. He was released by the British in 1944 and returned to duty with the Italian Army, eventually becoming a lieutenant general. Frattini died in Rome on 11 February 1980.

Gastone Gambara was born on 10 November 1890 in Imola. He attended the Military Academy in Modena from 1911 to 1913 and became a lieutenant in the 3rd Alpine Regiment. He fought during the First World War and was wounded and promoted to major. In 1918 he commanded the *29o Reparto Assalto* (29th Assault Detachment), consisting of *alpini*, and from 1919 to 1923 commanded an alpine battalion. From 1935 to 1937 he took part in the war in Ethiopia and was promoted to colonel; during the Spanish Civil War he became chief of staff of the Italian volunteer corps and was promoted to brigadier general. From 1939 to 1940 he was the Italian ambassador to Spain. With the outbreak of the Second World War he returned to active duty and took command of XV Corps, which fought against France, and then commanded VII Corps in Albania, being promoted to lieutenant general. In May 1941 he was transferred to Tripoli where he served initially as chief of staff under General Bastico, later assuming command of the *Corpo d'Armata di Manovra* (CAM, Maneuver Army Corps), later designated XX Corps. In March 1942 he returned to Italy, and in September took command of XI Corps in the Balkans. Following the 8 September 1943 armistice, Gambara collaborated with the Germans, surrendering Italian forces in Slovenia. He then joined Mussolini's Italian Social Republic, becoming chief of staff of the Republican National Army. He was taken prisoner by the Allies in 1945, and after his release moved to Spain in 1947. He later returned to Italy and died on 26 February 1962 in Rome.

Italo Gariboldi was born in Lodi on 20 April 1879. He joined the *Regio Esercito* in October 1896, attended the Military Academy in Modena and was commissioned as a second lieutenant in the infantry in October 1898, serving briefly in Libya as a captain in 1911. During the First World War he advanced in rank from major to colonel and received medals for bravery in action. He continued to be promoted, commanding several units and military schools. In 1936 he took command of the 'Sabauda' infantry division and took part in the Ethiopian campaign. In October 1936 he was reprimanded for being too lenient with the Ethiopian civilian population. On 11 June 1940 Gariboldi assumed command of the Italian 5th Army in Libya, and on 11 February 1941 he was appointed Commander-In-Chief of Italian forces in North Africa. As such, he was Rommel's superior, but he and Rommel disagreed as to how the war should be prosecuted; Gariboldi was somewhat cautious and believed that the Axis had to strengthen their forces prior to engaging in any offensive action, but Rommel believed in striking the British without delay. This disagreement led to Gariboldi's dismissal from North Africa on 20 July 1941. While in North Africa, he was very well liked by the Italian troops; he had a reputation for shunning publicity and for looking out for the welfare of the troops, who he visited often and who referred to him as '*il nonno*' ('the grandfather'). He subsequently went on to command the Italian 8th Army in Russia; after the defeat of the Italian forces in Russia, Gariboldi returned to Italy. Following the armistice on 8 September 1943, he was arrested by the Germans for refusing to cooperate with them and was imprisoned. He escaped shortly before the end of the war, retired from the army and died in Rome on 9 February 1970.

Alessandro Gloria was born in Rome on 7 July 1883. He attended the Military Academy in Modena, graduating as a second lieutenant in the artillery corps on 7 September 1903. In 1911–1912 he served with the 7th Field Artillery Regiment in Libya and later fought in the First World War, earning the rank of major. From 1920 to 1939 he held a number of command positions in artillery units as well as serving in staff assignments in Rome. In January 1940 he assumed command of the 37th 'Modena' mountain infantry division. On 25 August 1941 he was transferred to Libya as commander of the 25th 'Bologna' infantry division, which he commanded until its destruction in November 1942. Gloria was considered to be a very capable officer and was well regarded both by his fellow officers and his men; he often spent hours at a time in the most exposed areas among his troops. He returned to Italy in December 1942 and was later assigned command of the V Army in Dalmatia. In May 1943 he returned to Rome and was then reassigned to command of XXXV Corps in Bolzano where he was captured by the Germans following the 8 September armistice and interned in Germany at Camp 64/Z for generals at Shokken. He was repatriated to Italy in October 1945 and retired from service on 7 July 1956. Gloria died in Genoa on 24 October 1970.

Francesco La Ferla was born on 22 April 1886. He received a law degree in 1909, after which he joined the army and became an officer in the *Bersaglieri*. He served in Libya during the Italo–Turkish war in 1911-12, fought in the First World War, and in 1938, as a general, commanded the 'Frecce Azzurre' division in Spain during the civil war there. He commanded the 101st 'Trieste' Motorized Division during the 1942 Gazala battles in North Africa; in May 1943 he was taken prisoner at Enfidaville in Tunisia and was released in 1944. He died on 22 March 1962.

Enrico Maretti, despite being a legendary figure in the annals of the 'Ariete' armoured division, has little biographical information available relating to him. He was a native of Varzi (Province of Pavia), where a street has been named in his honor. He is known to have participated in the Italo–Turkish war in Libya and to have served as an officer in the First World War. During the Second World War he served throughout the North African campaign with the 'Ariete' armoured division, first with the 32nd Tank Regiment and later, from September 1941, as a lieutenant colonel in command of the 132nd Tank Regiment. He remained its commander throughout the rest of the regiment's existence in North Africa, allegedly winning the respect and admiration of Rommel himself. He had a reputation for being fearless, tireless and never ordering his tankers to do anything that he himself would not do. He did not give frivolous orders but did expect that the orders he gave be obeyed without question; the troops revered him for his fairness and his boldness. He was promoted to colonel in the spring of 1943. Postwar Italian accounts sometimes refer to him as the 'Italian Desert Fox'. He was the recipient of many Italian and foreign awards. Maretti died on 12 December 1978 at Finale Ligure, in the province of Savona.

Giovanni Messe was born in Mesagne, in southern Italy, on 10 December 1883. He joined the army as a sergeant in 1901, and like many of his contemporaries, saw action in Libya and in the

First World War. He was involved in the creation of the *arditi*, which were elite infantry assault units, and commanded an *arditi* unit during the war, reaching the rank of lieutenant colonel. From 1923 to 1927 he was aide-de-camp to King Vittorio Emanuele III, subsequently commanding the 9th *Bersaglieri* Regiment as a colonel. He then commanded a brigade in the second Italo–Ethiopian war and subsequently, as a major general, commanded the 3rd Cavalry Division. In 1939 he served in Albania, and in 1940–1941 he commanded a corps during the Italian invasion of Greece. On 14 July 1941 he was designated commander of the Italian Expeditionary Corps in Russia, a post he retained until November 1942, and in February 1943 he replaced Rommel as the commander of the *Armata Corazzata Italo–Tedesco* (Italo–German Tank Army), and the army's designation was changed to the *1a Armata Italiana* (Italian 1st Army). Messe, a realist, is said to have referred to the appointment as the '*Comandante degli sbandati*' ('the commander of the stragglers') and was well aware of the probability of being beaten, losing his reputation and falling prisoner as a result of the appointment. On 12 May 1943 he was promoted to *Maresciallo d'Italia* (Marshal of Italy). Messe fought a skillful delaying action against the Allied forces, but the overwhelming superiority enjoyed by the Allies in terms of men and equipment ultimately made his efforts useless, and on 13 May Messe formally surrendered to the Allies and was indeed taken prisoner as he had predicted. He was released by the British in autumn of 1943. Because of his performance both in Russia and in North Africa, Messe is considered by many historians to have been the best Italian general of the war. In September 1943 he was made chief of staff of the Italian Co-Belligerent Army. From 1953 to 1955 he served as a senator in the Italian senate. He died on 18 December 1968 and is buried in Rome.

Ugo Montemurro was born in Portoferraio in 1891, attended the Military Academy from 1910 to 1913 and was commissioned as a lieutenant in the *Bersaglieri*. During the First World War he commanded the IV Bicycle Battalion. During the battle of Caporetto, Montemurro was taken prisoner by a German lieutenant named Erwin Rommel, but managed to escape, then participating in the battle of Vittorio Veneto. In 1939, as a colonel, he took command of the 8th *Bersaglieri* Regiment. At the battle of El Mechili in April 1941 Montemurro's *Bersaglieri* captured British Brigadier Michael Gambier-Parry, along with Brigadier E.W.D. Vaughan; some 3,000 other prisoners were also taken. Rommel awarded the Iron Cross First Class to Montemurro as a result. Sometime around June 1941 he was sent back to Italy due to illness, and he later served on the Eastern Front, in Russia. In 1946 he was promoted to general and placed on the reserve rolls. He died on 7 September 1979 in Sirmione, a small town on Lake Garda, in the province of Verona.

Enea Navarini was born in Cesena on 1 April 1885. In 1905 he became a second lieutenant in the infantry, was promoted to first lieutenant in 1911 and fought in Cyrenaica in 1912. He was promoted to captain in 1914, fought and was wounded several times during the First World War, and reached the rank of lieutenant colonel by 1918. He was awarded numerous medals for his actions. Promoted to colonel in 1927, he was commandant of the Military School in Rome. He was promoted to brigadier general in 1936 and was stationed in Somalia; in 1938 he became a major general and assumed command of the 56th 'Casale' infantry division. In 1941 he became commander of Italian XXI Corps in North Africa, was promoted to lieutenant general in February 1942 and became one of Rommel's most trusted assistants. He returned to Italy on 14 October 1942 but was asked by Rommel to return to North Africa and again take command of XXI Corps. He later returned to Italy where he took command of XIX Corps responsible for defense of the coast of the Campania region until it was disbanded following the 8 September 1943 armistice. Navarini then fled to northern Italy where he joined Mussolini's Fascist armed forces, becoming commander of the training center for RSI special units. In April 1945 the new Italian government stripped him of his rank, but later that year he was reinstated. Navarini died in Merano on 22 March 1977.

Leopoldo Pardi was born in Novara in 1898. He arrived in Tripoli on 14 January 1941 as a major. He gained fame as an Italian artillery officer who, along with German Major Wilhelm Bach (known as 'Padre Bach' because of his pre-war occupation as a Lutheran minister) who led *Kampfgruppe Bach* in the defense of Halfaya Pass, warded off a series of determined attacks by the British to seize the pass in during Operations Brevity and Battleaxe, from May to June 1941. At Halfaya, Pardi commanded the I Group of the *2a Articelere 'Emanuele Filiberto Testa di Ferro'* equipped with 100/17 guns. Pardi subsequently took command of the II Group of the *1a Articelere 'Eugenio di Savoia'*. Promoted to lieutenant colonel on 9 July 1942, he was seriously wounded the same day and died of his wounds at El Daba on 12 July 1942. Pardi was greatly esteemed by Rommel, who personally tried in vain to get Pardi the urgent medical attention he needed to save him. Pardi was awarded various Italian medals as well as the German Iron Cross Second Class and First Class.

Costantino Ruspoli (Costantino Carlo Michele Agostino dei Principi Ruspoli) was born in New York City on 8 July 1891, son of Mario dei Principi Ruspoli, the 2nd Prince of Poggio Suasa. Costantino moved to Italy with his family at an early age. He was an Italian cavalry officer during the First World War but left the army following the war. He rejoined upon Italy's declaration of war in 1940 and was assigned to his former regiment as a captain, but upon learning that his younger brother had joined the paratroopers, also joined the newly formed specialty. Although he was more than 50 years old he outdid many of the younger officers while training as a paratrooper. He commanded the 11th Company of the 'Folgore' parachute division at El Alamein. He had the habit of wandering about the front lines smoking a pipe filled with English tobacco. He was killed in action at Deir El Munassib on 26 October 1942.

Marescotti dei Principi Ruspoli, the younger brother of Costantino Ruspoli, was born in New York City on 17 October 1892. He served in the First World War as an Italian cavalry officer, participated in the Ethiopian campaign in 1935, and served in Yugoslavia during the Second World War. As a lieutenant colonel, he commanded a battle group of the 'Folgore' parachute division during the battle of El Alamein in October 1942 and was killed in action on 24 October 1942.

Camillo Santamaria Nicolini was born in Maddaloni, in the province of Caserta, and fought in the First World War as a second lieutenant in the 7th Alpine Regiment. He was awarded the Bronze Medal for Valor for his actions during the battle of Monte Tambolin of 6 July 1916. He gained some fame during the early days of the North African campaign when as a major commanding a reconnaissance group of the 'Ariete' division he participated in the very earliest mixed German–Italian probes conducted by Rommel in February 1941, and continued to lead the reconnaissance group, the precursor of what ultimately became the *Reparto Esplorante Corazzato*, under the designation of the 'Colonna Santamaria'. During the fighting in North Africa he was wounded several times and earned a number of medals, including the Gold Medal for Military Valor. Following the September 1943 armistice between Italy and the Allies, Nicolini joined the army of Mussolini's Italian Social Republic (the RSI) as a lieutenant colonel, serving as a *Questore* (police chief); he was wounded in a partisan ambush in February 1944 but survived. Because of his affiliation with the RSI, after the war all of his medals were revoked except for his First World War Bronze Medal.

Bibliography

Primary Sources

Montanari, Mario, *Le operazioni in Africa Settentrionale, Vol. 3. El Alamein (gennaio-novembre 1942)* (Rome: Ufficio Storico, Stato Maggiore Esercito, 1989)

Second World War Official Histories, *Australia in the War of 1939–1945, Series 1-Army* (Canberra, various years)

Ufficio Storico dello Stato Maggiore Italiano, *Seconda controffensiva britannica in Africa Settentrionale e ripiegamento italo-tedesco nella Sirtica orientale* (Rome, 1949)

Ufficio Storico dello Stato Maggiore Italiano, *La 1a Armata italiana in Tunisia (11 novembre 1942–13 maggio 1943)* (Rome, 1950)

Ufficio Storico dello Stato Maggiore Italiano, *In Africa Settentrionale. La preparazione al conflitto. L'avanzata su Sidi el-Barrani* (Rome, 1955)

Ufficio Storico dello Stato Maggiore Italiano, *Terza offensiva britannica in Africa Settentrionale. La battaglia di El Alamein e il ripiegamento in Tunisia* (Rome, 1961)

Ufficio Storico dello Stato Maggiore Italiano, *La prima offensive britannica in Africa Settentrionale (ottobre 1940–febbraio 1941)* (Rome, 1964)

Ufficio Storico dello Stato Maggiore Italiano, *La prima controffensiva italo–tedesca in Africa Settentrionale (15 febbraio–18 novembre 1941)* (Rome, 1974)

Secondary Sources: Books and Journals

Agar-Hamilton, J.A.I. and Turner, L.C.F., *The Sidi Rezeg Battles, 1941* (Cape Town: Oxford University Press, 1957)

Alexander, Field Marshal Earl, *The Alexander Memoirs, 1940–1945* (New York: McGraw-Hill, 1962)

Anon., *31° Reggimento Carri 'Centauro'* (Bellinzago: Tipografia La Grafica)

Anon., *Fronte Terra: carri armati 2/II. Carri leggeri, carro veloce 33-35 – le operazioni belliche* (Rome: Edizioni Bizzarri, 1974)

Antares (pseudonym), *La 'Littorio' a El Alamein* (Milan: Storia Militare No. 288, September 2012)

Bagnasco, Erminio and de Toro, Augusto, *The Littorio Class: Italy's Last and Largest Battleships, 1937–1948* (Barnsley: Seaforth, 2011)

Bandini, Franco, *Gli italiani in Africa* (Mondadori Editore, 2014)

Barr, Niall, *Pendulum of War: The Three Battles of El Alamein* (Woodstock: Overlook Press, 2005)

Battistelli, Pier Paolo, *Rommel's Afrika Korps: Tobruk to Alamein* (Oxford: Osprey, 2006)

Bechi Luserna, Alberto and Caccia Dominioni, Paolo, *I ragazzi della Folgore* (Milan: Longanesi, 1970)

Beevor, Antony, *The Battle of Arnhem* (New York: Viking, 2018)

Beretta, Davide, *Batterie semoventi alzo zero* (Milan: U. Mursia, 1968)

Bierman, John and Smith, Colin, *War Without Hate: The Desert Campaign of 1940–1943* (New York: Penguin Books, 2004)

Bongiovanni, Alberto, *Battaglie nel deserto* (Milan: Mursia Editore, 1978).

Borgiotti, A. and Gori, C., *La Guerra aerea in Africa Settentrionale 1940–41* (Modena: S.T.E.M. Mucchi, 1972)

Bovington Tank Museum, *Tank Museum Guide, Part V, Tanks of Other Nations* (Bovington: Royal Armoured Corps Centre, various years)

Bradford, George R., *Armor Camouflage and Markings, North Africa, 1940–1943, Volume One* (Preston, Ontario: Progress, 1971)

Brescia, Maurizio, *Mussolini's Navy: A Reference Guide to the Regia Marina, 1930–1945* (Barnsley: Seaforth, 2012)

Brown, Peter, *British Cruiser Tanks A9 and A10* (Warsaw: Model Centrum Progres Poland, 2017)

Caccia Dominioni, Paolo, *El Alamein, 1933–1962* (Milan: Longanesi, 1963)

Caccia Dominioni, Paolo, *Le trecento ore a nord di Qattara* (Milan: Longanesi, 1972)

Caccia Dominioni, Paolo and Izzo, Giuseppe, *Takfir* (Milan: Longanesi, 1972)

Campini, Dino, *Nei giardini del diavolo* (Milan: Longanesi, 1969)

Cappellano, Filippo, *Autoblindo AB40, 41 e 43* (Parma: Albertelli Edizioni Speciali, 2011)

Cappellano, Filippo and Battistelli, Pier Paolo, *Italian Light Tanks, 1919–1945* (Oxford: Osprey, 2012)

Cappellano, Filippo and Battistelli, Pier Paolo, *Italian Medium Tanks, 1939–1945* (Oxford: Osprey, 2012)

Carroll, John and Davies, Peter J., *The Complete Book of Tractors and Trucks* (London: Hermes House, 2002)

Castagnoli, Renato, *I Granatieri di Sardegna 1659–1981* (Associazione Nazionale Granatieri di Sardegna, 1981)

Clifton, George, *The Happy Hunted* (London: Cassell, 1952)

Cloutier, Patrick, *Regio Esercito: The Italian Royal Army in Mussolini's Wars, 1935–1943* (Middletown, DE:, 2018)

Crippa, Paolo, *Carristi italiani in Spagna, 1936–1939* (Fidenza: Mattioli 1885 SpA, draft, 2020)

Crisp, Major Robert, *Brazen Chariots* (New York: W.W. Norton, 1958)

Crociani, Piero and Battistelli, Pier Paolo, *Italian Soldier in North Africa, 1941–43* (Oxford: Osprey, 2013)

Culver, Bruce, *Sherman in Action* (Warren, MI: Squadron/Signal, 1997)

Dunning, Chris, *Courage Alone: The Italian Air Force, 1940–1943* (Manchester: Crecy, 2009)

Finazzer, Enrico, *Basti in groppa! L'artiglieria someggiata dall'Armata Sarda all'Esercito Italiano* (Trento: Gruppo Modellistico Trentino, 2018)

Finazzer, Enrico, *Light Trucks of the Italian Army in WWII* (Sandomierz: Stratus, 2017)

Finazzer, Enrico, *Guida alle artiglierie italiane nella 2a guerra mondiale 1940–1945* (Genova: Italia Storica, 2020)

Finazzer, Enrico and Riccio, Ralph, *Italian Artillery of WWII* (Sandomierz: Stratus, 2015)

Fletcher, David and Sarson, Peter, *Crusader Cruiser Tank, 1939–1945* (Oxford: Osprey, 1995)

Ford, Ken, *Operation Crusader 1941: Rommel in Retreat* (Oxford: Osprey, 2010)

Ford, Ken, *Gazala 1942: Rommel's Greatest Victory* (Oxford: Osprey, 2008)

Ford, Ken, *El Alamein 1942: The Turning of the Tide* (Oxford, Osprey, 2005)

Ford, Ken, *The Mareth Line 1943: The End in Africa* (Oxford, Osprey, 2012)

Galbiati, Fabio, *Il contrasto ai trasporti aerei tedeschi in Africa Settentrionale* (Milan: Storia Militare N. 291, 1 December 2017)

Garello, Giancarlo, *Guerra aerea sulle dune. La Regia Aeronautica in Africa del Nord 1940–1943 (Prima Parte)* Unpublished

Giannone, Elicia, *Cultural Disparity and the Italo–German Alliance in the Second World War* (Calgary, Alberta: University of Calgary, Thesis, 2015)

Graham, Andrew, *Sharpshooters at War: The 3rd, the 4th and the 3rd/4th County of London Yeomanry, 1939 to 1945* (London: Sharpshooters Regimental Association, 1964)

Gravina, Igino, *Le tre battaglie di Alamein* (Milan: Longanesi, 1971)

Greene, Jack, *Mare Nostrum: The War in the Mediterranean* (Watsonville, CA: Jack Greene, 1990).

Griffith, Paddy, *World War II Desert Tactics* (Oxford: Osprey, 2008)

Holmes, Richard, *Bir Hakim: Desert Citadel* (New York: Ballantine Books, 1971)

Jones, Tobias, *The Dark Heart of Italy* (New York: North Point Press, 2004)

Jowett, Philip, *The Italian Army, 1940–45 (2): Africa, 1940–43* (Oxford: Osprey, 2001)

Kitchen, Martin, *Rommel's Desert War* (Cambridge: Cambridge University Press, 2009)

Kühn, Volkmar, *Rommel in the Desert: Victories and Defeat of the Afrika Korps* (Atglen: Schiffer, 1991)

Kurowski, Franz, *Das Afrika Korps. Erwin Rommel and the Germans in Africa, 1941–43* (Mechanicsburg, PA: Stackpole Books, 2010)

Latimer, Jon, *Operation Compass, 1940: Wavell's Whilrwind Offensive* (Oxford: Osprey, 2000)

Latimer, Jon, *Tobruk, 1941: Rommel's Opening Move* (Oxford: Osprey, 2001)

Loi, Salvatore, *Aggredisci e vincerai: Storia della divisione motorizzata Trieste* (Milan: Mursia Editore, 1983)

Macksey, Kenneth, *Beda Fomm: The Classic Victory* (New York: Ballantine Books, 1971)

Macksey, Kenneth, *Afrika Korps* (New York: Ballantine Books, 1968)

Macksey, Kenneth and Batchelor, John H., *Tank: A History of the Armored Fighting Vehicle* (New York: Ballantine Books, 1971)

Madeja, W. Victor, *Italian Army Order of Battle, 1940–1944* (Allentown, PA: Valor, 1990)

Martinelli, L., *Gruppo Squadroni 'Cavallegeri di Lodi' (15°) Cenni Storici* (Vercelli: SETE)

Mels, Pierluigi Romeo di Colleredo, *Da Sidi el Barrani a Beda Fomm 1940–1941. La Caporetto di Mussolini* (Zanica: Soldier Shop)

Messe, Giovanni, *La mia armata in Tunisia: Come finì la guerra in Africa* (Milan: Mursia Editore, 2004)

Military College of Science, *Preliminary Report No.14, Semovente* (Chertsey: Military College of Science, School of Tank Technology, July 1943)

Military Intelligence Service, *The Libyan Campaign, November 1941 to January 1942. Campaign Study No. 1. August 25, 1942* (Washington, DC: War Department, 25 August 1942)

Mitcham, Samuel W. Jr., *Rommel's Desert War: The Life and Death of the Afrika Korps* (Mechanicsburg, PA: Stackpole Books, 1982)

Mitcham, Samuel W. Jr., *Triumphant Fox: Erwin Rommel and the Rise of the Afrika Korps* (Mechanicsburg, PA, Stackpole Books, 1984)

Molinari, Andrea, *Desert Raiders: Axis and Allied Special Forces, 1940–1943* (Oxford: Osprey, 2007)

Mollo, Boris, *The Sharpshooters* (London: Historical Research Unit, 1970)

Montgomery, Sir Bernard Law, *The Memoirs of Field Marshal Montgomery* (New York: Da Capo Press, 1958)

Moorehead, Alan, *The Desert War: The Classic Trilogy on the North Africa Campaign, 1940–1943* (London: Aurum Press, 2017)

Moreman, Tim, *Desert Rats: British 8th Army in North Africa, 1941–43* (Oxford: Osprey, 2007)

Moreman, Tim, *Desert Rats, 1940–43: British and Commonwealth Troops in North Africa* (Oxford: Osprey, 2011)

Morisi, Paolo, *The Italian Folgore Parachute Division: Operations in North Africa, 1940–43* (Solihull: Helion, 2016)

Naglieri, Vittorio, *Carri armati nel deserto* (Parma: Ermanno Albertelli Editore, 1972)

Newsome, Bruce Oliver, *Valentine Infantry Tank, 1938–45* (Oxford: Osprey, 2016)

Pafi, Benedetto, Falessi, Cesare and Fiore, Goffredo, *Corazzati italiani 1939–1945* (Rome: D'Anna Editore, 1968)

Perrett, Bryan, *British Tanks in N. Africa, 1940–42* (London: Osprey, 1982)

Pignato, Nicola, *Atlante mondiale dei mezzi corazzati: i carri dell'Asse* (Parma: Ermanno Albertelli Editore, 1983)

Pignato, Nicola, *Atlante mondiale dei mezzi corazzati: Italia e Germania nella Seconda Guerra Mondiale* (Parma: Ermanno Albertelli Editore, 1971)

Pignato, Nicola, *Motoriii!!! Le truppe corazzate italiane 1919–1994* (Trento: Guppo Modellistico Trentino di studio e ricerca storia, 1995)

Pignato, Nicola, *Italian Medium Tanks in Action* (Carrollton, TX: Squadron/Signal, 2001).

Pignato, Nicola, *Italian Armored Vehicles of World War Two* (Carrollton, TX: Squadron/Signal, 2001)

Pignato, Nicola and Simula, Colonel Cesare, *Armour in Profile, Number 14, M13/40* (Great Bookham: Profile Publications Ltd)

Pignato, Nicola and Cappellano, Filippo, *Gli autoveicoli tattici e logistici del R. Esercito italiano fino al 1943. Tomo primo* (Rome: Stato Maggiore dell'Esercito, 2005)

Pignato, Nicola and Cappellano, Filippo, *Gli autoveicoli tattici e logistici del R. Esercito italiano fino al 1943. Tomo secondo* (Rome: Stato Maggiore dell'Esercito, 2005)

Pitman, Major Stuart, *Second Royal Gloucestershire Hussars: Libya–Egypt, 1941–1942* (London: Saint Catherine Press, 1950)

Playfair, Major-General I.S.O., *The Mediterranean and Middle East, Volume III: British Fortunes Reach Their Lowest Ebb (September 1941 to September 1943)* (Uckfield: Naval & Military Press, 2004)

Riccio, Ralph, *Clash at Bir el Gobi* (Bennington, VT: Military Journal, Vol. 1 No. 6)

Riccio, Ralph, *Italian Tanks and Combat Vehicles of World War II* (Fidenza: Mattioli 1885 SpA, 2010)

Riccio, Ralph and Pignato, Nicola, *Italian Truck-Mounted Artillery in Action* (Carrolton, TX: Squadron/Signal, 2010)

Rizzo, Giuseppe, *Buche e croci nel deserto: Apoteosi della divisione cr. 'Ariete'* (Verona: Tip. Editrice 'Aurora', 1969)

Roggiani, Fermo, *Storia dei Bersaglieri d'Italia* (Milan: Cavallotti Editore, 1973)

Sears, Stephen W., *Desert War in North Africa* (New York: American Heritage, 1967)

Smith, Peter C., *Massacre at Tobruk* (London: William Kimber, 1987)

Sweet, John Joseph Timothy, *Iron Arm: The Mechanization of Mussolini's Army, 1920–1940* (Mechanicsburg, PA: Stackpole Books, 2007)

Tallillo, Andrea, Tallillo, Antonio and Guglielmi, Daniele, *Carro L6. Carri leggeri, semoventi e derivati.* (Trento: Gruppo Modellistico Trentino, 2019)

Tallillo, Andrea, Tallillo, Antonio and Guglielmi, Daniele, *Carro M. Carri medi M11/39, M13/40, M14/41, M15/42. Semoventi e altri derivati. Volume primo* (Trento: Gruppo Modellistico Trentino, 2010)

Tallillo, Andrea, Tallillo, Antonio and Guglielmi, Daniele, *Carro M. Carri medi M11/39, M13/40, M14/41, M15/42. Semoventi e altri derivati. Volume secondo* (Trento: Gruppo Modellistico Trentino, 2012)

Trizzino, Antonino, *Gli amici dei nemici* (Milano: Longanesi, 1959)

Trye, Rex, *Mussolini's Afrika Korps: The Italian Army in North Africa, 1940–1943* (Bayside, NY: Axis Europa Books, 1999)

Van Creveld, Martin, *Supplying War: Logistics from Wallenstein to Patton* (New York: Cambridge University Press, 1977)

Walker, Ian W., *Iron Hulls, Iron Hearts: Mussolini's Elite Armoured Divisions in North Africa* (Ramsbury: Crowood Press, 2006)

Young, Desmond, *Rommel: The Desert Fox* (New York: Harper & Brothers, 1950)

Zaloga, Steve, *Stuart: US Light Tanks in Action* (Warren, MI: Squadron/Signal, 1979)

Zaloga, Steven, *Kasserine Pass 1943: Rommel's Last Victory* (Oxford: Osprey, 2005)

Zapotoczny, Walter S., *The Italian Army in North Africa: A Poor Fighting Force or Doomed by Circumstance* (Stroud: Fonthill Media, 2018)

Correspondence

Boris Mollo to Riccio, undated, Subject: Bir el Gobi

Captain F.C.J. Crowley (3 CLY) to Riccio, 10 May 1971, Subject: Bir el Gobi

Captain F.C.J. Crowley (3 CLY) to Riccio, 21 May 1971, Subject: Bir el Gobi

A.N. Gillman (4 CLY) to Riccio, 28 July 1971, Subject: Bir el Gobi, personal recollections

D.H. Jackson (3 CLY) to Riccio, 5 May 1971, Subject: Bir el Gobi

Riccio to F.C.J. Crowley, A.N. Gillman and D.H. Jackson, 25 April 1971, Form letter requesting personal recollections of battle of Bir el Gobi

Riccio to Ward Rutherford, 23 January 1971, Subject: *Kasserine, Baptism of Fire*

Ward Rutherford to Riccio, 6 April 1971

Electronic Sources

D.A.K. War Entries 1941, The Crusader Project <https://rommelsriposte.com/d-a-k-ware-entries-1941>